Marketing Database Analytics

Marketing Database Analytics presents a step-by-step process for interpreting data to gain insights that drive business decisions. The book establishes the importance of database analytics, integrating business and marketing practice. Demonstrating both concepts and techniques, this book will serve both graduate students of marketing research and practitioners well.

Andrew D. Banasiewicz is a senior lecturer at the Metropolitan College at Boston University and instructor at Harvard Extension School at Harvard University, USA. He has held senior level positions in marketing, database management and risk management organizations, and has authored two other books, as well as numerous articles. He holds a PhD in Business from Louisiana State University.

Marketing Database Analytics

Transforming Data for
Competitive Advantage

Andrew D. Banasiewicz

Routledge
Taylor & Francis Group

NEW YORK AND LONDON

First published 2013
by Routledge
711 Third Avenue, New York, NY 10017

Simultaneously published in the UK
by Routledge
2 Park Square, Milton Park, Abingdon, Oxon OX14 4RN

Routledge is an imprint of the Taylor & Francis Group, an informa business

© 2013 Taylor & Francis

Library of Congress Cataloging in Publication Data
Banasiewicz, Andrew D.
    Marketing database analytics : transforming data for competitive advantage /
    Andrew D. Banasiewicz.
        p. cm.
    Includes bibliographical references and index.
    1. Marketing—Databases. 2. Marketing—Data processing. 3. Database management.
    I. Title.
    HF5415.125.B347 2013
    658.800285'574—dc23   2012030597

ISBN: 978–0–415–65787–7 (hbk)
ISBN: 978–0–415–65788–4 (pbk)
ISBN: 978–0–203–07646–0 (ebk)

Typeset in Garamond
by Swales & Willis Ltd, Exeter, Devon
Printed and bound in Great Britain by
TJ International Ltd, Padstow, Cornwall

To my wife Carol, my daughters
Alana and Katrina and my son, Adam.

Table of Contents

List of Illustrations

Figures

Tables

Mini-Cases

About the Author

Andrew Banasiewicz is a quantitative risk and marketing analyst, focused primarily on predictive analytics and the design of data-intensive decision support and business measurement systems. He holds a Ph.D. in business from Louisiana State University and has over fifteen years of experience in the area of statistical modeling, with the bulk of it spent helping Fortune 500 companies, such as The Coca Cola Company, Conoco Phillips, Ryder, Hospital Corporation of America, Ralston Purina, Kellogg, Nabisco, Southern Company, IKEA, Ryder, Marriott International, General Motors, MGM Grand Hotel & Casino, Nevada Power, Altria, GE Capital or The World Bank design effective predictive analytical capabilities. Dr. Banasiewicz authored three books in the area of business analytics as well as multiple methodological and topical journal articles and industry white papers; he is also a frequent speaker at regional and national professional meetings. He held senior-level positions in marketing, database management and risk management organizations. Currently, in addition to his industry work, he serves as a senior lecturer and the director of the business continuity and risk management program at Boston University. He is also an instructor at the Harvard Extension School, Harvard University. He lives in Bristol, Rhode Island, with his wife, Carol and their three children, Alana, Katrina and Adam.

Preface

Anyone thinking of writing a book will at some point grapple with the question of "why?" For most, which is to say those of us whose primary occupation does not revolve around publishing, writing tends to "cut into" time spent with our families and friends, not to mention taking away from the much needed "down time." Why do it then? Well, I imagine there are as many reasons as there are writers—the reason I decided to embark on this and other book-writing projects was to build a "home" for what is best described as the coming together of my academic training and professional, "on-the-job" experience. Over the years, the interplay of those two factors has led me to conclusions that often contradicted various established business analytical practices, and this book is a forum in which I feel I can discuss and—hopefully—resolve at least some of those conflicts.

I began my business career with a large, multinational research and analysis firm as a quantitative business analyst, which I felt was one of the best places to allow me to make use of what I believed was a robust body of academic knowledge. Looking back at those days (or years) in retrospect, I can clearly recall how this introduction to the world of applied business analyses and consulting left me with an enduring sense of amazement, stemming from a sizable gap separating the academic and practical conceptions of data analyses. I found the somewhat tenuous character of academic research conclusions to be in sharp contrast to the strongly definitive, deterministic findings of applied research, just as I found the nearly fanatical attention of academics to methodological considerations to be in stark contrast to the near-disinterest in the said matters permeating the business world. Perhaps most surprising to me, however, was the asymmetry between the quality of data and the methodological sophistication. Much of the academic business research continues (as it did during my years as a student and subsequently a young faculty member) to rely on informationally limiting convenience samples of student opinions or projections, all while employing complex, cutting-edge analytic techniques. On the other hand, the applied research tended to tackle far more informationally rich sources of data, but often relying on comparatively simplistic analytic methods.

As the context of my work began to broaden to include merchandising mix, pricing elasticity and promotional allocation estimation, customer acquisition and value segmentation, promotional mix optimization and, most recently, risk management and mitigation, I began to formulate some specific approaches to tackling these common business challenges. I became particularly interested in the development of methodologically rigorous, multi-sourced (i.e., combining multiple, often dissimilar sources of data) analytic solutions, capable of taking the full advantage of the depth and diversity of the available data, rather than merely "scratching the surface" with more informationally limited single-(data)source analytics.

As I became familiar with a growing number of data sources, I began to note that although a large number of specific data types were available, the bulk of the true decision-shaping insights continued to come from a relatively small subset of data. It seemed like yet another validation of the Pareto principle, which suggested to me the possibility of realizing considerable informational gains by bringing together a relatively small number of well-chosen types of data. Primarily, those included different transaction-recording sources, such as UPC-scanner-sourced product movement data, customer/member transactional databases, SEC financial filings (e.g., 10K, 10Q, etc.) filed by publicly traded companies, corporate governance and litigation, U.S. Census, third-party overlays (e.g., geodemographics, psychographics, etc.), consumer panels, Web click stream and consumer feedback survey data. I grew convinced that "digging deeper" into these individual data types, coupled with pulling together carefully selected subsets of all available data would lead to considerable informational synergies. Along the way, I described and published a handful of specific applications, including approaches to segmentation selection, loyalty measurement, high value customer identification and new customer acquisition or securities class action risk scoring and impact simulation. These sporadic contributions began to suggest to me the existence of a more general database analytical framework, one that business organizations could use as a blueprint to guide their efforts of translating raw data into competitively advantageous knowledge.

At the same time, working in a wide cross-section of industries, including automotive, energy, financial services and banking, consumer packaged goods, hospitality and casinos, healthcare, pharmaceutical, insurance, telecommunications, retail, high tech and consumer services, I began to notice a certain pattern, namely that the degree of effort (which usually means the monetary amount of spending) put into building large and often complex data reservoirs was rarely accompanied by a corresponding degree of effort dedicated to putting all that data to a productive use. And even in the instances where data analyses or data mining were pursued vigorously, the methodological rigor often fell short of the level required to assure adequate validity and reliability of findings. I witnessed numerous examples of haphazard applications of statistical concepts to the analyses of large databases, which often resulted in the outstretching of those methods' usability limits, resulting in empirically unfounded conclusions. It became clear to me that the advent of electronic transaction systems gave rise to data streams that did not always fit neatly into classical statistical approaches, with the latter often stretched beyond their applicability limits. In a sense, it seems as if the data analysis practice is getting ahead of theoretical developments, which points to the need of developing methodological standards governing the analysis of large business databases.

The "copy and paste" approach to marketing analytics, where theoretical concepts, such as statistical significance testing are "imported" into database analytics without a proper due diligence, does not instill confidence in the quality of results. All too often, concepts of critical importance to the robustness of database analyses are employed with little regard to their usability limits or even the appropriateness of use. In a more macro sense, the very process of systematically extracting insights out of the often diverse (not so much in terms of meaning, which is expected, but more in terms of basic measurement properties, such as the level of aggregation or the type of the measurement scale) datasets has not been adequately formalized, leaving the door wide open to result validity and reliability problems. For instance, what steps should be taken to merge data elements representing different levels of aggregation into a single, analyses-ready file? What are the most appropriate strategies for dealing with missing value problems, across different situations and data types? How can we quantify the amount of specific action-attributable lift? The list goes on and on . . .

I came to the conclusion that the reason behind these apparent deficiencies is the relative "newness" of the database analytics as an applied discipline. Naturally, I am not suggesting that quantitative analysis of data, as a broadly defined field of study is new, which is obviously not the case. What is new, however, is the application of those methods to the analysis of large, transactional business databases, which themselves are relatively new. We should not lose sight of the fact that the electronic transaction systems that are a source of large, transactional databases became commonly available only in the last couple of decades, and a big part of what now constitutes data-driven business decision making (particularly as it relates to topics such as customer valuation, promotional mix allocation or behavioral segmentation) emerged as the result of the said transaction digitalization. As a result, the ability to create these highly specific types of informational inputs is contingent on the ability to combine the elements of the "old" quantitative data analysis methods and the "new" types of data and informational demands. And this is precisely where the process often breaks down—the "traditional" conceptions are at times ill-suited to the task at hand, but are used nonetheless.

The conventional data-analysis-related texts tend to be of relatively little help as well. First and foremost, the vast majority of these books were written with the demands of the ad hoc quantitative data analysis in mind, which means they tend to be domain-specific, offering an exhaustive treatment of a particular subject, but relatively little data and usage contextualization. Statistics texts offer a good example: Heavily focused on methods of crunching data, they tend to devote very little attention to potentially significant data type influences and the resultant outcome-related considerations. For the most part, data is rarely treated as more than a background used to illustrate the inner workings of statistical techniques, when in fact, it is a co-determinant of the efficacy of data analytic results. Occasional examples aside, the key sources of business data, such as UPC-scanner-sourced transactions, geodemographic and lifestyle overlays, online click streams or SEC public filings are rarely explored to an appreciable depth. Equally little attention is given to the challenges associated with bridging and amalgamating otherwise dissimilar data sources, an undertaking commonly referred to as "multi-source analytics."

I am not suggesting that the currently available, domain-centric texts are inadequate per se—my point is that these texts only focus on select "bits and pieces" of a broadly defined organizational knowledge creation process. While offering topically exhaustive treatment of their respective domains, such as statistics, database management or strategic planning, these sources are ultimately just about statistics, database management and strategic planning, respectively; as such, they fall short of capturing a broader database analytical process that borrows from each, but is not limited to a single one. Hence, it is my stated goal to present here a multidisciplinary approach to marketing database analytics that covers all aspects of transforming generic data into unique and competitively advantageous knowledge.

ADB

1 The Informational Advantage

Timely, pertinent and accurate information is critical to effective decision making. Conceptually, this claim is intuitively obvious to most of us, yet, having access to "right" information is hardly the norm in many business decision contexts. The reason for that is that as much as the idea of timely and accurate information being readily available is compelling, making it a reality is an involved and a potentially complex undertaking. Still, even the most operationally challenging problems can be solved, as evidenced by a number of organizations that were able to develop superior decision-aiding informational resources.

This chapter tackles the key conceptual and operational challenges of developing superior informational resources. It begins by expressly differentiating between "information" and "knowledge," with the goal of drawing attention to a common—and incorrect—practice of using these two terms interchangeably, followed by the discussion of "knowledge imperative," which captures the ever-growing importance of decision-aiding knowledge to business decision making. Lastly, the emerging field of database analytics is also discussed.

The Age of Data

Knowledge is the currency of the Information Age. In business, it is the foundation of effective decision making, and as such, an increasingly dominant predictor of organizations' success. Across industry sectors, firms that "know more" earn higher returns on their invested capital, simply because they can focus their energies and resources on the most beneficial courses of action. Within the realm of product and service promotions, superior insights enable organizations to grow the size and profitability of their customer bases by more effective targeting and fine-tuning of individual promotional mix vehicles. In short, better customer and promotional mix knowledge leads to greater productivity of the organization's promotional efforts.

Much of the decision-aiding knowledge comes from insights derived from the so-called "transactional" data, which encompasses a wide range of business-to-consumers and business-to-business interactions.[1] Thanks in a large part to the brisk growth of *electronic transaction processing* (ETP) systems, transactional data became ubiquitous over the past couple of decades. Starting with the introduction and subsequent proliferation of barcode-reading electronic scanners (first used in an Ohio supermarket in 1974), and further fueled by rapid advances in computing and data storage technologies, the ETP systems now generate enormous amounts of relatively accurate and detailed business transaction-describing data.

ETP was taken to a new level by the explosive growth of online commerce, which contributed volumes of transactional and related (such as the so-called "click-stream") data not seen before. Online commerce, however, is not just yet another source of transactional data—it also enables the levels of "trackability" of promotional imprints that were previously not possible. In other words, in contrast to the (very) hard to estimate number of impressions associated with television or billboard advertising, online promotions afford a far greater precision of promotional exposure estimation. Ironically, the otherwise virtual world of online business can be very tangible when it comes to the basic "who," "what" and "when" of business interactions (which spurred a rather intensive information privacy debate).

Another important aspect of the widespread adoption of ETP as the primary mode of processing business transactions has been the commoditization of the resultant data. Stated differently, most organizations competing in a given industry have comparable data assets, hence it follows that any cross-organization data-related knowledge differences are most likely a function of data analytical advantages. Just about every organization has lots of data, but some are simply better at squeezing competitively advantageous insights out of it.

It seems fair to say that, at an organization level, data crunching capabilities evolve primarily in response to organizational priorities and the growth in the availability of data. It follows that as more data becomes available, data crunching capabilities of organizations will also steadily expand. However, since the expansion of data analytic capabilities is also contingent on organizational priorities, not all companies will develop at the same pace. In the end, a common pool of data brought about by the afore-mentioned proliferation of electronic transaction processing systems (such as barcode readers widely used in retail) will bring about some common-to-all, generic data analytical capabilities, while at the same time creating competitive disparity in terms of more advanced data analytical competencies.

This trend is particularly evident in the area of marketing promotion evaluation. The vast majority of organizations that have access to the requisite data will typically also have "basic" data analytical capabilities, usually built around data summarization and reporting. Chances are that marketing managers at firms competing in the same industry are looking at very similar sales reports. Much of that basic informational parity can be attributed to the proliferation of third-party developed reporting applications, such as the widely used "business intelligence" tools offered by a number of different vendors, such as Business Objects, Cognos or MicroStrategy.

By all accounts, the convergence of widespread data availability and reporting capabilities should have produced a leveled informational playing field—in other words, most firms competing in a particular area ought to have comparable informational competencies. Yet, that is not the case. As detailed below, in virtually all industries only a handful of firms are able to consistently use data—readily available to most—to their advantage. To paraphrase an old cliché: *Most companies are* (still) *data-rich, but information-poor*. Even though data is accessible to the vast majority of organizations, it tends to widen the competitive divide rather than narrowing it. Hence, as pointed out in a growing number of popular business texts, such as Davenport's *Competing on Analytics* (2006), Levitt and Dubner's *Freakonomics* (2005) or Ayres' *Super Crunchers* (2007), advanced analytical "know-how" has become one of the key determinants of firms' marketplace competitiveness.

As noted earlier, in the knowledge-intensive environment, informationally competent firms are able to consistently outperform their competitors, primarily because they are able to make better use of organizational resources. Whether it is better understanding of consumers' needs and preferences, a more accurate assessment of the impact of competitive actions or more impactful allocation of promotional dollars, better information typically leads to better decisions. Knowing less, on the other hand, tends to introduce an element of randomness into the organization's decision making process (as the shortage of robust information necessitates guessing), which over the long run translates into a more uneven organizational performance. And last but not least, informational competency enables organizations to take a more proactive decision making stance, which is generally viewed as a prerequisite to both winning and maintaining market leadership. The lack of reliable decision insights tends to impose a more reactive decision making mode, which in turn tends to force organizations into playing catch-up with their better informed rivals.

It is important to note that persistent informational deficiency does not just negatively impact the organization's performance—it may actually pose a threat to its very survival. The steadily accelerating pace of globalization coupled with the broadening trend of deregulation continues to stiffen the competitiveness of markets, which in effect is raising the cost of poor decisions. Under most circumstances, there is simply too little time and too much competition to practice "trial and error" decision making.

As demonstrated by the likes of Microsoft, Proctor & Gamble or Marriott, timely, accurate and unique business insights are among the key pathways to sustainable competitive advantage. The degree to which market leaders are able to consistently outperform their competitors is now inextricably tied to their proficiency in translating large volumes of data into decision-guiding insights. The speed and precision with which an organization can translate raw data into decision-guiding insights determines whether it will be able to pinpoint competitive weaknesses and to identify the most advantageous courses of action, or be among the first to spot and take advantage of emerging trends and opportunities. And as the marketplace competition continues to heat up, fueled by growing privatization, accelerating product innovations and the widening trend of deregulation, it is not just the success, but even the very survival of organizations that is becoming increasingly more dependent on their ability to make sound and effective decisions. In a sense, all organizations are now in the information business but their competencies in that area are highly uneven.

In view of the enormous scope and the depth of what can be included under the broad label of "marketing analytics," this book does not pretend to offer a "one size fits all" solution that could be applied to all data-analysis-related business problems. In fact, given the wide range of potential topical areas, industry- and company-specific circumstances and the types of data, such a "theory of everything" solution does not appear feasible, at least at this time. With that in mind, this text is concerned with one particular area of business knowledge—the "how-to" of efficient, objective and reliable promotional programs evaluation. The ideas put forth here are built around the belief that organizations can use rational planning and evaluation processes and analytic techniques to optimize the productivity of their promotional mix. More specifically, thoughtful promotional managers can increase the net revenue contribution of their promotional mix. The journey toward that end objective starts with an explicit investigation into what constitutes knowledge.

The Believability Factor

There are some very hard to believe facts associated with folding an ordinary sheet of notebook paper. First, regardless of the size of a sheet, no one has been able to fold a sheet of paper more than twelve times.[2] However, what is even more extraordinary about paper folding is the height of the resultant stack. Starting with an appropriately sized sheet of ordinary notebook paper, folding it seven times (the number of folds once believed to constitute the upper limit) will result in a stack approximately equal in height to the thickness of an average notebook. Another three folds will result in the stack height about the width of a hand (thumb included), and an additional four (for a total of fourteen folds) would push the height of our stack to be roughly that of an average person. If we were to continue to fold our sheet of paper, the expected results become very hard to believe: Seventeen folds would produce a stack the height of an average two storey house; another three folds (for a total of twenty) would yield a stack reaching approximately a quarter of the way up the Sears Tower. If folded over thirty times, the resultant stack would reach past the outer limits of Earth's atmosphere; and lastly, if folded fifty times, our ordinarily thin, albeit extraordinarily large in terms of area (to allow a large number of folds) sheet would produce a stack of paper reaching . . . all the way to the Sun. That is roughly 94 million miles!

For most of us, years of schooling imprinted our minds with a variety of abstract notions, while also conditioning our psyche to accept a considerable amount of intangible truths. So long as those scientific and other truths do not come in conflict with our "common sense" of reality, most of us are generally willing to accept even somewhat far-fetched claims. However, when that is not the case—that is, when a particular claim violates what we consider to be reasonable, the result is *cognitive dissonance*. We just can't accept a particular fact or a claim as being true. Even if the underlying rationale and the empirical method both seem acceptable and correct, it can be still very, very hard to believe a conclusion that "does not make sense". That is precisely the case with the paper folding exercise. It is an example of *exponential growth*, which is a phenomenon where the rate of growth rapidly increases as the quantity (e.g., the above stack of paper) gets larger. Since it is a well-defined mathematical property we can compute its values without the need for physical measurements, which is the reason we are able to estimate the height of the stack of paper, even though we are not physically able to fold a sheet of paper fifty times. I am going to venture to say that those of us who at some point in our educational journey were exposed to the notion of exponential growth found it to be intuitively clear and reasonable; furthermore, once properly explained, the computational steps also made sense, which is to say their logic did not clash with our view of the world. Yet when put to a bit of an extreme test, that otherwise acceptable concept can yield unacceptable conclusions. Folding a thin sheet of paper a relatively small number of times simply cannot result in such a staggeringly high stack. . .

This example underscores both the value and the challenge associated with using data analysis derived knowledge as the basis of decision making. It is very easy to accept the findings that fall in line with our existing beliefs, though it could be argued that little incremental value comes out of such "discoveries". It is altogether a different story when findings contradict our a priori beliefs: Is there a problem with the data? Is the approach flawed? Are there any errors. . .? To be fair, data can be corrupted, an approach can be flawed and we all certainly make mistakes. At the same time, however, if none of that could be the case—what then? Oftentimes, doubts linger and what could have become an inspiration for a competitively advantageous decision, joins the repository of many other research initiatives, all dutifully written up, but never acted upon.

Yet taking the leap of faith and acting in accordance with objectively validated insights can be quite beneficial. Much of information technology that permeates our professional and personal lives is "powered" by quantum mechanical predictions; in fact, quantum theory is, in terms of the accuracy of its predictions, the most accurate scientific theory ever constructed.[3] At the same time, it is among the most bizarre, hard-to-believe frameworks in terms of its postulates. In the quantum theoretical world, objects can exist in two states or places simultaneously (a condition known as "superposition"), in addition to which, objects are also instantaneously "aware" of distant other objects (an effect known as "quantum teleportation"). It is akin to saying that a person can be simultaneously alive and dead and furthermore, that a person's physical existence is entangled with consciousness of others. What then determines whether someone is alive or dead? The act of looking, stipulates quantum mechanics. In other words, perception creates physical reality. Does that sound believable?

To Einstein these were "spooky interactions" which is a term he coined deriding the quantum theory. In fact, the great scientist spent more time trying to disprove the quantum theory than he did crafting his own theories of general and special relativity. But in the end, he failed. As much as it is hard to intuitively come to terms with the bizarre postulates of the quantum world, the equations describing its mechanics are extremely reliable. Microchip-powered computing devices, like the laptop on which I am typing this text, work undeniably well, because of the accuracy of quantum mechanical predictions, even though most of us have very hard time accepting the picture painted by the underlying theory.

Obviously, this is not a text on quantum mechanics or paper folding trivia. However, these two examples point to an interesting assertion: The believability of analytically derived explanations should not always be the ultimate determinant of whether or not we accept—and more importantly, act upon—the findings. This is not to say that we should totally disregard our intuition, for that would mean depriving ourselves of lifetime worth of accumulated, though not always well catalogued, knowledge. Quite to the contrary—I am arguing that true edge-producing knowledge needs to combine the elements of truths that might be intuitively obvious to us with those that may not make sense to us, but have been shown to be empirically true. In other words, why not try to get the best of both worlds?

Data, Knowledge and Decisions

As ably detailed by Quinn and his colleagues,[4] success of organizations depends more on their intellectual and systems capabilities than physical assets. To a large degree, Quinn's conclusion is somewhat intuitively obvious: Physical assets are, for the most part, generic, thus it is the application or deployment of those assets that determines the overall success of organizations. Stated differently, it is the uniqueness of organizational "know-how," coupled with the ability to utilize that knowledge that are the greatest influencers of success. Hence it is of considerable importance to organizations to systematically develop competitively advantageous insights in a way that will aid their decision making processes.

It is not an easy task. Unlike the objectively measurable physical assets, knowledge is highly abstract and difficult to measure, both in terms of quality as well as quantity. In the organizational context, it is often either confounded with individuals or buried deep inside various reservoirs holding it. An even more fundamental challenge is knowing what we know, especially given the pervasiveness of the use of terms such as "data," "information," "facts," "insights" or "knowledge." When is what we know an inconsequential (as far as the ability to enhance the quality of decisions), informational tidbit and when is it a true, difference making insight? The next section hopes to provide some clarification.

What is Knowledge?

Plato[5] defined *knowledge* as "justified true belief." The *Oxford English Dictionary* lists several different definitions of knowledge: 1. "expertise, and skills acquired by a person through experience or education; the theoretical or practical understanding of a subject," 2. "what is known in a particular field or in total; facts and information," and 3. "awareness or familiarity gained by experience of a fact or situation." Wikipedia offers probably the simplest definition, by equating knowledge with "what is known."

Oddly (in view of its 2,500 years or so vintage), Plato's definition of knowledge comes the closest to what it means to business decision making. In business in general, and marketing management in particular, decision making is necessitated by a plurality of alternatives—if there are no alternatives, defined here as substitutable courses of action, there are no decisions to be made. In view of that, knowledge can be construed as the degree of understanding (of relative advantages and disadvantages) of the competing options, or in Plato's terms, beliefs that are "justified and true" regarding the value of alternatives. The possession of such robust understanding leads to selecting the "best" alternative, or the option yielding the greatest net benefit.[6] Hence from the standpoint of marketing decisions, *knowledge represents justified and true beliefs regarding the relative efficacy of competing courses of action*.

Taking this line of reasoning a step further, knowing more will give rise to *informational advantage*, which is *the ability to make more effective decisions stemming from better understanding of the potential outcomes of competing courses of action*. In other words, deeper insights or better know-how on the part of promotional management will contribute to the organization's competitiveness—in fact, under some circumstances, it could be a source of competitive advantage. However, in order to have that type of a profound impact, organizational knowledge has to exhibit several broadly defined characteristics—most notably, it needs to be codifiable, teachable and systemic.

Codifiability of knowledge is its ability to objectively encode facts and inferences into clear behavioral guides. In a practical sense, it is a degree to which a particular set of insights or know-how can exist independently of those creating it. Examples of codifiable knowledge include multivariate statistical models-generated behavioral expectancies or propensities, such as the probability of adverse development of recently filed liability claims or the likelihood of securities or employment practices class action. On the other hand, marketing managers' experience or intuition are not easily, if at all, codifiable. As discussed in the next section, not all knowledge can be encoded and as a result, communicated.

The *teachability* of knowledge reflects the degree to which it can be absorbed by the organization. In general, the more understandable and parsimonious the knowledge, the simpler it is to teach. That said, we sometimes do not draw a sufficiently clear line of demarcation between knowledge creation and its application, which is particularly the case in business analytics, where many potentially valuable insights are lost in the web of methodological complexities. In most circumstances, there is a significant difference between teaching how to conduct analyses and how to use the results, which is an important distinction explored in more detail in subsequent chapters. For now, let it suffice to say that insights communicated in a user-friendly format and dispensed in manageable quantities tend to be easy to absorb by the organization, which means that over the long haul they will have more impact on decisions.

Lastly, knowledge has to be *systemic*, which is to say that it needs to permeate the organization. This is important simply because organizations are effectively systems of diverse functions that need to act in harmony to meet its stated objectives. For example, in order for the knowledge of the expected impact of marketing activities to contribute systematically to the growth in revenue and/or profitability, it needs to be made accessible (and taught) to multiple organizational functions, such as marketing and brand management, CRM (customer relationship management) and others.

Components of Knowledge

The creation of knowledge will continue to be a largely human endeavor for the foreseeable future. I am not trying to say that information technology will not play a progressive bigger role in the development of organizational know-how; instead, I am trying to draw attention to an important distinction between *knowledge* and *information*, which are often used interchangeably (both notions are discussed in more detail in the *Data Basics* chapter). Definitionally, information is best described as facts placed in a context, while knowledge is the sum of interpreted information—in other words, information constitutes input while knowledge is the final outcome. It means information is singular and for the most part non-evaluative (i.e., it contains no cause–effect delineation), while knowledge is cumulative and interpretive (i.e., observed outcomes are presented as results of specific actions). Hence, while information technology will certainly play an ever-increasing role in the generation and dissemination of information, the creation of decision-guiding, competitively advantageous knowledge is simply too complex, and to some degree too intangible to be automated, at least in the foreseeable future.

The cumulative character of knowledge gives rise to what is often called *explicit knowledge*, which is factual, objective and relatively easily codified and communicated. In essence, it is an analog to a database. The interpretive dimension, on the other hand, is evident in what is known as *tacit knowledge*. It is a subjective though uniquely human aspect of knowing that is hard to codify, teach and systematize, exemplified by skills, intuition and experience (hence the aforementioned intangibility of knowledge creation). In short, what we tend to regard as knowledge is essentially a product of the interplay between "hard facts" and "fungible interpretation," as shown below in Figure 1.1. Combining these two quite different though equally important dimensions is the primary difficulty in automating the creation of knowledge processes, which is the reason for my earlier claim that the creation of knowledge will remain a largely human endeavor, at least in the foreseeable future.

A somewhat different way of thinking about the building blocks of knowledge is to look at it from the standpoint of epistemology, which is a branch of philosophy concerned with the nature and scope of knowing. An epistemological definition points to four distinct types of knowledge: logical, semantic, systemic or empirical. *Logical*

Figure 1.1 The Components of Knowledge

knowledge is the result of the understanding of how ideas relate to one another. Here, knowing manifests itself in applying accepted rules of logic, which stipulate additional truths. For example: All human beings are fallible. John is a human being, therefore, John is fallible. *Semantic knowledge* is the result of learning the meaning of words, which is simply the familiarity with definitions. The definition of epistemology mentioned earlier is an example of semantic knowledge. *Systemic knowledge* is the learning of a particular system, its symbols and their interpretations. For instance, one's mathematical skills are an example of systemic knowledge. Lastly, *empirical knowledge* is the learning resulting from our senses. Much of the scientific knowledge falls under that umbrella— in the fact the scientific method discussed later relies heavily on empirically derived understanding.

Yet another way of categorizing knowledge is to think of it in terms of a broadly defined purpose it serves, which can be either descriptive (also called declarative) vs. procedural. The former captures the essence of our understanding of "what is," while the latter encompasses our understanding of "how to" accomplish something. For example, knowing the frequency of certain types of loss-generating events and/or the severity of those events constitutes descriptive knowledge; knowing how to reduce the said frequency and/or severity exemplifies procedural knowledge. In the area of marketing database analytics, much of what falls under the umbrella of descriptive knowledge constitutes relatively generic information—the truly competitively advantageous insights usually exemplify procedural knowledge.

Knowledge Creation

How is knowledge created? Although specific mechanisms are probably too diverse and numerous to summarize here, knowledge creation can be either a conscious, end-objective-guided endeavor or it can be a result of an unintended "accident." In other words, knowledge is created purposefully or incidentally. The former is quite familiar to most in the business world, as it is the primary means of generating decision-guiding insights in business. For instance, we notice a sudden upturn in the sales of a particular brand, which then precipitates the question of "why." The process of answering this question is essentially the process of creating purposeful knowledge. On the other hand, the insight that ultimately led to the invention of the now-ubiquitous microwave oven was an unintended by-product of unrelated research into physical properties of very short wavelengths, i.e., microwaves.[7] The researchers were not seeking to gain an understanding of the heating or cooking properties (they were researching radar properties of microwaves; in fact, the first commercially sold microwave oven was called Radar Range), and it was a pure accident that one of the researchers put a candy bar in his shirt pocket which began to melt as a result of direct exposure to microwave radiation. . .

Stories like the accidental microwave invention certainly stir our imagination, but— at least in business research—it is the often painstaking, systematic, purposeful pursuit of knowledge that can contribute to the creation and sustainment of competitive advantage. Stated differently, to be effective, analyses of business data should be directed toward answering specific questions. Thus as approached in this book, knowledge creation is a teleological[8] process, which needs to be directed at a specific purpose to yield worthwhile results.

It all seems straightforward, though it is not. Most organizations are far more adept at capturing data than they are at turning it into decision-aiding insights; in fact, the sheer volume and diversity of the available data can get in the way of using its informational content productively. Strategies often get lost in a sea of "interesting," albeit accidental findings generated and disseminated not because they support specific objectives, but simply because they are. . .well, interesting. More importantly, these often trivial informational pursuits tend to draw the same level of vigor (frankly, oftentimes even more as "interesting" tends to be more captivating than "important") as does the pursuit of insights to guide the firm's stated strategic goals. Hence in some instances it is not the scarcity but the overabundance of data that impedes the creation of competitively advantageous knowledge, which when coupled with ineffective information filtering processes can significantly diminish the potential value of corporate data.

And thus the challenge: To create a hard to imitate knowledge base to serve as a foundation of sustainable competitive advantage, by means of injecting unique insights into the organization's decision making processes. As pointed out earlier, it means the pulling together of the two, frankly quite different dimensions of knowledge: explicit and tacit.

Starting with the former, the creation of a robust *explicit knowledge* reservoir requires the translation of data-derived information into higher level insights. This entails two somewhat different and temporally sequential steps. First is the *informational reduction*, which is a set of statistical procedures-based activities (discussed in more detail in subsequent chapters), designed to expressly differentiate between facts that are critical to reaching the stated strategic objectives and those that are not. The second step is that of *meta analysis*, which entails summarizing the critical results (based on informational reduction), but still too granular information into higher-order insights. The entire data-to-explicit-knowledge process is depicted in Figure 1.2.

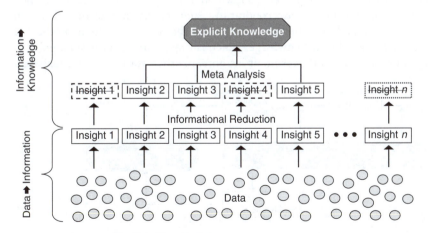

Figure 1.2 Creating Explicit Knowledge

Explicit knowledge alone, however, rarely gives rise to competitive advantage because it is still devoid of experience-based fact interpretation, thus it is usually not sufficiently indicative of the most advantageous courses of action. In other words, the absence of the experiential dimension, such as an experience in a particular industry to help contextualize company-specific loss experience, or hands-on claim management or loss-prevention experience may both limit the potential applicability of the fact-only-based explicit knowledge. This is particularly important considering that in many industries most of the competitors have access to a wide array of fundamentally the same information; hence, working from the same factual base, they are likely to arrive at similar insights, if their knowledge creation pursuits are limited to the explicit dimension of knowledge.

Adding the experiential or tacit component of knowledge into the knowledge creation mix helps to draw attention to what matters from a competitive standpoint. Thus to gain informational advantage over its competitors, an organization has to develop proprietary sources of factual information or find an effective method of "personalizing" its factual knowledge by combining it with the elements of *tacit knowledge*. There are numerous examples of successfully pursuing both alternatives. The world's largest retailer, Walmart, in contrast to most of its competitors has consistently refused to sell its store movement data (i.e., sales data collected from the point-of-sale devices) to the outside syndicated information aggregators (most notably, AC Nielsen and Information Resources) to assure the uniqueness of its knowledge. The results are self-evident. . . On the other hand, Capital One Bank, working fundamentally with the same type of data as its competitors invested heavily in its own, proprietary data analytical processes (i.e., tacit knowledge) which enabled it to consistently deliver above average financial results. The competitive and other circumstances in which these two companies operate pushed them in somewhat different directions, but both organizations made the most of their circumstances, largely because they were purposeful and systematic.

Harnessing the value of tacit knowledge is in many regards more challenging as so much of it is subjective and difficult to codify. That said, a systematic process, framed in the larger context of marketing analytics can serve as a conduit to extracting, normalizing and ultimately, incorporating the tacit dimension into the overall organizational knowledge base. The recommended process is depicted in Figure 1.3.

As suggested earlier and graphically shown in Figure 1.3, the broadly defined analytical process can be construed as a conduit to systematically transforming data into information and, ultimately, (explicit) knowledge. Furthermore, it is also as a source of the more experience-based tacit knowledge, which is important from the standpoint of maintaining the objectivity of the resultant insights. In other words, the data analytical

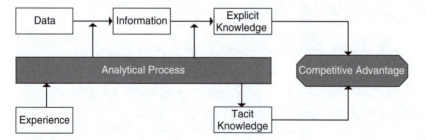

Figure 1.3 Analysis of Data as a Knowledge Creation Conduit

skill set (*analytical process*), coupled with accumulated industry and related expertise (*experience*) support both the process of extracting explicit knowledge out of data (*data* → *information* → *explicit knowledge* progression) and the accumulation of tacit knowledge. The end goal of the knowledge creation efforts—which is sustainable *competitive advantage*—is the product of a unique combination of explicit and tacit knowledge at the organization level. In a conceptual sense, the entire process outlined above is a reflection of the teleological nature of business knowledge creation and accumulation: competitively useful knowledge creation is directed at a specific purpose, rather than "fishing" for whatever can be found in the seemingly endless ocean of data.

Theory or Data Driven?

How do we know that we know? Ascertaining the validity and reliability of what is considered "knowledge" is probably one of the oldest controversies in science. At issue here is not only the availability of objective evidence—i.e., knowledge—but also its believability. In other words, how do we separate facts from fiction? Consider the so-called "Galileo Affair"[9] to appreciate the potential difficulty of distinguishing between objectively verifiable facts and subjective beliefs. The Galileo Affair is anchored in the idea of empirically testing the key postulates of the heliocentric system proposed by Copernicus. As the inventor of the telescope, Galileo was the first to be able to gather closer celestial observations and more precise measurements empirically verifying the accuracy of Copernican thesis. Yet lacking an appreciable understanding of optics, many of Galileo's contemporaries were skeptical of his findings, suspecting the apparent celestial phenomenon to be tricks of the lenses. And so in their eyes, a great scientist was a heretic.

Obviously, our understanding of the world in which we live has increased immensely over the nearly four centuries that elapsed since Galileo's struggles. Yet as we continue to push the limits of our knowledge, we continue to struggle with the same basic task of being able to differentiate between objectively verifiable knowledge and subjective beliefs.

From the standpoint of philosophy of science, the creation of objective knowledge can be either *theory* or *data laden*. The former is carried out by means of hypothesis testing, which is a method of empirically assessing specific theory-derived claims. It means that theory laden knowledge creation springs from the foundation provided by a particular conceptual and rational paradigm—and, it is limited to testing specific claims of predictions derived from that framework. It also means that results of empirical analyses are interpreted within the confines of the theory being tested. There is a certain amount of intuitive appeal associated with that stance, but more importantly, it is supported by neuroscience studies detailing the "mechanics" of the functioning of the brain. These studies suggest that cognitive processing of information requires that our brains hold some beliefs about reality, as absent those, we would be unable to learn from the available information.[10] In other words, the human knowledge creation process appears to be somewhat confirmatory, i.e., theory laden, in nature.

In the way of contrast, the *data laden* approach assumes no existence of an underlying theory and instead approaches the analysis of the available data as a purely exploratory endeavor. Hence the resultant knowledge is built "from scratch," as it is cobbled together from individual insights found while exploring the available data. The data laden approach certainly has merit, but at the same time it is more likely (than the theory laden approach) to be blotted by data imperfections, which is a significant drawback, both in science and in business.

Business analysts need to carefully consider the strengths and weaknesses of these two competing knowledge creation frameworks. The theory laden method requires the availability of a somewhat "mature"—i.e., testable—theoretical framework. It is important to keep in mind that a handful of loosely stated suppositions or insights generated by past analyses do not necessarily constitute a "theory," at least not one that can offer an adequate explanation and/or prediction of the phenomenon of interest. On the other hand, often there can be multiple competing theoretical frameworks available, which can be confusing, to say the least. This brings us back to the earlier-made distinction between "purposeful" and "incidental" knowledge. Directing knowledge creation efforts toward clearly stated objectives, analysts can usually take advantage of conceptually robust and empirically validated conceptual frameworks emanating from a long list of business-related disciplines, such as psychology, economics and neuroscience. In fact, the marketing database analytical framework outlined in this book makes a heavy use of several such frameworks, most of all the *persuasion theory*, the *theory of reasoned action* (both "imported" from psychology) and the *equimarginal principle* ("borrowed" from economics).

The challenges faced by the data laden approach to knowledge creation are more formidable, which is a result of the combination of heightened dependence on the accuracy of data associated with this approach and the inherent imperfections of most databases. As it is intuitively obvious, greater dependence on open-ended exploration of data will create significantly more stringent data quality requirements. In purely exploratory (i.e., open-ended) data analyses, the absence of a supporting theoretical framework makes the task of differentiating between actual and spurious relationships particularly difficult, at times even impossible. Hence the question asked earlier—how do we know that we know?—becomes particularly difficult to answer.

Especially important to the assessment of the overall informational correctness of data are the notions of quality and representativeness. The *quality of data* manifests itself through data accuracy and completeness. The former represents the degree to which the coded values comprising a dataset are error-free, while the latter communicates the availability of actual (as opposed to "missing") data values for all records contained in a file. *Representativeness of data*, on the other hand, is an outgrowth of the inherent "incompleteness" of virtually all business databases. Even the largest data reservoirs contain, in effect, only a subset of all events of a particular type (such as marketing promotions), which then raises the question: How representative is a particular sample of the overall universe? However, unlike the previously discussed data quality, which tends to limit the reliability of overall findings, the representativeness of data plays a role in the generalizability of insights.

All of these considerations can be distilled to a few key takeaways. First and foremost, of the two competing knowledge creation approaches, *data laden knowledge creation* is significantly more demanding in terms of data quality and representativeness. Hence, relying on this approach to the creation of business knowledge will result in a higher likelihood of arriving at erroneous conclusions, when the available data is imperfect either in terms of quality or representativeness. This limitation is well illustrated by the drawbacks of automated data mining applications frequently used in conjunction with large transactional databases. It is one thing to flag statistically significant effects, it is yet another (and a significantly more difficult task) to reliably differentiate between persistent relationships and spurious ones.

Theory laden knowledge creation is certainly not immune to the dangers presented by poor data quality, but it is significantly less impacted by it, for a number of reasons. First and foremost, virtually no theory is ever validated or refuted on the basis of a single test, or even a handful of tests, which obviously reduces the danger associated with a single, low quality dataset. Secondly, a single study will typically test multiple hypotheses derived from the theory of interest and, under most circumstances, not all of the hypotheses being tested would be impacted in the same fashion by data imperfections.

Perhaps most importantly, theory laden approach takes fuller advantage of the cumulative nature of knowledge creation. It offers a way of leveraging previously uncovered and validated insights and building on that base with the help of additional analyses. Overall, it offers a more effective way of distilling the available data into competitively advantageous insights.

Knowledge as a Strategic Asset

An organization that "knows" how to produce something at a lower cost than other producers will enjoy cost advantage over its competitors. If its goal is to grow market share, the cost advantage will give it the ability to do so without sacrificing profitability, or it can simply enjoy higher margins and use the resultant profits elsewhere. Either way, being able to make the same product for less is clearly advantageous—does the same reasoning hold true for promotional activities? I believe so.

As noted earlier in this chapter, much of the decision-aiding knowledge comes from insights derived from the so-called "transactional" data, which encompasses a wide range of business-to-consumers and business-to-business interactions. A *transaction* is an exchange, agreement or communication carried out between separate entities and, typically, involves flow of items of value, such as goods or services. In the database sense, a transaction is an electronic record encapsulating the key descriptive characteristics of an exchange, an agreement or a communication. To comprise a distinct record, a *database transaction* has to be complete, distinct and permanent.[11]

The widespread adoption of electronic transaction processing (ETP) systems mentioned earlier has led to transactional data becoming ubiquitous over the past couple of decades. Fueled by rapid advances in computing and data storage technologies—and more recently, an explosive growth of online commerce, the ETP systems now generate enormous amounts of relatively accurate and detailed business transaction-describing data.

However, it is important to keep in mind that transactional data is outcome-oriented—stated differently, it "speaks" to what happened, but not to why it happened. This is a particularly crucial distinction from the standpoint of marketing management, best understood in the context of "chance" vs. "reason." Consider an abnormally strong performance of a particular marketing campaign—was it due to factors best described as random chance (e.g., it so happened that due to unforeseen supply chain problems, the key competing product was temporarily out-of-stock in major markets), or was it a manifestation of a particularly sound promotional strategy (e.g., the "right" offer delivered to the "right" audience)? To answer this question, one has to look beyond the realm of single-source data.

Multi-Source Analytics

It is intuitively obvious, if not altogether axiomatic that combining multiple sources of data will lead to deeper insights. From the standpoint of knowledge creation, the advantage of integrating different sources of data is the possible deepening of the understanding of the root causes of observed buyer and/or prospect behaviors. Whereas individual data silos—such as buyer behavior or demographic, psychographic and other metrics—enable one to examine the different aspects of what jointly comprises "consumer behavior," fusing together those stand-alone data sources will enable viewing consumers as integrated decision-making systems.

An *integrated decision-making system* is an analytic conception of consumer decisioning looked at from the standpoint of the available data. It captures the impact (on observed outcomes, such as product purchase or promotional response) of the relatively static characteristics, such as demographic descriptors, as well as situational factors, such as attitudinal states. In the analysis sense, it also supports the estimation of the impact of individual drivers of behavior viewed in isolation from other factors and in combination with the other factors.[12]

Integrated system analytics has been employed in a wide variety of fields, including meteorology (e.g., to analyze violent storms), geosciences (e.g., to map shorelines), medicine or aerospace design. That said, however, fusing together different sources of data with the goal of attaining deeper understanding of outcomes of interest is, under most circumstances, operationally challenging for a number of reasons, including:

- **Variability in precision.** As will be explored later (particularly in the *Data Basics* chapter), data sources typically vary—often quite significantly—in terms of their measurement accuracy. For example, due to the "what" (product purchases) and "how" (machine scanning) it captures, UPC scanner data is relatively accurate; at the same time, the often-used consumer geodemographics (basic demographic indicators, such as age, income, education, ascribed to physically proximate groups of households, the so-called "census blocks," discussed in more detail later) are relatively inaccurate.
- **Spatiotemporal differences.** Essentially all data have been collected at a particular place (the "spatio" part of "spatiotemporal," from the Latin term "spatium" for space) and time (the "temporal" part, from Latin "temporalis" for time) and the individual data sources will commonly differ on either or both dimensions. For instance, purchases and attitudes will almost always differ in terms of time of capture; promotional response and purchase data will frequently differ in terms of both the place and time of capture.
- **Unit of measurement dissimilarity.** The basic organizational schema of data is a two-dimensional grid, where, typically, rows delimit individual "records" or "cases" and columns delimit individual "measures" or "variables." The data type specific "unit of measurement," which is what constitutes the individual rows in the data layout grid, may be an individual product (as is the case with retail scanner data), a consumer promotional response (e.g., direct mail response data) or a geographic area estimate (as is the case with geodemographics).
- **Attributional schema inversion.** One of the key operational cross-data source differences is the nature of "entity-to-action" ascription or assignment, which determines whether observed outcomes or attitudinal states are operationalized as

attributes of entities (e.g., buyers or responders) or the other way around. This is a relatively technical concept discussed at length in the *Data Basics* chapter—for now, let it suffice to say that fusing together different sources of data is contingent on the individual data sources boasting comparable attributional schemas.

- **Data imputation strategy.** Once combined, multi-sourced data will often amplify individual data sources' missing value problem. Virtually all statistical analyses require an a priori (i.e., prior-to-analysis) resolution of the missing data challenge, which under most circumstances can take either of the two routes: 1. elimination of records containing missing values, or 2. imputation of missing values (both discussed in more detail in the *Analytic File Creation* chapter). Although at the level of an individual data source finding an acceptable solution to the missing value problem is rarely exceedingly vexing, finding a common-to-all (data sources) solution may be significantly more difficult.

The above outlined potential difficulties associated with the pursuit of multi-source marketing analytics should not be overlooked or underestimated—that said, the potential informational benefits are simply too substantial to ignore. As noted earlier, fusing together different sources of consumer data is a necessary prerequisite to transforming generic (i.e., available to all) information into unique (i.e., available to only a few, or even just a single organization) decision-aiding knowledge.

An old Taoist proverb teaches that "*a journey of a thousand miles begins with a single step*"; here, the journey toward the development of a robust marketing analytical capabilities starts with an explicit recognition of the tacit differences separating raw data, information and finally, decision-aiding knowledge.

From Data to Information to Knowledge

Although often used interchangeably, the notions of *data, information* and *knowledge* all convey fundamentally different meanings. From the standpoint of decision making utility, *data is potential information, information is potential knowledge*, and *knowledge is potential competitive advantage*. Implicit in these differences is a tacit value creation progression, where the initially low value *raw data* is being transformed into higher value *information*, and ultimately into the "finished product," which usually takes the form of competitively advantageous *knowledge*. Hence the notions of data, information and knowledge are all linked together by the value-adding transformation of the low impact, generic commodity (data) into high value, decision-aiding corporate asset (knowledge). The cross-firm invariance in informational proficiency is in itself a manifestation of differences in firms' analytic capabilities. An analytically proficient organization has the requisite skills and processes allowing it to reliably and consistently turn the competitively generic data into competitively unique and advantageous knowledge, while an analytically deficient organization lacks either the necessary skills or processes. Hence the attainment of informational proficiency is rooted in the development of a *knowledge creation process* as the primary conduit to the establishment of a fact-based decision making framework.

Within the confines of business—and specifically, marketing management, the knowledge creation process is defined as a *set of operationally clear data analytical activities aimed at extracting unique, competitively advantageous insights out of the otherwise generic raw data*. The operationally clear data analytical activities are further defined as *specific statistical techniques or computational algorithms*[13] *offering the most effective and efficient means of transforming specific types of data into well-defined decision inputs.* As implied in the above definitions, the data analytical process makes an extensive use of a variety of quantitative techniques, with the goal of bringing about edge-producing insights, not readily available to others in the marketplace. Culled together into a single reservoir, the collection of these insights comprises the *organizational knowledge base*, which is an increasingly important component of organizational equity. As it is intuitively obvious, the quality of the organizational knowledge base is highly dependent on the robustness of the process producing it, which as discussed later, is one of the primary drivers of cross-firm informational inequalities. Perhaps less intuitively obvious is that the ultimate measure of its efficacy is the degree to which the results attributed to that knowledge contribute to the establishment or maintenance of sustainable competitive advantage.

Some of the most revolutionary and admired companies, including General Electric, Walmart, Microsoft, Google or Amazon can attribute much of their success to informational proficiency and the impact it has had on their decision making. Although operating in vastly different industries and governed by considerably dissimilar operating models, these organizations nonetheless have one thing in common: They excel at extracting knowledge out of data and using it to their advantage. In fact, in most industries, knowledge leaders are also performance leaders, because knowing more means making better decisions in anything from resource allocation to opportunity identification. It is important, however, to consider their informational proficiency in the confines of their respective industries to account for cross-industry data inequalities. Some sectors of the economy, such as retailing, financial services or hotel and hospitality are transactional data-richer than some other ones, such as energy or materials. (This difference is primarily due to the dominant transaction type distinctiveness—e.g., retail entails business-to-consumer sales of specific items, while the materials industry is most often characterized by bulk business-to-business sales.)

In addition to data availability inequalities, the individual segments of the economy are also characterized by dissimilar levels of competitive intensity. Retail, hospitality, consumer package goods, financial services or gaming and entertainment sectors tend to be among the most competitive, in terms of the sheer number of firms offering directly substitutable products. Operating in more competitively intense environments results in firms having a greater incentive to invest early and invest more in data-supported decision-aiding infrastructure. Not surprisingly, the best known and probably the most compelling and talked about examples of unique knowledge-driven competitive advantage come from those industries. Household names, including Walmart, Capital One, Proctor & Gamble or Marriott became recognized performance leaders in their respective industries as a direct consequence of first becoming data-based knowledge leaders. These companies had the foresight to invest in the development of superior business intelligence systems and also had the discipline to make objective information the bedrock of their decision making. They have been able to consistently outperform their competitors because they are in a position to better read the marketplace and make more effective use of their resources. To them, as well as a host of other, analytically advanced data users, informational proficiency simply diminishes the amount of guesswork in such critical areas as pricing, merchandising, promotional allocation or new product design, which offers ample competitive cushion to knowledge-enabled firms.

It is remarkable that in spite of the compelling evidence pointing to significant competitive benefits associated with superior, fact-based knowledge, so many organizations continue to bet their future on intuition of individual decision makers. Obviously, there is value in the accumulated experience, but its impact can be considerably more pronounced when coupled with broader learning stemming from objective data. The goal of building a robust organizational knowledge base is not to replace the decision maker, but rather to enhance his/her efficacy by systematically reducing the level of uncertainty inherent in virtually all decisions. Knowing more enables one to spot and take quicker and fuller advantage of emerging marketplace opportunities and it is well-known that the "first mover" advantage often translates into higher profits (which is an obvious consequence of no or very few competitors). And last, but certainly not least: *Superior knowledge is also more difficult to replicate by the competition than other sources of competitive advantage.* Successful products can be copied relatively quickly, just as eye-catching promotional campaigns can be mimicked and winning strategies imitated, but because superior information is the "invisible" force behind better products or more effective campaigns, it is extremely difficult for others to replicate. Not surprisingly, firms that mastered turning data into better decisions continue to outpace their peers.

Sources of Proficiency

Informational competency is rarely, if ever, a product of an accident. Its genesis can be usually traced to careful planning of data capture/acquisition, strong execution of data analytical strategies and disciplined, system-wide embrace of fact-based decision making. It all translates into a well-defined set of "hard" and "soft" assets. In terms of the former, superior knowledge requires robust computer hardware and software, both of which are needed to support data capture or acquisition, compilation and the initial processing of the accumulated data as well as the subsequent in-depth analyses. The latter entails the availability of an appropriate data analytical skill set, without which, even the "best of breed" hardware and software will not catapult the organization to informational competency. In other words, it is entirely possible that an organization could make substantial investments in information technology and still only keep up with the competition. That is because getting ahead of the competition in terms of decision-aiding knowledge—i.e., gaining and sustaining informational, and ultimately, competitive advantage—requires looking beyond the "common-to-many" data analytic mindset in search of unique, advantage creating insights. It means pursuing a more ambitious, forward-looking informational vision.

But what does a "forward-looking informational vision" mean? In broad, conceptual terms it amounts to looking at a right problem in a right way. In more precise analytical terms, it is simply the creativity surrounding the analysis of the available data.

Knowledge leaders work at being at the forefront of informational proficiency by molding data to questions posed by critical business challenges, rather allowing computational convenience to dictate what type of information is extracted from the data on hand. They seek specific, decision-aiding insights into such key competitive-edge-producing problems as quantification of incremental sales or revenue impact of competing price and promotion strategies. They understand that in many regards, the pursuit of business knowledge is the antithesis of mass-producing generic reports that capture every imaginable nuance and detail contained in the raw data, while answering few if any of the outcome-deciding questions. That is why organizations that ultimately become performance leaders have the drive, conviction and skills to enable them to leave the comfort of the "tried and true" traditional—i.e., generic—data reporting and analyses to look for answers not yet found by their competitors. They are not satisfied with knowing as much as their competitors—instead, they search for unique, competitive-edge-producing insights. That, in a nutshell, is the essence of a "forward-looking informational vision."

Similar to other mold-breaking behaviors, analytic innovation has its own share of impediments that need to be overcome. Probably the most significant, at least from the behavior-changing standpoint is the organization's ability to sharpen its informational focus. In short, there is a fundamental difference between the *availability* and *applicability* of information. This distinction is important when thinking about data analysis (i.e., information creation) vs. data usage (i.e., information deployment). In principle, edge-producing analytics entail the inclusion of all available data, but the effective use of the resultant insights is contingent on focusing on only the subset of all available knowledge that is directly related to the decision at hand. Quite often, to know more at the decision time demands "setting aside" the bulk of the available information. Frankly, this is among the reasons that broad-base reporting tends to be an ineffective decision aid. Organizations that become knowledge leaders cultivate not only robust knowledge creation, but also rational and disciplined information usage guidelines. In a nutshell, making better decisions calls for specific, decision-related set of insights—everything else, interesting or not, is superfluous to that process.

It is a lot easier said than done, though. Many organizations' MIS/IT functions are permeated by the "volume production" mentality, which usually manifests itself in a string of detailed reports that overwhelm most, while informing only a few. It is the unspoken, though enduring belief that generating large volumes of information represents a "return" on the often hefty data infrastructure expenditures. In one form or another, the emphasis on volume is quite common, which is in a large part due to the often significant divide separating those who create information from those ultimately using it. This *analyst–user divide* is one of the reasons that the often significant investments in database and reporting technologies rarely translate into noticeable marketplace benefits. Stated differently, technologically advanced database management systems (DBMS) can be a source of *informational parity,* but not of *competitively advantageous* knowledge. This is a critical distinction and one of the key reasons behind the development of the analytical process outlined in this book.

In a strange sort of a way, the trend toward DBMS application standardization is to some degree "responsible" for the low business impact of many of these often pricey data management systems. The ever more robust capabilities of the off-the-shelf applications along with their progressively greater ease of usage, vis-à-vis the mounting technological challenges of the custom-built data processing solutions[14] have led to the virtual disappearance of the latter. Though otherwise a very positive development, the wide-spread adoption of generic decision support systems also carries with it some not-so-positive consequences, such as the informational conversion. Simply put, similar (at times, identical) data combined with generic data management and analysis systems often lead to very similar informational bases, quite unintentionally "shared" by organizations competing in a given industry. In the end, multiple firms competing for more-or-less the same customers and offering functionally very similar products often end up trying to outwit each other with the help of fundamentally the same information.

Still, as mentioned earlier, a relatively small but highly successful segment of companies have found a way to consistently extract competitively unique insight out of the otherwise generic data. Their data and data management systems are usually quite similar to their competitors', but their knowledge creation is typically far ahead of the rest. The key to those organizations' success lies in how they approach the task of mining data. Unlike their less able peers, the analytically proficient firms tend to look beyond the *retrospective* (i.e., a detailing of past results), metric-centric report generation, instead focusing on *prospective* (projections supporting future decisions), business issue-centric and decision-directing insights. Reflecting fundamentally different informational paradigms, the retrospective and prospective data analytical postures differ on a number of key dimensions, with the two most important being the *degree of informational specificity,* or the *volume of the resultant information*.

It is axiomatic that the more tailored the information is to the business problem at hand and the specifics of the organization, the more it will benefit the organization's decision making. Particularly, in order for data analyses to make positive contributions to the firm's success, its outcomes have to be objectively evaluative of competing courses of action. This means that the resultant knowledge should be sufficient to point the decision maker in the direction of the greatest anticipated benefit. Although it seems like a simple enough task, making this conceptual goal an operational reality can be complex. The reasons behind the complexity are rather apparent: Many of the "traditional" data analytic techniques are ill-suited to the realities of modern transactional databases and the informational demands of the fact-based decision making. As shown throughout this book, some of the more basic techniques, such as statistical significance testing or impact (i.e., lift) quantification, are at odds with the intended use of the resultant insights—in other words, usage limitations imposed by computational processes conflict with the intended or desired business applications. Some other techniques, such as experimentation, are not per se at odds with business applications, but their usability limits are often outstretched by informational demands placed on them.

The area demanding perhaps the most fundamental re-evaluation is the broadly defined results or outcomes reporting. Virtually all organizations rely on tabulating and trending their period-by-period revenue performance, which is often "sliced and diced" in a myriad of ways. Although it is certainly important to keep abreast of historical performance metrics, this information is of little help in forward-looking decision making. Choosing among competing courses of action, such as different promotional allocation schemas, requires the decision maker to be able to quantify the schema-specific expected impact to be able to estimate their respective returns on investment, yet such insights cannot be discerned from aggregate performance results. Stated differently, making better choices demands objective estimates of *action-attributable incrementality*, which is the ultimate measure of the *worthiness* of competing alternatives. The striking dissimilarity between the basic result reporting and the objective lift assessment becomes even more pronounced upon a closer examination of both.

Action-Attributable Incrementality

The basic sales reporting is best exemplified by what has come to be known as *management dashboards*, which are reader-friendly, graphics-intensive[15] summarizations of key performance indicators. These reports are typically built around outcome tabulations, such as sales or promotional expenditures and side-by-side comparisons, where the selected metrics are broken down by type or geography. Management dashboards are clearly beneficial to decision makers insofar as they can—if well designed—present a relatively comprehensive snapshot of the business, in a highly parsimonious format. The vast majority of dashboards, however, tend to be inconclusive. They focus on easy to measure outcomes, such as sales, revenue or expenditures while failing to address the underlying *causes*. This is a considerable limitation. A brand commonly has multiple promotional vehicles at work at any given time, thus knowing which—if any—of those mechanisms had a measurable impact on the outcome of interest is quite important to future marketing mix planning.

To be more beneficial to the promotional planning process, management dashboards should be built around *action-attributable sales incrementality* assessment. In terms of the previously mentioned knowledge creation continuum, the sales incrementality assessment provides decision makers with future action guiding knowledge by linking specific outcomes with the most pronounced promotional causes. It is, however, considerably more complex methodologically. It also represents a shift in information generation philosophy: The traditional "observable outcome oriented reporting" is focused on churning out reports encompassing all that *can be known*, while the "action-attributable sales incrementality focused reporting" advocated here is focused on specific insights into *critical to know* areas.

In practice, the difference between these two methodologically and substantively distinct result-measurement approaches translates into two fundamentally dissimilar sets of activities: The former are typically built around simple metric-by-metric tabulation and summarization of aggregate results, while the latter emphasize the translating of large volumes of either inconclusive or incomplete pieces of data into probabilistic cause–effect estimates. From the analytical standpoint, the observable outcome-based reporting is computationally straightforward and nowadays the task is almost always handled by highly automated, functionally elegant data reporting software packages. The opposite is true for action-attributable incrementality assessment-based reporting, which demands highly involved, often complex and manual statistical modeling preceded by a considerable amount of data preparation. Although some parts of the requisite process are prone to standardization (hence this book), action-attributable incrementality estimation is considerably more effort and expertise intensive. That said, as exemplified by Dell, Amazon or Procter & Gamble in addition to the above-mentioned Walmart, Capital One or Harrah's, the payback on the more involved knowledge creation process investment can be both significant and long-lasting.

Volume

The volume of information also matters. Interestingly, more often than not there tends to be an inverse relationship between the sheer amount of information and its business utility. This may sound counterintuitive, particularly considering our enduring belief that it is better to know more rather than less. The pitfall in this line of thinking, however, is the implicit assumption that more information translates into deeper knowledge. This is simply not true, mainly because a considerable amount of the available information often has very little to do with a particular business decision (or any decision, for that matter). For instance, the decision of which of several competing promotional alternatives should be selected when the end objective is that of profitable sales growth will not draw much help from anything other than an objective assessment of the individual promotion's anticipated lift. Other insights, such as last year's sales trends or cross-outlet sales distribution comparisons might be deemed "interesting," but ultimately they offer little-to-no help in identifying the most effective of the promotional choices. In principle, one can have lots of information but little-to-no knowledge. It follows that to yield the maximum benefit, information creation needs to be rooted in the give-and-take considerations of quality over quantity and need-directed problem solving over propagating spurious informational details. Frankly, it is counterproductive to disseminate interesting but not decision-aiding informational tidbits, simply because processing it takes time and attention away from the task at hand, while making no substantive contributions to decisions at hand.

From the viewpoint of science, there is nothing new about the notion of less being more. As one of the key tenets of scientific inquiry, this idea traces its philosophical roots to Occam's Razor,[16] a centuries-old axiom guiding the process of scientific theory building. Better known as the *principle of parsimony*, this basic "keep it simple" prescription tells us that the best explanations are those that involve the fewest number of concepts or informational details. A business decision maker will benefit much more from a relatively few, but highly action-directing insights than from a large number of mostly inconclusive and often unrelated details.

This is not to say that whatever information is not applicable to an issue at hand should be discarded—quite to the contrary, more effort should be put into cataloging and meta analysis as the means of making effective use of all informational assets. Of the two, the latter can be particularly beneficial, though it is rarely used in applied business research. Operationally, *meta analysis* is data about data, which in essence is the exploration of results of data analysis in search of underlying patterns and other communalities. It can be particularly beneficial to database analyses because it offers a robust and an objective method of summarizing the often quite voluminous basic insights. It can serve both as the means of uncovering of new insights as well as succinctly communicating of the otherwise excessively detail findings.

Clearly, informational excellence can be quite beneficial to firms' economic well-being which brings us to an obvious question: What is required of an organization for it to develop a high level of informational proficiency? Or, stated differently: What separates informationally advanced organizations from their less analytically proficient competitors?

Analytics

Informational competency is rarely, if ever, a result of data access inequalities. As previously discussed, most organizations today have access to more-or-less that same type of raw data, largely due to the fact that the vast majority of it comes from functionally generic sources.[17] For instance, the bulk of Walmart's data comes from its point-of-sale systems which are functionally quite the same—i.e., capture the same type of basic data—as are those used by K-Mart or other major discounters (after all, these are standard applications sold and developed by outside vendors). In that sense, Walmart's informational superiority should not be attributed to (raw) data inequalities, as the previously noted standardization of electronic transaction processing systems just about guarantees that most competitors in an industry will have access to the same types of transactional data.

That is not to say that there are no instances of firms enjoying access to unique sources of data. There are a number of examples of organizations systematically supplementing their "generic" data sources with additional, often somewhat idiosyncratic (i.e., decision type-specific) data types. For instance, Harrah's enriches its basic hotel, casino and entertainment folio details with in-market experimentation results, which are then used extensively as the basis for making promotional and other decisions. The data associated with such experiments, exemplified by total dollar amounts and visit frequencies attributed to different combinations of incentives, requires specific and often complex setup and administration procedures. It means that in contrast to the "generic" transactional details passively collected by the POS and other systems, the capture of the "special purpose" data is contingent on highly specialized skill set. This means that organizations pursuing the collection of such data are typically already far more informationally proficient than their competitors. In other words, the capture of the "special purpose data" is more a result of informational competency than its precursor.

Another possible source of informational proficiency could be the broadly defined data infrastructure, which is comprised of data storage as well as data processing hardware and software. Probably even more than data access, the data processing infrastructure is extremely unlikely to be the source of informational advantage for two basic reasons: First, over the last several years the widespread standardization of ware-housing and reporting applications has led to a certain degree of functional conversion, which means that differently branded applications are nonetheless quite similar in terms of their capabilities. Secondly, even the largest organizations more-or-less abandoned the earlier trend of developing from scratch their uniquely own (and thus different) decision support systems in favor of standardized, outside vendor-supplied solutions. In other words, there is little-to-no cross-user infrastructure differentiation.

In the end, neither the mere access to raw data, nor the availability of a "state-of-the-art" data processing infrastructure are likely to be a source of a sustainable informational advantage. This leaves only two other plausible explanations: 1. organizational culture, and 2. the data analytical *know-how*.

Culture, defined here as the institutionalization of fact-based decision making, holds quite a bit of intuitive appeal as the source of the cross-firms knowledge disparity. After all, if an organization does not value information, in the sense of embracing data-driven decision making, it could not possibly develop a superior data-based knowledge foundation. However, one could also argue the flip side of this reasoning, namely, that it is unrealistic to expect a rational firm to value anything prior to the existence of convincing evidence. Since both sides of this argument have merit, this has the characteristics of the proverbial "chicken and egg" circular argument, with no clear way of settling "which came first." However, looking to organizational culture as the source of informational proficiency implicitly assumes that the organization has the skills required to extract uncommon insights out of the otherwise common data. And this indeed could be the crux of the problem—many firms do not.

To put it simply, the biggest single source of informational advantage is the superior *knowledge creation know-how*. Overall, the most significant factor that consistently explains why some data-rich organizations are also knowledge-rich while other, equally data-rich and technologically enabled firms are comparatively knowledge-poorer is the advanced data analytical skill set of the former. At the time when data is ubiquitous and the basic data processing increasingly informationally generic, it is the ability to go beyond the basic data crunching functionality that is the key determinant of the value of the resultant information.

Though manifestly important, the knowledge creation know-how is arguably the least developed and certainly the least formalized aspect of the new, digital world. Many will balk at this statement, as after all, quantitative data analysis itself is a well-established, long-standing field of study. And indeed it is, in the academic sense. However, as shown throughout this book, it is not in the practical business sense. Similar to a number of other fields of study, quantitative methods tend to be inwardly oriented and primarily focused on methods, rather than outcomes. Those trained in it tend to acquire substantial amounts of domain-specific knowledge, but very little understanding of the contextualizing influences of different data types or business objectives. Analysts' understanding of even the most rudimentary characteristics of modern business databases tends to lag far behind their comprehension of the specific inner-workings of the individual quantitative analysis methods, which is to some degree a reflection of many academics' limited exposure to the more complex business data sources. Frankly, that poses a problem as extracting unique and competitively advantageous insights is as dependent on the in-depth knowledge of statistical techniques as it is on the comparable knowledge of data. In short, database analytics may have the makings of a new discipline, which though heavily rooted in statistical data analysis nonetheless draws heavily from a host of other business disciplines, ranging from database technology to economics.

The Knowledge-Based Decisioning Imperative

One of the most persistent indicators of the informational maturity of organizations is their outlook on data, and particularly sales transactions. Though virtually all firms recognize the importance of this source of information, not all take a full advantage of its informational content. To the vast majority, transactional data needs to be *reduced* to be of value, which means tabulated, summarized, described and distributed via a wide range of reports, such as those showing total sales, sales per geography, time period, etc. On the other hand, a relatively smaller set of organizations take a far more *expansive and exploratory* approach to transactional data. Their more inquisitive stance stems from the desire to understand the causes of the observed outcomes, rather than merely tabulating unexplained results. Not surprisingly, their data mining capabilities are, almost always, far more developed, particularly in the sense of a wide-scale (i.e., organization-wide) use of multivariate statistical analyses and experimental design. These are the knowledge leaders discussed earlier—the organizations whose "data crunching" capabilities evolved beyond the often pointless report propagation in search of unique, competitive-edge-producing knowledge.

Interestingly, both types of organizations, the causal knowledge seekers and the result summarizers tend to speak of data as a corporate asset. In case of the former, exemplified by firms such as Capital One, Marriott, Proctor & Gamble or Walmart, data is clearly a corporate asset—after all, those firms were able to gain and maintain competitive advantage through an innovative and an effective use of data. Looking at data "asset-worthiness" through that prism, it is hard to see how the latter category of companies, the result summarizers, can make the same claim. If the firm's competitive position has not been enhanced by data, is that data really an asset to the organization? Probably not.

The reason for that is simple: Data, as a digital representation of certain outcomes (e.g., purchases) or states (e.g., demographics) is merely a raw material with a *potential* to inform the firm's decision making. Absent the know-how necessary to extract competitive-edge-producing insights out of it, raw data offers little-to-no utility to an organization, in addition to which, its informational (and any monetary) value diminishes over time.[18] For instance, 10-year-old product purchase details offer little in a way of insight into present-day product repurchase propensity or price elasticity. In other words, virtually all business data have a certain period of applicability, beyond which its informational contents become simply too dated and in effect, obsolete. At the same time, just "having" data (i.e., its capture, storage and ongoing maintenance) can be quite costly, often requiring millions of dollars of capital expenditures on computer hardware and software, not to mention dedicated stuff (database administrators, programmers, etc.). These considerations point to the question of business value: If the data residing in our IT systems does not make clear and consistent contributions to sales, or other revenue-generating activities, why should it be considered an asset? After all, basic business logic suggests that an asset should not consume more than it either currently or potentially can contribute. Let's take a closer look.

Is Data an Asset?

An *asset* is defined as something of economic value that the organization owns and controls and that is expected to provide future benefits. In an investment sense, an asset increases the value of a firm or benefits the firm's operations. Although data can be viewed as having intrinsic economic value since in many instances it could be sold in the marketplace, that argument is only applicable to a certain subset of firms (i.e., retailers often sell their transactional data to outside vendors, such as AC Nielsen or IRI, who then re-sell it, typically as packaged solutions, to manufacturers) and data types. In a broader context, it is fair to say that few if any organizations would be willing to sell their product sales data or promotional response results, as any potential monetary gains would be far outweighed by the potential competitive self-hindrance. Furthermore, there are a number of regulations governing sharing of certain types of data, such as the recently enacted Shelby Act which places severe limitations on the use of vehicle registration data. All considered, outside of the data service provider industry, few companies decide to invest in data capture and its ongoing maintenance capabilities because of the expectation of deriving an income stream from future sales of that data.

Under most circumstances, the real "asset-worthiness" of data stems from its potential to improve the firm's operations through the generation of unique knowledge, which in turn can give rise to competitively advantageous decisions. This leads to an obvious conclusion that data that do not contribute, meaningfully, to the development of competitive advantage should not be considered an asset. In fact, keeping in mind the often high cost of its capture and maintenance, poorly utilized data could even be viewed as an expense from a strictly cashflow point of view. There simply is no getting around the obvious conclusion that unless properly used, data investments can lead to an economic loss when evaluated in the confines of basic cost–benefit analysis.

All considered it is then more realistic to think of data as a *potential* asset, as such a categorization highlights the importance of the analysis of the available data. This more tenuous expression of data's asset-worthiness underscores the obvious fact that without a significant amount of effort put into analytics, even the "best" data will not contribute enough to the organization's well-being to warrant an unconditional asset designation. Also, thinking of data as a potential, rather than an actual asset draws attention to the importance of taking steps to extract economic benefits out of data that are at least equal to data's "cost of ownership."

Furthermore, thinking of data as a potential asset has a secondary benefit of redirecting the emphasis away from storage and maintenance infrastructure and toward the usage. Since the 1980s, organizations across industries have been investing heavily into data capture and maintenance-related infrastructure, while dedicating disproportionately little effort and resources to data exploration. It has been estimated that approximately 85%–90% of total data-related expenditures were directed at the hardware and software infrastructure, with only the remainder going toward extracting insights out of data. In other words, only about 10¢ out of every $1 of data-related spending went toward actually making data into a true organizational asset. As a result, the well-known expression of a firm being "data-rich, but information-poor" is often quite true.

But even the 10% or so of the total information technology expenditures that in one way or another was dedicated to data exploration has not always been utilized as much as possible. Oftentimes, a good part of that spending went toward the production of generic information (e.g., the standard, measurable outcome-focused management dashboard reports discussed earlier) that could bring the organization up to the level of competitive parity, though not sustainable competitive advantage. Some of that is due to the previously discussed convergence of technological data capture and storage platforms (e.g., UPC scanners, POS and DBMS or the recently emerging campaign management and tracking systems) combined with a generic approach to data analysis, together leading to additional informational convergence. Further fueling the informational convergence is the recent proliferation of third-party analytics, or data analysis vendors offering fundamentally the same type of information to multiple competitors in an industry. Unlike the technological standardization, however, the degree of analytical convergence varies across industries, as it tends to reflect of the availability of data to vendors. Nonetheless, there is a distinct trend of relatively few, large data providers and aggregators providing informationally non-distinct analytical products and services to a wide cross-section of the marketplace.

The slow but persistent process of technological and informational convergence underscores the importance of the earlier discussed forward-looking informational vision built around analytically innovative approaches to data analysis. Raw data has the potential of becoming an asset, but its asset-worthiness hinges on the organization's analytical skills. Data is an asset to organizations that are able to systematically extract competitive-edge-producing insights out of it. To others, specifically those whose data crunching capabilities are limited to standard, off-the-shelf tools and whose informational vision does not extend beyond basic outcome reporting, data is yet another component of the cost of doing business.

Data as a Source of Competitive Advantage

The last couple of decades have been particularly eventful from the standpoint of business information. Some of the more noteworthy trends, from the standpoint of knowledge creation, include the following:

- A combination of rapid gains in data processing capabilities, decreases in storage and processing costs and the proliferation of powerful software applications are leading to database technology becoming affordable to an ever growing number of organizations.
  - Result: *Leveraging customer and competitive data became a key ingredient of firms' product and market strategies.*
- The growing digitalization of business processes, including sales and customer interactions, is spawning an overabundance of transactional data often leading to potential users "drowning in data but lacking information."

- Result: *Organizations spent large sums on customer data warehouses, yet to-date only a handful truly leverage their data assets.*
- The forces of deregulations coupled with growing business globalization are leading to considerable increases in the level of competition, ultimately amplifying the importance of timely and accurate customer and market information.
  - Result: *Increasing competition accentuated the need for speedy extraction of actionable business insights from databases.*
- Information availability and immersion are becoming a part of everyday business culture and data analysis techniques slowly making their way into common business lexicon.
  - Result: *As database analytics is no longer a domain of a few, large organizations, the demand for skilled analysts exploded.*

Taken as a group, these developments are to a large degree responsible for the growing importance of unique (to a given organization), fact-based knowledge in building and sustaining competitive advantage. In a sense, *all organizations are now in the information business*, to the degree to which their competitive well-being has increasingly grown dependent on the access to timely and accurate decision-guiding insights. Stated differently, knowledge surrounding the key decisions, such as product design (i.e., what is the most desirable bundling of product attributes?), promotional mix allocation (i.e., how should the finite promotional dollars be allocated across the available promotional alternatives to deliver the highest incremental benefit?) or the customer acquisition and retention strategy (i.e., what are the most cost-effective tools/tactics?) is now among the most pronounced determinant of firms' success.

In a recent, insightful look at the impact that the persistent and well-thought-out data analysis—defined as reliable conversion of raw data into competitively advantageous knowledge—can have on organizations' long-term success, Thomas Davenport delineated a number of key factors characterizing information-driven organizations.[19] These include the widespread use of modeling and optimization, enterprise-wide deployment of data-derived insights and solid support from the top echelons of management. Of those, the *widespread use of modeling and optimization* comprises the general set of skills needed to translate the mounds of often dissimilar raw data into useful information. As detailed by Davenport, the quality of the resultant analyses requires the coming together of three key components: the right focus, the right people and the right technology. Implicit in the interplay of those three information-quality shaping forces is the analytic know-how, which is that somewhat intangible quality that on one hand calls for strong quantitative methodological skills, while at the same time contributing a healthy amount of problem solving creativity. A disciplined and rational left brain meets the spontaneous and untamed right brain. . .not impossible, but at the same time, not an everyday occurrence either.

As previously outlined in the *Sources of Proficiency* section, organizations that excel at extracting competitively advantageous knowledge out of the otherwise generic data are able to do so because of their data analytical prowess and the organization-wide fact-based decision making discipline. Processes ranging from high-level strategic planning to tactical decisions surrounding product mix, logistics, inventory and distribution or promotional mix spending allocation are all making increasingly better use of the available data. As mentioned earlier, one of the key drivers that fueled Walmart's growth and its eventual ascendance to the world's largest retailer and the Fortune #1 organization (based on gross revenue[20]) was its early embrace of the information-driven decision model. While its competitors continued their march forward (or so they believed), guided mostly by their intuition, anecdotal evidence and rarely empirically validated generalizations, Walmart looked to objective and representative data insights for decision cues. As a result, its merchandising mix consistently outperformed its peers, while its simulation- and optimization-based supply chain management mercilessly squeezed unnecessary inventory and stock-out costs, enabling it to offer competitive prices while still generating attractive returns for its shareholders. It is no surprise that the now industry-leading organizations such as Dell and Amazon emulated Walmart's supply chain philosophy as one of the engines catapulting them to the position of prominence.

But Walmart's way is not the only way—frankly, blindly copying methods of successful companies' practices can be a slippery slope, as it cannot be assumed that just because a particular practice or a method works well in one instance, it will work equally well in other instances. Inherent in the development of effective data mining capabilities is a certain element of organizational self-discovery, which entails the identification of the most adaptable (to the specific of the organization) ways the organization can use data to gain and sustain competitive advantage. After all, the retail industry's dynamics are quite different from the pharmaceutical, financial or other sectors of the economy, as is the available data. Neither are any two firms in a given industry exactly the same, particularly in the cultural sense (for instance, some firms are highly centralized while others are de-centralized in terms of their decision making models; some are overt risk takers in terms of heavy emphasis on new, trend setting products, while others are risk avoiders, preferring instead to focus on the "tried and true" ideas or technologies). Therefore, the specifics of "what" data and "how" it can be used effectively are shaped by both industry-wide forces (e.g., what type of data and data insights can offer the greatest potential competitive levers?), as well as by company-specific competencies and goals (e.g., company's intrinsic capabilities and its organizational culture).

Capital One, as one of the leading credit card issuers in the U.S. and one of the leading credit card industry innovators has consistently delivered above average results by an almost religious dedication to objective data analysis, especially customer mix optimization. Harrah's, a major casino entertainment organization and a relative risk-taker in its industry, systematically improved its profitability by using data analysis to attract and retain customers with the greatest profit potential. A resource-constrained baseball club, the Oakland A's consistently posted one of the league's best regular season records by identifying the otherwise undervalued players that could perform the desired assortment of tasks, something Oakland was able to do in spite of working with a far-below-average budget. Honda developed a second-to-none brand loyalty by using data for early detection of potential problems, thus greatly increasing the reliability of their automobiles. A leading hotel chain, Marriott, uses advanced analytics to optimize the price–profitability relationship, while Novartis, the giant pharmaceutical firm leverages data analysis to improve the quality and the efficacy of its R&D efforts. Last but not least, Procter and Gamble, a leading consumer packaged goods manufacturer continues to prosper in a very competitive, mature industry segment in a large part due to organization-wide embrace of data-driven new product development, as well as promotional mix allocations and evaluation practices.

The Emerging Field of Database Analytics

The rate at which the data is accumulated vastly exceeds the rate at which it is analyzed. The ever expanding digitalization of business transactions, manifesting itself in the growing number of data-creating technologies, such as POS systems or campaign tracking software resulted in an exponential growth in the sheer amount of raw data. In addition to the "involuntary" data capture, systematic data "creation" has exploded, both in terms of types as well as volume. Specialized databases, such as consumer geodemographics, psychographics, spending or wealth estimates are widely touted as potential sources of the "whys" behind the "whats" offered by transactional data.

Yet as mentioned earlier, on average, out of every $1 spent on databases, no less than $0.85 goes to storage infrastructure and only roughly up to $0.15 is allocated to extracting insights out of the data. Some of this spending allocation disparity can be attributed to the more capital-intensive nature of data capture and storage infrastructure; however, that reasoning does not extend beyond the initial acquisition and setup costs. In other words, once the data capture and storage systems are in place (and paid for), the infrastructure vs. analysis resource allocation inequality should begin to disappear. But that rarely happens in practice, which is a manifestation of an enduring—and incorrect—organizational mindset equating "information" with "data." It is common for organizations to believe that continuing to pour money into data capture and maintenance infrastructure will lead to better decisions and, ultimately, higher revenue or profitability. The empirical evidence, however, does not support that assertion, as there is no clear cause–effect linkage between the organization's IT expenditures (defined as hardware- and software-related spending) and its marketplace success. Operating system, processor or storage hardware upgrades may enhance the organization's data capture, storage, retrieval and processing capacities, just as business intelligence data reporting software will likely increase the ease, the speed and the usability of basic database reporting. In the vast majority of cases, these are the real informational benefits of the aforementioned $0.85: more data—more accessible—more quickly.

The ever larger and more numerous organizational databases are not only expensive to build and to maintain, but can also be analytically taxing. In fact, if the data they contain is not analyzed correctly, unreliable or even invalid inferences can be drawn. For instance, it is now commonplace to rely on the notion of statistical significance to attest to effect coefficients' (such as promotional response lift) "validity," which as detailed later often outstretches the test's application limits (which is usually due to either the sheer size[21] of the analysis universe or the nature of the data,[22] both of which require controlling steps that are rarely taken in practice). Ultimately, when subjected to a closer scrutiny, a good many of the seemingly "robust" findings end up being nothing more than spurious relationships misinterpreted as facts.

The analysis of large corporate databases can also present significant interpretational challenges. The explosion in the availability of data associated with the advent of electronic transaction processing made possible an objective evaluation of a wide range of promotion-related and other types of behaviors, but doing so oftentimes necessitates the use of complex, probabilistic multivariate statistical models. These approaches tend to make heavy use of abstractly defined "statistical effects" that require a considerable amount of interpretation before becoming meaningful to non-technical business audiences. This is particularly the case with statistical models employing interaction (i.e., combinations of variables expressed as separate metrics) or non-linear (i.e., effects where the change in one metric is accompanied by a disproportionate change in another) terms. Though no one knows with certainty, it is believed that more than 50% of database modeling findings never mature beyond the initial, technically framed presentation. Hence it follows that the attainment of an acceptable level of the decision making utility is tied to the adequacy of "model translation" efforts, or the re-casting of obtuse statistical effects into more interpretationally clear business terms. And that in turn is dependent on the adequacy of the analyst training.

On-the-job training is still the most popular means of training junior analysts in working with large volumes of heterogeneous data filling up the plethora of databases found in many of today's business enterprises. Obviously, it can be very beneficial for the more experienced employees to pass their knowledge onto their less experienced colleagues; however, it can also contribute to the institutionalization of flawed practices. Moreover, it promotes "learning without understanding," a highly undesirable practice for any organization aspiring to glean competitively advantageous insights out of its data.

An obvious alternative to on-the-job training is more specialized academic preparation. Unfortunately, business schools have been relatively slow to both recognize and embrace (in the sense of teaching) database analytics. More often than not, university-level statistics courses teach the theory in a relative isolation from the idiosyncrasies of different data types and, when using data, rely on overly simplistic datasets. In the end, the bulk of the graduates end up being ill-equipped to tackle the complexities of modern business databases.

What steps should data-rich organizations take to also become information- and (more importantly) knowledge-rich? Make better use of the available data resources through the development and institutionalization of robust data analytical capabilities. Doing so, however, requires a couple of key steps: First, organizational knowledge creation needs to be approached as an ongoing process, rather than a sporadic event. In other words, an organization aspiring to become a knowledge leader in its industry needs to put in place a process linking organizational goals, informational objectives, data analyses and knowledge proliferation. Secondly, insight validation and predictive reliability processes need to be established, and need to be capable of differentiating between spurious associations and true competitively advantageous insights. This will call for the proverbial "thinking out of the box" to adapt statistical methods and processes to the characteristics of large corporate databases and the demands of business decision makers. This book offers an outline of a database analytical process, designed expressly to help business organizations increase the impact of their marketing promotions.

The Uniqueness of Marketing Database Analytics

As an emerging, practice-oriented field, database analytics draws on multiple disciplines ranging from statistics to database technology, promotional campaign management and strategic planning. As a subset of the larger database analytical process, promotion analytics relies on largely the same universe of skills and knowledge, with a particular emphasis on the following:

Technical Skills

- **Statistics.** Database analysts are expected to be proficient in a wide range of the univariate and multivariate techniques, the sampling theory and the experimental test design.

- **Campaign measurement.** Probably one of the least developed areas within the field of database analytics, it focuses on measuring sales incrementality attributable to individual promotional treatments, programs and campaigns.
- **Online analytics.** Typically focused on Web traffic analysis, tends to be somewhat idiosyncratic in terms of tools and to a lesser degree, methodologies.
- **Database technology.** Although database analytics practitioners do not need the level of technical proficiency of developers or programmers, knowledge of the basic level of relational or event database structure is important to make the most of the data they contain—i.e., to translate the often voluminous data into sustainable competitive advantage, which is the theme of this book.

General Promotion Knowledge

- **Promotional strategy, targeting and segmentation.** The knowledge of the basic conceptual frameworks along with practical applications.
- **Campaign design and management.** The basic flows and processes; differentiation between offer, treatment and campaign.
- **Direct marketing.** The basic design, fielding, tracking and measurement techniques.

Experience-Based Knowledge

- **Promotion analytics "rules of thumb."** Is 20% a reasonable campaign response rate to a repurchase campaign targeting lapsed brand buyers? Sometimes, to be able to pinpoint a truly successful result or a finding that falls outside what is normally considered to be a "reasonable" range, an investigator needs to have some degree of familiarity with "typical" or "normal" values for given outcomes.

Why is it important for a data analyst to develop such a wide-ranging set of skills and proficiencies? The short answer to this question is because all of those factors play a role in transforming generic information into unique, competitively advantageous knowledge. More on that in the next section.

The Marketing Database Analytics Process

As convincingly argued by Peter Drucker, one of the most preeminent management thinkers, a business enterprise ultimately just has one goal—to create a customer. Doing so requires management to perform two critical functions in every organization: 1. to foster innovation, and 2. to effectively market the organization's products and/or services. Management teams that perform these two tasks better than their competitors will win a larger share of the overall customer base.

It follows from the above rationale that effective promoting (of products or services) entails using the least amount of resources to win the largest number of customers. This intuitively obvious notion is at the root of what is generally referred to as "promotional productivity," often objectified through the promotional ROI (return on investment) metric.

Reaching—and more importantly—sustaining above average levels of promotional productivity requires a considerable amount of specific knowledge, such as buyer purchase or repurchase propensities, price elasticity, anticipated promotional lift, etc.

That said, the seemingly long list of the potentially useful decision-aiding insights can be reduced to a relatively small set of well-defined critical promotional success factors. However, what constitutes critical success factors for marketing is in itself a function of the role of marketing vis-à-vis the organization at large.

When looked at from the standpoint of business utility, marketing promotions (as a functional area within an organization) are expected to offer a set of tools to aid the organization in reaching the stated performance objectives. In other words, promotions are means to an end, where the end represents reaching or exceeding the said business goals. And although business enterprises vary significantly in terms of what and/or how they produce, their goals can nonetheless be reduced to one or more of the following three general categories:

1. Sales/revenue growth.
2. Profit growth.
3. Market penetration.

Naturally, most organizations will be concerned with all of the above, but at any given time, any one of those goals will be more pronounced than the remaining two. For instance, a relatively new and small organization will typically emphasize sales growth and market penetration over near-term profitability, while a more mature and established firm will typically be more concerned with increasing the profitability of its operations. And ultimately, since all organizations have to make tradeoff-entailing resource allocations, the resource constraints will usually "force" them to prioritize their objectives.

Whatever the stated business objectives, the role that marketing promotions usually play in reaching those goals falls into one of the three distinct sets of activities:

1. New customer acquisition.
2. Current customer retention.
3. Customer value maximization.

Not surprisingly, larger organizations tend to have somewhat separate functions, or departments, each tasked with new customer acquisition, current customer retention as well as cross- and up-sell (customer value maximization). Whether that is the case or these somewhat different tasks are all concentrated in the hands of the same group, the role of promotional analytics is nonetheless to supply marketing personnel with actionable knowledge that can be used to enhance the efficacy of the aforementioned key promotional endeavors.

Hence it follows that a generalizable marketing database analytical process should contribute to the efficiency and the effectiveness of the above-delineated promotional objectives, and by extension, the broader organizational goals. This is particularly important from the standpoint of drawing an objective line of demarcation separating the "truly impactful" from the merely "interesting" insight-generating analytic endeavors. In other words, the exploration of the available data that is not directed toward specific informational needs is likely to produce a plethora of intellectually curious, but practically insignificant findings, all of which will contribute very little toward increasing the efficacy of promotional efforts.

The process-based approach to effective analyses of large marketing databases summarized below was developed within the constraints imposed by the above

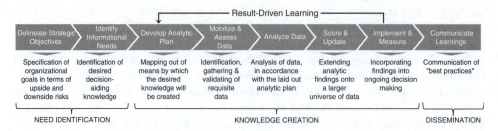

Figure 1.4 Marketing Database Analytics Process

considerations. It outlines the means of translating raw data into, initially, *informational insights* and ultimately, into *competitively advantageous knowledge*. The overall process flow and its key components are depicted in Figure 1.4.

A more in-depth discussion of the database marketing analytical process shown above is presented in the next chapter.

About This Book

This is a "how-to" book: How to use commonly available data to get unique insights into commonly asked marketing promotion related questions. Given its analytical focus, the bulk of the book's contents are related to quantitative data modeling. That said, non-statistical modeling issues are explored with a comparable level of depth and care, as the creation of truly unique and valuable business insights necessitates a solid understanding of elements of other supporting domains, such as strategic planning, data warehousing and economics.

Many of the solutions presented here stem from hands-on practical experience of working with numerous, large organizations from a cross-section of industries, including financial, energy, automotive, packaged goods, insurance, banking, telecommunications, high tech, retail, consumer durables and hospitality. The overall analytical process and its individual components are expressly "calibrated" to take into account the most commonly used data sources, with the primary emphasis on large transactional data warehouses, such as the UPC scanner product movement data typically associated with retail point-of-sale systems. Also explicitly considered are other common business sources of data including sample-based surveys, such as consumer satisfaction or product quality studies; data aggregator-compiled "causal overlays" exemplified by consumer geodemographics; public financial filings and disclosures, such as the Standard & Poor's Compustat database tracking quarterly and annual financial filings that are required of publicly traded companies. In the data sense, the basic premise of the database analytical process presented in this book is the amalgamation of dissimilar sources to form the basis for creating the otherwise-beyond-reach knowledge.

Content-wise, I draw upon the work of multiple disciplines, including statistics, business strategy, database technology and management and to a lesser degree from other areas, such as industrial psychology. In my discussion and recommendations I rely heavily on practical database analytical consulting experience, based on my work with large corporate databases of Fortune 500 organizations from a wide cross-section of industries mentioned earlier. I make extensive use of database analytical examples drawn from real-life analysis and modeling projects to illustrate the shortcomings of some methods and processes and to underscore the advantages of other approaches.

As stated above, this book is about the "how-to" of database analytics. Although it offers theoretical descriptions and rationales behind the recommended approaches, the focus throughout this text is on the hands-on, systematic process of answering specific business questions. It is important to note that, as detailed in Chapter 2, the end goal of the marketing database analytical process, depicted above in Figure 1.4, is not a mere translation of data into information, but rather it is to create a source of unique and thus competitively advantageous organizational knowledge, added to and updated on an ongoing basis.

My secondary objective is to contribute to a re-focusing of analysts' attention away from the "modeling" part of the process and toward the "usage" of the resultant knowledge. This is not to say that I am advocating modeling carelessness, far from it, as the subsequent chapters show. I am merely trying to shine the spotlight on the utility of the end product of analysis, recognizing that an abstractly defined statistical model—in and of itself—rarely offers meaningful amount of utility to its end users, unless the results are properly framed and communicated.

Organization

The basic organizational framework of this book follows the general outline of the framework depicted in Figure 1.4 above. Although the content is of relatively technical nature, the presentation is (hopefully) easy-to-follow.

The next chapter (Chapter 2) offers a more in-depth discussion of the marketing database analytical process shown in Figure 1.4. The remaining chapters are grouped into three broad sections that make up the marketing database analytical process: 1. Need Identification; 2. Knowledge Creation; and 3. Dissemination.

The first two chapters of the *Need Identification* section, *Organizational Objectives and Informational Needs* (Chapter 3) and *Skills and Tools* (Chapter 4), kick-start the marketing database analytics process by drawing attention to the importance of rooting the analysis of data in specific organizational needs, all with the goal of increasing the chances of the resultant insights making a substantive and material contribution to the marketing action-related decision making.

The second section—*Knowledge Creation*—comprises the bulk of the book's content, nine chapters in total (Chapters 5–13), as it details the individual components of the systematic transformation of raw marketing data into decision-aiding insights. Chapter 5, *Analytic Planning*, describes some key considerations entailed in laying out not only what analyses are to be done, but also any prerequisites that need to be satisfied. Chapter 6, *Data Basics*, weaves together a number of concepts from database design, information theory and database management all aimed at forming an objective foundation of the basic concepts surrounding electronic data storage and manipulation. Chapter 7, *Analytic File Creation*, offers an in-depth treatment of specific data cleansing and preparatory steps, geared toward assuring the accuracy of input data as well as the attainment of distributional and other data properties that are essential to assuring robustness of statistical analyses of data.

Chapters 8 through 11 detail the heart of the marketing database analytical process—the actual analysis of data. Chapter 8 presents a discussion of what should be the initial data analytical step—*Exploratory Data Analyses*, the discussion of which is geared toward establishing the foundation of the informational content of the earlier created data file. Building on those initial, exploratory insights, is a relatively broad *Segmentation* discussion (Chapter 9), followed by a more focused review of *Behavioral Predictions* (Chapter 10), which is built around key (to marketing analytics) multivariate statistical techniques. Next (Chapter 11) comes a discussion of *Action-Attributable Incrementality* approaches, focused on the challenge—and the available solutions—of estimating the net impact of marketing promotions, followed by an overview of *Database Scoring* (Chapter 12), which is an application of analysis-derived insights to the entire customer/prospect universe. Lastly, capping the "analysis" part of the marketing database analytical process is the detailing of the steps that are necessary to translate the often esoteric analytic results into actionable, decision-aiding knowledge (*From Findings to Knowledge*, Chapter 13).

The third and final section, *Dissemination*, focuses on "packaging" of the resultant insights into parsimonious and easy to follow dashboard and scorecard reports, targeted at specific informational consumers. It represents a culmination of a single iteration of the decision-aiding knowledge creation process depicted in Figure 1.4.

Beginning with Chapter 5, each chapter is capped with a practical Mini-Case, the goal of which is offer real life illustrations of concepts discussed within those chapters. Although all individual Mini-Cases use real-life data and examples, some of the details, such as names, are changed in view of the competitive sensitivity of the information.

2 The Marketing Database Analytics Process

Successful completion of a task usually depends on developing a robust understanding of it, in terms of what is to be done and why, as well as the availability of requisite skills and tools. Keeping in mind that the ultimate objective of any business organization is winning and retaining customers, the creation of the requisite knowledge—i.e., how to attract and retain profitable customers in an economically sound manner—forms the basis of an effective marketing strategy. In other words, the attainment of broadly defined informational advantage is the key to competitive advantage.

The marketing database analytics process first introduced in the previous chapter is discussed in more detail in this section. The process, which lays out an approach of systematically translating raw data into decision-guiding knowledge, offers the operational means of realizing informational advantage; its conceptual roots and the overall rationale are discussed next.

Approach and Philosophy

The ideas outlined in this book are rooted in the belief that analyses of business data in general—and marketing analytics in particular—are most effective when framed in the context of explanation-based prediction coupled with multi-source analytics. Definition-wise, *explanation-based prediction* is making probabilistic estimates regarding future outcomes based on explaining past ones, while *multi-source analytics* is the use of amalgamated, though otherwise diverse types of data as the basis for analyses.

Process

Taking a closer look at the key epistemic[1] issues, it is important to keep in mind some of the fundamental differences between the purely scientific goal of theory creation and testing, and the focus of applied marketing analytics, which is that of estimating the likelihood of outcomes of interest along with the delineation and parameterization of key drivers of those outcomes. Stated differently, our goal is not to search for universally true and longitudinally invariant (i.e., unchanging over time) generalizations, but rather, to make reasonably accurate estimates in relation to future states of certain outcomes that are of interest to us. In fact, it is usually assumed that much of what we find today is going to change in the future given the dynamic nature of market behaviors. Hence process-wise, the logic of marketing database analytics can be depicted as follows:

The process depicted in Figure 2.1 illustrates the notion of explanation-based prediction: Exploratory analysis-generated findings give rise to a prediction, which is

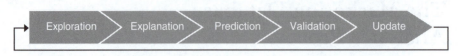

Figure 2.1 Generic Process of Database Analytics

followed by validation. In practice, exploratory analyses will yield a causal model which in turn forms the basis for a scoring equation which generates forward-looking estimates, which are validated against the known outcomes. Once the new batch of behavioral data is available, the analytical process is restarted to take into account any changes in (data-contained) behavioral patterns. This process is inherently reductive, which is to say it focuses analytic efforts on the most disaggregate elements of companies' marketing mix, such as an individual coupon drop or a direct mailing.

Methods

The two framing aspects of the analytic approach described in this book—explanation-based prediction and entity-specific estimation—carry a number of implications. First, the estimation of the outcomes of interest will encompass the use of multiple metrics, both quantitative and qualitative, to enhance the accuracy of future states' predictions and the completeness of the underlying causal explanation. Second, analytic conclusions will be geared toward improving the business efficacy of future decisions, measured in terms of the expected impact on earnings. Third, the interrelationships among the individually estimated marketing actions will be assessed in the context of a dynamic system capable of propagating future changes.

Method-wise, the above translate into the following considerations:

1. Focus on multi-source, multivariate analyses

The approach outlined in this book is expressly focused on developing all-inclusive marketing database analytical capabilities. Stated in more operational terms, it means the marketing database analytics process shown in Figure 1.4 is built around multi-variate, or multi-variable, analyses of dissimilar sources of data. *Multi-source data* is a necessary prerequisite to analyses of the organization's marketing mix. *Multivariate analyses*, on the other hand, are necessary to the development of reliable explanation of the observed outcomes. Theoretically, this reasoning is rooted in the modern *measurement theory*,[2] the basic tenets of which advocate the use of multiple indicators in situations where the phenomenon of interest is illusive in nature (i.e., the so-called "latent" or unobservable constructs) or when no single indicator is a perfect predictor of the outcome of interest.

As a broadly defined family of analytic tools, multivariate statistical analyses can be thought of as mathematical techniques designed to simultaneously estimate the effects of multiple measures, in such a way as to allow to: 1. take into account possible cross-variable interdependencies, and 2. quantify the net effect that can be attributed to each measure. In a context of individual marketing mix elements (such as direct mail), multivariate analyses will yield insights that are maximally complete (given data limitations), while containing a minimum amount of explanatory redundancies. Hence

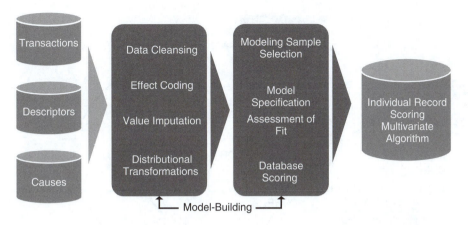

Figure 2.2 Predictive Parameterization Process

extended over a number of different promotional mix elements, multivariate analytical techniques will yield the maximally explanatory and most accurate predictive capability. Figure 2.2 offers a graphical summary of the predictive analytical estimation processes detailed later.

2. Estimation of marketing mix-wide interrelationships, supporting system-wide propagation of future changes

As noted earlier, the individually estimated promotional and related marketing effects are subsequently integrated into an overall system combining effect-specific impact estimation with the assessment of interdependencies among the individual effects, or marketing mix components. Furthermore, in order to be able to accommodate the ongoing updates depicted in Figure 1.4, the said system needs to be capable of propagating changes to one or more "connections" onto the entire network. Consider Figure 2.3. In the hypothetical multi-event network depicted, the individual promotional vehicles—Vehicle A, Vehicle B, etc.—are connected by lines showing their interdependencies, along with magnitudes of those interdependencies ($CORR_{AxB}$, etc.). The interdependencies are measured in terms of bivariate correlations, which are non-directional. The arrow-expressed directional cross event type connections denote future propagation of changes to any of the bivariate relationships onto the entire network.

Validity and Reliability

The vast majority of advertising promotions—one of the key elements of marketing mix—are geared toward eliciting specific attitudinal changes, with the ultimate goal of bringing about the desired behavioral outcomes. The seemingly ubiquitous automotive or consumer product (such as breakfast cereal or soda) ads attempt to create a positive affect toward specific brands, which in turn should increase the probability of selecting the advertised brand at the time of purchase. However, unlike the easily observable behaviors (a product purchase is a very unambiguous outcome), attitudinal changes are elusive, from the measurement standpoint. Given the very intangible nature of attitudes,

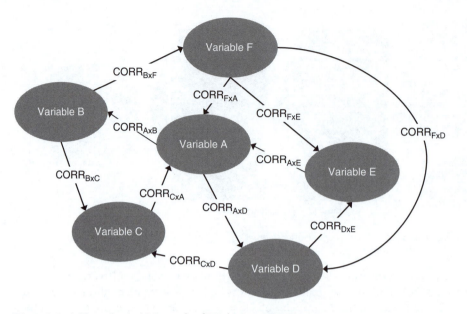

Figure 2.3 A Hypothetical Network of Marketing Mix Elements

their measurement—both in terms of their state as well as any promotion-related changes—necessitates very close attention to the notions of *validity* and *reliability*.

Consider the following measurement challenge: An automotive manufacturer, typically known for economical, lesser expensive vehicles decided to introduce a premium brand extension—a luxury, four-door sedan. In the months preceding the launch of the new car, the company ran a string of television and online ads geared toward altering consumers' perceptions of its product, hoping to infuse ideas such as "quality," "comfort" and "prestige" into the psyche of the buying public. Did the ads have a desired effect?

Abstract notions such as "quality" or "prestige" are difficult to ascertain because they do not necessarily convey a universal meaning. In other words, one person might equate "quality" with "reliability," while another with the vehicle's fit and finish. Hence, to be able to ascertain consumers' attitudes, as well as attitudinal changes, it is necessary to expressly identify unambiguous, tangible indicators of abstract (also known as "latent" in the jargon of psychometric measurement) constructs, such as the aforementioned quality, comfort or prestige. Graphically, this can be expressed as follows (see Figure 2.4):

In essence, the challenge entailed in answering the above-posed question ("Did the ads have a desired effect?") is twofold: First, it is to find the "right" indicators (Observable Measure 1, Observable Measure 2, etc., in Figure 2.4), which are the tangible, easier to assess proxies for the event in question. Second, it is to ascertain the accuracy of those indicators—in other words, how good a proxy for the Latent Construct is Observable Measure 1?

The attitudinal assessment challenge posed above is illustrative of two key and distinct measurement considerations: reliability and validity. *Reliability* captures the repeatability or consistency of a particular operationalization. A measure (such as Indicator A or Indicator B) is considered reliable if it gives us the same result over and over again, of course assuming that what we're measuring (Latent Construct) is not changing.

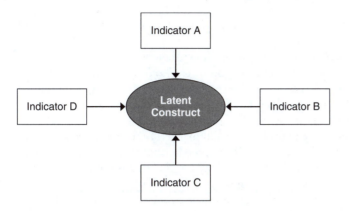

Figure 2.4 A Hypothetical Latent Construct Measurement Problem

Conceptually then, reliability is a ratio of "true level of the measure" to the "entire measure." In practice, however, the "true" measure is rarely known, hence in the applied sense, the best way of estimating reliability is to express it as a correlation among multiple observations of the same measure. There are several different types of reliability—internal consistency, test-retest reliability, parallel forms and inter-rater reliability—from the standpoint of marketing measurement, the inter-rater reliability is of most importance.

The other of the two key aspects of latent construct measurement is *validity*, which captures the degree to which the construct's conceptualization and operationalization are in agreement. Simply put, it is the quality of measurement. Conceptually, validity is both broader and a somewhat more elusive idea, hence it can be looked at from a number of different angles, which reflect two key underlying questions: 1. Is the operationalization a good reflection of the construct? 2. How will the operationalization perform? These two broad questions can be broken down into several, more specific question-expressed types of validity considerations (see Table 2.1).

Table 2.1 Types of Validity

Type	Description
Face Validity	On their face value, are the indicators (Indicator A, Indicator B, etc., in Figure 3.5 as a whole a good reflection of the latent construct?
Content Validity	Is the informational content of individual indicators in keeping with the meaning of the latent construct?
Discriminant Validity	Are these measures of the latent construct operationally different from other sets of measures?
Predictive Validity	Will the operationalization be able to predict the outcome of interest with a reasonable degree of accuracy?
Convergent Validity	Do predictions generated by the operationalization converge with other, related predictions?
Concurrent Validity	Can the operationalization distinguish among types of outcomes?

The Marketing Database Analytics Process

The process-based approach to effective analyses of large volumes of multi-sourced marketing data is summarized in Figure 2.5.

The *marketing database analytics (MDA) process* shown below is comprised of eight distinct stages, which are grouped into three categories: 1. *Need Identification*, 2. *Knowledge Creation*, and 3. *Dissemination*. Although as shown above in Figure 2.5 the individual stages comprise a continuous process, each of the three broad subsets of the process is framed in the context of some unique demands and characteristics.

The goal of the *Need Identification* part of the overall marketing database analytics process is twofold: First, it is to bring forth the agreed upon (by the executive management) strategic goals of the organization. To be clear, the focus of this step is not to initiate any discussions regarding the appropriateness of those goals, but to simply list the strategic objectives that have been embraced by the organization. Second, it is to translate the delineated strategic objectives into specific informational goals. Implicitly, this step recognizes that a successful achievement of the organizational goals is, to a large degree, dependent on the attainment of a high degree of decision making clarity. The overall goal of the *Need Identification* stage of the MDA process is to distill the agreed upon strategic goals of the organization into a clear set of informational demands.

The goal of the second, broad stage of the marketing database analytics process—*Knowledge Creation*—is that of meeting the informational demands that stem from the organizational objectives (or more specifically, marketing goals). That is both a tall order and a very broadly scoped endeavor. It encompasses five distinct process stages, *Analytic Plan Development, Data Mobilization and Assessment, Data Analysis, Scoring and Update, Implementation and Measurement,* which as shown in Figure 2.5 is also a recurring or an iterative process. In fact, the *Data Analysis* part of the *Knowledge Creation* part of the overall process is itself comprised of several distinct stages, as shown in Figure 2.6.

The *Analysis* stage is comprised of four purpose- and methodologically-distinct sub-stages: 1. *Exploratory Analyses*, the goal of which is to supply initial assessment of the underlying metrics and relationships; 2. *Segmentation,* the focus of which is the identification of economically actionable consumer (current as well as prospective customers) segments; 3. *Behavioral Predictions*, tasked with making forward-looking projections of quantitatively estimatable outcomes; and 4. *Incrementality Measurement*, which aims to quantify action-attributable impact of marketing actions. Much like the more general process steps depicted in Figure 2.5, the sequencing and contents of the analysis-specific stages of the MDA process are both intended to support speedy, objective and robust methods of translating raw data into usable, decision-aiding knowledge.

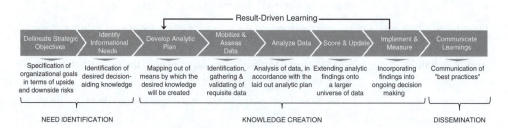

Figure 2.5 The Marketing Database Analytics Process

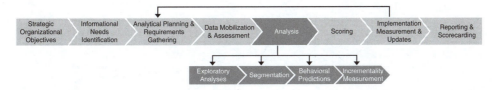

Figure 2.6 Components of the "Analysis" Stage

Returning to the overall marketing database analytics process depicted in Figure 2.5, the role of the third and final process stage—*Dissemination*—is to "package" the earlier created knowledge into a maximally impactful set of end user reports. At the risk of sounding tautological, it is both easy and difficult. It is easy insofar as piecing together of a picture is not particularly hard when all of its pieces are readily available; at the same time, it is difficult because different end user constituents can have quite dissimilar preferences and appetites for detail.

It is worth emphasizing that the development of robust organizational knowledge bases is a piecemeal process, with each single step contributing a successively closer approximation of the objective "truth", as it builds upon and refines previous findings. The ongoing utility of the accumulated knowledge is dependent on a systematic feedback gathering system (i.e., the *Result-Driven Learning* feedback loop), which is necessary to keep up with the ever-changing and evolving business, economic and regulatory environments. Furthermore, it is also worthwhile to emphasize that since marketing analytics, as described in this book, is an ongoing learning process, rather a pursuit of isolated facts, the methodologies described within each of the above depicted process steps represent a subset of all methods that could be potentially employed within a context of each of the process stages. In other words, the goal of this book is not to offer an all-inclusive delineation of all methods that could potentially be used to analyze marketing-related outcomes, but rather to direct readers' attention to specific techniques that have been proven to be the most appropriate in estimating the outcomes relating to the design and management of marketing programs.

PART I
Need Identification

3 Organizational Objectives and Informational Needs

The ultimate goal of marketing analytics is to contribute to the creation of sustainable competitive advantage by providing economically actionable, decision-aiding knowledge. Doing so necessitates, among other things, rooting of data analytics in the stated organizational objectives and the resultant informational needs.

This is a lot simpler than it may sound, because from the standpoint of marketing actions, organizational objectives can be grouped into three distinct clusters: 1. acquisition of new customers; 2. retention of existing customers; and 3. optimizing the value of customer relationships. Obviously, this is not an "either-or" listing, as most organizations will pursue, or will want to pursue all of those objectives concurrently; however, from the standpoint of marketing analytics—and more specifically, the creation of decision-aiding knowledge—each of these objectives entails a different set of analytic activities. Hence it follows that in order for the outcome of marketing analytics to have the maximum decision making impact, it needs to be "tailored" to the organizational objective-driven informational needs. This chapter offers an outline of the key considerations entailed in systematically cataloguing marketing database analytics-related organizational objectives and the resultant informational needs.

Organizational Goals

It was noted in the opening chapter that a business enterprise ultimately just has one goal—to create a customer. To do so, a business organization needs to perform two critical functions: 1. to foster innovation, and 2. to effectively market the organization's products and/or services. The latter of the two imperatives is the domain of marketing, and depending on the degree to which the task of promoting of the organization's products and/or services can be effectively carried out using the least amount of resources to win the largest number of customers, marketing will have contributed to the organization's competitive advantage. This can be viewed as an "offensive" aspect of the broadly defined marketing function.

As much as winning new customers is critical to business organizations' growth and prosperity, retaining current customers is just as important. In fact, anecdotal evidence suggests that, on average, it is about four times more expensive to win a new customer as it is to keep an existing one—stated differently, without an effective (customer) retention strategy, even the most successful acquisition efforts might not be economically sustainable over the long run. Just consider the case of the U.S. automakers who, during much of the 1990s and the early part of 2000s were locked in a three-way (GM, Ford and Chrysler) discount-based customer acquisition war, which ultimately led to GM (actual) and Chrysler (de facto) bankruptcies, as well as the overall erosion of the U.S.-based automakers' share of the U.S. market.

A perhaps less clear-cut marketing-related organizational goal is to "economize" customer relationships, which means increasing the profitability of individual customers. Doing so might entail migrating select customers toward more profitable products/ services (e.g., from entry-level to a luxury sedan for an automaker or from basic to premium programming options for a TV cable operator), reducing promotional subsidies, such as manufacturer coupons used widely in consumer packaged goods, or increasing the frequency of repurchase, which is often the goal for travel and leisure products and services.

Whatever the stated business objectives, the role that marketing promotions usually play in reaching those goals falls into one of the three distinct sets of activities:

1.   New customer acquisition.
2.   Current customer retention.
3.   Customer value maximization.

As noted in Chapter 1, most organizations will be concerned with all of the above, but at any given time, one of those goals will be more pronounced than others. For instance, a relatively new and small organization will typically emphasize sales growth and market penetration over near-term profitability, while a more mature and established firm will typically be more concerned with increasing the profitability of its operations. And ultimately, since all organizations have to make tradeoff-entailing resource allocations, the resource constraints will usually "force" the prioritization of objectives.

Informational Objectives

One of the biggest challenges of database analytics is that of effectively dealing with the divide separating the analysts and the users of information. As expected, the former tend to view analyses of data as a technical task governed almost entirely by data and method characteristics, while the latter are typically consumed, again almost entirely, by business implications. Naturally, both viewpoints have merit: Technical modeling issues are critical to the robustness of ensuing results, just as the practical applications of findings are the ultimate determinant of their value. Unfortunately, the often limited understanding of each other's priorities and issues tends to lead to analysts guessing their way through projects' practical substance-related considerations, at the same time as the future business users are glazing over the results' research methodology-related limitations. Not surprisingly, such Babylonian efforts commonly yield poorer overall results for organizations than multi-million hardware, software and data investments could otherwise produce.

So what can be done about it? To use Plato's utopian vision: Should kings become philosophers, or should philosophers become kings?[1] Frankly – neither. For the most part, given the depth and the relative complexity of quantitative data analytical methodologies and related topics, it seems unreasonable to expect the users of information to become methodological experts. At the same time, considering the typical detachment of analysts from the practical applications of their analyses, it is not likely that they will reach the users' level of business need understanding. That leaves only one feasible avenue to improving the less than ideal analyst—user level of cooperation; namely, to put in place a systematic process of defining informational needs that can reliably "translate" business informational needs into operationalizable analytical activities. Unfortunately, it is not quite as easy as it may sound.

There are a couple of general, highly interrelated challenges that need to be overcome. The first one can be broadly described as the *level of informational precision*. While business needs are typically stated in somewhat general—if not ambiguous—terms, data analysis needs precision and specificity, if it is to hit the "informational bull's eye." For example, let's consider a question commonly asked by marketers: *"How are my campaigns performing?"* To a business user this seems to be a perfectly clear, self-explanatory question, yet to an analyst, its meaning is far from obvious. Looking at it from a standpoint of having to make the most appropriate data and method selection, an analyst will realize that there are numerous, operationally distinct approaches that can be used here, each yielding a considerably different answer. For instance, counting the number of campaign responders is one of the potential analytical avenues, often picked because it offers the simplest way of assessing an aggregate performance of a promotional campaign. A (far) more analytically involved alternative involves the quantification of the campaign specific lift, or sales incrementality attributable to a particular treatment, as a way of comparing the performance of individual campaigns. Another approach sometimes used entails surveying consumer awareness changes or satisfaction levels, with the implicit assumption that heightened awareness/satisfaction levels will translate into higher sales. The point here is that what might seem to be a clear-cut business question can be analytically quite ambiguous.

The second obstacle is even more fundamental, as it involves timely and complete *a priori delineation of business informational needs*. As defined here, it is a relatively broad endeavor encompassing the distilling of the big strategic picture into more granular tactical components, clearly stating data and methodological requirements, followed by the sketching out of an analytical roadmap. Taken together, the component parts of the a priori delineation of business informational needs can be thought of as a continuum to which both the analysts and business users of information can contribute, as shown below:

Business users are responsible for putting forth strategic and tactical objectives, which is the point of departure in developing a robust informational foundation. At this point, the emphasis is on presenting a comprehensive picture of the high-level business objectives. Next, the strategic and tactical objectives need to be translated into specific informational requirements. For instance, the high level strategic goal of increasing the brand's profitability may translate into the need to identify the most profitable potential new buyers (informational need #1), the most effective promotional mix vehicles (informational need #2), or a delineation of robust performance metrics (informational need #3). The success in this stage depends on the business users and analysts working together earnestly to add a dimension of analytical precision to the stated informational needs.

Once the informational needs have been defined and operationalized, analysts are then responsible for addressing data and methodological requirements. It all boils down to

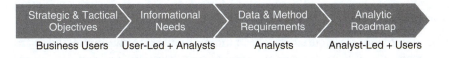

Figure 3.1 Delineating Informational Needs: The Team Continuum

answering a basic question: *What are the data and methodological requirements that are necessary to deliver against the stated informational needs?* The last step in the process—the development of an analytic roadmap—puts forth a clear plan for how those goals will be accomplished, spelling out the timeline, resource requirements, means and dependencies as well as the final deliverables. It makes it possible for analysts to describe the upcoming deliverable and solicit feedback before committing to a specific analytical course of action.

An optimist looks at what appears to be a problem as a potential opportunity to bring about improvements. The degree to which analysts and users of analyses-based insights do not sufficiently communicate with each other presents a challenge insofar as the value of data analysis is concerned. At the same time, being able to pinpoint the specific deficiencies stemming from the said poor communication—the level of informational precision and an a priori delineation of business informational needs—offers a blueprint for an effective remedy, outlined earlier in Figure 3.1.

Delineation of Strategic Goals and Tactical Means

Baldrige defines strategic objectives as *"an organization's articulated aims or responses to address major change or improvement, competitive issues, and business advantages."* Paralleling an advertising slogan, database analytics does not "make" strategic objectives—it "helps" in turning them into reality.

A well-defined set of strategic goals includes the appropriate operationalizations, or tactical means by which the stated objectives are to be reached. For instance, the goal of growing the brand's sales can be tactically reached by lowering prices, increasing promotional intensity or targeting new consumer segments.[2] In fact, it is the tactical means to the organization's stated strategic goals that are the true point of departure in the database analytics planning process, simply because tactics are more tangible and as such, more indicative of the requisite informational needs. In that sense, the goal of database analytics is to aid in the identification and execution of tactics driving the stated strategic objectives.

The task of delineating the focal strategies and tactics belongs to business users, with a particular emphasis on those accountable for reaching the stated goals. Goal specificity is highly desired.

Uncovering Informational Needs

Once the organization's overall strategic goals and their tactical means have been clearly enunciated, specific informational needs can be identified. In general, those will fall into one of the following two categories:

1. Explanation and prediction.
2. Ongoing assessment.

Explanation and Prediction

This is a broad category of potential analyses, ranging from relatively simple univariate (i.e., one variable at a time) investigations to complex multivariate (i.e., simultaneously considering multiple variables) predictive models and simulations. For instance, a frequently encountered business goal that relies heavily on exploratory analytical capabilities entails brand pricing decisions, typically framed in the larger context of stimulating sales. It is well known that most products exhibit some level of price elasticity, which means that a price decrease can be an effective sales stimulant. The challenge, of course, usually revolves around the identification of that optimal tradeoff between a lower per unit profit level (due to price decrease) and the increase in aggregate sales, and total profit. From an analytical point of view, a key inference-based input into these decisions is the appropriately operationalized price elasticity.

Predictive analytical capabilities, on the other hand, are exemplified by the seemingly ubiquitous need to grow sales through new buyer acquisitions. Here, database analytics are often looked to for the identification of high brand conversion or trial likelihood prospects. In other words, for a brand with a X% market share in a product category Y, Y—X typically represents the universe of prospects, which means that for a number of widely used products, such as breakfast cereals, cellular phones or automobiles, the "available" prospect pool can be both large in terms of size and diverse in terms of preferences. Certain types of predictive models, described in depth in Chapter 7, can be used to focus the acquisition efforts on a subset of prospects deemed (i.e., predicted) to be most likely to convert, which will obviously increase the efficacy and the efficiency of those endeavors.

In general, the exploratory and predictive analytical capabilities supply decision making inputs prior to taking a particular business action—in other words, they are helpful in making better informed decisions. In the way of contrast, the ongoing performance assessment set of capabilities discussed below helps to assess the impact of decisions that were made by objectively quantifying their impact. As discussed throughout the subsequent chapters, the two sets of capabilities are the cornerstones of the database analytical process described in this book.

Ongoing Assessment

Frequently referred to as the "back-end program measurement," this is a family of methods focused on objective quantification of the impact of the organization's strategies. Depending on data availability and the level of methodological sophistication, it can range from a simple tallying of promotional response rates to a relatively involved quantification of the treatment-attributable sales incrementality.

In contrast to the innovation-focused exploratory and predictive capabilities, the ongoing impact assessment "values" cross-time and cross-treatment standardization. In other words, the most effective back-end measurement capabilities are those yielding results that are comparable across the different types of initiatives and across time.

Both the exploratory and predictive capabilities, as well as the ongoing impact assessment are most effectively planned through a close cooperation between business users and analysts. Combining the knowledge of the two early in the analytical planning process will likely bring about greater efficiencies later by zeroing in on what questions should be asked and which ones can actually be answered in view of the ever-present data and methodological limitations.

Assessing Data and Method Requirements

The notions of data availability and methodological readiness can themselves be depicted in terms of a continuum representing the degree of data availability or methodological readiness. Oftentimes, the transactional data is immediately available as it tends to reside on the organization's systems, and as such it is ready for extraction and deployment. By the same token, data representing an enhancement offered by an outside third-party, such as consumer credit bureaus, geodemographic or lifestyle research firm, etc., is available in the sense of being acquirable, which simply means that considerably more time may elapse before it is physically in the possession of an analyst. In addition, outside data appending frequently involves an a priori target extract preparation, post hoc assessment of the hit rate,[3] not to mention a potential contract-negotiation-related slowdown. Often glazed over as banal or mundane, these details should be expressly considered as a part of the analytical planning because as uninteresting (to both analysts and business users of information) as they tend to be, they have the potential of derailing the timing of even the simplest analyses. And gaining a leg up on the competition means not only having the right insights, but also having that knowledge available at a time when using it can make a difference.

On the methodological readiness side, it is important to acknowledge that the depth of expertise and the methodology-specific experience can vary—at time substantially— across analysts. Keeping that in mind is not only one of the key prerequisites to effective analytical planning (discussed next), but may also lead to questions surrounding the "do in-house" vs. "outsource" decisions.

An often overlooked consideration involves tool requirements. As the available statistical analysis software grew more powerful over the years, it also grew more expensive, modularized (i.e., divided into a base system plus add-on modules) and specialized (i.e., the general purpose SAS and SPSS statistical analysis packages vs. a limited purpose tools, such as MARS or CART). Consequently, many organizations opt to initially purchase scaled-down versions of the more expensive software and add additional modules as the need arises. Again, it is worthwhile to consider the informational objectives in the context of the required tools to avoid last minute surprises.

Analytic Roadmap

A crucial step, but one not always taken, is the development of a comprehensive analytic roadmap, an Analytic Plan. This document, which represents a "contract" between the analysts and the user community, should be prepared by the former with the full participation and the ultimate buy-in from the latter. At the very minimum, a well-crafted analytic roadmap should contain the following:

- An explicit delineation of the individual analytic initiatives with a clear linkage to specific informational needs and ultimately, the organization's strategic objectives.
- An overall completion timeline showing the starting and completion dates for each project.
- A description of how each initiative will improve the decision-making process.
- Data, special tool and other requirements.
- Analytic and business owners of each initiative, identified by name.
- Brief functional description of the end state of each initiative.
- Brief methodological description of individual initiatives.

The purpose of the roadmap is twofold: On the one hand, it serves to set clear expectations among the business users, both in terms of the specific upcoming deliverables as well as the approximate completion time. In that sense, it also minimizes disruptive clarification user demands, thus allowing analysts to concentrate on the task at hand.

The second key purpose of preparing an explicit analytic roadmap document is planning efficiency. Analytic staffing needs, external data and additional tool requirements or outsourcing needs can be identified ahead of time and action can be taken in a more cost-efficient manner. Business users can also plan around the scheduled availability of the new informational assets.

4   Skills and Tools

A critical part of any process-based endeavor is the availability of requisite skills and tools. Within the realm of the marketing database analytics processes discussed earlier, the most essential informational skills and tools are those that enable the completion of the individual phases of the knowledge creation process, in a manner that leads to competitively advantageous outcomes.

The goal of this chapter is to develop a general framework that can be used to systematically examine the character of the most pressing informational needs and the skills and tools necessary to develop robust analytic insights. The "skills and tools" framework discussed next represents a subset of the earlier outlined marketing database analytical process.

Skills & Tools

Its potential notwithstanding, databases do not always have the expected business impact. Although the list of specific reasons can be long, in general, they tend to cluster into two general groupings: insufficient analyst skill set and inadequate analytic tools. Consider Figure 4.1 ('+' denotes the level of importance, with '+' indicating comparatively low and '+++' comparatively high impact).

Analyst skills are defined as the sum of all competencies necessary to translate raw data into competitively advantageous knowledge, while *analytic tools* are any software or hardware enablers of the processing of data. Both have a significant influence on the knowledge creation process, as shown above, but of the two, analyst skills have a stronger impact than tools, which means that a skilled analyst with poor tools will accomplish

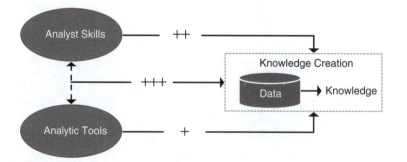

Figure 4.1 When Database Analytics Under-Delivers

more than poor analyst with excellent tools. However, it is the interaction between human skills and data processing tools that has the most determinant impact on the quality of the resultant analytic insights. In other words, the ability of the organization's knowledge creation process to yield unique, edge-producing insights is highly dependent on the availability of requisite analyst skill level and access to appropriate data analytical tools.

What constitutes a requisite analyst skill set and appropriate data analytical tools? Probably the most accurate "no-answer answer" is that it depends on the task at hand. For instance, high-value customer identification or treatment-attributable sales incrementality quantification requires somewhat different analyst skills than option pricing or survival analyses. For that reason, the best way to delineate the critical analyst skill set and to identify the most appropriate tools is by considering the demands of the individual steps in the database analytical process, first presented in Chapter 1. The overriding principle employed here is that the *skills–tools* combination is shaped by the demands of creating competitively advantageous knowledge base.

The Skills–Tools Assessment Process

Given that database analytics, as a process, is focused on translating data into unique, organizational knowledge supporting the stated organizational objectives, analyst skills and any analysis-enabling tools should include all that is necessary to complete the goals of database analytical initiatives. It means that, as implied in Figure 3.1, the ideal skill set should range from the "softer" skills, such as cross-functional team work, to an array of "harder" skills, including experimental design, statistical analysis and data manipulation. And lastly, it also means that the success of database analytics—and of knowledge creation overall—is also contingent on analysts' access to specific data manipulation and statistical analysis tools. Figure 4.2 delineates stage-by-stage skill and tool requirements.

A cursory look at the range of skills outlined above might paint a picture of a modern day "Renaissance man," rather than a quantitative business analyst. In some way, such a conclusion attests to a common problem with the widely held conception of quantitative data analyses: The analysts' skills and their attention both tend to be focused on "crunching data," with little-to-no attention being paid to aligning the resultant information with broader organizational needs. If I had a dollar for every statistical model that was never put to a good, or any use. . .

The database analytical process described in this book is about a lot more than using statistical analysis tools to crunch data. As detailed before, it is about consistently producing unique knowledge to give an organization a basis for gaining and sustaining

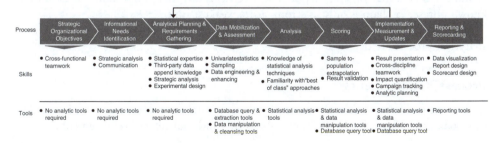

Figure 4.2 Database Analytical Process and Skill Requirements

a competitive advantage. It is a lofty goal and it does require a skill set that goes beyond the traditional "model-building." It has implications both for individual analysts as well as entire data analysis departments.

The former would be well advised to make an effort to think of themselves more as information workers and less as data analysts/crunchers. The distinction between the two is particularly pronounced in the context of preparing data analyses reports: Data analysts tend to favor process description, while information workers tend to focus more of their energies on conclusions. In practice, it translates into, among other things, putting more effort into "findings and recommendations" of the analysis and frankly, devoting less time to methodological descriptions. All too often, final data analytic presentations devote as much as 80% of their content to discussing the "how we did" and a comparatively trivial amount of coverage and thought is given to "what it all means" or "what should be done with it."

Interestingly, in spite of the often seemingly obscurantist attention to methodological details, a significant proportion of business analyses is methodologically flawed. Whether it is a choice of an inappropriate methodology or outstretching of the applicability limits of an otherwise appropriate technique, the validity and reliability of results of various business analyses are quite frequently suspect. Hence although it is argued to devote less of the "presentation coverage" to how analyses were conducted, the importance of making better thought out methodological decisions is emphasized. To that end, potential applicability limits of some of the more commonly used statistical techniques or concepts, such as business applicability of statistical significance testing are discussed in depth in Chapters 5 and 8.

The knowledge creation process also has implications for the organizing and staffing of quantitative data analysis division within an organization. Specifically, two somewhat opposing notions need to be balanced: The idea of having an adequate "bench depth" should be moderated by the notion of "diversity of competencies." In other words, under most circumstances it is undesirable for a data analysis division to put "all of its eggs into a single basket" in terms of the overall skill range. Obviously, staff turnover and other factors often challenge the service continuity demand placed upon the firm's analytic capabilities. That said, the ongoing competitively advantageous knowledge creation capabilities demand a range of skills, as outlined in Figure 4.2, which brings to light the importance of well thought out analyst recruitment and ongoing training. It would be potentially detrimental to the quality (i.e., business impact) of the resultant knowledge for the department to have a lot of "bench strength" in one particular area, such as behavioral predictions, at the cost of being deficient in another one, such as incrementality measurement. Although some parts of the knowledge creation process might be more involved than others, they are not necessarily any more important. To use a well-known phrase, "a chain is only as strong as its weakest link."

Next, specific skill- and tool-related process requirements of the marketing database analytical process are detailed.

Process Requirements

Each of the eight stages comprising the marketing database analytics process detailed in this book carries with it clearly identifiable skill- and tool-related requirements.

Strategic Organizational Objectives

Skills

All too often, analysts work in nearly total isolation from the rest of the organization, which often leads to limited user acceptance of results. Good analyses are rooted in a strong understanding of user needs, as only then can the right questions be answered in the correct fashion. To be an effective tool to the organization at large, the analytical planning process needs to be anchored in cross-functional cooperation. Although as shown in Figure 3.1 the delineation of strategic goals is the responsibility of users, analysts should be involved in that process to have the opportunity to ask questions, all with the goal of developing an intuitive level of understanding of the specific questions they are expected to answer.

As will be discussed later, the process of translating high-level strategic goals—such as increasing the brand's penetration—is highly interpretative and thus inherently subjective. The efficacy of the analyst-led decisions relating to data and analytical methodologies is highly dependent on the planner's understanding of the specific needs of the various organizational constituent. Thus it is important to build and maintain relationships with the future users of analytic results as a way of fostering the clarity of analytic planning.

Tools

In the age of the seemingly endless availability of tools and gadgets, there are still no good substitutes for a simple listing of key objectives. Here, a sheet of paper and a pencil can be as potent a tool as a computerized spreadsheet. Of particular importance to strategic objective delineation are thoroughness and operational clarity.

Informational Needs

Skills

A competent analyst is a master of a few trades and a jock of few others, including strategic analysis. Traditionally, strategic analysis has been viewed as a separate business analytical area, rather than a part of the database analytical process. There are several general strategic evaluative frameworks with the two best known being the SWOT (strengths, weaknesses, opportunities, threats) analysis and Porter's "five forces." These are excellent macro view tools offering a natural point of departure by helping organizations pinpoint sources of sustainable competitive advantage by systematically evaluating the firm's competitive environment as well as its own capabilities. Their open-ended nature, however, makes them less than ideal for direct application to a more targeted endeavor of the knowledge creation process. In other words, these frameworks cannot provide the level of operational detail demanded by data analytical initiatives.

A philosophically similar, though tactically more narrowly focused framework that can be used as a basis for identifying specific user informational needs in the context of the stated organizational goals can be anchored in three distinct sets of activities: *initiative prioritization, critical success factor analysis* and *scenario planning*. The analysts' proficiency with each of these informational-need delineation tools is the key to successfully translating the usually somewhat vaguely stated firms' strategic goals into operationally precise informational imperatives.

Initiative prioritization entails being able to differentiate between the "competitively critical" and "interesting but not essential" informational dimensions, as well as assessing the difficulty or plausibility of putting together the desired informational assets. This goal is accomplished by means of evaluating individual initiatives in terms of the previously delineated informational attributes, resulting in initiative-specific scoring and a subsequent rank-ordering.

The second of the three strategic analytical tools is the *critical success factor analysis*, which serves to map out the knowledge creation process and identify specific weak links in the process. In contrast to initiative prioritization, which is fundamentally a database analytics endeavor planning tool, the critical success factor analysis is a development optimization tool, whose goal is to ease the process of crafting the previously selected set of initiatives.

Lastly, in order maximize the user benefit and acceptance of the results of analytic efforts, a competent analyst should also be able to carry out effective a priori *scenario planning* of the actual end user solutions. An initiative "productization" tool, it serves to identify the optimal functionality, or "look and feel" of the specific informational end deliverables. It allows the analysts to better align the end deliverable's functionality with the end users' specific informational needs.

Thus in the context of database analytics, strategic planning encapsulates a prioritization of the potential analytic developmental efforts, effective analytical developmental process planning skills and robust a priori end user functionality assessment skills. Admittedly, that is a lot to expect of a single person. It is not, however, a lot to expect of a department comprised of multiple analysts. In other words, the individual tasks could be spread across multiple analysts, in accordance with individual levels of experience and expertise. However, a gradual acquisition of those skills should be a part of an analyst development and mentoring process, ultimately leading to training well-rounded knowledge creators, rather than mere developers of low impact informational tidbits.

Last but not least, the *Informational Needs Identification* stage of the database analytical process is also very communication-intensive. Because they are highly intangible and somewhat subjective, informational and other needs are inherently elusive, which means that uncovering "true" needs can be somewhat more challenging than merely asking. An effective method of honing-in on the most critical set of informational needs can be best described as "persistent dialectic," or an ongoing user-analyst communication. In-depth interviews with the key stakeholders or mini focus groups with groups of stakeholders have been shown to be effective needs identification platforms, through which analysts can develop an intuitive level of understanding of the informational needs of end users.

Tools

Primarily a mission of discovery of latent end users' information needs, the *Informational Needs Identification* process does not require database analytics-specific tools.

Analytic Planning and Requirements Gathering

Skills

Matching the end users' anticipated benefits and functionality with the analysts' vision is the key to developing usable and competitively advantageous knowledge. This critical step rarely gets sufficient amounts of explicit attention, due in a large part to its highly intangible content. Yet when the otherwise robust analytic solutions fail to adequately reflect the needs of end users, whether in terms of content or functionality, the likelihood of their acceptance diminishes significantly.

As shown in Figure 4.2, the success of this stage of the database analytics process is contingent on a several diverse skill sets, specifically:

- Knowledge of statistical data analysis.
- Familiarity with third-party data appends.
- Communication.
- Strategic analysis.

Knowledge of Statistical Data Analysis

The knowledge of statistical analysis methods is a skill set that is probably most readily associated with analytical endeavors, for obvious reasons. Of particular importance to effective analytic planning is the comprehensiveness of the analyst's knowledge—i.e., familiarity with a wide range of techniques—as well as the technique-specific depth of data-requirements-related understanding. It is common for analysts to have a great deal of familiarity with some methods and little-to-none with others, or have deep experience with one data type, such as transactions, but little to none with others, such as campaign results. The biggest disadvantage of such methodological narrowness is its correlation with the general inability to "think outside of the box," to use a well-worn expression. Once again, transforming large and diverse volumes of data into unique knowledge requires a fair amount of analytic creativity, which means taking innovative steps without compromising the robustness of results.

Familiarity with Third Party Data Appends

An effective analyst has a high level of familiarity with idiosyncrasies of different data types. All too often the focus of data analysis is on single source of data, such as transactions, promotional campaign results or consumer satisfaction. As important and insightful as such analyses are in their own right, their maximum benefit cannot stretch beyond relatively generic and specific information, easily mimicked by competitors. The true nuggets of gold are to be found in the analyses of interactions among those idiosyncratic pieces of information, which is the most likely source of competitively advantageous knowledge. Hence a truly skilled statistical analyst will have the ability to jointly analyze diverse sources of data.

The ability to analyze diverse data types is rooted in the basic level of understanding of the makeup of the more commonly used sources of data. Although many organizations routinely capture considerable amounts of data on an ongoing basis, it is important to keep in mind that the bulk of data capture tends to be a by-product of organizations' operations thus rarely is it available or presented in a ready-to-use format, as it is often scattered around multiple systems. At times, an analyst will need to acquire a working knowledge of multiple data access and manipulation system as a means of accessing of the different aspects of the otherwise internally available data. Oftentimes, different third-party data appends, such as lifestyle, general purchase propensities, wealth or geodemographic indicators will also need to be brought in to add additional explanatory dimensions to the in-house data. A competent analyst should have a general level of familiarity with the available data sources and types, their strengths and weaknesses, typical match rates[1] and a general analytic content appropriateness level.

Communication

Implicit in the development of the sufficient level of data knowledge is the ability to communicate effectively. Unfortunately, communication effectiveness is a skill that is rarely given much weight among quantitative analysts. Frankly, that is a problem. Data due diligence is a fairly communication-intensive process, which often requires clearly conveying the statistical inner-workings in order to understand the appropriateness of the data types of interest. The analysis and modeling processes are usually relatively technically complex, which makes them particularly challenging to explain to those with limited technical knowledge in the field.

A similar logic extends to being able to communicate the advantages and disadvantages of the contemplated courses of action. There are no "one size fits all" solutions in quantitative analysis, thus any selected approach will carry with it a set of advantages and drawbacks, all of which need to be clearly communicated to form the basis for informed consent. In other words, the only way of making sure that the analyst-selected methodologies will yield the end-user-desired information is through the analyst developing a strong understanding of the users' needs while clearly conveying the expected functionality of the planned solutions. In order for a productive dialectic to follow, a level playing field of understanding needs to be formed, an integral part of which is the ability to communicate complex concepts in an easy to understand language.

Strategic Analysis

Strategic analysis, a skill set critically important to the previously outlined *Informational Needs Identification* stage is also important in this stage of the database analytics process. Recalling the three general strategic analysis methods— initiative prioritization, critical success factor analysis and scenario planning—the a priori scenario planning is of particular importance during this stage of the process. It is a highly effective method of assessing the degree to which the analysts' operationalization of the end users' informational needs is optimal. Combined with effective communication skills, the a priori solution scenario planning enables the analysts to fine tune their analytic plan and arrive at the maximally impactful end solutions.

In some instances, the proficiency in experimental design can also be necessary. As an area of knowledge, experimentation can be thought of as an operational extension of strategic analysis, where an objectively derived, though usually not fully empirically tested hypothesis can be subjected to a thorough evaluation. In situations where the stated organizational strategic objectives can be sufficiently supported with the knowledge extracted out of data that is either currently available or potentially available from an outside source, the experimental design skill is not critical. On the other hand, in situations where it is necessary to set up a specific test or an experiment in order to be able to capture the needed data, the analyst familiarity with at least the basic test[2] design principles and processes is crucially important.

Tools

Much like the two previous stages of the database analytical process, the success of the *Analytic Planning and Requirements Gathering* stage is not contingent on any analytics-specific tools.

Data Mobilization and Assessment

Skills

Garbage in—garbage out. It is true in many aspects of business, but particularly so in the analysis of data. Poor quality of data can render meaningless the most ambitious and innovative analytic plans, yet surprisingly little effort is put into its assessment. Before data can be translated into information and ultimately, competitively advantageous knowledge, it must be first molded into a clean and comprehensive analytical data file. Doing so involves two separate, yet highly complementary steps: data mobilization and data assessment.

Data mobilization is the process of extracting representative samples from individual data files or data warehouses. The database analytics process, as defined in this book, is directed at creating specific knowledge assets directed at supporting the stated organizational objectives. As discussed in depth in Chapter 1, the most fundamental difference between knowledge and information is the degree of uniqueness and specificity, with knowledge representing insights that are unique to the organization and focused on a specific goal. At the most rudimentary data level, knowledge creation requires pulling together of as many different elements of data as are available and deemed helpful in crafting maximally unique and insightful knowledge. Critical to data mobilization is familiarity with basic *sampling concepts* and the knowledge of *data manipulation tools*.

The second key aspect of creating a robust analytical data set is *data assessment*, which essentially is a series of steps geared at determining the accuracy, representativeness and coverage of the individual variables, a process jointly referred to as the *data quality control*. Picking up where the data mobilization efforts left off, data assessment cleanses the individual data elements by recoding (e.g., converting mixed values into numeric ones) quantitatively non-analyzable variables, enhancing missing value, identifying outlier and clarifying the meaning of all mobilized data. Critical to effective data assessment are basic *statistical tool proficiency* and the previously mentioned *data manipulation* skills.

Although statistical and data manipulation tools tend to often be embedded in a single software package—such as SAS or SPSS—the underlying skill sets are considerably different. Data manipulation requires the ability to process often large data files, merge multiple files, perform data aggregation (such as rolling up individual purchases to household level or UPC to brand level) and value indexing. On the other hand, statistical tool proficiency—considered in the context of data preparation—refers to the knowledge of data engineering techniques, such as variable frequency distribution assessment, missing value replacement or outlier and influential value identification. It also entails computing of basic univariate descriptive metrics, such as the measures of central tendency or variability.

A more abstractly defined skill set—familiarity with basic sampling concepts—is of key importance to determining the appropriate size and composition of the individual database extracts. Using the entire content of a data warehouse as an input into multi-source data analytics is usually size-prohibitive and methodologically unnecessary, which means that the database analytical process will require a selection of multiple subsets of larger data files. In order for the individual samples to be valid reflections of their respective universes, their composition has to closely mimic that of the source files, and their effective sample sizes also have to be sufficient.[3] Familiarity with basic sampling schemas, such as random, cluster or stratified, minimum sample size and unit determination procedures and the post-selection population-sample homogeneity assessment are all necessary to robust data assessment, as those skills are crucial in ascertaining the representativeness of individual samples.

Related to the investigations of the data already in-hand is the assessment of the desirability of adding additional data elements. *Data appending* is typically done for two distinct reasons: The first and most common goal is to expand the potential informational base by supplying more potentially explanatory or predictive elements. The second reason is to replace poor quality, currently owned data. The key data append skill set is the knowledge of what is available as well as the appropriateness of the different assets to the end goal of specific analytic initiatives.

Tools

The first of a series of "data hands-on" database analytical process stages, *Data Mobilization & Assessment* usually calls for two sets of analytical tools: database query and data manipulation means.

Database query tools enable an analyst to access and extract specific data contained within a database. These can range from a relatively generic structured query language (SQL) to more specific applications embedded within database management and reporting systems, such as MicroStrategy, Oracle or Cognos environments. The specific programming skill set is contingent upon the type of a database or a data warehouse and the data management system, yet it all boils down to a simple statement: effective database analytics is aided by a free access to any relevant data contained within the database of interest.

A far more important database-analytics-related skill set is the ability to freely manipulate the data to be used in analyses, as it is rare that the data files are extracted out of a database in an analytically ready-to-use format. Among the common, data-manipulation-related steps are: file merging, missing value identification and substitution, variable indexing, disaggregate data householding, indicator creation and the univariate assessment. While some data files might be relatively small (in terms of the number of cases and the number of variables per case) and clean (i.e., few missing values and outliers, variables exhibiting undesirable distributions, etc.), other ones may require a considerable amount of cleaning, summarizing and indexing. Transactional data, which is usually one of the most potent sources of decision insights, often falls into the latter category, which is why robust data manipulation tools, such as SAS or SPSS, are invaluable.

Analysis

Skills

Analysis is the very heart of database analytics—it is the engine that powers the conversion of low-value data into high-value knowledge, a process that is particularly skill and experience dependent. As such, it requires two, very broadly defined skill sets: the knowledge of statistical analysis techniques and the familiarity with the "best of class" analytical approaches. The former is most often a result of a formal statistical training, while the latter is usually acquired through "hands-on," practical experience.

There are numerous conceptualizations of statistical analysis and modeling—the one that is perhaps most appropriate in the context of database analytics emphasizes the use of appropriate statistical techniques, being mindful of assumptions made by each technique, performing hypothesis tests, interpreting data and reaching valid conclusions. In the context of the database analytical process outlined in this book, statistical analyses can be categorized based on end objectives of individual analytic endeavors, as shown in Figure 4.3.

As suggested below, a skilled analyst should be adapt at *univariate* (e.g., measures of a single variable's central tendencies and dispersion, value frequency distribution, etc.) and *multivariate* (e.g., pairwise correlations, cross-tabulation, regression) techniques to be able to extract exploratory insights out of the data. Often seen examples of exploratory analytics include descriptive customer segmentation and profiling, customer value migration or buyer demographic distributions. In a methodological sense, these efforts are focused on developing a basic informational foundation.

The second main branch of database analytics—predictive analyses—often calls upon more complex statistical methodologies, which naturally translates into deeper statistical expertise on the part of an analyst. The more advanced statistical techniques, such as loglinear or latent class models are usually more difficult to fit and interpret and are often built around more stringent assumptions. In addition, as shown in Figure 4.3, predictive analytics are frequently used as means of hypothesis testing, which adds the additional

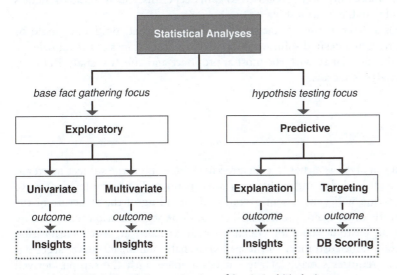

Figure 4.3 A High-Level Categorization of Statistical Techniques

requirement of familiarity with the appropriate testing principles. Lastly, a subset of predictive analytics—the targeting-focused efforts—adds yet another layer of skill requirements, which is the ability to translate sample-based analytic results into a population-level (i.e., the entire database) scoring algorithm.

The second of the two broad analysis-specific skill sets depicted in Figure 4.3 is the familiarity with the "best of class" analytic approaches. Over the past couple of decades, a number of specific analytic solutions were developed, each one focusing on a common business problem. Examples include customer lifetime value segmentation, treatment-attributable incrementality measurement, high value customer identification and targeting, etc. The difference between these approaches and the previously described general statistical technique knowledge is that the former represent tested methods of combining specific techniques, data manipulation steps and information deployment guidelines to bring about the maximally effective results in the context of a specific promotional initiative. In other words, they help to eliminate, or at least greatly diminish, the typical trial-and-error process of identifying the most effective method of solving a particular problem.

Tools

Advanced analytics require advanced tools. There are a number of tools an analyst can use, depending on the type of data or analytic complexity. Overall, the three most comprehensive and best known statistical analysis packages are SAS (which once stood for *Statistical Analysis Software*), SPSS (which originally was an acronym for *Statistical Package for Social Sciences*) and R (an open-source data analysis language). These all-in-one packages give the analyst a broad range of data manipulation, transformation and statistical analysis capabilities. There are a number of other packages that grew up around more specific objectives. For example, MINITAB focuses primarily on quality improvement consideration (such as Six Sigma), while CART (Classification and Regression Trees) and MARS (Multivariate Adaptive Regression Splines) focus on decision-tree-based predictive modeling. An example of an even more idiosyncratic application is Amos, a structural equation modeling (SEM) tool used to gain deeper insights into causal models and the strength of variable relationships.

In short, there is a diverse array of statistical analysis tools that could and should be used to speedily arrive at a desired solution. More than in other stages of the knowledge creation process, the familiarity with the most appropriate and effective analytical tools is critical to the analyst's success.

Scoring

Skills

The end goal of any analysis is either to generate knowledge about the subject matter at hand, or to generate knowledge and enable a certain capability. For example, descriptive customer segmentation will generate an overall understanding of the structure of the customer base; on the other hand, predictive lifetime value segmentation will generate the knowledge of the customer base, but in addition, it will also support identification and selection of high-value customers (or prospects) to enable a more effective targeting. The latter scenario requires scoring of the entire database with the sample-derived customer valuation and categorization.

Database scoring, as it relates to data analysis, is the process of extending sample-based findings onto the entire database population; it is almost always associated with predictive, multivariate statistical models. Operationally, scoring entails the solving of the sample-calibrated equation for each of the remaining database records. As shown in Figure 4.2, it entails two somewhat distinct skill sets: 1. The sample-to-population value extrapolation, and 2. Result validation.

The *sample-to-population extrapolation* combines the elements of the statistical technique knowledge of the Analysis stage and data manipulation of the Data Mobilization & Assessment stage. The analyst has to be able to apply the sample-calibrated relationships (e.g., a regression equation or another statistical model) to the entire database population, which usually requires the ability to manipulate large volumes of data, as well as the ability to apply the appropriate statistical procedures.

The *result validation* requires the ability to generate the appropriate diagnostics, such as computed values' frequency distributions, and the ability to interpret the results. In the event of problems, such as the identification of values falling outside the acceptable or reasonable ranges,[5] the analyst has to be able to take the appropriate steps to remedy the situation, which may involve re-estimating of the statistical model of interest or identifying and correcting for database (i.e., population) outliers.

Tools

The tool requirements of this stage are a combination of the Analysis and the Data Mobilization and Assessment stages. Similarl to data analysis, scoring is usually conducted outside of the database itself because solving of the sample-calibrated equations for the entire database population can usually be accomplished far more expeditiously within a particular statistical analysis environment. In other words, an appropriate data manipulation tool will be required.

Furthermore, since the scoring process is in essence an application of a specific statistical technique, such as linear or logistic regression, the appropriate statistical analysis software is also required. As previously mentioned, some of the comprehensive data analysis and modeling packages such as SAS, SPSS or R combine both functionalities. It is worth pointing out, however, that there are certain types of analysis, such as decision trees, that are more effectively handled by the more sophisticated (in that regard), special purpose applications such as the previously mentioned CART or MARS methodologies. Thus while in some situations data manipulation and the actual sample-to-population score extrapolation can be accomplished within a single analytical environment, such as SAS or SPSS, in other situations, two separate software tools may need to be deployed.

Implementation, Measurement and Updates

Skills

From the standpoint of needs and tools assessment, the final phase of marketing knowledge creation, as operationalized by the marketing database analytics process detailed in this book is the broadly defined "use and maintenance." A bit of a "catch-all" stage, in terms of the requisite skills it is a combination of art and science—the former most evident in the somewhat loosely defined result implementation, while the latter best exemplified by the well-defined skills requisite of ongoing impact measurement.

IMPLEMENTATION

The most important implementation-related skills are effective presentation and communication. Effectively communicating potentially competitively advantageous findings, in an easy-to-understand manner is often the weak link in the knowledge creation chain. Database analytic presentations tend to be skewed toward abstract process steps, overly technical details and delineation of informational tidbits rather than describing the underlying knowledge.

Being able to emphasize the most pertinent dimensions of the findings often requires close collaboration with the end users of analytic insights. Analysts have a deep understanding of interpretational limits of the information they create, while the end users have a similarly strong understanding of the intended application of it. Distilling information into competitively advantageous knowledge requires close cooperation between the two, as only then can the results be accurately and reliably molded.

MEASUREMENT

Effective ongoing measurement of the efficacy of analyses-driven changes requires strong impact quantification and campaign-tracking-related skills. Quantifying the impact of specific actions can be relatively straightforward or highly complex, depending on the type of action being measured, the metrics and the desired level of precision and data availability. For instance, pricing changes usually have a relatively direct impact on subsequent sales levels, while revamping of brand positioning (as communicated via general advertising) presents a far more complex measurement problem. Thus the ability to objectively quantify the incrementality attributable to specific promotional actions will frequently call for a solid foundation in experimental test design.

It goes without saying that before the impact of any action can be quantified, the results need to be tracked and captured across time. The campaign tracking skills entail the ability to make the appropriate provisions in data capture mechanism to allow for an objective attribution of outcomes to actions. This includes setting up unique promotional codes and linking responses and purchases to those codes.

UPDATES

Knowledge creation is an ongoing, cumulative process, which progresses by means of successive approximations. To be a source of sustainable competitive advantage, database analytical insights also need to be adaptive to the ever-changing competitive realities. All of that requires cyclical updates to the initial analytic plan to sharpen and possibly change its focus based on the results of current action-turned-insights. In that sense, the database analytical process is circular, as the end of one knowledge creation cycle leads to the initiation of the next one.

Tools

Taken as one, implementation, impact measurement and updates call for the availability of statistical analysis and database manipulation as well as database query tools, both of which have been previously discussed (in the context of Data Mobilization and Assessment and Analysis process stages, respectively).

PART II
Knowledge Creation

5   Analytic Planning

There is an often told story illustrating the importance of expertise (it's probably entirely fabricated, but nonetheless it illustrates the point quite well). It goes like this: A homeowner had a problem with a squeaky floor—specifically, there was one, relatively small spot that seemed to defy any repair attempts. The owner of the house retained a long succession of craftsmen, but in spite of what seemed like a simple and a very contained problem coupled with multiple repair efforts, the floor kept on squeaking. Undeterred by repeated failures, the homeowner persisted in his efforts to fix the squeaking floor. And surely enough, eventually yet another craftsman came along and following a careful examination of the potential causes, hammered a handful of carefully placed nails and the floor stopped squeaking! The initial elation of the owner of the house to finally get the squeak fixed turned into dismay upon the receipt of the craftsman's bill of $1,020. He demanded an explanation and the breakdown of the total charge, following which he received an itemized bill which read as follows:

$20:   Nailing squeaky floor boards
$1,000:   *Knowing* where to nail

This is the essence of the *analytic know-how*, which is the knowledge of the most appropriate (to the task at hand) data management, amalgamation and engineering, modeling and interpretation skills. The goal of this chapter is to outline a conceptual analytic planning framework, which is an extremely critical step to the degree to which the fulfillment of future analytic needs is contingent on specific steps being taken earlier in the data analytical process.

Analytic Planning

Planning is one of the essential building blocks of rational, intelligent behavior. There are two key aspect of planning: The first is the psychological process of thinking about future states or outcomes, as well as the means and impediments of getting there. The second is the creation of a structured action map, or a plan, aimed at achieving stated goals.

The process of planning has several benefits. Thinking that is focused on future states or outcomes of interest spurs the identification of numerous considerations that might not have otherwise been noticed. Structuring of an action plan, on the other hand, brings about procedural clarity through the delineation of process steps, dependencies and the timeline.

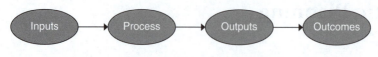

Figure 5.1 A General System Model

Probably the most productive way of looking at analytic planning is through a system approach. A *system*, defined here as an organized set of interrelated elements, is comprised of inputs, processes, outputs and outcomes, all linearly organized as shown above.

Inputs include both resources (human, capital, etc.) as well as the stated organizational objectives, discussed in earlier chapters. *Process* is a collection of means of transforming inputs into something else, namely, outputs. *Outputs* are tangible results produced by the processes embodied by the system. And lastly, *outcomes* are the benefits derived by end users.

The marketing database analytics approach detailed in this book is ideally suited to the systems-based analytic planning because of the implicit determinism embedded in that process, as evidenced by a priori delineation of informational needs, which are derived from organizational goals. The marketing management actions or activities are themselves limited in scope, as they entail evaluation of past activities, identification of the most pronounced drivers of the observed outcomes and using those insights to shape future promotional decisions. In that context, the goal of an analytic system is to generate maximally effective, decision-aiding knowledge.

Planning vs. Plan

Sometimes we confuse the "how" something is produced with "what" is being produced. Naturally, the process of planning should produce a plan—that much is obvious. What gets overlooked, however, is the implicit temporal distinction between the two, namely, that the process of planning should be viewed as being antecedent to the outcome, which is a plan. This is not just a semantic distinction, particularly when placed within the realm of the ongoing nature of the marketing database analytics process detailed here, which demands both flexibility as well as longitudinal consistency. Stated differently, to be effective, an analytic plan has to stem from a robust planning framework, capable of supporting the ongoing marketing mix changes and corrections in a manner that will retain the requisite measurement consistency across time.

Planning Framework

Consider the general systems model depicted in Figure 5.1 above—it is composed of several, serially arranged elements: Inputs, Process, Outputs and Outcomes. Now, consider the marketing database analytics framework (MDA), first depicted in Figure 1.4. As shown in Figure 5.2 below, the two conceptualizations are closely related.

Let's dig deeper into the above graphically depicted conceptualization. Considering the tenets of the general systems model in the context of the MDA process, we can establish the following interdependencies:

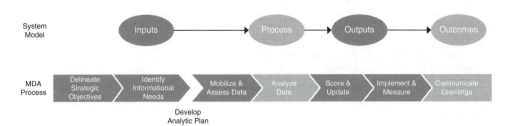

Figure 5.2 System Model vs. MDA Framework

Inputs → Informational Objectives and Data
The creation of decision-aiding knowledge is, to a large degree, shaped by two mutually independent forces: 1. Stated information objectives, which essentially represent questions in need of answers, and 2. The available data, which effectively constrains the validity and the reliability of the resultant insights.

Process → Methods
In many regards, this is the most straightforward part of the analytical plan development—it entails the identification of the most appropriate data analytical methodology or methodologies, given the stated informational objectives and constraints imposed by the available data.

Outputs → Analytic Results
The purpose of this stage is the delineation of expected analytical (statistical) outputs and the assessment of the validity and reliability of those outputs. In particular, it is to "spell out" specific means or tests for establishing non-spuriousness of inferences drawn from data.

Outcomes → Decision Inputs
From the standpoint of end user value, this is a particularly important aspect of the analytic planning process: What steps should be taken to "translate" the often highly abstract, esoteric data analytical outcomes into unambiguous decision-aiding knowledge? It is often both the most overlooked and challenging aspect of the overall data analytical endeavor.

The value in expressly describing the conceptual linkages or interdependencies connecting the MDA process and the systems model is in it laying the objective foundation for a generalizable planning template, discussed next.

Generalizable Planning Template

Although the specifics of any initially developed analytic plan will more than likely change over time, a considerable amount of objectivity and consistency can be instilled by setting up a general planning template. An example of an analytic planning template is shown below—it is worth noting that the essence of that template is to bring about a reasonable amount of standardization, which is particularly important in view of a potential analytical team discontinuity (i.e., a change in the composition of the project team).

Table 5.1 Sample Analytic Planning Template

Input	Analysis	Outcomes
Information Needed: – Exploratory – Predictive	Most appropriate analytical methods	Anticipated analytical/ statisical outcomes
Available Data – Limitations		Reliability & validity checks
	Business Insights	
	Anticipated decision aiding knowledge	

Additional Considerations

A helpful way of thinking about analytic planning is to consider the resultant plan to be a "contract" between the analysts and the end user community. Hence in addition to the above delineated system consideration, a well-crafted analytic plan might also contain the following:

- An explicit delineation of the individual analytic initiatives with a clear linkage to specific informational needs and ultimately, the organization's strategic objectives.
- An overall completion timeline showing the starting and completion dates for each analytic project.
- An explicit description of how each initiative will improve the decision-making process.
- Analytic and business owners of each initiative, along with their respective roles and responsibilities.

It is worthwhile to remember that the purpose of an analytic plan or a roadmap is twofold: On the one hand, it sets clear expectations among the ultimate business users of the to-be-derived insights, both in terms of the specific upcoming deliverables as well as the approximate completion time. In that sense, it serves to minimize disruptive "clarification" demands, thus allowing analysts to concentrate on the task at hand.

The second key purpose of preparing an explicit analytic roadmap is efficiency. Clear directions go a long way toward streamlining the actual conduct of analyses and reducing potential re-work. Perhaps even more importantly, clarity enhances the quality of data analyst–business user communication, which is the key to timely and cost effective analytics.

Mini-Case 5.1: Analytic Planning and Customer Loyalty Programs

A local, independently owned clothing outlet is considering putting in place a customer loyalty program, both as a defense mechanism against what it sees as an onslaught of national chains, but also as a mean of thanking its repeat patrons. The management likes the idea, but it is concerned that it might be too taxing to administer and thus would like to get a better understanding of what's involved in getting such a program up-and-running. With that in mind, they hired an experienced consultant who outlined the following scenario for them:

Timely and robust information is at the core of any loyalty program, because the essence of those initiatives is captured by the *quid pro quo* (meaning, "this or that" or "give and take") idea: Those consumers showing repeated willingness to repurchase the product or service are rewarded for their patronage with price discounts and other offerings. This entails—on the part of the brand—being able to identify its loyal buyers as well as knowing those buyers' purchase characteristics, such as average spend, repurchase frequency and lifetime value. Typically, those insights are not available, or not fully available at the onset of the program, thus one of the key aspects of loyalty program development is the anticipation of future informational needs and creation of appropriate data capture mechanisms. It all boils down to three simple questions: What do we need to know to be able to assess the efficacy of the program? What data do we currently have and what additional data do we need to capture? How should we structure the data that is to be captured (i.e., specific metrics) and what mechanism will we use to capture and store the additional data? Let's take a closer look at each question.

The first question—the identification of key informational needs—draws attention to the definition of "success" for a loyalty program. By and large, a loyalty program's success is defined in the context of customer retention and value maximization. For a retail outlet, the former may be a bit fuzzy (attrition and long re-visit cycles may be hard to tell apart), but the latter of the two considerations is quite operationally meaningful, as it captures the amount of spending per unit of time. Hence it follows that the management should be focused on being able to quantify cross-customer value.

The second of the three questions—what data are currently available and what additional data need to be captured—is fairly straightforward to answer. The store already makes use of an electronic transaction processing system (UPC scanners), which means that individual purchases are being captured—of course, what is being captured is the "what," rather than the "who," unless the payment is in the form of a credit card. It is important to point out that the once-pervasive "reverse credit card appending" (matching of credit card numbers to a database containing person-identifying information) is no longer legal, but using the card holder's name in conjunction with his/her ZIP code offers a legal and a fairly accurate workaround. Of course, "fairly accurate" might be adequate for the purposes of a direct marketing campaign, but not for the purposes of loyalty tracking; furthermore, not all customers will pay for all their purchases with credit cards. In short, the retailer will need a reliable and consistent method of identifying individual purchasers, which can typically be accomplished with a store-issued loyalty card.

The third and final question—how should the newly captured data be structured and captured—points toward more technically esoteric considerations dealing with measurement properties of new data and specific means of capturing, storing and properly attributing the newly defined metrics. For example, if the management is interested in amassing customer demographics (in addition to purchase details), individual metrics need to be operationally defined (e.g., if "customer age" is one of those measures, should it be captured as a continuous-measured, exact value, or a categorical range?) and their capture mechanism identified (e.g., a "required" field on card application; a point-of-sale query, etc.). An important consideration here is to think in terms of informational outcomes that are expected in the future—for example, if "customer age" is captured as a categorical range (e.g., < 18 years of age, 18–25, 26–35, etc.), future comparisons of "average customer age" might become unexpectedly tricky, as simple arithmetic average (i.e., mean) cannot be computed for categorically coded variables.

6 Data Basics

One of the visible consequences of the rapid proliferation of electronic transaction processing systems is the ubiquity of business data. It has been estimated that, on average, the volume of data doubles about every eighteen months—not surprisingly, data storage and management expenditures can be quite significant. What is, however, surprising is how comparatively little many organizations spend on "transforming" data into actionable insights—typically, only about 5% of data-related expenditures are allocated to analysis of data. It seems there is a tendency to overlook the obvious, namely, that unless it is utilized to guide the organizational decision making, the expenditures necessitated by the ongoing data capture can create a drag on earnings, rather than contributing to the firm's competitiveness. The reason for that is the relative immaturity of the broadly defined marketing analytics, and more specifically—database analytics.

Robust database analytics require a degree of understanding of not only statistical techniques, but also the fundamentals of data, including data structures and the key characteristics of the different types of data. This chapter offers a broad overview of the latter.

Data and Databases

Organizations in virtually all industries allocate considerable economic resources to their database informational infrastructure, all with the goal of trying to become more "fact-driven" in the business decision making process, particularly within the realm of marketing. Capturing, storing and managing of business data is a centerpiece of a thriving industry, which encompasses (data) capture and storage hardware, (data) manipulation and reporting software and (data) exploration-focused consulting. However, the results of billions of dollars of aggregate database infrastructure spending are all too often disappointing—they turn out a barrage of descriptive reports that individually and cumulatively yield disproportionately little predictive, decision-aiding knowledge.

Today, virtually all mid-size and larger business organizations either already have in their possession or have access to a variety of transaction-recording and/or descriptive data. In fact, the vast majority of these organizations own multiple databases, maintained and used by numerous functional areas, such as sales, claims management, human resources, industry analysis, marketing and so on. And, as pointed out in the opening chapter, most organizations subscribe to the flawed belief that "data is an asset," which is to say that they hold on to the belief that the often considerable expense required to capture, store and maintain the ever-growing volumes of diverse data is justified as an investment in "organizational intelligence." Underscoring that unwavering conviction is the fact that, in total, over the past 25 years or so, businesses in the U.S. alone invested in excess of $1 trillion in data-related infrastructure, but with very mixed results. Some, including Walmart, Google, Capital One, Harrah's or Marriott, to name a few, clearly benefited from their data-related investments; many others, however, ended up putting a lot more into the database endeavor then they ever were able to get out of it. In fact, it could be argued that, overall, the database revolution did more for the fortunes of data service suppliers than it for the competitiveness of an average database using organization.

Let me reiterate the point I made in the opening chapter: Data is not an asset—it is a *potential* asset, just as having talent is only an asset if and when it is put to a productive use. In other words, data is a resource, a raw material of sorts, which needs to be made into something useful before it can have value to its holder. Walmart did not overtake K-Mart because it had more data—it did so because it was purposeful and methodical about systematic analysis of its data (which, by the way, was not fundamentally different than K-Mart's). In short, the then-up-and-coming retailer made the exploration of its sales and other data the very heart and soul of their decision making. In other words, Walmart managed to "squeeze" a lot more out of its data, which in turn greatly increased the efficacy of the company's decisions.

Getting more out of data is a function of two, somewhat related considerations. First, it requires what could be called "an intimate knowledge" of data sources. Do not forget—the vast majority of data capture is a by-product of business process digitization, particularly what is broadly termed "electronic transaction processing." It means that business databases tend to be large in terms of size and esoteric in terms of content. Typically, they encompass millions, often billions, of records and hundreds or even thousands of individual metrics, many of which are far from being intuitively obvious. The bottom line: The attainment of robust knowledge of a particular database requires dedicated effort, which is perhaps why an average user will just "scratch the surface". . .

The second prerequisite to getting more out of data is the amalgamation of dissimilar data into a singular analytical source. Now, if getting to know a single database seems like a lot of work, getting to know several and finding a way of combining their contents could well be considered a Herculean undertaking. And frankly, it can indeed be a hard and an arduous process. Is it worth it? Any organization not convinced it is, should probably reconsider stockpiling data in expensive databases.

As illustrated throughout this and the remaining chapters, the most significant difference between information-savvy organizations and their data-rich but information-poor counterparts is the data analytical *know-how*. In other words, while virtually the same hardware and software technologies are available to all organizations; it is the power of the subsequent data exploration and utilization that determines the ultimate return on the overall data infrastructure investments. And it all starts with a solid grasp of the available data.

Databases in a Nutshell

A *database* is an organized collection of facts. Although we tend to associate databases with modern computer applications, databases as such existed long before the advent of modern electronic computing. Definition-wise, a telephone book found in nearly every household is as much a database as Walmart's 583 terabyte[1] mega system. In other words, a database can range from a simple listing of your friends' phone numbers written down on a single sheet of paper to a large corporate or governmental computerized system.

A *business database* is defined here as an electronically stored collection of facts that requires its own management system (i.e., commonly known as database management system, or DBMS for short) and specialized query and analysis tools. Furthermore, due to their size and complexity, most business databases also require specialized skills for ongoing reporting and knowledge extraction.

There are multiple ways of describing databases: by data type, purpose, content, organizational structure, size, hardware and software characteristics, etc. From the standpoint of database analytics, the most pertinent aspects of a database are its:

- *scope*, which considers differences between data warehouse and data mart;
- *content*, which specifies the form of encoding, such as text, multimedia or numeric;
- *data model*, which details the basic organizational structure of a database, including entity-relationship, relational and object-oriented.

Each of the key defining qualities of business databases are discussed next.

The Scope: Data Warehouse vs. Data Mart

Even limiting the database definition to business applications, database is still a very general designation. Overall, business databases can be grouped into the following two categories, briefly described in Table 6.1.

Table 6.1 Categories of Business Databases

Database Type	Description
Data Warehouse	Broadly defined as comprehensive data repositories focusing on enterprise-wide data across many or all subject areas. They tend to be subject-oriented (e.g., purchases, customers), time-variant (i.e., capturing changes across time) and non-updatable in the sense of new replacing the old (i.e., read-only and periodically refreshed with a new batch of data). Data warehouses are usually data- rather than task-oriented, application independent (i.e., can be hierarchical, object, relational, flat file or other), normalized or not (database normalization is a reversible process of successively reducing a given collection of relations to a more desirable form) and held together by a single, complex structure. "Custom" database analytical initiatives typically source their data from a data warehouse, but the analysis itself almost always takes place outside of its confines.
Data Mart	These are specific purpose data repositories limited to a single business process or business group. Data marts tend to be project- rather than data-oriented, decentralized by user are and organized around multiple, semi-complex structures. An example is a direct marketing data mart containing details of the customer base, individual campaigns (e.g., target list, offer specifics, responses), customer contact history, etc. Usually, a data mart contains a sub-set of the contents of data warehouse, which makes it informationally more homogenous and application-ready. Data marts can serve as just data repositories or, in conjunction with business intelligence applications can support ongoing performance dashboarding.

The term "database" is sometimes used to denote a data warehouse, and at other times a data mart. Even worse, it is not uncommon for an organization to expect data mart-like functionality from a data warehouse, simply because in view of some, a database is a database. Yet in the knowledge-creation sense, there is a vast difference between these two general types of databases. A *data warehouse* is merely a repository of facts, usually centering on transactions and related data. A *data mart*, on the other hand, is a specific application of a subset of all data warehouse contents, designed with a particular purpose in mind, such as product/service promotion. The hierarchical and functionality differences between the two are summarized below in Figure 6.1.

Database Content

Content-wise, there are a number of different types of databases, comprising several of distinct categories, detailed in Table 6.2 below.

Bibliographic and full text databases are traditionally associated with library informational services, such as ABI/Inform or LexisNexis, containing summaries or full texts of publicly available published sources, such as newspapers, professional journals, conference proceedings, etc. In a business sense, they offer a referential source of information rather than ongoing decision support. Multimedia and hypertext databases are one of many Internet and the World Wide Web related informational innovations that tend to be used more as businesses communication/(i.e., promotional) vehicles, rather than sources of decision-guiding insights. Although at this point these type of databases offer limited utility to marketing managers, the emergence (albeit, slow) of the Semantic Web[2] may radically reshape that.

The last of the four broad types of databases, numeric, is the primary decision support engine of organizational decision making. The content of numeric databases, such as the earlier described transactions, behavioral propensities or basic descriptors, coupled with the easy-to-analyze coding make these databases both statistically analyzable and informationally rich.

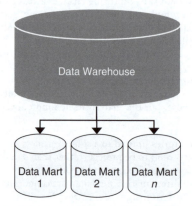

Figure 6.1 Data Warehouse vs. Mart

Table 6.2 Types of Databases

Consideration	Description
Bibliographic	Used to organize published sources, such as books, journals or newspaper articles; contains basic descriptive information about those items. Mostly used in library cataloging. Bibliographic databases are reference sources, not analyzable with traditional statistical techniques discussed here.
Full text	Contain complete texts of publications, such as journal or newspaper articles. Examples include Lexis database or *Encyclopedia Britannica*. Great qualitative sources of knowledge, full text databases can be sources of quantitative coded data, but are not directly statistically analyzable.
Multimedia & Hypertext	The most recent database type, largely responsible for the explosive growth of the World Wide Web. It supports creative linking of diverse types of objects, such as text, pictures, music, programs, into a single expression. These types of databases are representative of the modes of electronic, online content delivery, this are indirectly analyzable within the context of campaign management. However, they require a considerable amount of preparation prior to analyses.
Numeric	Used to store digitally coded data, such as purchase transactions, demographic information or survey responses. It is the staple of business database infrastructure and the focus of the analytical processes described here.

Data Models

Business databases that are designed to store transactional and augmenting data are almost always explicitly or implicitly numeric.[3] The information these data reservoirs contain can be organized in accordance with one of several data organizational models, which can be grouped into three general categories of entity-relationship, relational and object-oriented.

1. ENTITY-RELATIONSHIP DATA MODEL

The most basic data model, the entity-relationship model is built around parent–child hierarchical typology; it identifies basic organizational objects, such as a customer, transaction, age, account number and specifies the relationships between these objects. It is the simplest and the oldest of the three models, which means it is relatively easy to set up but also offers limited usability. The model's general logic is illustrated below:

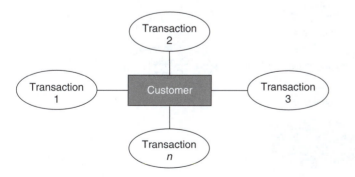

Figure 6.2 Entity-Relationship Data Model

2. RELATIONAL DATA MODEL

The relational model represents facts in a database as a collection of entities, often called tables, connected by relationships in accordance with predicate logic and the set theory. The relational model is more conducive toward automated, templated report generation, but it is also more restrictive in the sense of "on the fly" report generation, as the relationships need to be specified and programmed in advance. The term "relational" conveys that individual tables are linked to each other to enhance the descriptive value of a simple flat file. It is a lot more complex to set up than the entity-relationship model, but offers far greater levels of utility. Its general logic is illustrated in Figure 6.3.

3. OBJECT-ORIENTED DATA MODEL

In many regards, this is the most evolved data organizational model, but it is also least analytically flexible. The data structure is built around encapsulated units—objects—which are characterized by attributes and sets of orientations and rules, and can be grouped into classes and super classes, as illustrated in Figure 6.4. Although the individual "objects" exhibit a considerable amount of usage flexibility, their preparation requires a considerable amount of programming.

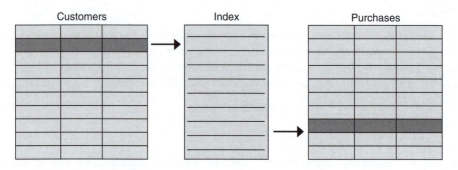

Figure 6.3 Relational Data Model

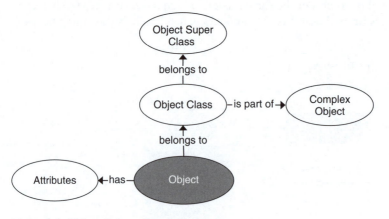

Figure 6.4 Object-Oriented Data Model

Database types and data model differences certainly contribute to the level of difficulty associated with developing a solid level of understanding of the fundamentals of database analytics. However, although these considerations have a significant impact on the database's querying and reporting capabilities, they exert only a relatively marginal impact on analytics. The primary reason for that is that querying and reporting are conducted within the confines of the database itself with the help of the database management system, or DBMS, while data analytics is usually carried out outside of the database. Thus the organizational structure of the database is of interest to database analysis only insofar as the identification and proper classification of the available data.

Data: Types

What is data? Quite simply, *data is facts*. Naturally, there is an enormous, almost infinite variety of data, which can be broadly categorized along two basic dimensions: *qualitative* or *quantitative* (dimension 1) and *root* or *derived* (dimension 2), as shown below in Figure 6.5 (the horizontal axis captures the "quantitative vs. qualitative" distinction, while the vertical axis shows the "root vs. derived" one).

Qualitative vs. Quantitative

Qualitative data represents facts recorded in a non-numeric fashion. In the business context, qualitative data often represents opinions, beliefs or feelings captured through structured or unstructured interviews, ethnographic research or simple observation—nowadays best exemplified by social networking data (e.g., Facebook, Twitter, etc.). In a scientific sense, it is typically used as the basis for deriving initial hypotheses, which are then tested on a more representative and larger sample.[4] While qualitative data captures a greater depth of a single individual's state, such as individual beliefs, it tends to be non-projectable (i.e., extrapolated onto a larger population) due to either small, usually non-representative sample size or cross-record informational dissimilarity. Also, due to the fact that it often needs to be extracted or inferred by a researcher, it is additionally prone to the researcher's interpretative bias. The most common business application of the qualitative data format takes the form of focus groups, frequently used in new product/idea testing. Due to its non-numeric format, qualitative data is not statistically analyzable[5] at the level required by robust knowledge creation.

Quantitative data are facts recorded in a numerical fashion. In business, the single most valuable source of quantitative facts are ongoing operations, which generate transactional

transactions campaign results survey opinions	Quantitative & Root	Qualitative & Root	focus groups interviews video tapes
propensities sales aggregates geo-demographics	Quantitative & Derived	Qualitative & Derived	emerging themes observational interpretations

Figure 6.5 High-Level Data Categorization

records often referred to as the "secondary" data (so-named because its capture was secondary to business operations, such as sales, that generated it). Other, often used sources of quantitative business data include *surveys* (usually referred to as the "primary data," which reflects its purpose-specific origination) and the so-called *individual differences*, such as demographics and lifestyles or propensities to engage in specific behaviors. In general, quantitative data is statistically analyzable[6] and projectable, which is to say that it can support broader (i.e., stretching beyond the confines of a particular sample) generalizations.

The distinction between the quantitative and qualitative data types points to fundamentally different methods of collecting and codifying facts. The former offers a high degree of respondent representativeness and a numeric, objectively analyzable format, while the latter delivers non-numerically coded depth of an individual respondent's insight. As previously mentioned, qualitative data is often used as a basis for forming hypotheses, which are then tested with the help of quantitative data. For example, focus groups (a commonly used qualitative data capture mechanism) can be used to pinpoint a desired set of characteristics for a new product (i.e., to generate hypotheses about bundling individual product attributes), and a subsequent in-practice pilot (a good source of quantitative data) can offer an objective, generalizable estimate of the new product's market potential.

Although in principle both the qualitative and quantitative data types are potentially important sources of insights, applied marketing analytics tends to be primarily concerned with the analyses of the latter, for a couple of obvious reasons. First and foremost, corporate databases are essentially repositories of quantitatively coded or quantitatively codable data, which is a consequence of the systemic properties of most of the electronic business systems. Secondly, digitally coded data is easier to analyze objectively, as data and data analytical methods are independent of one another, which is to say that two different analysts applying the same method to the same dataset should arrive at identical or nearly identical results (assuming invariance in terms of any data imputation or re-coding). Analyses of qualitative data, on the other hand, are essentially inseparable from the analyst, as they represent subjective evaluation and/or interpretations, both of which can vary considerably across analysts. The inability to replicate and thus cross-validate a particular set of findings is a significant hindrance to marketing analytics; it effectively makes it impossible to compile sufficient amount of corroborating evidence for findings that might be hard to accept on face value.

Root vs. Derived

In contrast to the *qualitative–quantitative* distinction, the *root* vs. *derived* continuum represents the difference of "degree," rather than "type." Specifically, this distinction points to the degree of data aggregation, which is the process of combining multiple, typically narrowly operationalized elements into a new, single and more aggregate data point. In view of the fact that the aggregation process usually involves mathematically manipulating data, it is typically associated with quantitative data. The purpose for summarizing disaggregate data may vary across situations, but usually it is at least in some way related to the desire to increase the data's informational value, aid handling of large data files or to comply with legal requirements.[7]

Root data represents the most disaggregate form of storing facts in a database and it usually corresponds to the form in which data was originally captured. Depending on the source, such as individual purchase transactions, survey responses or product inquiries, this general data form can exist at varying levels of detail and abstraction.

Let's consider the purchase transaction data. The vast majority of larger retail outlets are equipped with electronic barcode scanners, which record individual transactions at the Stock Keeping Unit (SKU) level, which is the actual physical product being purchased.[8] The root data collected by those systems are the individual product–time–place–cost conjoints, which represent unique product transactions captured at a particular place and point in time. For instance, a 6-pack of 12 oz. cans of Diet Coke sold at 5:45 pm on March 21, 2012 at Kroger store #21034 for $2.99 is an example of root transactional data.

Clearly, root data can be quite voluminous. An average supermarket, for instance, stocks around 50,000 individual SKUs on a single store basis, while an average supermarket chain carries in excess of 150,000 SKUs overall (the difference reflects regional as well as store size variability). In terms of data, a mid-size chain of 500 or so stores captures several million transactions[9] daily, which adds up to several billion records in just a single year.

Although not quite that voluminous, accident-related claim data is another example of disaggregate root data. To stay with a retailer example used above, a large volume of "foot traffic" will also generate a considerable amount of (mostly minor) accidents, such as "slip and fall" and others. A large retailer with hundreds or thousands of location will quickly accumulate thousands of individual liability records.

Thus although powerful in terms of its informational content, data stored in root format can be extremely cumbersome to work with, in large part because of its size and detailed character. It has high potential value, but the insights it contains are far from self-evident. On a practical level, the management is rarely interested in tracking performance at the individual item level (e.g., individual accident claim, SKU) and in many cases it is simply not feasible due to the very high numbers of individual items. As a result, it is common to aggregate the root data to a more meaningful (and manageable) levels, such as a brand or a category. Doing so effectively converts root into derived data, because the sales levels attributed to the more aggregate entities of a brand and a category are in effect *derived* from the sales of their disaggregate components.

As previously remarked, the distinction between root and derived data types is best looked at in terms of difference of degree, or specifically, their respective levels of aggregation which ultimately translates into measurement precision. In general, the lower the level of aggregation of data, the higher its informational precision, simply because the process of data aggregation invariably inflates the amount of noise in the data, becuase exact disaggregate quantities (e.g., individual-level accidents) are replaced with less exact aggregate-level quantities. Hence, the root vs. derived level of precision differential tends to be inversely proportional to the amount of aggregation that might be deemed necessary. For example, rolling up individual item data (e.g., 2-liter bottle of diet Coke) to progressively more aggregate levels as represented by, for instance, the brand (Coca-Cola) and then the manufacturer (The Coca-Cola Company), will render the resultant data successively less accurate. Hence while on one hand data aggregation is necessary from the standpoint of informational parsimony, it carries with it an (often significant) amount of precision decay.

The reason for the precision decay is the error additivity associated with the data aggregation process. It increases the amount of imprecision embedded in the data because it is based on compounding of disaggregate data values (many of which may contain some level of imprecision), which typically involves averaging. Hence, the necessary evil of data aggregation should be considered in the context of the following:

1. Averaging creates data error, as the more precise disaggregate value are replaced with less precise aggregate ones. For example, computing average income for a particular consumer segment will lead to less accuracy for every individual household in that segment.
2. Compounding can magnify the already existing data errors, particularly systematic omissions, such as not capturing sales of certain SKUs, non-traditional channels, or counting promotional giveaways as sales (e.g., buy one, get one free). Overall, summary-based derived data may be inappropriate for certain transactional data-based statistical applications, such as the estimation of action-attributable impact. In that sense, correct data categorization can have a strong impact on the accuracy of analytic results.

The reasoning presented above may seem somewhat counterintuitive in view of the conventional statistical "error cancellation" provision, where randomly distributed error terms sum up to zero as "over" and "under" estimates cancel each other out. This notion is one of the central provisions of the least squares estimation methodology employed by some of the most commonly used statistical procedures, such as regression. However, when applied without a proper due diligence to the analysis of large, transactional databases, the otherwise sound error cancellation rationale can lead to erroneous conclusions as it gets inappropriately stretched beyond its applicability limits. It all stems from a handful of fundamental differences between the nature and the behavior of statistical estimates and the actual data often found in large corporate systems.

First of all, as the name implies, *statistical estimates* are mathematically derived values, while data are facts. The former is arrived at by means of (usually) unbiased computational processes calibrated to ensure a random distribution of errors around the expected values, while the latter has no built-in error randomization provisions. Secondly, the term "error" carries vastly different meanings in the context of statistical analyses and transactional data.

Webster's Dictionary defines *error* as a *"departure from what is true, right or proper,"* in other words, a mistake. In statistics, *error* is a difference between two values, such as actual and expected or a single estimate and a group mean. It is interpreted as (a typically expected) variability rather than a (typically unexpected) mistake, which means that quite often the former is a desired and a necessary prerequisite to statistical analyses. In contrast to that, an *error* in the context of raw, transactional data is simply a mistake in the everyday sense of the word. It is neither desired nor necessary, rather it is an unintended consequence of data capture and much effort is put into eliminating and correcting it.

What is of more importance to robust data analysis is that a purposeful statistical error exhibits predictable properties and behaves in an equally predictable fashion, which effectively eliminates the likelihood of aggregation-related skewing[10] (assuming, of course, a sufficiently large sample size). However, the "behavior" of fact-based data aggregation is quite different from that, insofar as data mistakes do not necessarily behave in a predictable fashion (i.e., are not randomly distributed). Thus it is not reasonable to expect that under-reporting of the purchase frequency of Brand A will be cancelled out by over-reporting of the purchase frequency of Brand B, when both are aggregated up to the level of a store or a region. Frankly, it would make more sense to expect that a process which under-reports the purchase frequency of one brand will also under-report the purchase frequency of another brand.

In the end, there will always be compelling reasons to aggregate detailed data up to a more meaningful level. It is important, however, to keep in mind the proportional increase in the likelihood of data errors associated with rolling up of disaggregate data. And since much of the database analytical effort ultimately translates into numerical conclusions, such as sales lift quantification or a propensity score, appropriately categorizing the data inputs on the "root vs. derived" continuum will go a long way toward, well, reducing the amount of error in those conclusions.

Data: Contents

There are multiple ways of categorizing data: by source, type, usage situation, etc. From the standpoint of (potential) informational content, data can be broadly divided into the *behavioral core* and the *causal layer augmenting the core*. The former are essentially transactions (such as purchases) or other behavior-denoting interactions; the latter encompasses a somewhat broader, type-wise, variety of metric classes, ranging from individual or geo-level demographics (or firmographics for businesses), attitudes and lifestyles (or industry classification for businesses), satisfaction surveys, field information (e.g., outgoing telemarketing for consumer markets or direct sales for businesses) and other types of action- or actor-describing details. Hence while the behavioral core metrics convey observed or observable outcomes, the (outcome) augmenting causal layer variables hide the potential causes, or at least correlates of the observed behaviors.

These rudimentary differences between the behavioral core and the augmenting causal information are indicative of the informational value of the two data types. Behaviors, particularly purchases or promotional responses, are typically the central component of any database analysis since they are most closely tied to revenue (i.e., they reflect actions tied directly to earnings) and as such can attest to the ultimate success or failure of business strategies. More specifically, from the standpoint of marketing strategy, the attainment of competitive advantage is analogous to realizing the greatest revenue or profitability gains at the lowest possible cost; hence it follows that explaining and predicting behavioral outcomes is at the nexus of marketing analytics.

This is not to say that the causal data is of trivial value—far from it. The root causes of behavioral outcomes and patterns can rarely, if ever, be understood without the explanatory power of causal descriptors, such as demographics, lifestyles, attitudes or NAIC (North American Industry Classification) codes for businesses. In that sense, the behavior-augmenting causal data contributes the "why" behind the "what." It is intuitively obvious that without the ability to single out specific precipitators of observed behavioral patterns, those patterns could not be understood beyond a series of hard-to-predict outcomes spuriously associated with business actions. Needless to say, it would be difficult, if not altogether impossible to derive competitively unique knowledge.

Ultimately, it is the synergistic effect of the *behavioral core–augmenting causal data* combination that is the most fertile source of business insights. However, to realize its full potential, a strong understanding of each of two rudimentary data sources is necessary.

The Behavioral Core

Most databases have highly operational origins and it is particularly true to the behavioral outcome-focused ones. Consider the rapid proliferation of bar-code-based point-of-sales (POS) scanner technology (first introduced in mid-70s), the electronic order processing systems and the virtual explosion of Web-related capabilities—all of those developments and resultant trends output massive amounts of data, largely as a by-product of their operations. As discussed in the opening chapter, organizations tend to gravitate toward the belief that data, in and of itself, is an asset that warrants investing considerable monetary and human resources. As a result, quite a few organizations amassed tremendous amounts of behavioral information, often warehoused in multiple systems or a single, distributed albeit networked data reservoir. For instance, the Walmart Corporation has what is by many believed to be the largest non-governmental transactional database in the world, with its size estimated to have surpassed the 500 terabytes[11] mark. And although Walmart's database obviously represents an extreme in terms of its sheer size, many transaction-intensive organizations, such as those in retail or banking industries have amassed transactional databases ranging in size from 10 to around 50 or so terabytes of data. This is an incredible amount of analyzable data, which as shown later, can benefit the organization's knowledge pursuit on one hand, while limiting the applicability of some "staple" statistical techniques on the other.

Entities as Attributes of Events

Behavioral metrics are essentially actions, and depending on the source of data they can take on a different form, reflecting the two key dimensions of "who" (e.g., an employee, a customer, an organization) and "what" (e.g., a sale of a 48oz. box of Cheerios). From the standpoint of a database, behaviors represent "transactions" and as such, an individual record is comprised of a specific "event," such as a purchase, as well as a varying number of "attributes" associated with that event, such as the date or the amount. However, because the capture of these individual data elements is a by-product of electronic transaction processing, many of the individual data tidbits may reside in separate transaction files, or even multiple data-recording systems, rather than a single, central data warehouse. For example, customer purchase, demographic and promotional response details routinely reside in separate files. Although largely an infrastructure-related consideration, it also has a profound impact on the subsequent analyses of the behavioral data, insofar as it leads to *data organizational schema inversion*, where *customers are coded as attributes of events* (e.g., transactions, promotional responses, etc.), rather than *events being attributes of customers*. Consider Figure 6.6.

   In the hypothetical diagram shown above, the "event," such as an in-store purchase (a product) is the central unit of analysis of the resultant record, while the multiple "entities" represent individual customers. In other words, the database transaction is structured in such a way that the "who" is an attribute of "what." This is a tremendously important consideration, both from a philosophical as well as practical data manipulation and analyses standpoints. In regard to the former, it is simply illogical for customers to be attributed to products for the obvious reason that it leads to lumping of the otherwise dissimilar purchasers. Doing so diminishes the analyst's ability to reliably differentiate between different customers, which is ultimately the goal of behavioral predictions. In other words, the customers-as-attributes-of-events type of data organizational schema forces analysts to look at data from the standpoint of "what transpired"

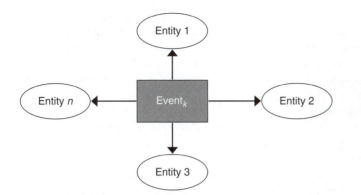

Figure 6.6 Entities as Attributes of Events

rather than "who engaged in a particular behavior," which severely limits the efficacy of the resultant insights.

Attributing customers to events also carries with it important practical data manipulation considerations. On the one hand, it is conducive to event-level reporting (hence the widespread use of reporting-oriented business intelligence tools), while at the same time, it makes customer-level analyses far more difficult, because of the extensive data re-coding requirements (detailed later in this chapter). In a sense, it "pushes" data users into outcome-based database reporting (i.e., generic information) and impedes the more competitively advantageous explanatory analytics, and ultimately, the edge-producing knowledge creation.

However, because so much of the behavioral data is passively collected by the various electronic transaction processing systems, the customers-as-attributes-of-events data organizational schema is very common, as are reports summarizing product purchases without tying any of these behavioral outcomes to specific causes.

Events as Attributes of Entities

As pointed out above, viewing customers as properties of events is clearly neither rational nor conducive to insightful analyses; hence the relationship needs to be reversed so that actions associated with different events (i.e., behaviors) can be attributed to those engaging in the behaviors of interest. However, before that can be done, a considerable amount of data engineering is needed, in part because of the re-coding task itself, but also because there is quite a bit of invariance among the individual behavioral core data types. The *cross data type invariance* is particularly evident when attempting to amalgamate attitudinal "causes," best exemplified by survey-captured opinions, with transactional "effects," such as in-store purchases.

The most important, and at times most difficult step is that of attributing multisourced data elements to one another to establish a "cause–effect" relationship. In many instances it requires extensive additional data coding, particularly when analyzing high repurchase frequency products. Consider the product purchase cycle (e.g., awareness, consideration, trial, etc.) and the related, though separate in the database sense, promotion response behaviors (e.g., exposure, processing, etc.). At the time, a purchase will represent a response to promotional exposure, yet that "cause–effect linkage" is not

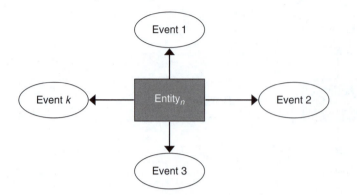

Figure 6.7 Events as Attributes of Entities

expressly set up in the data. Unless individual behaviors or actions are appropriately coded and the corresponding behaviors are attributed appropriately, it may not be known which, if any, action caused the specific outcome.

Once the source-specific data has been properly set up, the resultant data structure needs to be redefined from event-centric to entity-centric, as shown in Figure 6.7.

Expressing events as properties of entities, rather than the other way around, is more reflective of the underlying processes. Marketing management is about paying attention to specific events that impact the outcomes of interest to the organization. Some transactions represent events directly impacting those outcomes, while others may represent attempts at trying to manage their effects. To maximize the productivity of marketing programs—i.e., to bring about the greatest possible revenue or profit gains at the lowest possible cost—the organization has to have a way of quickly and efficiently "drilling" into the cost-precipitating events, which in turn requires an appropriately structured behavioral data. Ultimately, it means that database analytics initiatives need to be built around outcome-causing entities.

The desirability of focusing source-specific data on the "who" (i.e., customers), as opposed to the "what" (i.e., products) is also evident from the standpoint of informational efficacy. In particular, it is critical to making a transition from a mostly single-topic reporting (such as sales or promotional response rates) to multi-source data analytics (e.g., delineating and quantifying the drivers of sales variability or response rates). The latter requires the merging together of multiple, typically dissimilar data files, which in turn calls for the common-to-all organizational unit needs to be identified. In the vast majority of cases, the only consistent threat connecting the otherwise dissimilar data files is the "who," which means that expressing events as properties of entities is a necessary precondition of multi-source analytics.

Reconciling Dissimilar Data Attributional Schema

In most data types, there is a need to establish attributional relationships, akin to the cause–effect connection. For instance, the rudimentary unit of analysis in a transactional database is a transaction, which necessitates the attributing of an event, such as a store purchase, to another entity, such as a household or an individual consumer. The reason this seemingly redundant step is necessary has to do with the disparity between how transactional data is collected and how it should be analyzed. Regarding the former, virtually all transactions are captured one-at-a-time, as individual records. In other words, two distinct purchases made at different times by the same buyer will be treated as two distinct database records—in fact, in some databases each product within a "shopping basket" (all products purchased at the same store, at the same time and by the same consumer) may comprise a separate record. In a database sense, two purchases made by the same customer are treated the same way as two purchases made by two different customers. Obviously, the two scenarios yield different conclusions in the context of frequency and severity management. For that reason, the initial data capture steps have to include express rules for attributing (i.e., connecting) outcomes to sources. This is the *data source attributional schema* due diligence consideration.

In the realm of the emerging enterprise data infrastructure, a need typically exists to combine multiple sources of data in a single database environment, which gives rise to somewhat more involved *enterprise data attributional schema* considerations. The bulk of marketing systems' transactional data is a by-product of the digitization of business processes discussed earlier, where the "natural unit of analysis"—or the basic organizational structure of data—is an individual purchase, response or other action, rather than entities (e.g., buyers, promotional responders) behind those actions. As noted earlier, in those systems two or more purchases from the same source (e.g., a person) are treated as separate entities. Of course, each such database record typically contains the appropriate outcome-to-source linking identifiers, yet the outcome-to-source attribution is usually not expressly established. But again, because this data was not captured for analytic purposes per se (hence the often used name, "secondary data" given to transactional metrics), explicit steps need to be taken to make sure that the differences between independent, source-wise, and dependent events is expressly recognized.

This is generally not the case with behavioral, lifestyle or attitudinal surveys, all of which are examples of data that has been captured expressly for its own value (often referred to as "primary data"). In the database sense, it means that the aforementioned outcome-to-source attribution is usually already in place.

Aside from the collection method, these two data sources—i.e., primary vs. secondary—are separated by an important distinction: The former's organizational schema implies that outcomes are attributes of sources (which is the way we would typically think about the outcome-to-source attribution), while the latter's schema implies the opposite—namely, that sources are attributes of outcomes. This attributional schema difference—or the dissimilarity in the way that differently sourced data elements relate to one another is an important consideration in making the enterprise data model more "analysis-friendly."

Figure 6.8 visually contrasts the two schemas.

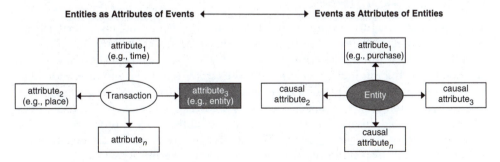

Figure 6.8 Entities as Attributes of Events vs. Events as Attributes of Entities

The above distinction is important because the knowledge creation process typically involves the culling of dissimilar data types, which requires resolving attributional schema disparities, which is one of the reasons the otherwise powerful databases often yield little unique knowledge. Frankly, it is far simpler to analyze individual data sources separately, in effect limiting the informational insights to a single, or a handful of schematically similar data sources. Taking information to the next level—which is turning it into competitively advantageous knowledge—usually calls for a satisfactory resolution to the seemingly inescapable data schematic dissimilarities. Overall, the inability to systematically synthesize multi-sourced data is among the most significant impediments to making that transition to the higher level of information utility (in practice, it is one of the key impediments getting in the way of enterprise databases models or the so-called "360° view" of customers becoming operational realities). As a topic of a considerable importance to the overall database analytics endeavor, transforming schematically dissimilar data types into a single format is fully discussed in the next chapter.

Let's look at a couple of specific and commonly encountered data types. The first is the transactional data which exemplifies the *entities as attributes of events* organizational schema. Here, purchases captured at an item level constitute the primary unit of measurement, with other aspects of behaviors acting as descriptors contextualizing the transaction. So, for instance, the purchase of item #12345 is associated with store $_p$, time $_p$, location $_p$, price $_p$, etc. In terms of the data matrix, rows constitute individual purchases while columns (variables) are the individual purchase characteristics. This type of organizational schema makes the basic outcome reporting relatively straightforward (hence, the widespread use of the automated business intelligence tools in this realm), but explanatory or predictive analyses (discussed in latter chapters) cannot be attempted without a considerable amount of data rearranging.

The second main organizational schema is one where *events are expressed as attributes of entities*, and is exemplified by behavioral and attitudinal surveys. In contrast to the above, sources (e.g., consumers) are the central unit of measurement to which everything else is attributed. In the practical sense, this means that in a basic data matrix, database records are individual survey responders, while columns are the record-describing variables. In other words, unlike the *entities as attributes of events* organizational schema describe above, this data model makes predictive analyses relatively easy to carry out. The challenge, of course, lies in establishing attributional unity between the two data types—doing so, entails two distinct data engineering steps:

1. MASTER-TO-EVENT THREADING

The process of structuring multi-sourced data into a coherent organizational schema requires *master-to-event threading*. In a sense, this process can be thought of as the establishment of a *hierarchical attributional schema,* where temporal or causal connections are established linking individual *events* and the *master* record. For instance, individual purchases or promotional responses (i.e., events) are all "threaded" to a single *master* (typically, a customer or a household identifier) linking together all of those data pieces. The purpose behind this data preparatory step is to establish cross-record standardization to support future *cause–effect* analyses. This is particularly pertinent for organizations wishing to establish an enterprise-wide view of their marketing activities.

2. VARIABLE CODING

Yet another data capture-related preparatory consideration relates to *variable coding*, which is the assignment or an explicit recognition of specific measurement properties to individual data elements. As a general rule, if measurement properties need to be assigned, the most analytically flexible scale should be used, which might be intuitively obvious, but unless the measurement property specification rules are expressly stated, less-than-ideal choices can be made during the initial data capture efforts.

From the statistical data analysis standpoint, numeric data can be either *continuous* or *categorical* (also called *metric* or *non-metric*, respectively). The former is comprised of variables measured either with interval or ratio scales, often referred to as *metric* data, while the latter can be measured with *nominal* or *ordinal* scales, and it is also called *categorical* data. In the knowledge creation sense, metric data has far greater informational value than the non-metric data, primarily because it permits a wider range of mathematical operations, making it analyzable by a wider range of analytical techniques. Table 6.3 summarizes the types of variables along with their most important characteristics.

In general, interval and ratio scales-measured variables are both assumed to be continuously distributed for the purposes of data analysis, while the nominal and ordinal ones are treated as categorical. It is important to note that while continuously distributed variables (i.e., metric) can be easily converted into categories[12] (i.e., non-metric), discrete metrics cannot be made into continuous ones. As a result, once data has been coded as categorical, certain commonly used statistical techniques cannot be deployed to analyze it.[13] Given its obvious importance, this topic is discussed in more depth later.

Causal Data

One of the most important lessons in statistics is that *correlation is not causation.* This statement captures the belief that term "causation" carries a burden of proof that goes

Table 6.3 Types of Scales

Trait	Categorical		Continuous	
	Nominal	*Ordinal*	*Interval*	*Ratio*
Definition	Labels of states that can be expressed numerically, but have no "numeric" meaning	Rank-ordering-based categorization; intervals between adjacent values are indeterminate	Fixed distance (with respect to the attribute being measured) rank-ordered categories	A scale in which distances are stated with reference to a rational zero
Permissible Operations	counting	*greater than* or *less than* comparisons	addition and subtraction	addition, subtraction, multiplication and division
Example	gender, marital status	movie ratings (PG, R)	degrees F; attitude	degrees K; distance
Analysis	cross-tabulation	frequencies	mean	coefficient of variation

far beyond what is required to ascertain a simple, though persistent association, aka, correlation. Hence, what makes certain types of data "causal"? The answer begins with an up-close look at the basic tenets of the concept of causation.

Ascertaining Causation

Given its central role in knowledge creation, the notion of *causality* or *causation* has been a subject of centuries-long debate among scientists and philosophers alike. At the core of the debate has been the line of demarcation separating cause-and-effect from just simple concurrence-based relationships. Is factor A causing B, or do the two merely coincide? According to Hunt,[14] an explanation has to meet four separate criteria before it can be classified as causal. Those are shown in Table 6.4.

As pointed out above, temporal sequentiality and associative variation have a very simple meaning and application, in spite of the somewhat foreboding names. Occurring in sequence (A followed by B) and doing so persistently is both intuitively obvious and relatively easy to demonstrate. For instance, if certain marketing actions (such as a direct mail campaign) precede, time-wise, observed business outcomes and that relationship is recurring, that would generally constitute sufficient basis to attest to temporal sequentiality and associative variation.

It is less so with the remaining two causality thresholds: non-spurious association and demonstrated theoretical support. Even though many behaviors tend to be somewhat repetitive, the mere fact that they tend to be a part of a larger set of behavioral interdependencies makes the requirement of proving their non-spurious nature a difficult one.

Table 6.4 Causality Criteria

Criterion	Description
Temporal Sequentiality	Changes in factor A to be used to causally explain factor B must precede in time the occurrence of changes in B. Thus an attributed action must precede the observed outcome before it can be considered a cause of it. It is an intuitively obvious and an easily established requirement in practical business analysis.
Associative Variation	Changes in factor A must be systematically associated with changes in factor B. In other words, in order to conclude that certain types of promotions lead to higher sales, one must be able to observe systematic sales increases associated with those specific marketing actions. Again, a logical and usually relatively easy to meet requirement.
Non-Spurious Association	If A causes B, then there must be no factor C which, if introduced into the explanation would make the systematic A–B association vanish. Thus if a particular direct mail campaign is indeed one of the causes of sales gains, factoring out another metric, such as online advertising, should not nullify the *direct mail campaign–sales increase* relationship. Unlike the previous two requirements, this is a far more difficult condition to meet, primarily because data is not always available to make that determination and even when it is, its quality can vary considerably among sources.
Theoretical Support	If A causes B, is it consistent with an established theory X? If the aforementioned direct mail campaign indeed leads to higher sales, what is the theory that explains that dependence? Since practical business analyses are typically not concerned with abstract theoretical explanations, this particular requirement is rarely satisfied, though it is worthwhile to keep in mind.

In addition, many of these activities are highly pragmatic—i.e., they do not espouse to adhere to specific general theories and their roots are often in fact, spurious ideas and decisions. Frankly, the pursuit of competitive advantage demands that firms take steps that are uniquely more advantageous to them than their competitors, rather than pursuing strategies that have been proven to work the same way for everyone else.

So what is the conclusion? Establishing *causality* in business analyses should be held to a somewhat different, frankly lower standard than in theoretical research. This may sound almost blasphemous to some, but let's consider some of the hallmark differences between practical and scientific endeavors. First and foremost, business analyses are typically concerned with uncovering unique though sustainable sources of competitive advantage, in contrast to scientific investigations which almost always are focused on formulating and testing generalizable, i.e., universally true, knowledge claims. This means that business and theoretical analyses both share in the requirement of ascertaining temporal sequentiality and the associative variation of the potentially causal relationships, but it also means that in contrast to the theoretical pursuits, business analyses can conclude that the relationships of interest are causal without conclusively demonstrating a clear theoretical support or the non-spurious nature of the said association. In other words, a particular cause–effect relationship does not need to be universally true (meaning, equally valid for all other organizations) in order to be a source of competitively advantageous decisions by a particular organization—it only needs to be persistent, or hold up across time.

Second, scientific worthiness of findings is demonstrated through their generalizability and only implicitly through longitudinal stability, while the value of practical business analyses is demonstrated almost exclusively through longitudinal persistence of results. To a firm, it matters little whether particular dependencies can be generalized to other firms or industries (frankly, as suggested above, the pursuit of a competitive edge would argue the opposite), but it is tremendously important that these relationship hold as expected when resources are invested into future business initiatives, whether these are promotional programs or other capital expenditures. In other words, while theoretical research aims to create universally applicable knowledge, business research strives to uncover the few dimensions of knowledge that are uniquely applicable—i.e., advantageous—to a particular firm.

Third, marketing analytics are contextualized by focus and data. Even the largest organizations only compete in a subset of all industries and their data and data analyses are a reflection of the scope of their operations. In other words, the focus of business analyses is the world in which a given organization operates, while the focus of theoretical investigations naturally transcends any idiosyncratic industry or a set of industries. Thus the resultant knowledge claims—including causality—should be evaluated in the proper context.

Therefore, as it is used in this text, the term "causal" will apply to data that can be used as the basis for establishing or validating enduring relationships demonstrating temporal sequentiality and associative variation. The same standard will be applied to ascertaining causality in the context of the database analytical process.

A Closer Look

In the context of marketing analytics, *causal data* are any data elements that systematically contribute to explaining the variability in the core data, most notably, in frequency and severity of loss-causing events. Causal data allow us to look past *what* happened to trying to understand *why* it happened, which is a crucial step in the development of predictive analytical models.

Overall, causal data encapsulate entity traits, preferences and propensities. *Entity traits* are the basic descriptors such as demographics or location. *Preferences* are either demonstrated or attributed choices, exemplified by psychographics, lifestyles or preferred product categories. And lastly, *propensities* represent modeled probabilities of engaging in a particular course of action, such as the likelihood of a particular consumer or a household responding to a specific marketing incentive.

Content-wise, causal data can be broadly categorized as either business- or individual-focused.[15] At the center of the *causal business data* is a collection of basic individual or household characteristics collectively called *demographics*, which includes the basic descriptive traits such as age, income, education, etc. A second important grouping of business causal data falls under the umbrella of *demonstrated propensities*, which include the willingness to catalog-shop, buy online, respond to direct mail solicitations, etc.

In terms of its *source*, causal data can be either observed or derived. *Observed data* is factual and usually it is reported directly by entities, such as individuals or businesses—examples include the demographic information supplied by consumers through product registration, or the lifestyle groupings into which individuals self-select. *Derived data* is probabilistic and it typically is a result of sample-to-population or geographic area-based generalizations, as illustrated by promotion response propensities or geodemographics.

The *level of aggregation* reflects the granularity of the data, which can be individual, a group of individuals or a particular area. Individual-level causal data reflects the characteristics of a single individual, usually the customer in the context of marketing. A group of individuals, such as household, reflects the characteristics of the group that is expected to engage in a shared decision making. Lastly, area- or geography-based causal data represents location-derived estimates of individual characteristics, such as geodemographics, which are block-level (typically about 20–30 households, on average) estimates of the key descriptors derived from the more granular U.S. Census data.[16]

The considerable differences in data granularity across the three levels of aggregation suggest a number of tradeoffs, most notably between accuracy and coverage of the individual-level causal data, as shown in Figure 6.9.

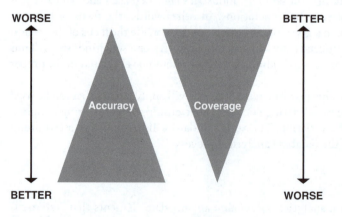

Figure 6.9 Accuracy vs. Coverage Tradeoff

As depicted above, there is an inverse relationship between accuracy and coverage: As one increases, the other one decreases. The most disaggregate consumer data is available at the individual level—obviously, it is the most accurate information because it is factual, insofar as it depicts the actual characteristics of those engaging in behaviors of interest. However, it is also the scarcest, i.e., it is only available for a relatively small fraction of all individuals, and at times it may not be accessible, for legal and other reasons. Group-level data is less accurate because it is probabilistic, i.e., it expresses the most likely, rather than actual characteristics. But at the same time, it offers a better coverage since it is not limited to observed outcomes. Lastly, geography-based causal data is least accurate since its values represent estimates derived for large groups of households, but it offers the most complete coverage because it is derived from the U.S. Census, which covers the entire country.

Naturally, the quality of data plays a significant role in the validity and reliability of analytical insights. Causal data plays a particularly important role because it is suggestive of actions that can enhance the performance of marketing initiatives. Furthermore, in a strictly technical sense, it also has a pronounced impact on the quality of statistical models it helps to power, particularly as it relates to what is known as "model specification" (fully discussed later). In essence, a correctly specified model will have a relatively small number of statistically and substantively potent predictors, which is a logical as well as practical consequence of the *principle of parsimony* discussed in the opening chapter. Poor quality causal data will translate into poor explanatory power on one hand, while also contributing to an unnecessary inflation in the number of predictors (while offering little additional explanation).

It Is Not About the Digits

For all their complexity and the often hefty price tags, databases are fundamentally nothing more than large collections of digitally encoded facts, which require considerable effort and skill before they are of any value to decision makers. Although the investment in the database infrastructure is manifestly about the creation and dissemination of decision-aiding information, the amount of effort and resources put into knowledge creation activities pales by comparison to how much is spent on hardware and related infrastructure. Consider that on average about 85% of all database-related expenditures are consumed by hardware (i.e., storage), about 10% is spent on software and only as little as 5% on the analysis of stored data. As a result, a typical scenario looks something like this: A mid-size or a large organization spends millions of dollars (many millions, in case of the latter) to erect complex and expensive data storage and management facilities, but stops short of committing comparable resources to harvesting the raw material locked away in various databases. Nor is our hypothetical organization overly concerned with the lack of compelling evidence to suggest that these expensive databases are worth the investment. . . Once again, virtually all organizations have data, yet only a small subset of them are able to turn it into a source of competitive advantage.

Yet overtly, the reason organizations make database investments is to outwit their competitors, or at the very least, maintain competitive parity. Hence the database paradox: *The larger, more complex and comprehensive a database, the less likely it is to give rise to competitive advantage.* It is another way of saying that organizations tend to "choke" on the amount of data at their disposal. Quite often, large data volumes give rise to an even larger volume and array of reports, which tends to amount to nothing more than color-coding of raw data, which is the practical consequence of reporting on outcomes without clear cause delineation (which almost always requires more involved analytics). Untold man-hours are spent pouring over disparate pieces of information, but ultimately very little competitive-edge-producing knowledge is created, all while decisions continue to be driven more by intuition than by facts. Under this (common) scenario, building and maintaining of large corporate data reservoirs becomes a goal in itself, with the creation of competitively advantageous knowledge getting lost in the shuffle.

Obviously, not every organization falls into that trap. As mentioned earlier, Walmart's database, believed to be the largest of its kind at an estimated 600 terabytes (and growing) helped to propel it to the elite group of the most dominant (as measured by revenue) and most influential (as measured by market power) organizations in the world. Walmart's efficacy at persistently extracting knowledge out of the otherwise overwhelming quantities of raw data clearly illustrates the power of systematic and skillful data exploration. It also illustrates that merely translating digits into text—i.e., converting data into information disseminated as reports—is not enough to gain competitive advantage. To truly reap the benefits of its database investments, an organization must develop complementary knowledge-extraction capabilities.

The Data–Information–Knowledge Continuum

Utility-wise, databases exist for two basic reasons: First, they enable an ongoing capture and storage of facts; second, they serve as platforms for inferential knowledge creation. When both reasons are combined, databases become conduits for transforming data into information, some of which may lead to decision-aiding knowledge, ultimately giving rise to competitive advantage. Figure 6.10 below summarizes the *Data → Information → Knowledge* progression, shown in the context of each of the step's incremental value to users, interpretational challenges and the level of benefit.

From the standpoint of users, raw data, which is simply a repository of digitally coded (in the case of business databases) facts, represents the lowest level of utility. It is both the most interpretationally challenging (obviously, thousands or millions of seemingly random digits mean very little) and it embodies the least amount of user benefit, precisely because it does not clearly communicate anything . . . Regardless of its format (i.e., root vs. derived), source (i.e., transactions vs. surveys) or organizational model (i.e., relational or other), raw data will just about always present a considerable interpre-

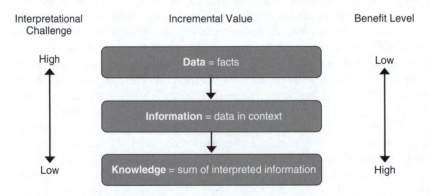

Figure 6.10 The Data–Information–Knowledge Continuum

tational challenge because of its sheer volume, cryptic nature and the lack of self-evident differentiation between important and trivial facts.

However, once the raw data are converted into information, the resultant inter-pretation becomes easier and it is of more benefit to users. Its value increases as a result, but it still might be hampered by limited actionability. For example, translating individual purchases (raw data) into period or store-level summaries (information) certainly increases the benefit and lightens the interpretational challenge, but the resultant information is still of little benefit to decision makers as, in this case, it says little about the potential driver of the observed outcomes. In other words, while useful, information still needs additional "refinement" before the value of the database invest-ment is truly maximized. In the example used here, that point is reached when the purchase-detailing information is combined with attitudinal details, promotional history and demographics as well as other individual difference variables, such as past purchase history or promotional response propensity, to ultimately give rise to *knowledge* hinting at the most effective marketing strategies. In a more general sense, information represents extracting findings out of raw data, while knowledge corresponds to application of these findings in the decision making process, a progression first described in the first chapter.

Hence the value progression implied in Figure 6.10 can form a foundation for thinking about data analyses. The *Data "Information" Knowledge* value continuum can be used to illustrate the most fundamental difference between database reporting and database analytics: The former enables the conversion of raw data into information, while the latter facilitates the creation of knowledge, which is the ultimate expression of the value of data. Figure 6.11 illustrates this distinction.

The informational value creation process outlined above carries important usage considerations surrounding large, corporate databases. At the most rudimentary level, databases can be used to support ongoing business performance reporting through performance "dashboards," usually built around a pre-selected set of metrics of most importance to the organization. Such reports are of particular interest to line managers with vested interest in keeping an eye on operational aspects of business. The format of these reports, as well as their content and frequency, tend to be shaped by factors such as data availability, industry characteristics and the organization-specific needs. In general, database reporting tends to be data type specific (e.g., point-of-sales data is used to create brand-, product-, period- or location-specific sales summaries, while direct mail details are used to create promotional impact reports), making it difficult to cross-reference key pieces of information, and altogether impossible to draw cause (promotion)–effect (sales) conclusions. In essence, basic data reporting provides important though generic infor-mation, which means it is not likely to give rise to sustainable competitive advantage. However, many of these reports or dashboards can be produced with highly automated

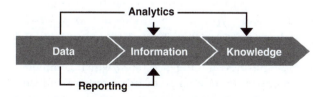

Figure 6.11 Data Value-Added Progression

business intelligence software, thus requiring little-to-no advanced data analytical capabilities, which is one of the reasons behind their popularity.

Going beyond the mere status quo reporting, a more robust analytical set of processes can help in translating the often disparate pieces of information into higher level inferences, or knowledge. Of course, it is not quite as easy as it may sound. As pointed out earlier, the ability to distill large volumes of markedly dissimilar information into specific, competitive-advantage-producing insights hinges on a combination of a forward-looking informational vision and a robust analytical skill set. Converting raw data into (competitively) generic information can be handled, for the most part, with the help of highly automated, commercially available database tools. Funneling the often still voluminous and almost always inconclusive information into unique knowledge cannot be handled by standardized, off-the-shelf database reporting applications for reasons ranging from extensive data preparation requirements to the intricacies surrounding multivariate analyses (discussed in later chapters). Furthermore, the creation of competitively unique knowledge quite often necessitates the amalgamation of multiple (and otherwise disconnected) data sources into a single, yet multidimensional causal chain, which in turn requires the establishment of cross-factor correlations, cause–effect relationships as well as the more technically obtuse interaction and nonlinear effects.

It follows that it is considerably more difficult to develop robust *information-to-knowledge* conversion processes than it is to put in place robust database reporting, or data-to-information conversion capabilities. Of course, the higher level of difficulty carries with it more substantial benefits. As exemplified by Walmart, Capital One or Harrah's, it enables a migration from just generating competitive parity type of insights and toward the establishment of a source of sustainable competitive advantage. In a financial sense, the ability to systematically translate generic information into unique knowledge vastly increases the implied return on database-related investments.

More on Reporting vs. Analytics: Tools and Applications

The simplest way to extract information out of a database is to query it. *Querying* involves relating individual data elements to create specific information. For example, to get at the "cost by region" information, the DBMS used to run the queries needs to divide all available sales into the appropriate regional "buckets," create region-by-region summaries and return appropriately formatted information. The speed and the agility of database querying capabilities vary across the type of data model used, with the entity–relationship model offering the lowest levels of querying speed and agility, while the relational model tends to deliver the highest levels of performance in that regard.

Database querying is a somewhat manual process, requiring some level of technical proficiency. For example, accessing of a relational database, which is arguably the most dominant data storage mechanism in business today, requires familiarity with querying protocols of the particular relational database type, such as Microsoft Access, Oracle, IBM DB2 or MySQL. Combined with the repetitively ongoing nature of many of the informational needs, much of the ad hoc *database querying* is usually replaced with standard, automated *database reporting*. Business intelligence tools, which commonly provide the automated reporting functionality, rely on standard templates and pre-defined process to repeatedly generate the same set of reports, often in fixed time intervals. Thus rather than querying the database about period-by-period and/or region-by-region sales manually, an automated sales report is generated without the need for manual querying.

Unfortunately, such generic, standard database reporting processes are frequently confused with database analytics, so much so that in the eyes of many, analytics is synonymous with reporting. Although there are certainly similarities between the functions—both entail manipulating and translating raw data into the more meaningful information—there are sharp differences separating these two types of endeavors. Perhaps the most important is the type of data processing. Reporting relies primarily on summarization, tabulation and contrasting, all with the goal of generating basic *descriptive* conclusions about the underlying data. More analytically advanced data exploration often starts with basic descriptive analyses as well, though its ultimate goal typically entails forward-looking extrapolations and predictions. In other words, database analytics goes far beyond the status quo reporting, by offering causal explanations and making decision-guiding predictions. In that sense, basic database reporting offers descriptive summaries of past events, while the inferential knowledge-focused database analytics supports *probabilistic interpretation* of data, as illustrated by Figure 6.12.

Different missions call for different tools. Database querying and reporting typically utilize the database's own DBMS capabilities, usually in the form of outside database reporting tools known as "business intelligence solutions," or BI tools for short (technical fields love acronyms!). These tools, exemplified by Business Objects, MicroStrategy or Cognos, help to automate report generation while also deepening database exploration. It is important to note, however, these tools effectively become a part of the DBMS and as such, operate within the database itself. In addition, the resultant reports are externally consumed and are not used to enrich the informational value of the database itself.

The necessary coupling of hardware and software applications that are required to support an operational database environment gave rise to a new class of database computational devices known as *database appliances*. The fundamental difference between a database appliance and a traditional stand-alone hardware and software approach is that the former is a turnkey solution integrating the hardware and software components into a single unit, an appliance. The single unit performs all the functions of a database, a server and a storage device considerably faster[17] and thus might be preferred in situations where large volumes of standard reports need to be generated under tight time constraints. From the data analysis standpoint, the fundamental underlying assumption of this class of database devices is that it is desirable to analyze the contents of the entire

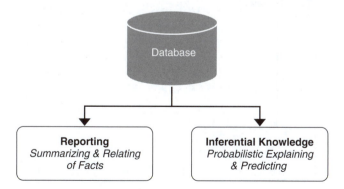

Figure 6.12 Factual vs. Probabilistic Data Exploration

database (i.e., to use all available records), and it is in the context of such "full database queries" that the greater speed of database appliances is most appreciated. However, as will be shown in the subsequent chapters, the database analytical process of translating data into competitive-edge-producing insights makes a heavy use of appropriately selected samples, the drawing of which can be quite cumbersome in a database appliance.

Although the specific characteristics of the database management may impact the speed and the ease of performing certain operations, data analysis and modeling are ultimately impacted far more by the power and the efficacy of the statistical analysis applications. The three most dominant and widely used systems—SAS, SPSS and R—are functionally independent of the DBMS and are in effect, open-ended methods of addressing data-related issues, rather than means of funneling data into pre-defined templates (although all three can be incorporated in most database designs, including the aforementioned appliance and used for basic reporting). What differentiates SAS, SPSS and R from lesser-known applications is their depth and comprehensiveness, in particular as it relates to data processing, management and manipulation, statistical analysis and modeling, database scoring and output management.

From the standpoint of the resultant information, all data management systems, inclusive of the earlier discussed business intelligence as well as the data analysis and modeling applications, can be used for either *descriptive* or *predictive* purposes. The former is focused primarily on retrospective outcome summarization and tabulation, while the latter is typically tasked with forward-looking decision support. Although both tend to be labeled "analytics," it is more correct to refer to retrospective outcome summarization as "reporting" and forward-looking decision support as "inferential knowledge" As depicted in Figure 6.13 below, reporting functionality tends to be database-resident, as it is quite conducive to automation.

Hence the business intelligence solutions mentioned earlier—e.g., MicroStrategy or Business Objects—are embedded in the database itself. On the other hand, the statistical data analysis systems—e.g., SAS and SPSS—tend to be stand-alone applications, primarily because the knowledge creation process they enable is not conducive to automation.

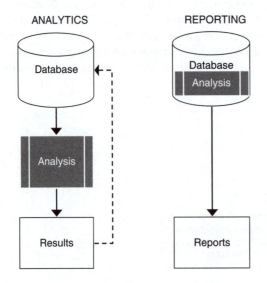

Figure 6.13 Database Reporting vs. Analysis

The Case of Data Mining

One particular aspect of database analysis called "data mining" does not fit in with the rationale outlined above. Broadly defined, *data mining* is an information extraction activity designed to uncover hidden facts contained in the data with the help of an automated system combining statistical analysis, machine learning and database technology (it should be noted that data mining can certainly be performed manually, but in the eyes of many, the term itself became synonymous with automated data pattern identification capabilities). So although data mining resembles database reporting in terms of its degree of automation, its methodological engine aligns it more closely with inferential knowledge discovery. At the same time, its goal of "roaming the database to find noteworthy relationships" differentiates it sharply from conventional database analytics focused on testing specific hypothesis in support the organizational strategy-driven informational needs. Overall, data mining is distinctly different from the goal-driven database analytical process described in this book, yet it is an alternative inferential knowledge creation avenue, as shown in figure 6.14 below.

I should point out that data mining received a lot of attention over the past decade or so, particularly in the area of "enterprise data management." Leading software business applications developers, including the two largest statistical analysis software vendors, SAS and SPSS (the latter now a part of IBM), invested in complex systems built expressly to sift through large volumes of data in search of (statistically) significant relationships. However, there are a couple of key hurdles that, to the best of my knowledge, have not yet been overcome.

The first one is methodological in nature. In order to differentiate between "significant" and "not significant" relationships, data mining applications employ established statistical significance tests (of which there are different types, tied to data characteristics), which as a group are a set of techniques for determining if a given relationship is spurious (i.e., it represents a chance occurrence) or persistent (those tests are discussed in more detail in subsequent chapters). As fully discussed later, the reliability of statistical significance tests is negatively impacted by sample size, which leads to

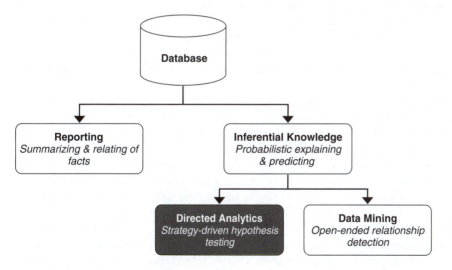

Figure 6.14 Database Exploration Venues

practically trivial relationships (e.g., extremely small correlations or differences) being deemed as "significant," in a statistical sense. Given the "pass vs. fail" nature of statistical significance tests, all "significant" relationships are deemed to be important, which will lead to lumping together of the truly important and trivial, or even spurious findings. In the context of a large database, for which data mining was intended, the resultant listing of statistically significant findings may be so extensive that finding the truly important ones may prove to be quite taxing.

The second key shortcoming of automated data mining is of more pragmatic nature, reflecting the relative inability of such systems to deliver sustainable informational—and ultimately, competitive—advantage. Recall the data and application commoditization discussion. The bulk of the transactional and related data is not organization-unique, just as electronic transaction processing systems generating the data are not unique. Similarly, data mining applications are commercially available applications. Combining two relatively generic entities will lead to generic outcomes, just about guaranteeing the lack of unique, competitively advantageous insights.

The limitations of machine search-based systems notwithstanding, these technologies proved to be tremendously important insofar as they paved the way to the exploration of the largest, though historically inaccessible source of data: text. The next section offers a closer look at what has come to be known as "text mining."

Textual Information

An important, though often largely inaccessible (for large scale analyses) source of data is *text*, defined here as words treated as data. In contrast to numerical data, the bulk of which is a product of machine-to-machine communication, textual data is a result of human communication, which means it is ubiquitous and analytically challenging. There are numerous reasons for why textual data is analytically challenging, but they can be reduced to two primary factors, which are *structural variability* and *volume*. The former encapsulates the intricacy of human communication—the interweaving of explicit and implicit elements, structured vs. unstructured modes, the multiplicity of meanings associated with many commonly used terms, to name just a few. The latter is self-evident, though perhaps it might be instructive to more explicitly define that quality: The World Wide Web contains more than 7 billion indexed primarily text containing pages[18]; Google, the widely recognized online search leader (accounting for about half of all internet searches) grows its search database by more than 100 million searches per day; the Library of Congress, the world's largest library (boasting more than 130 million items, such as books, maps, photographs, etc.) contains an estimated 20 terabytes[19] of textual data. Yet perhaps the most telling illustration of the volume of textual data is social media, where Facebook alone sits atop of more than 30 petabytes of data—more than 3,000 times the size of the Library of Congress.

Textually encoded information, as exemplified by social networking data, is important to marketing analytics as it contains "unfiltered" expressions of consumer motivational factors that play a key role in determining consumer marketplace behaviors, especially as it relates to brand and other choices. In fact, within the confines of consumer products, it could be argued that the broadly defined *consumer voice*, which encompasses all electronically captured consumer communications, is one of the strongest predictors of the future performance of consumer brands. Historically, consumer voice was qualitative and non-generalizable in nature—the former referring to the subjectivity of its analysis, while the latter underscoring non-representativeness of the resultant conclusions.[20] That said, the relatively recent emergence of wide scale *social networking*,[21] coupled with advances in text mining analytic technologies is beginning to reshape how we think about—and how we analytically approach—non-numeric, or qualitative consumer data.

Social Communication and Marketing Analytics

Social networking, as a field of academic inquiry, is built around an idea (really, an axiom) that the key to understanding social interactions is to focus on properties of relations among network participants, rather than on the participants themselves. However, when trying to develop an understanding of social-network-encapsulated interactions in the context of a brand, product type or company, it is myopic to focus exclusively in social relations. To a business entity (a company, a brand, etc.), the "who" of social networking is as important as the "what" because the former contextualizes the latter. For example, the management of a consumer brand would want to differentiate between qualitatively expressed opinions of the brand's high-value customers and those of its current non-purchasers or casual (i.e., low-value) buyers for a number of reasons, such as to get a better understanding of the brand's "perception gap." This is suggestive of two somewhat distinct outcomes of analyses of text data: 1. qualitative-research-like extraction of the "emergent themes"; and 2. digitization of key text-encoded metrics. The former can be considered an end outcome in and of itself, while the latter is an input into broader analysis, where insights gleaned from text analysis are related to those garnered from analyses of consumer behaviors. In more operational terms, it means that textually and numerically encoded data need to be—ultimately—amalgamated into a single analytic dataset. Under most circumstances, doing so is a fairly tall order—to appreciate why that is the case, it is instructive to take a closer look at some of the fundamental analytical properties of text data.

Structured vs. Unstructured

Much like a typical numeric data file, text data files are two-dimensional matrices, where columns demark individual variables and rows delimit successive cases. Given that, a key consideration in machine-aided analysis of text is the organizational composition of data files, with a particular emphasis on the relationship between successive rows and individual columns in the data matrix. Within the confines of the successive rows vs. individual columns layout, text files can be categorized as either structured or unstructured.

Structured data follows a repeatable pattern where each successive data record (row) mimics the layout of the previous one and columns demark distinct variables. Form-based information, such as warranty cards that accompany household appliance purchases are a good example of this category of text—each purchaser completes the same type of information captured in the same manner. Naturally, given the fixed and repeatable format of structured data files, it stands to reason that so-formatted files are far more amenable to machine processing, though at the same time, the informational value of outcomes of those analyses might be somewhat limited. Why? Structured data files' computer processing malleability is rooted in their layout—as mentioned earlier, to be considered "structured," a text data file has to follow a basic two-dimensional matrix layout where columns contain distinct fields and rows enumerate successive data records. Given that, the only truly meaningful difference between structured text and numeric data is that the individual data fields (i.e., variables) comprising the former contain text rather than digits. Although somewhat less obvious, it also means that the informational content of those fields tends to be skewed toward categorical, rather than syntactical substance[22] (think of the warranty cards that usually accompany household appliance purchases). As a result, the output of the analysis of structured text tends to be limited to the identification of patterns and/or communalities across records, which is obviously worthwhile, though at the same time only represents a fairly small subset of the informational content of text-encoded communications. Hence, the task of reliable machine-aided analysis of structured text data is a fairly manageable one, but the resultant insights tend to be fairly limited.

Unstructured data, which are by far the most common form of text files,[23] do not adhere to a recognizable layout schema. The layout of individual records comprising unstructured data can be characterized as being amorphous and lacking discernible organizational schema—it is non-repeatable in the sense that each successive record is independent of the previous one and any similarity is coincidental; furthermore, individual columns do not delimit distinct and repeatable variables. Examples of unstructured or free-flowing text abound, as most of the written human communication, ranging from books, newspapers and the like to contents of billions of web pages and social communications tend to fall within that category. The lack of structure coupled with the inherent ambiguity of "natural" (meaning, used in human communication) language makes unstructured data quite difficult to deal with algorithmically, primarily because, in principle, each data record is different from all other records, both in terms of the layout as well as content.[24] The upside to the absence of a rigid organizational schema is that unstructured text tends be syntactically rich, which means that although it is possible to focus the mining efforts on the identification of cross-record patterns and communalities (as is the case with structured text), the true value in analyzing unstructured text often lies in surmising the "deeper meaning" hidden in what and how is being communicated. However, it can be a daunting task, primarily because natural language depends heavily on "common sense knowledge," which is the understanding of the implied meaning of expressions that goes beyond technical definitions of individual terms. This is one area where precision-demanding machine processing is—in spite of over-promising terms such as "artificial intelligence"—far inferior to the human mind. Thus, unlike the relatively manageable task of categorizing structured text, unstructured textual data is exceptionally hard to encode logarithmically, which means it does not succumb to traditional data analytic techniques.

Given the considerable differences separating structured and unstructured text, it follows that there are a number of different methods that can be used to machine-process large volumes of text data. Broadly referred to as "text mining," these techniques are summarized next.

Text Mining Approaches

Text data are very common—by some estimates, a typical business organization has anywhere between two and ten times more textual than numeric data. Analyses of textual data, which are overwhelmingly exploratory (as opposed to hypothesis testing) in nature, are commonly referred to as *text mining*, which itself is considered a subset of a broader category of *data mining*.[25] As applied business analytic notions, both data and text mining tend to be associated with machine-aided processing, largely because of the computer applications first introduced in the 1990s by companies like SAS, SPSS[26] or IBM; though in principle, those terms apply to all exploratory analyses, whether or not aided by machines. Thus, an analyst using a computer-based application to explore a large repository of text data, such as customer comments posted on a brand's website, or a researcher reading a transcript of a focus group are both examples of text mining. Naturally, "manual"—reading and summarizing by humans—mining of text or other data is only operationally feasible when the quantity of data is fairly small.

In many regards, business organizations (and others) tend not to think of text as explorable data, primarily because systematic and wide-scale analyses of large volumes of text-encoded data have been largely out of reach. For the vast majority of companies, the only meaningful exposure to non-numeric data analysis usually came in the form of qualitative marketing research, as exemplified by focus groups or other forms of *ethnographic research*.[27] From the standpoint of decision-guiding knowledge, the very attribute (i.e., data quantity that is small enough to be manually analyzable) that makes qualitative marketing research studies analytically manageable also diminishes the utility of is informational outcomes. For instance, an average focus group engages a group of 8–12 people in a guided discussion spanning about 90–120 minutes, which yields the amount of data that is small enough to allow "manual" processing, which usually means a properly trained researcher or a team of researchers reading and summarizing participants' text-expressed opinions and comments with the goal of arriving at a set of findings, commonly referred to as "emergent themes." Of course, even with a fairly small dataset it is nonetheless a time-consuming and a laborious process—even more importantly, however, such analyses are also permeated by readers' subjectivity, which is an inescapable consequence of the stated goal of qualitative research: to "interpret" the comments/opinions contained therein. In practice, there is no meaningful method of quantifying, much less eliminating researcher bias, which means it is a problem without a clear solution. Hence, even if it was operationally feasible to "manually mine" large text databases, such as the totality of consumer comments relating to a particular brand, the potential reviewer bias, or more specifically, inter-reviewer variability (given that such endeavor would require many raters in order to be completed within a reasonable amount of time) would clearly cast doubt on the validity of conclusions.

The above considerations underscore that to be operationally feasible as largely free of *rater bias*, analyses of large reservoirs of text (and numeric) data require machine processing. Thus, although as pointed out earlier any exploratory analysis of text data can be characterized as "text mining," within the confines of the marketing database analytics process detailed in this book it refers to the discovery of trends and/or patterns in (typically) large quantities of textual data with the help of automated or semi-automated means.

Process-wise, mining of textual data entails four distinct steps: 1. retrieval, 2. summarization, 3. structural mining and 4. digitization. *Retrieval* pertains to searching for records of interest that are hidden in large repositories, such general or topical databases; the outcome of the retrieval efforts will usually take the form of an extract. *Summarization,* on the other hand, involves the condensing of otherwise large quantities of (textual) data; its outcome typically takes the form of an abstract or a synopsis. *Structural mining* is probably the broadest, as well as most complex aspect of text mining as it involves converting voluminous text data into (statistically) analyzable, categorized metadata.[28] Depending on the combination of purpose and the type of data (discussed below), structural mining can mean searching for predetermined expressions or attempting to surmise the deeper meaning hidden in the syntactic structure of text. Lastly, *digitization* refers to the process of number-coding of metadata, or converting non-numeric data values into numeric ones. The ultimate goal of that conversion is to facilitate amalgamation of form-dissimilar (i.e., text vs. numeric), but complementary-in-meaning text-mining-derived insights and already digitally coded numeric data, with the goal of enabling *multi-source analytics*.[29]

Function-wise, text mining can be performed with several different outcomes in mind, such as: 1. *summarization*: identifying co-occurrences of themes in a body of text; 2. *categorization*: reducing documents' content to pre-defined categories; 3. *clustering*: reducing documents' content to emergent (i.e., based on documents' content, rather than being pre-defined) categories; 4. *visualization*: re-casting textually expressed information into graphics; 5. *filtering*: selecting subsets of all information, based on predetermined logic. It is important to note that, though quite dissimilar, the individual text mining functions can be viewed as complements, as each delivers a distinctly different end-user informational utility.

Method-wise, mining of text data can take the path of either frequency count and tabulation or natural language processing. The *frequency count and tabulation* approach itself can take one of two paths: 1. "tagging" of a priori identified expressions, or searching a body of data for specific expressions or terms that have been spelled out in advance of the search; or 2. "term funneling," where instead of using a priori lists, the starting point of the analysis is the generation of comprehensive frequency counts of all recurring terms. The former—*tagging*—requires a substantial amount of knowledge on the part of the analyst, to the degree to which specific expressions or terms have to be identified as important ahead of the search; as such, it is deductive in nature, which is to say it is focused on answering specific questions stemming from the hypothesis formed at the outset of analyses. Furthermore, simply searching for terms that have been identified as important beforehand is not conducive to uncovering new "truths," as the focused mechanics of deductive search make it difficult, if not practically impossible, to notice unexpected results. The latter of the two frequency and tabulation data mining approaches—*term funneling*—requires no prior knowledge hence in contrast to tagging it is inductive in nature, but it can produce overwhelmingly large quantities of output (tens of thousands of terms and/or expressions), which in turn will demand a substantial amount of post-extraction processing. It follows that it is not only time-consuming, but also likely to infuse potentially large amounts of the earlier discussed *rater bias*, effectively reducing the objectivity of findings. Overall, their differences notwithstanding, tagging and term funneling are focused strictly on pinpointing of terms without considering the context or the way in which those terms are used. In other words, using the frequency count and tabulation method, it might be difficult, if not outright impossible to distinguish between positively and negatively valenced lexical items.[30]

The second broadly defined approach to text mining—*natural language processing* (NLP)—attempts to remedy the limitations of the frequency count and tabulation methodology by attempting to extract insights from the semantic[31] structure of text. NLP is an outgrowth of computational linguistics (itself a part of a broader domain of artificial intelligence), which is statistical and/or rule-based modeling of natural language. The goal of NLP is to capture the meaning of written communications in the form of tabular metadata amenable to statistical analysis—as such, it represents an inductive approach to knowledge creation, well adept at uncovering new "truths." Given the significantly more ambitious goal of natural language processing, namely, objectively summarizing and extracting the meaning of nuanced human communications, the level of difficulty associated with this endeavor is significantly higher, which means that the reliability of findings will typically be proportionately lower.

Although NLP clearly offers a potentially deeper set of insights, it is also fraught with difficulties that directly impact the validity and reliability of the resultant findings—on the other hand, the comparatively more superficial frequency count and tabulation is straightforward to implement and can deliver a fairly consistent—keeping its limitations in mind—set of insights. All considered, both text mining approaches have merit and in order to gain a better understanding of the applicability of both methods, a more in-depth overview of presented next.

Frequency Count and Tabulation

As outlined earlier, the goal of frequency count and tabulation approach to text mining is to identify, tag and tabulate, in a given body (known as "corpora") of text, pre-determined terms and/or expressions. Conceptually, it can be thought of as a confirmatory tool as it is focused on finding concepts that are already (i.e., prior to search) believed to be important, rather than identifying new ones—i.e., pinpointing concepts that were not previously believed to be important. As a result, the efficacy of the frequency count and tabulation approach is highly dependent on prior knowledge, as manifested by the completeness of the a priori created external categories.

However, even the most complete external schemas in no way assure robust outcomes as the search or the mining process itself can produce incomplete findings due to ambiguity stemming from wording or phrasing variability and the potential impact of synonyms and homographs. The *word* or *phrase variability* is a syntax (principles and rules used in sentence construction) problem stemming from the fact that the same term or an idea can oftentimes be written in somewhat different ways. A common approach to addressing word- or phrase-related variability is to use the so-called "stemming algorithms" which reduce words to their Latin or Greek stems with the goal of recog-nizing communalities. *Synonyms*, which are yet another potential source of search ambiguity, are terms that have a different spelling but the same or similar meaning, while *homographs* are terms that have the same spelling but different meaning. The most common approach to addressing those sources of possible confusion or ambiguity is to create external reference categories, which are de facto libraries of terms delineating all known synonyms and homographs for all a priori identified search terms. Clearly, a rather substantial undertaking. . .

Process-wise, the frequency count and tabulation approach to mining textual data makes use of *text transformations*, defined here as the process of translating words into digits, where each word is an attribute defined by its frequency of occurrence.[32] This process is built around a notion of "bag-of-words"—a transformation-simplifying assumption which posits that a text can be viewed as an unordered collection of words, where grammar and even the word order are disregarded. Considered in the context of the two types of textual data discussed earlier—structured and unstructured—text transformation can take on somewhat different operational meanings: Transforming structured data typically involves supplanting textual fields with numerically coded and a priori delineated categories, which effectively translates textual expressions into numeric values. In that context, it is a relatively straightforward process because structured textual data tends to exhibit relatively little ambiguity, due to heavy reliance on predetermined lexical categories.[33] At the same time, the process of transforming unstructured data is considerably more involved because of an open-ended nature of that source of data—in principle, terms appearing in unstructured data can be thought of as unconstrained choices, as opposed to those representing selections from a predetermined (i.e., closed) menu of options, as is often the case with structured text. A direct consequence of unconstrained nature of unstructured text is a far greater need for *disambiguation*, which is resolving of potential conflicts that tend to arise when a single term or an expression can take on multiple meanings. Conceptually, disambiguation is somewhat similar to the earlier discussed notion of term/phrase variability, but operationally it is quite a bit more complex as it necessitates anticipating the potential conflicts ahead of knowing what terms can appear in what context.

Overall, the frequency count and tabulation approach to text mining entails a considerable amount of analyst input, while at the same time its primary focus is on the identification and re-coding (from text into digits) of identifiable and definable terms and expressions, all while skipping over any deeper meaning that might be hidden in the semantic structure of text. As noted earlier, this broadly defined approach offers, in principle, no clear way of contextualizing or otherwise qualifying search-identified terms, beyond merely pinpointing their occurrence and counting the subsequent recurrences. Looked at as a sum of advantages and disadvantages, frequency count and tabulation method can be an effective approach to extracting numerically analyzable details out of the otherwise inaccessible textually expressed data, but overall it is not an effective mean of discovering new knowledge.

Natural Language Processing

Perhaps the most obvious limitation of the frequency count and tabulation approach to text mining is the embrace of the bag-of-words idea, which leads to lumping together of stem-related but differently valenced terms (i.e., the same term used in the positive vs. negative context). The stripping away of grammar linking together individual—i.e., merely counting the recurrence of terms without regard for their order or a broader context—inescapably leads to loss of information, which in turn diminishes the quantity and the quality of the resultant insights. Hence an obvious (and challenging) path to substantially enriching the depth and the breadth of newly discovered knowledge is to set aside the limiting bag-of-words assumption and to expressly consider the syntactical structure of text, which means to process what is known as "natural language."

Broadly conceived, *natural language* is human communication that is distinct and different from "constructed languages," best exemplified by computer programming or mathematical logic. In general, natural language can be spoken, written or signed, though text mining is obviously only concerned with the written aspect of it—more specifically, unpremeditated descriptions of states, outcomes and/or phenomena that comprise textual data. Formally defined, *natural language processing* (NLP) is an exploratory process of extracting meaningful insights out of the semantic structure of a body of text. Approach-wise, NLP can take one of two broadly defined forms: 1. supervised machine learning-based automated classification, or 2. unsupervised mining. At their core, both types of methodologies expressly consider words, word order and grammar in trying to discern generalizable rules that can be applied to distilling large quantities of text into manageable sets of summarized findings; however, they are quite different in terms of operational mechanics.

The first of the two NLP approaches, *automated classification*, can be thought of as a "pseudo-exploratory" methodology as it is a type of supervised learning where an algorithm (a decision rule) is "trained" using a previously classified text. The training task is essentially that of establishing generalizable rules for assigning topical labels to content, where the efficacy of the resultant algorithm is, to a large degree, dependent on the balancing of two important, though somewhat contradictory notions of accuracy and simplicity.[34] There are two distinct schools of thought as it regards the development of automated text classification systems: 1. *knowledge-based*, which relies on codification of expert-derived classification rules; and 2. *learning-based*, where experts supply classified examples rather than classification rules. Within the realm of the marketing database analytics process detailed in this book (as well as the broader context of marketing analytics), knowledge-based systems are generally deemed more workable, primarily because the requisite training inputs are more obtainable[35] (under most circumstances, it is prohibitively difficult to compile adequately representative classification samples that are required by learning-based systems). It is important to note that to be effective as a classification tool, the initial algorithmic learning cannot be overly tailored to idiosyncrasies of the training file (a condition known as "overfitting"), as doing so will lead to poor generalizability—yet, it needs to exhibit adequate classificatory accuracy (hence the need to balance the two somewhat contradictory notions of accuracy and simplicity).

Unsupervised mining, the second of the two general types of machine learning techniques, can be thought of as a "purely exploratory" text mining approach (in contrast to the above-described pseudo-exploratory automatic classification). However, even the purely exploratory text mining mechanisms do not represent, in a strict sense of the word, truly independent machine-based processing of human communications. These methods leverage similarity/difference heuristics—such as hierarchical clustering techniques—that are informed by text records' content which are emergent from data, rather than being based on learning from already classified text. That said, it is important to note that although the mining itself is unsupervised, the general rules within which it is conducted are governed by explicit vocabulary control, which typically takes the form of an a priori constructed (by human experts) thesaurus. The individual terms commonly comprising a particular thesaurus are noun phrases (i.e., content words), with the meaning of those terms restricted to that most effective for the purpose of a particular thesaurus, which in turn is shaped by the context of the search (e.g., a search of a database of customer comments might be focused on pinpointing drivers of brand users' satisfaction and/or dissatisfaction). In terms of *lexical inference*, or deriving meaning from grammar-connected word combinations, the human-expert-provided thesaurus also needs to expressly define three main types of cross-term relationships: equivalence, which is critical to resolving synonym-related ambiguity, as well as hierarchy and association, both of which play important roles in extracting semantic insights by imbuing meaning to multi-term expressions.

A choice of a specific approach notwithstanding, the goal of natural language processing is to go beyond enumerating categories by extracting kernels of syntactical meaning out of textual data. Hence, in the vast majority of cases NLP is used with semantically rich unstructured text, although in principle it could also be employed with structured text. In practice, however, the frequency count and tabulation text mining techniques discussed earlier are more appropriate—and probably more effective, all considered—to use with the categorization-friendly structured text.

Machine processing of natural human communications is a lofty goal and the NLP approaches briefly outlined above should be viewed as a probabilistic science yielding a moderate degree of success. In general, the quality of outcomes of syntactical analyses is highly dependent on the nature of data and the desired utility of findings: In general, the higher the specificity of data and the expected utility of results—the better the efficacy (in terms of validity and reliability) of outcomes. The reason for that dependency is that, under most circumstances, greater specificity translates into lower variability between the inputs (e.g., classification rules, examples or thesauri) provided by human experts and the raw data used in the analysis. Overall, in contrast to numerically encoded data, which can be analyzed with the expectation of highly valid and reliable results, analyses of the often highly nuanced and context-dependent text data cannot be expected to yield comparable (to the aforementioned numeric analyses) levels of result efficacy. In fact, the very task of objectively assessing the validity of text mining results is fraught with difficulties, not the least of which is the scarcity of evaluative benchmarks. More specifically, whereas the results of numeric analyses can be cross-referenced in a manner suggesting possible inconsistencies, the use of such evaluative methods is rarely feasible within the confines of text mining.

Still, its limitations notwithstanding, machine processing of written human communication offers an opportunity to peer into previously inaccessible domains of data, ultimately further enhancing the efficacy of the decision making process. And as suggested by the history of technological progress, the text mining technologies will continue to improve, which means that the validity and the reliability of machine-created insights will continue to get better.

Single- vs. Multi-Source Analytics

The explosive growth in the volume and diversity of data brought to light yet another important data-related consideration: single-source vs. multi-source analyses, briefly discussed earlier. Although rarely receiving much more than a cursory mention, this is a tremendously important consideration from the standpoint of creating competitively advantageous knowledge. Let's take a close look at the nature of multi-sourced analytics.

To start, it is important to ask what constitutes a data source. For the most part, it is *uniqueness* and *homogeneity*. To constitute its own source, data needs a unique point of origin. The so-called UPC (Universal Product Code) scanner data owes its name to its unique origin, which is a barcode-reading scanning device. It is also homogenous in the sense that individual records have fundamentally the same informational content. Hence the UPC data constitutes a unique source-based and informationally homogenous category of data. A more recent (UPC scanners have been in use since the mid-1970s) variation of technology-spurred data is exemplified by the radio frequency identification tags, or RFID tags for short. An RFID tag is an object that can be applied to or incorporated into a product, animal, or person for the purpose of identification and tracking using radio waves. (Some tags can be read from several meters away and beyond the line of sight of the reader; active RFID tags contain a battery to supply power for ongoing transmission, while passive RFID tags do not contain a battery.)

Similar to scanner data, *demographics* can be thought of as a unique and homogenous data source, to the degree to which individual (demographic) metrics are manifestations of different physical characteristics of a population; in a similar manner, *psychographics* represent another unique, though complementary data source, capturing the intangible characteristics of a population, such as values, attitudes or lifestyles. Yet another example of a distinct data source is consumer creditworthiness information, which is a reflection of consumers' borrowing and bill-paying behaviors collected and aggregated by consumer reporting agencies known in the United States as "credit bureaus."

All of these individual data sources—buying behaviors, demographics, psychographics or creditworthiness—are naturally self-delimiting, hence their distinctiveness is fairly obvious. That is not necessarily the case with the textual data discussed in the previous section, which can also be considered a distinct data source to the degree to which it provides otherwise unavailable measures. Of course, "text data" is a general designation as there are numerous distinct sources of text-encoded metrics, hence there numerous unique and homogenous text data venues, such as the now-ubiquitous consumer product reviews or other sources of open-ended commentaries.

It follows that there are multiple types of data available to businesses that could be used for broadly defined purposes of marketing analytics. For instance, individual-level metrics such as purchases, promotional responses, behavioral surveys, psychographics, lifestyles or credit bureau information can all be used to derive robust estimates of buyer behavior. In the vast majority of cases, the analysis of these and other data types takes place in a single-source context, simply because it is a lot more straightforward than concurrent analyses of multiple, diverse data types. In some instances, single-source analyses are indeed quite appropriate, namely, when informational needs can be adequately met in that fashion. However, there are many other instances where multi-source analyses would reveal insights that cannot be gleaned from single-source explorations. In fact, the goal of developing cost-effective and impactful marketing strategies—and enabling tactics—demands causal knowledge, which cannot be attained by delving into one data source at a time. In other words, to understand the totality of consumer behavior it is necessary to simultaneously consider all of the possible behavioral determinants, which points toward multi-source analytics. However, for many organizations, the idea of amalgamating source-dissimilar data into a singular source of insights continues to be just that—an elusive idea. . .

A theme that is repeated throughout this book is that single-source analyses—i.e., analyses of a unique and homogenous data type carried out separately from analyses of other unique and homogenous data types—facilitates conversion of data into information, while multi-source analyses make possible information-to-knowledge conversion. Consider Figure 6.15 below:

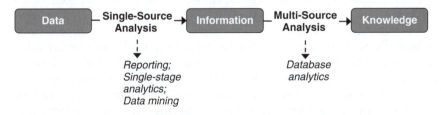

Figure 6.15 Multi-Source Analytics as the Source of Unique Knowledge

Conversion of raw data into usable information is the essence of single-source analytics—it is also the staple of business analytics. To the degree to which being in business is synonymous with selling of products and/or services, and the lion's share of sales transactions are carried out electronically, it should not be surprising that the vast majority of business organizations collect sales-related (i.e., single-source) data. Perhaps the most obvious informational utility of that data source is, broadly defined, *tracking and reporting* of outcomes of interest, such as sales by brand, product/service category or geography. The resultant time- or geography-based sales summaries have been a staple of business analytics for many years, and the more recent proliferation of data management and reporting technologies made the basic data reporting functionality essentially ubiquitous. A natural extension of the basic reporting functionality, *single-stage analytics*, entails looking beyond the "what is" basic reporting, typically focusing on estimation of responsiveness of outcomes, such as sales, to known (i.e., captured as data) stimuli, such as the various forms of sales incentives. In more methodological terms, single-stage analyses are usually confined to a predetermined set of outcomes and possible influencers of those outcomes, which is suggestive of a *hypothesis testing*. In other words, to the degree to which the analytic goal is to determine if any one or more of a predetermined set of factors has a measurable impact on the outcome or outcomes of interest,[36] the underlying analytical processes and methodologies can be characterized as *confirmatory*.

Still, analyses of single-source data are by no means limited to testing of a priori delineated hypotheses—an equally important and potentially informationally fruitful source of insights can be *data mining*, or an open-ended search for insights. In contrast to confirmatory hypothesis testing, mining of a set of data is purely *exploratory* in nature, as it is geared toward identifying previously unnoticed relationships with the goal of expanding current levels of understanding of a topic or a set of topics. An open-ended search for insights can be particularly effective when the amount of data (variable-wise) is large, as is usually the case with the earlier discussed UPC scanner data.[37] In such situations, an exploratory "consider-all" looks beyond the realm of already recognized interdependencies, in the hope of spotting new insights that could be suggestive of previously unconsidered marketing options (for example, exploratory data mining could identify new cross-product-type promotional opportunities by isolating previously unnoticed purchase interdependencies among seemingly unrelated products).

All considered, single-source analytics can certainly be a spring of worthwhile information—however, considering individual sources of data in isolation from one another invariably results in the forgoing of potentially important informational synergies, which is perhaps the most fundamental shortcoming of single-source analytics. As suggested in Figure 6.15, amalgamating unique data sources into a broader, source-dissimilar but meaning-interconnected informational reservoir is the first step in evolving the organization's data analytical capabilities from a function focused on pursuing of topical insights to one that is capable of creating competitively advantageous, decision-guiding knowledge.

As discussed in the opening chapter, the fundamental difference between information and knowledge is that the former sheds light on "what happened," while the latter is capable of explaining "why it happened." Naturally, it is immeasurably more beneficial to have the understanding of the underlying causes than to merely be well-informed regarding outcomes or events of interest, given that causal knowledge can inform future decisions, which is generally not the case with explanation-lacking outcome information.

This is the essence of multi-source data analytics imperative—it offers the means of realizing the long-heralded but rarely realized value of data.

The notion of multi-source analytics is suggestive of yet another emergent business concept—a *marketing ecosystem*.[38] The following section offers a closer look.

Marketing Ecosystems

There is a long, though not always glorious, tradition of likening different aspects of business to natural phenomena, of which the idea of an *ecosystem* is one of the more recent examples. As a scientific concept, an ecosystem is the totality of living organisms and nonliving elements inhibiting a particular area; in a given ecosystems, organisms interact with each other and with nonliving elements. The natural—i.e., biological—definition of an ecosystem implies a certain degree of distinctiveness of the system as well as a certain degree of interconnectedness among the living and nonliving components of the system. If an ecosystem can be assumed to have a purpose, then it would most likely be to perpetuate itself and by extension, the purpose of its living elements can be assumed to be that of survival.

Given the basic outline of a natural ecosystem, it is easy to see its close parallels with business: "the totality of living organisms and nonliving elements inhabiting a particular area" can be likened to "the totality of firms competing in a particular industry"; the ecosystem's purpose of "self-perpetuation" is essentially the same as it is for any industry, as is the case with "survival" being the goal of individual ecosystem "members." The application of the concept of ecosystem to a somewhat narrower context of marketing retains those similarities: A *marketing ecosystem* can be thought of as the totality of promotional means, encompassing platforms, channels and techniques, which individually and jointly contribute to the fundamental purpose of marketing—to win and retain a customer.[39] Those promotional means are striving for relevance as they are confronted with an array of adverse developments, including continual emergence of new alternatives, progressively more fragmented media usage and ever-rising targeting precision expectations. In a sense, like the organisms in a biological ecosystem, individual promotional elements are trying to survive as viable marketing ecosystem participants.

Within the realm of marketing, perhaps the most obvious application of the notion of ecosystems is to characterize the totality of the industry, as exemplified by a comprehensive Booz & Company research study, "Marketing & Media Ecosystem 2010."[40] The study, which focuses on the changing dynamics of the marketing and media industry as a whole, likens the broadly scoped industry—encompassing service providers (advertising agencies, marketing service organizations and the like) and media content providers (MTV Networks, The Disney Company, Facebook and others)—to a marketing ecosystem, where individual "organisms," or companies, compete and, to a lesser degree, collaborate with each other.

A somewhat different way of thinking about a marketing ecosystem is to consider the concept from the point of view of a brand. As suggested earlier, the goal of a brand is to win and retain profitable customers, with broadly defined marketing activities aiding in reaching that objective. The gradual but persistent shift toward "always on" promotional communication formats, coupled with the almost dizzying proliferation of promotional media and related options are effectively redefining the traditional conception of *marketing mix*. The persistently used, decades-old conceptualization of the four focal elements of marketing,[41] the *four Ps* of marketing (product, price, promotion and place) no longer offers an adequately clear way of thinking about the impact of marketing activities. There are several reasons for that: First, it reflects a producer-centric view, which is not in keeping with the reality of consumer-centric economy. Second, the conceptualization lumps together brand communication strategy (promotion) with what can be viewed as constraints (product, place and price) placed upon that strategy. In other words, the role of marketing, as a business function, is to devise maximally impactful brand promotional communications, subject to the offering's (a physical product or an intangible service) core attributes—or the "product" part of the four Ps—in addition to its price and distribution.

Perhaps most importantly, the four Ps conceptualization conveys a largely deterministic picture of the brand's world, one which is not in keeping with today's highly fluid business environment. More specifically, the four Ps framework implicitly assumes that, at a point in time, the bundle of attributes comprising the product of interest (or several varieties of that product), as well as the product's price and distribution are all effectively fixed. However, that is not today's reality: The advent of mass customization (the use of flexible, computerized manufacturing systems to produce output tailored to a specific order) is changing the way we think about products, as product attributes at a point in time can vary, reflecting individual buyers' preferences. The rise of ecommerce has had a similar impact on the notion of place (distribution), which also lost a lot of its clarity, largely because to a consumer ordering a product on the internet from the comfort of his or her home, the distribution channel for that product is mostly invisible and practically irrelevant. Although more tacitly, the four Ps conceptualization also fails to capture the changing character of brands' communications: The past trend of brands both initiating and controlling promotional communications is also largely giving way to a more interactive model, where both brands and consumers initiate and control brand-related communications—the former by the way of consumer-targeted promotions and the latter through brand-related, largely online social interactions. Yet, even that distinctiveness is beginning to fade, as the traditionally "one-way" media, such as television, are moving in the direction of true interactivity.[42]

All things considered, internet-driven technological innovations are fundamentally reshaping the marketing paradigm—away from the narrowly defined, somewhat static and producer-centric *marketing mix* concept and toward a considerably more expansive *marketing ecosystem*. One of the more compelling depictions of a marketing ecosystem was proposed by Mullen, a Boston-based integrated advertising agency (see Figure 6.16).

Perhaps the most important aspect of the ecosystem conceptualization is that a consumer is at the center of a multimedia swirl, where multiple communication channels both compete for attention and collaborate with each other to bring about the desired outcomes. It is a "yin and yang"[43] world: Individual promotional channels, such as print, direct mail, online, mobile or out-of-home (public place advertising, such as billboards) are both in competition, as each is hoping to attract the largest possible share of advertisers' budget, while at the same time they reinforce each other by offering multiple exposure points to advertisers' messages. Mullen's depiction captures what is nothing less than a staggering number of communication alternatives available to marketers; the graphic's life-resembling layout also hints of the fluidity of the system. Perhaps most importantly, the ecosystem representation draws attention to the essence, or the core of marketing's mission: To allow brands to communicate with their current and prospective customers.

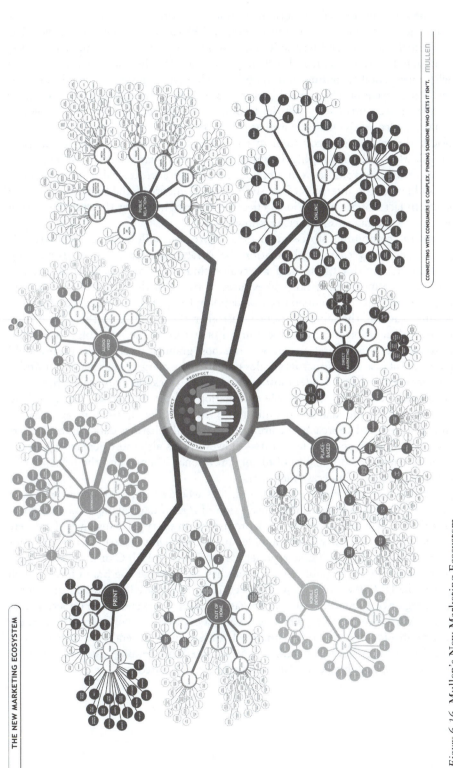

THE NEW MARKETING ECOSYSTEM

Figure 6.16 Mullen's New Marketing Ecosystem

Source: Mullen. Reprinted with permission. www.mullen.com

Given the sheer number of promotional options, how does one decide which vehicles to lean on and which ones to, possibly, de-emphasize? Aggregate trend-wise, there has been a gradual though persistent shift away from the "old" media—traditional TV, print, radio and to some degree, direct mail—and toward the "new" communication channels, most notably online and mobile.[44] However, aggregate trends are not necessarily indicative of which media vehicles are likely to work best for a particular brand—the answer ultimately lies in thorough assessment of the effectiveness of individual vehicles, individually as well as collectively.

Consider the marketing ecosystem in the context of earlier discussed *multi-source analytics*. Clearly, combining highly dissimilar data sources is far from easy, but not rising up to that challenge would be tantamount to forgoing a great deal of informational richness hidden in the interplay of the individual elements of the brand's marketing ecosystem. In fact, robust promotional effectiveness insights are at the core of creating competitively advantageous marketing knowledge.

Process-wise, combining of dissimilar data sources can follow one of two paths: 1. disaggregate, or 2. aggregate amalgamation. *Disaggregate amalgamation* entails merging two or more files into a single data reservoir using a common-to-all link, such as customer ID. The merger generally takes place at the most disaggregate level of data hierarchy (see the earlier discussion of *root* data) and requires the existence of a case-unique link, such as the aforementioned customer ID. Given that the goal of disaggregate amalgamation is increase the number of attributes (i.e., variables) that could be used to analyze cross-case relationships at the most granular level, ideally there should be high degree of case-overlap across all files that are to be merged together, to minimize potential data distortions.[45] Under most circumstances, cases that only appear in one file should be closely examined for possible elimination to keep the proportion of missing values in the post-merger dataset to a minimum. All considered, disaggregate amalgamation is the preferred approach to combining physically distinct data files as it offers the greatest amount of analytic flexibility—however, it is also most demanding in the sense that it requires communality of file organizational schemas and the presence of a common-to-all (files) unique case identifier.

Aggregate amalgamation involves combining files where cases represent summaries of more detailed records (see the earlier discussion of *derived* data). Under most circumstances, this type of a merger tends to be a product of necessity—for instance, if we were to combine sales and coupon redemption files and the former was organized by UPC but the latter by brand (i.e., each case represented an individual UPC or a brand, respectively), it would only be possible to combine these two files at the brand level (which means that the UPC-level records would need to be aggregated, or "rolled-up" to the higher aggregate of a brand). Hence, aggregate amalgamation should be undertaken at the most detailed level possible, which is usually the lowest level of aggregation that is common to all files that are to be combined. In fact, it is generally advantageous to combine data at lowest level of detail, simply because more detailed data can always be aggregated, but once aggregated, data cannot be disaggregated.

Mini-Case 6.1: Multi-Source Analytics

One of the U.S. wireless carriers recently embarked on a major customer relationship management (CRM) initiative to develop a "360-degree customer view," defined as *providing all organizational stakeholders with the consistent view of the customer.* At its core, the initiative entails amalgamating multiple customer-related, but source-dissimilar data sources in a manner where each set of data represents a different customer dimension—needless to say, it is a considerable informational undertaking. As is the case with other, large, multi-department organizations, the wireless carrier's approach to data capture is highly functional, to the degree to which much of the data capture is a passive consequence of electronic transaction processing. That, coupled with the fragmentation of data (i.e., different parts of the organization focusing on just certain subsets of all customer data) has led to a great deal of under-utilization of data as a decision-guiding resource. Among the undesirable consequences of that status quo is that the same customer might appear to be more or less attractive to the organization, depending on who in the organization is looking. In other words, since different parts of the organization are focused on different slices of the overall customer data, when taken out of the "total data" context, those individual data slices will likely tell a different story. . . Not only can such relativism lead to conflicting conclusions, it stands in the way of implementing more "enlightened" CRM approaches, such as tying loyalty rewards to customer lifetime profitability. Those are among the reasons compelling the wireless carrier to invest in the *360-degree customer view.*

One of the key challenges in the wireless telecommunication industry is the distinction between a customer—which could be an individual person, a household or a business entity—and a telephone number. At present, the total U.S. population is a bit under 314 million, while the total number of active phone numbers is about 1 billion. Even when non-private (i.e., business, government, etc.) phone numbers are set aside, there is still a one-to-many relationship between a wireless subscriber and phone numbers, because many of today's popular communication devices, such as tablet PCs or mobile broadband modems for laptops, have phone numbers embedded in them (e.g., a broadband-enabled tablet PC uses a built-in phone number to connect to internet). Hence, a wireless subscriber might have a phone number associated with his/her wireless phone, another one associated with his/her tablet PC and yet another one associated with his/her mobile broadband modem. Furthermore, that subscriber can also have still other, separate phone numbers, such as those used by his/her children. . . In a data sense, many of those will usually exist as separate accounts (since the individual devices tend to be acquired and activated at different points in time), which means that a single wireless subscriber can be seen as several different customers. On top of that, each of those individual "customers" will usually yield a considerably different ARPU (average revenue per user), as a smart phone voice + text + data subscription generates about $100 monthly, while the data-only wireless internet access for tablet or laptop generates between $20 and $40 monthly. But the informational proliferation only begins here: Multiple accounts will then spawn a number of account-related "data derivatives," such as billing records, account service and management, customer interaction and other records. Add to that departmental data fragmentation—i.e., smart phones vs. feature phones vs. tablets vs. wireless broadband modems—the number of single-source data grows exponentially, as does the fragmentation of the customer view.

The first step in the journey to create the *360-degree customer view* is to construct a controlling master identification system, which in the case of the wireless carrier is a combination of the name and address associated with individual accounts. Once created, the "master ID" forms the basic unit of analysis—i.e., each individual row in the data matrix will delimit a subscriber; to the degree to which a particular subscriber might have multiple phone numbers associated with his/her account, those numbers will become attributes (variables in the data matrix context), as will other characteristics, such as account payment history, promotional responses, etc. In doing so, multiple-data records, where a single subscriber appears as an attribute of multiple phone numbers, are reconfigured into a single record where the individual phone numbers (and all details associated with those numbers) are attributed to the controlling subscriber ID. Once the amalgamation has been completed, no matter who in the wireless subscriber organization is looking at the customer base, the resultant picture will be the same.

7 Analytic File Creation

One of the common misconceptions in applied business analytics is that having the requisite data readily available marks the beginning of data crunching. Under most circumstances, having the data in-hand is merely the beginning of the process of creating an analyzable data file, rather than the beginning of data analyses. The reason for that is that, as discussed in Chapter 1, most data used in marketing analytics (as well as other aspects of business) is a by-product of the electronic transaction processing—in other words, the data layout, formatting and other characteristics reflect the inner-workings of those systems, rather than the demands of the ensuing analyses. Hence, before meaningful analysis can be initiated, an often significant amount of data engineering has to take place.

Taking the steps necessary to convert not-directly-analyzable raw data into, a still raw, but analyzable data file constitutes the creation of an analytic file. The extent of the required re-engineering will vary depending on the interplay between the characteristics of the original data and the informational demands at hand, but there are a number of specific considerations that needs to be addressed almost universally—those are discussed in the ensuing chapter.

Data Gathering

Data capture can be either *incidental* or *purposeful*. Data is collected incidentally when it is a by-product of ongoing business operations. Its capture is, to a large degree, a result of technological progress. For instance, stores equipped with barcode scanners capture product purchase data because the process of barcode scanning generates an electronic record, each time it occurs. Similarly, an online purchase creates a transaction record, just as an electronically placed manufacturer order generates a similar record. These data are generated each time a particular system is used,[1] even if there is no interest in data as an outcome.

On the other hand, the capture of other data types requires special effort. For instance, to get a valid and a representative view of buyer satisfaction or to uncover the attitudinal drivers of brand choice, a firm usually has to field a consumer survey. Such data is collected purposefully since its capture requires special provisions that are only put in place for the explicit purpose of capturing that particular information.[2] Thus in contrast to the incidental data capture, the gathering of the purposeful data is usually independent of the firm's operational systems. Under most circumstances, these data are only collected if they are to be used for a specific purpose.

The data acquired from outside data vendors is a little more difficult to classify. The commonly used geodemographics exhibit the characteristics of both the incidental and purposeful data. Being derived from the U.S. Census information makes it incidental, while being targeted at a relatively specific goal makes it purposeful. In the end, however, it is more reasonable to consider it purposeful because its creation requires an additional effort and if its sales ceased (due to a lack of demand), so would its creation.

The vast majority of the core data is incidental, as is some of the causal data—because of that, it also tends to be organized around events, rather than customers (see Figures 6.3 and 6.4). This is an important point to keep in mind while considering adding some additional, i.e., purposeful, data to the database. Whether the added data comes from an outside data vendor/aggregator or from a direct data capture (such as a survey), its coverage—defined as the % of all database customers for whom the specific purposeful data was added—will almost always be limited to only a subset of all customers in the database.[3] In order to assure the projectability of sample-based database appends, the originally event-centric core data needs to be reorganized into customer-centric matrix to allow for proper coverage and/or bias assessment, or the selection of an appropriate sample.

Analytic Dataset Creation

Some databases come "fully loaded" with a rich assortment of core and causal data, all organized in a customer-centric fashion and ready to be taken to the proverbial "next level." A more common scenario, however, is a database in need of additional, usually causal appends, and proper organization. In such cases it is more cost and time effective to create a database extract-based analytical dataset.

An *analytical dataset* is a subset of the database that has been enriched with the appropriate outside (to the database) data, properly organized and cleansed. In the data sense, it is the starting point for the database analytical process described in this book. As previously mentioned, its creation involves three separate steps:

1. Extracting a subset of the database.
2. Enriching the database extract.
3. Organizing and cleansing.

Extracting a Subset of the Database

The most common database type today is one built around transactional information. The majority of larger retailers keep track of their transactions, as do most manufacturers. The resultant data reservoirs are enormous—the previously mentioned Walmart database has been estimated to contain roughly 435 terabytes of data at the time of this book's writing. And although most other corporate databases are considerably smaller, quite a few of them are multi-terabyte systems, which can easily translate into tens of millions or even billions of records.

Although such large volumes of data can be helpful in assuring reporting accuracy, it can be a hindrance in more advanced statistical modeling. The first reason behind it is obvious and it requires little explanation: It is quite difficult and time-consuming to manipulate such large files, particularly while conducting exploratory data analysis involving a large number of individual metrics and tests. The second reason is somewhat less obvious, but it has more direct impact on the validity of findings: Large sample sizes have a potentially skewing effect on the robustness of statistical parameters and tests. In view of the potentially weighty implications of that dependence, a more in-depth explanation seems warranted.

Central to the estimation of many statistical parameters is the notion of *standard error*, which is an estimated level of imprecision of a particular statistic. In the computational sense, there are multiple methods of calculating standard errors, depending on the type of statistic used which in turn reflects different possible applications of this concept. In the realm of database analytics, probably the most frequent application of the notion of standard error takes place in the context of sample mean values estimation. In this case, the standard error is computed simply by dividing the sample standard deviation by the square root of the sample size. Interpretation-wise, the larger the sample size, the smaller the standard error. And that is the crux of the problem.

Standard error in and out of itself is of little interest to business analysts—however, it is one of the key inputs into a frequently used *statistical significance testing*,[4] the goal of which is to determine if the observed differences between means (such as the difference in the purchase rate between treated and control groups) are factual or spurious. As the standard error estimate decreases (due to a large sample size), the ever-smaller differences are deemed "statistically significant," which often leads the less experienced analysts to conclude that the otherwise trivially small differences (such as between treated and control groups in an impact experiment) represent meaningful practical findings (such as a positive treatment-attributable incrementality, in the case of the said experiment). In other words, excessively large sample size artificially deflates the size of the standard error estimates which in turn increase the likelihood of "false positive" findings—i.e., ascribing a factual status to trivially small, spurious differences.

The practical consequences of this dependence can be considerable—almost disproportionately large given the somewhat obtuse nature of the concept. For example, an organization might be led to believe that the initial tests of the contemplated strategic initiatives, such as pricing policy or promotional mix allocation changes, are encouraging enough to warrant a full scale commitment, when in fact the analysis (when properly executed) might not support such conclusions. Hence this seemingly trivial notion might be the database analytics' version of the Butterfly Effect,[5] which is why it demands a deeper treatment, presented later.

But for now, let's concentrate on the delineation of effective database extract selection rules, in view of the inappropriateness of using an un-pruned database universe as the basis for analysis.

Extract Selection Rules

The most important considerations in selecting a subset of an entire database are *representativeness* and *sizing*. The former speaks to the degree of compositional similarity between the database and the extract, while the latter spells out the minimum required number of records. Though different in terms of their focus, the two are highly interconnected. An extract-wide sample size is in a large part determined by the composition of the sample, specifically, the number of individual sub-segments and the nesting structure (i.e., how many tiers of sub-segments, or segments within segments, are there). The extract selection rules, therefore, should be framed in the context of the expected representativeness and sizing of the contemplated sample.

The often recommended—and used—*random selection* is actually rarely the best approach to take in selecting a subset of a customer/prospect database. The reason behind that counterintuitive statement is that this otherwise convenient approach is likely to lead to over-sampling of large customer/prospect groupings and under-sampling of the small ones. This is particularly the case when it comes to the very best customers, who usually comprise a relatively small proportion of the total customer base (see the Pareto's Principle, often referred to as the "80–20" rule). As such, the best customers are likely to be under-represented in a randomly-drawn sample, which would obviously inhibit a deeper understanding of their behaviors (not to mention contributing to a skewed interpretation of the overall findings).

To mitigate the possibility of such undesirable outcomes, the *stratified sampling* scheme can be used instead. This sampling technique offers a higher likelihood of bringing about the typically desired random selection, by building the selection logic around appropriately defined customer segments.[6] The specific stratified customer database extract selection steps are outlined below:

- Step 1: Explicitly describe the content of the customer database by identifying the following:
  - customer clusters (e.g., spending or lifetime value segments, etc.).
  - descriptive variables and their quality (i.e., % of coverage).
  - longitudinal depth of purchase data (i.e., how far back does the data go?).
- Step 2: Identify the most disaggregate customer cluster, i.e., what is the most narrowly-defined group of customers to be used as the focus of analysis?
- Step 3: Flag customer records in accordance with cluster membership and determine the number of records per cluster.
- Step 4: Select a random sample of 500–1,000 customers from each of the clusters.
- Step 5: Contrast the profile of the sample extract with the parent population by comparing the means and distributions of the descriptive variables outlined in Step 1. If differences exceed 1 standard deviation on the key variables' means and/or distributions are significantly different, re-sample.

An important consideration governing the appropriateness of the resultant sample is its analytic adequacy. In other words, will it support the most disaggregate, in terms of sample composition homogeneity, analysis? The general rule of thumb is to use the most narrowly defined group expected to be used in the ensuing analyses as the starting point and work up the level of aggregation chain to arrive at the final sample.

Once selected, the sample extract usually needs to be enriched with additional, typically causal data to enhance its explanatory power.

Extract Data Enrichment

Additional data can be added to the selected sample either from other internal systems or from outside partners or data suppliers. However, one should not lose sight of the fact that since much of the data organizations capture are by-products of their ongoing operations, data tend to be scattered throughout the organization's various systems. Common examples include campaign data (mail list, offers and responses), field sales information (customer visits, inquiries, etc.), outgoing telemarketing (contact lists, call dispositions, etc.), satisfaction surveys, complaints. Although many organizations have been trying to integrate much of that data into a single data reservoir—the so-called

"360° customer view"—it tends to be a slow process and more often than not much of that data remains scattered across various internal systems.

At the same time, it is often beneficial to look outside of the organization for sources of potentially explanatory data. Although there are dozens of data suppliers specializing in data compilation and aggregation, in general, the bulk of the third-party data can be classified as either U.S. Census derived aggregates or special interest survey extrapolations.

The *U.S. Census derived data* represents geography-based aggregation of the detailed resident and business information collected by the U.S. Census Bureau. The resultant descriptors, commonly referred to as "geodemographics," are built around metrics describing age, gender, marital status, children, education, income and employment, race and ethnicity, home values and home ownership. The finest level of granularity at which these data are made available by the Census Bureau is the block level, which is the smallest geographic unit for which the Census Bureau provides (to outside, commercial entities) 100% populated data tables. In urban areas it typically corresponds to city blocks bounded by streets. In total, as of the last U.S. Census (conducted in year 2000), the United States is divided into over 8 million individual blocks. The bulk of the publicly available—and thus commonly appended to commercial, transactional databases—U.S. Census data is at the block level.[7]

Due to privacy considerations, however, some of the Census data is only made available at the census tract level. As defined by the U.S. Census Bureau, census tracts are "*small, relatively permanent subdivisions of a county. . .*[which] *normally follow visible features, but may follow governmental unit boundaries and other non-visible features in some instances; they always nest within counties* [and] *average about 4,000 inhabitants.*" As of the 2000 U.S. Census, the United States was broken down into 65,443 census tracts.

The other, commercially available and frequently seen source of explanatory data often used to expand the informational value of transactional data extracts comes in the form of special interest, sample survey-based *behavioral and preference estimates*. One of the two main sources of these data are consumer panels, exemplified by AC Nielsen's scanner-based purchase tracking panel, Yankielovich consumer lifestyle tracking studies or Market Facts' online and catalogue purchase tracking panel. The main advantage of consumer panels, in general, is the breadth of topical coverage and longitudinal continuity, both of which support an assessment of longer-term trends. The most noteworthy drawbacks, on the other hand, are participant self-selection and demand effects, which are another way of saying that any panel-participant-reported facts or opinions may not accurately depict the actual behaviors or feelings of consumers at large. Overall, however, the good outweighs the bad, particularly when trying to understand observed consumer behaviors (i.e., database-contained purchases). The most frequently used panel-derived descriptors are consumer lifestyles and psychographics, online and catalogue purchase propensities and innovation adoption propensities, such as cell phone usage, broadband internet connection purchase for individuals or distributed computing for businesses.

The other main source of the commercially available, sample-based estimates are consumer and business credit reporting bureaus. On the business data side, organizations such as Dunn & Bradstreet make available a range of general industry characteristics and financial performance metrics, while on the consumer data side, the three main consumer credit bureaus (Experian, Equifax and TransUnion) make available consumer credit and financial-asset-related estimates. In addition to the mass data suppliers, a number of smaller firms offer sample-based estimates of the otherwise hard-to-quantify consumer metrics, such as household net worth, or automobile registration.[8]

The quality—defined in terms of coverage and accuracy—varies across the types of data. Consumer and business credit information sourced from the three major credit bureaus defines, naturally, the upper end of the quality spectrum, though its usage for analysis and other purposes is also highly restricted and tightly regulated. Other data types, such as household net worth, lifestyle or purchase propensity estimates are usually considerably less accurate, since they represent sample-based extrapolations. Overall, these data types hold some explanatory power if used in conjunction with other information and applied to groups of consumers or businesses, but tend to be relatively inaccurate at the individual entity level, such as a household.

Usage: Research vs. Marketing

A major consideration in acquiring database information-enriching outside data is its intended usage. Most commercial data aggregators and resellers adhere to a dual pricing scheme: Data that is only used for research and analysis is priced lower, often considerably, than the same data that is to be used for promotional purposes. The former is usually defined as the analysis of data leading to the creation of knowledge about consumers, their behaviors and preferences. The latter is usually taken to mean the using of the data supplied by the data provider as the basis for targeting specific consumers.

An even more important consideration in selecting the appropriate outside data are the potential legal constraints. As the privacy concerns are becoming more pronounced, there is a growing trend of limiting the usage of consumer data by commercial entities. That said, most of the restrictions tend to focus on unauthorized data transfers/selling and using personally identifiable information as the basis for promotional initiatives. One of the common means of enforcing privacy restrictions is the anonymization of data appends by means of removing all personally identifying information, such as names and addresses. However, even if the appended data were not stripped of all personally identifying information it is important to make sure that the usage of the data does not exceed the limits stipulated by the user license or the applicable laws.

Organizing and Cleansing

As previously discussed and illustrated in Figure 6.7, an analytic data file should be customer-centric (in the data structure sense), with individual events, such as purchases, promotional responses or outside-attributed propensities, relating to customers as attributes. Not only is that type of an organizational schema an expression of the intended focus of most database analytical efforts, but it also makes appending of outside data easier (by supporting file merging at an individual customer/household level). It follows that by the time the outside data has been added to the original database extract, the so-enlarged file is already properly organized. In the event that is not the case, the analytic dataset needs to be rearranged in accordance with the general rationale shown in Figure 6.8.

Once properly organized, the dataset needs to be cleansed before any meaningful analysis can take place. According to a TDWI report, "Data Quality and the Bottom Line," poor data quality costs U.S. businesses approximately $600 billion annually.

Obviously, data-quality-related losses are inherently difficult to quantify, hence it is possible that an actual magnitude of these costs might be somewhat higher or lower. That said, even if the "true" losses are only 50% or so of the above estimate, it is still a significant enough problem to be given a serious consideration. In a more abstract sense, it seems clear that adequate data quality controls should be a necessary component of the database analytics-driven knowledge creation processes, if the results are to be valid and reliable. The two key data quality due diligence steps are data cleansing and normalization. Technically, data normalization is a subset of data cleansing, but in view of both its importance and a certain degree of technical complexity it will be discussed as a stand-alone concept.

Data cleansing can be broadly defined as the process of repairing and normalizing of the contents of an extracted dataset. *Data normalization*, on the other hand, is the process of identification and removal of outlying and potentially skewing and influential data values and correcting for undesirable distributional properties by means of missing and derivative value substitution.

Data Normalization: Outlier Identification

An outlier is a value that falls outside of what is otherwise considered an acceptable range. Some outliers are illustrative of data errors, but others might represent accurate, though abnormally large or small values that are extremely rare. Depending on the size of the dataset (i.e., the number of observations), outliers can be visually identified by means of simple two-dimensional scatterplots, or can be singled out by means of distribution scoring, which is the process of "flagging" individual records whose values on the variable of interest fall outside of the statistically defined norm, such as ±3 standard deviations away from the mean.

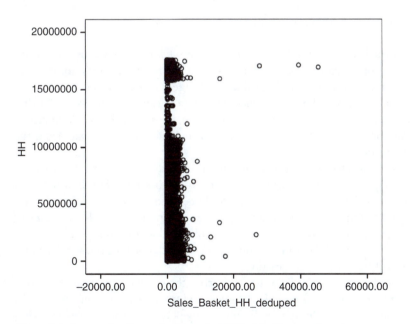

Figure 7.1 Scatterplot Example: Household Weekly Grocery Spend

Visual representations of data, such as the aforementioned scatterplots, offer the simplest method of identifying outlying observations, as illustrated below by a plot of household weekly spending levels at a grocery store chain.

However, the visual detection of outliers becomes practically impossible once the number of dimensions (i.e., defining variables) is greater than two and the data can no longer be easily shown as a simple two-dimensional plot. In addition, even when a two-dimensional representation is sufficient, there is an obvious difficulty associated with the reliance on the visual outlier detection, which is, where to draw a line between an outlier which should be eliminated and a large but retainable value. As illustrated by the above chart representing real-life data, the most extreme—i.e., the furthest to the right in the above illustration—values are easy to classify as outliers, yet the closer one gets to the bulk of the distribution, the more difficult and arbitrary the decision becomes. Outlier treatment needs to be approached with caution, as eliminating too many large values carries with it undesirable statistical and practical consequences. On the one hand, retaining too many excessively large values may cause an inflation of "average" and distributional measures, which in turn may lead to practically problematic consequences, such as unrealistically inflated high-value customer definitions. Still, excessive "large value clipping" will often reduce the variability of the data, which tends to diminish the explanatory power of the subsequent data analysis. In practical terms, it may exclude the very best customers, whose spending levels are considerably above the rest.

The best way to circumvent the subjectivity of visual outlier identification is through the aforementioned dataset flagging, which takes advantage of basic distributional properties of data to objectively identify not only the outlying data points, but those that may exert excessive amounts of *influence* on the analysis of data. In the context of database analytical applications, the influence of a particular database record is a function of that record's deviation from the norm and its leverage, expressed as:

Influence = Deviation from Mean * Leverage

In terms of individual values, influence of a particular value is determined by estimating the standard deviation of actual values (deviation from the mean) from the mean value and the leverage of (potentially) outlying values. Leverage is an expression of "outlying-ness" of a particular value, which is its distance away from the average value—the further away from the mean a particular value, the more leverage it has. Hence influence is simply a measure of the distance, expressed in terms of standard units, away from the center of the distribution.

The challenge associated with the above method—particularly in the sense of measuring the degree of non-conformity (i.e., the outlyingness of individual data points)—is the potential for *masking* of some outliers. In other words, since all data points, including any outliers, are used in computing a mean, it is possible that some of the "less extreme" outliers will be masked by artificially inflated mean values. It is important to point out that the masking problem occurs with both the physical distance and magnitude of difference-based measures.[9]

A relatively easy fix is available. Prior to computing the mean of a particular sample, rank-order all sample records and exclude the lower and upper 5%–10% of the records, prior to calculating the mean. Doing so will prevent any potential outliers from effecting the mean and thus eliminate the masking problem outlined above.

The appropriately computed mean can then be used as the basis for quantifying the extent of deviation from an expected level for each of the records in the analytical dataset. Of course, there are typically a number of candidate variables to be used as the basis for classifying a particular record as an outlier. To that end, it is recommended that only the behavioral metrics, previously described as the "behavioral core" variables should be used as the basis for the outlier determination. This is because these measures present the greatest danger of individual customer record misclassification or group level mis-characterization, which is why it is so important to define outlyingness in accordance with their particular characteristics.

The second broad category of data—the causal data—can be used as the basis for outlier detection, but it is generally not recommended. The primary reason for that is that although these types of metrics can be used for customer or prospect grouping (e.g., demographic or lifestyle segmentation), more often than not their role is to provide explanation and/or description of database records, which suggests an overall weaker skewing effect. In addition, in a "typical" database, a considerable proportion of the causal data represents third-party approximations or group-level estimates (e.g., block level geodemographics), both of which tend to be normalized in the process of their computation. In other words, causal metrics are considerably less likely to have outlying values.

The Process

Regardless of the approach used, the definition of what constitutes an outlier will always carry with it a certain level of ambiguity, or at least subjectivity. Hence outlier identification is as much about the process as it is about thresholds. Putting in place a single and consistent (across time and applications) method for detecting and remedying outlying values will at the very least diminish the possibility of introducing a selection-related bias.

In transactional databases the metric of interest is usually represented by an average or cumulative (customer/prospect) spending level, or an otherwise stated measure of sales/revenue. As pointed out earlier, value outlyingness can be operationalized in terms of the number of standard deviation units that the value of interest is greater or smaller than the appropriately computed mean value. (The appropriately computed mean computation excludes the two tail ends of the value distribution, typically 5% or 10% of the most extreme values. A similar adjustment should also be made when computing the standard deviation metric.).

What remains is the setting of outlier threshold—in other words, at what point an otherwise large value becomes an outlier? In thinking about this issue, consider the goals of the planned analysis and the general inner-workings of statistical methods to be used. Although both vary, a common objective is the identification of high-value current and prospective buyers for targeting purposes, which typically makes use of a variety of regression methodologies. Regression parameters are evaluated in terms of their level of significance (more on that later), which is ultimately tied to distributional properties, including the notions of standard error and standard deviation. The commonly used 95% significance level expresses the validity of an estimated parameter in terms of the likelihood of it falling within ±2 standard deviations away from the mean. Why not calibrate the acceptable value range to the anticipated level of precision? Using such an objective benchmark, only records falling outside the standard-deviation-expressed range of allowable departures from the mean should be flagged as abnormal. This rationale can be translated into the 4-step process outlined below:

- Step 1: Compute the mean and the standard deviation of the variable of interest.
- Step 2: Select the desired allowable limits; i.e., 3 standard deviations away from the mean = 95% of the values, 4 standard deviations away from the mean = 99% of the values, etc.
- Step 3: Compute the maximum allowable upper values: *mean + upper allowable limit* and the maximum allowable lower values: *mean – lower allowable limit*.
- Step 4: Flag as abnormal the records falling outside the allowable range, both above and below.

Demonstrably outlying records should be eliminated from the dataset. Before they are deleted, however, it is worthwhile to discern if they are more-or-less randomly distributed across the customer groupings, or concentrated in a particular group or groups. If it is the latter, the basic descriptive characteristics of the effected groups should be compared in terms of the before and after the outlier deletion. If significant differences are uncovered, such as mean differences in excess of one standard deviation, the sample-based analysis may not be representative of that group's entire population in the source database. The most obvious remedy is to re-draw that particular part of the sample or to exclude it from the extract if re-sampling is not feasible within the available timeframe. In addition, the reason behind the high outlier concentration should be investigated.

Data Normalization: Distribution Correction

First, let's take a minute to take a closer look at the general notion of a "statistical distribution" and its best-known form, the so-called "standard normal distribution." Statistics is in essence an application of rigorous mathematical techniques to a sample with the goal of making inferences that can be applied to the entire population from which a particular sample was drawn. Doing so necessitates the making of a number of substantive assumptions about the likelihood that the observed, sample-based quantities and relationships are representative of those to be found in the parent population. In order for the sample-to-population extrapolations to be reasonably accurate, values of individual variables must be distributed, i.e., scattered around a center such as the mean, in a predictable fashion. When the observed values of a particular variable follow a generalizable distribution they have a predictable likelihood of occurrence, which in turn forms the basis for sample-to-population generalizations.

It should be noted that density distributions represent empirically based generalizations, which means that they can take a variety of mathematically described shapes. *Normal distribution* is the best known and the most frequently used form of a continuous variable's probability distribution.[10] It can be transformed into a *standard* normal distribution with the mean equal 0 and a standard deviation (which is a scale-neutral unit of measurement) of 1 by re-expressing the original metric in a standard format of the so-called "z-scores" computed as follows:

$$z = \frac{x - \mu}{\sigma}$$

where,

x = an observed value
μ = mean
σ = standard deviation

The "popularity" of the standard normal distribution can to a large degree be attributed to the Central Limit Theorem, which states that a sample mean will follow an approximately normal distribution if the sample is large enough, even if its source population is itself not normally distributed. Standard normal distribution is also very simple, as it is described by only two parameters: a mean equal to 0 and a standard deviation equal to 1. This function is important to statistics because it lies at the root of many other continuous distributions. By extension, it is also of central importance to database analytics because most of the statistical techniques essential to knowledge creation require the data to be normally distributed. Normally distributed data is characterized by the familiar symmetrical bell-shaped curve, which implies a clustering of the majority of values around the center of the distribution; it also implies that the more outlying values are predictable as well as equal (i.e., balanced right and left departures from the mean). Figure 7.2 below depicts the generalized form of the standard normal distribution.

Somewhat complicating the notion of data distribution is the distinction between univariate (i.e., one variable) and multivariate (multiple variables) distributional characteristics. The two-dimensional conceptualization depicted in Figure 7.2 captures a univariate distributional view—i.e., a scattering of observed values is depicted in the context of single variable, such as the level of spending or period sales. Since most database extracts contain multiple continuous variables, the univariate distributional assessment would entail an equal (to the number of the said variables) number of single-variable distributions. However, as discussed in the subsequent chapters, the knowledge creation process described in this book calls for multivariate statistical techniques, which in turn entails the assessment of the underlying data's *multivariate normality*. It is important to note that a multivariate normal distribution is not a mere composite of univariate normal distributions. In other words, even if every variable in the dataset is normally distributed, it is still possible that the combined distribution is not multivariate normal. For that reason, the extract dataset's distributional properties should be

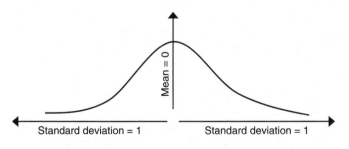

Figure 7.2 Standard Normal Distribution

evaluated in both the univariate and multivariate contexts. As detailed below, the univariate assessment can be easily carried out graphically (see Figure 7.4 below), but the multivariate examination requires a numeric test, such as the one suggested by Mardia,[11] now readily available as a part of standard statistical packages, such as SAS or SPSS.

In practice, many sample database extracts are often not normally distributed in regard to the key customer behavioral characteristics, such as spending or sales levels, while at the same time are approximately normally distributed with regard to many causal characteristics, such as demographics or firmographics. In other words, extract files are rarely multivariate normally distributed. One reason for that is the often-cited "80–20 rule" (Pareto principle), according to which, the top 20% of the firm's customers account for about 80% of its revenue. Naturally then, it will result in an asymmetrical clustering of data points, which is statistically undesirable but nonetheless quite common in transactional databases. Equally problematic is the excessive "flatness" of the distribution, which is typically a result of a monotonic value distribution sometimes associated with geodemographic descriptors.

Generalizing beyond the above examples, the analysis of the basic distributional properties of the normal distribution suggests two basic normalcy evaluation criteria: *Skewness*, which measures the symmetry (or more precisely, the lack of it), and *kurtosis*, which captures the peakedness of data relative to a normal distribution. A normal distribution is expected to exhibit an acceptable amount of symmetry (skewness) and "tightness" around the mean of the distribution (peakedness). As detailed in the next section, there are several graphical and numeric approaches available for assessing both distributional characteristics.

Normality of the distribution is important because many of the "staple" statistical techniques and tests used in database analyses require the underlying data to be at least "approximately normally" distributed. Absent that, the knowledge creation process can become considerably more challenging, as alternative data crunching methodologies may need to be identified. It is important to keep in mind, however, that the notion of distributional normalcy is associated with continuously distributed (also referred to as "metric") data. These are variables measured with either interval or ratio scales, as exemplified by Likert-type attitude measures or product sales, respectively. Discrete variables' (also referred to as "non-metric") properties are expressed with the help of other concepts, discussed later.

Skewness Identification and Correction

A distribution is *skewed* if one of its tails is longer than the other. A *positively skewed* distribution (also referred to as being "skewed to the right") is one that has a long tail extending to the left of the center, which occurs when the mean of the sample is greater than its mode.[12] It follows that a *negatively skewed* distribution (also referred to as "skewed to the left") has a long tail extending to the right of the center, as a result of the mode being greater than the mean. The general shapes of positively and negatively skewed distributions are illustrated in Figure 7.3.

In a statistical sense, a skewed variable is one whose mean is not in the center of the distribution. Both positive and negative skews can be operationalized by comparing the actual values against a null hypothesis of zero and testing the difference for statistical significance. A statistically significant actual-minus-null deviation is then taken as an indication of an action-demanding departure from normality. In practice, however, many

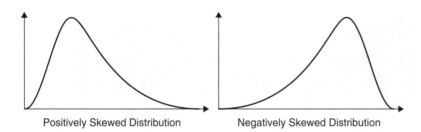

Figure 7.3 Negatively and Positively Skewed Distributions

commonly used statistical techniques, such as regression, have been shown to be relatively robust with regard to modest deviations from normality of the input data, while large-sample-based significance tests have been shown to be highly prone to yielding false positive results.[13] Thus in assessing skewness of the distribution of a particular continuous variable, the question should be: Not whether or not it is skewed in an absolute sense, but whether it is skewed in the sense of diminishing the validity and/or reliability of any subsequent analysis.

Put that way, there are no absolute skewness benchmarks or thresholds. Also, as noted above, most of the mainstream statistical techniques, such as the various regression formulations, are robust with regard to some departures from the expected normal data distribution. This eases the assessment of the quality of continuously distributed data, simply because more tolerance in distributional deviation places the focus on the identification of gross deviations from expected norms. At the same time, not all statistical techniques—as discussed in the ensuing chapters—require normally distributed data. However, the assessment of the extract's distributional properties should be undertaken without regard to ensuing statistical analysis, as it is a key step in ascertaining representativeness of the sample.

The notion of skewness takes on a somewhat different meaning when it comes to non-continuously distributed categorical variables. Often referred to as non-metric or qualitative data (measured with either a nominal or an ordinal scale), these variables are typically evaluated in terms of the relative proportions. In other words, for a dichotomously coded variable, such as gender (male vs. female) or a response indicator (yes vs. no), the ratio of the two response categories can be compared, with the same approach being applied to a larger number of response categories.

The simplest and perhaps the quickest method of assessing univariate distributional properties of the extracted dataset is a histogram, which can be used with both continuous as well as discrete metrics. A simple visual representation of the individual variable's response categories' frequency distribution, this method efforts a quick visual means of detecting skewed distributions, as exemplified below.

A histogram, however, can be inconclusive in many non-extreme situations, i.e., where the data is somewhat, but not strongly skewed, simply because it does not have built-in objective determination thresholds. In other words, relying only on visual depictions, it is often difficult to tell the difference between "somewhat skewed" and "approximately normal" distributions. Fortunately, there are several computational tests that can be used to measure the degree of skewness which circumvent the limitations of histograms and other visual methods, with the three best known ones shown below.

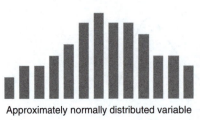 

Approximately normally distributed variable   Negatively skewed variable

Figure 7.4 Sample Histogram

1. Pearson's coefficient of skewness =

$$\frac{(mean) - (md)}{stdev} = \frac{3(mean) - (medium)}{stdev}$$

where,

md = mode
$stdev$ = standard deviation

2. Quartile measure of skewness =

$$\frac{Q_3 - 2Q_2 + Q_1}{Q_3 - Q_1}$$

where,

Q_1, Q_2 & Q_3 = quartile 1, 2 and 3, respectively

3. Coefficient of skewness =

$$\frac{\Sigma(x - \mu)^3}{N\sigma^3}$$

where,

μ = mean
σ = standard deviation
N = sample size

Although the above tests yield an objective quantification of the degree of skewness, they lack a normative threshold that analysts can use to identify unacceptably or excessively skewed distributions. Considering that skewness can be expressed on a continuum ranging from '0' for perfectly symmetrical, normally distributed sample to an infinitely large (at least in theory) positive or negative values, and also keeping in mind that some skewness can be tolerated even by methods requiring normally distributed data, an objective threshold is needed to guide an analyst in delineating the point at which skewness becomes a problem. The following decision rule is the recommended solution[14]:

$$\text{if } |skewness\ statistic| > \sqrt{\frac{6}{N}} \text{ then dataset is significantly skewed}$$

where,

N = sample size

In other words, if the absolute value of skewness statistic exceeds two standard errors of skewness, approximated by

$$\sqrt{\frac{6}{N}},$$

the dataset should be considered significantly skewed. If that is the case, two separate courses of action are available:

1. The previously detailed outlier detection and elimination.
2. Mathematical dataset transformations.

In general, *data transformation* can be defined as the re-expressing of the data in different units with the goal of bringing about desired data qualities, which usually means correcting for departures from normality. There are multiple types of mathematical transformations available and the selection of a method is usually driven by method-ological considerations (for instance, one of the key requirements of linear regression is that data follow normal distribution, while other statistical techniques impose no distributional requirements), empirical test results (such as the above discussed skewness tests) and proven empirical "rules of thumb" (for instance, it has been shown that frequency-count-based data can be made more normal by taking their square roots). A transformed value then is as a function of an original value and a type of a transformation used. In the data analytical sense, transforming data amounts to replacing an original value of a particular variable with a result of a specific transformation correcting for specific distributional deficiency. A word of caution: Although useful in correcting for undesirable characteristics of data and thus ascertaining the robustness of findings, the use of transformations can nonetheless lead to biased or outright improbable results. Furthermore, using transformed data as input into analyses results in an additional step of translating estimated coefficients into directly interpretable values (for instance, if log transformation, discussed below, was used in estimating a linear regression model, the resultant regression coefficients would need to be transformed back into a standard format by means of computing antilogs of their values before the results could be used in the manner outlined in the *Behavioral Predictions* chapter).

In general, transformations can be either linear or non-linear. A *linear transformation* changes the scale, but not the shape of the distribution, while a non-linear trans-formation changes the shape of the distribution. In terms of purpose, linear transfor-mations are typically used to *standardize* (or z-standardize) variables, which entails converting values expressed in original units of measurement to standard deviations from the mean. It is important to note that contrary to what is often believed, standardization does not normalize a distribution, hence a skewed distribution will remain skewed following variable standardization. This means that a linear transformation of data should be considered if the goal is to simplify cross-variable comparisons. On the other hand, a *non-linear transformation* should be considered if the shape of an underlying distribution needs to be changed, or more specifically, if non-normally distributed data is to be forced to assume the previously mentioned standard normal distribution.

As noted earlier, the primary benefit of linear transformation, such as the aforementioned standardization is enabling direct, side-by-side comparisons of otherwise not directly comparable measures. By re-expressing differently scaled (i.e., measured with magnitudinally dissimilar unit, such as miles vs. years) variables as standard-deviation-expressed z-scores, the relative influence of metrics can be assessed, ultimately enabling importance-based rank ordering of measures of interest. Other than variable standardization, linear transformation methods include adding a translation constant (adding a constant value to each raw data point with the goal of shifting of the origin of the X-axis) or a multiplicative constant (multiplying each raw value by a constant with the goal of scaling, which is expanding or contracting of the underlying distribution). Regardless of type, linear transformations are focused on re-scaling of individual variables without impacting the aggregate distribution.

Non-linear transformations, on the other hand, are focused on changing the shape of the underlying distribution. This is a somewhat more esoteric goal, driven less by practical demands of result interpretation and more by methodological requirements of statistical techniques. Depending on the type (i.e., skeweness vs. kurtosis) or the strength of non-normality, a number of different transformation options are available, all of which fall under either of the two broadly defined categories: *logarithmic transformations* (or log, for short) and *power transformations*. In the majority of cases, logarithmic (with natural, ln, and base-10, log10, being the most common ones) transformation can be an effective normalization-infusing treatment for positively skewed data. That said, if the degree of skewness is relatively mild, a logarithmic transformation may over-correct, in effect replacing positive with negative skewness (at the same time, severely positively skewed data may not be correctable with log transformation). Power transformations are usually a viable option in the instances where a logarithm fails to deliver the adequate degree of normalization. The following are the most commonly used power transformations, along with their targeted corrections:

- x^2 (raising the original value to the second power)—to reduce negative skewness
- x^3 (raising the original value to the third power)—reduces extreme negative skeweness
- $\sqrt{2}$ (the square root of the original value)—reduces mild positive skewness
- $-1/x$ (negative reciprocal of the original value)—reduces more extreme positive skeweness

However, unlike the outlier elimination which should be carried out as a part of any a priori data cleansing, data transformations are usually executed in conjunction with specific statistical techniques, because as noted earlier, not all methodologies make specific distributional assumptions. Hence the topic of data transformations will be revisited in subsequent chapters.

Kurtosis Identification and Correction

The second of the potential distributional data challenges is peakedness, or kurtosis of data, relative to normal standard distribution. Positive kurtosis indicates relatively peaked distribution, while negative kurtosis indicates a relatively flat one, as depicted in Figure 7.5 below.

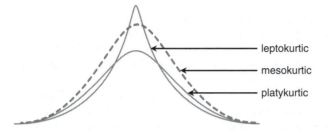

Figure 7.5 Mesokurtic, Leptokurtic and Platykurtic Distributions

Similar to skewness, normal distributions have approximately 0 kurtosis, and the departure from normality represents a movement along the 0-to-infinity continuum. A normally "high," in the physical sense, distribution (i.e., a shape that is neither excessive peaked nor flat) is usually called mesokurtic, in contrast to an abnormally high distribution which is called leptokurtic and an abnormally flat one which is called platykurtic.

The easiest method of detecting kurtosis is by visually examining a histogram of the distribution, but as it is the case with skewness, it is not always possible to visually differentiate between what might be an acceptably small deviation from the norm (i.e., not undesirably impacting subsequent analysis) and a significant departure. This difficulty can be to a large degree circumvented by employing a numerical kurtosis test, shown below:

$$\text{Kurtosis coefficient} = \frac{\Sigma(x - \mu)^4}{N\sigma^4}$$

where,

μ = mean
σ = standard deviation
N = sample size

Again, the question of "where to draw the line" arises: Since few distributions are perfectly mesokurtic, i.e., have 0 kurtosis, how large a departure from the idealized norm can be accepted before the validity and reliability of subsequent data analysis are negatively impacted? The following decision rule can be used[15]:

$$\text{if } |\text{kurtosis } \textit{statistic}| > \sqrt{\frac{24}{N}} \text{ then dataset excessively non-mesokurtic}$$

where,

N = sample size

In other words, if the absolute value of the kurtosis statistic exceeds two standard errors, approximated by

$$\sqrt{\frac{24}{N}},$$

the dataset should be considered significantly leptokurtic or platykurtic, as applicable.

Data Repairing: Missing Value Substitution

One of the key criteria for evaluating the initial analytic quality of database extracts is the degree of completeness, which is usually expressed at an individual variable level. For instance, if 1,000 individual records were extracted, with each containing 100 individual variables, what is the proportion of missing to non-missing values for each of the 100 variables across all 1,000 records?

Frankly, it is rare for an extract data file to be 100% complete. First, organizations vary in terms of their data capture and maintenance proficiency. But even those that excel in that area still need to contend with the inevitable "missing value" challenges. In other words, due to factors including human error, occasional technical glitches or imperfect data capture methods, virtually all data types will exhibit some degree of incompleteness. In general, the behavioral core data typically yields a smaller proportion of missing values than the causal enhancement data. At a more micro level, any electronically captured point-of-sales data, such as the UPC-scanner-based or online transactions will usually exhibit the highest level of completeness, with the typical missing value proportion of less (at time considerably) than 10%. On the other hand, the (behavior) augmenting causal data, such as demographics, firmographics, lifestyle or ascribed purchase propensities tend to yield considerably lower completeness rate, in some cases as low as 5%–10%, particularly for the third-party geodemographic overlays.

Most data analyses cannot proceed unless these "data holes" are filled (by default, some of the commonly used statistical software packages such as SAS or SPSS will eliminate all records containing missing values on variables used in the analysis, a process often referred to as "pairwise deletion"). These unintended deletions of missing data-containing records are obviously troublesome from the standpoint of maintaining a sufficiently large analysis sample size. Even if missing values are randomly scattered throughout the extract dataset, a (favorable) condition termed *missing completely at random* (MCAR), the analysis sample may become prohibitively small as a result of missing case deletion.

Another, even potentially more handicapping consequence of such unchecked elimination of missing value records is a systematic bias creation potential, which is a result of underlying—though usually not self-evident—commonalities shared by missing value cases. This might be particularly evident in the context of the previously outlined stratified sample, where the overall universe of database records is comprised of several, clearly discernible sub-categories. In this case, it is possible that any missing value driven record deletion would impact some segments noticeably more than some others.

And finally, even if the effective (i.e., post-deletion) sample remains robust in terms of its size and unbiased in terms of its composition, the amount of variability in the data will certainly have been reduced, which may potentially adversely affect the robustness of findings. In other words, since the amount of data variability is directly related to the explanatory and/or predictive power of data analyses (i.e., low variability attests to very few or very weak cross-record differences), reducing it runs the danger of diminishing the informational content of the data.

In view of these potentially significant missing value deletion consequences, the safest approach to dealing with missing data often turns out to be a reasoned *a priori replacement* strategy. However, for reasons detailed below it is not always possible to take this course of action and even when it is possible, it entails its own due diligence process.

First and foremost, each variable needs to be assessed in terms of its usability—i.e., does its coverage warrant inclusion in the ensuing analysis, or should it be outright eliminated. For instance, a metric which is 90% populated will almost always warrant inclusion in future analysis; on the other hand, a metric which is 90% missing will almost warrant exclusion from any analysis. In practice, however, most variables will fall into that grey area of indecision that tends to span the middle ground between the two extremes. What then?

To some degree, the answer depends on the type of variable. The behavioral core metrics should be held to a higher standard of completeness simply because they are manifestations of factual actions and in a statistical sense, tend to serve as predictive targets, or dependent variables that do not have immediate substitutes or proxies. A database record lacking transactional details lacks the most fundamental classificatory dimension enabling it to be correctly categorized, which renders its informational value null. Assigning any value, be it the mean, median or a regressed value would amount to creating data. In other words, database records with missing behavioral core metric values should be eliminated from further analyses.

Causal data, on the other hand, can be held to a less stringent standard. As enhancements to customer behaviors, these variables are descriptive (rather than classificatory) in nature and usually have multiple proxies or substitutes—i.e., they are a part of the multivariate mix, rather than being a univariate target. In a statistical sense they tend to be deployed as predictor (also called independent) variables, usually as a component of a large multivariable mix, as shown in later chapters. In other words, a record with missing values on some of the descriptive causal variables still makes a positive informational contribution with other, populated causal variables.

The question that arises, however, is what should be the upper limit of missing values (i.e., the proportion of missing) that should be deemed acceptable? There is no agreement among analysts (or among theoreticians, for that matter) as to what such a threshold should be and as a result, treatments vary widely across situations. That said, it is reasonable to assume that a missing value metric, which could be called "proportion of missing values" is a continuous, randomly distributed stochastic variable that could be examined within the notion of standard normal distribution. It also seems reasonable to conclude that basic distributional properties of the normal distribution can be used as bases for identifying an objective missing value evaluation threshold. In particular, the proportion of all observations accounted for by the set number of standard deviations away from the mean seems particularly appropriate, as it expresses the probability of the actual value falling within a certain range. Of course, the choice of how many standard deviations away from the mean may constitute an outlier is usually somewhat arbitrary.

As shown in Figure 7.6, roughly two-thirds of all observations can be accounted for within ±1 standard deviation away from the mean, which increases to about 95% of all observations within ±2 standard deviations and more than 99% within ±3 deviations away from the mean. Although 95% or even 99% would be the ideal standards, in practice, setting the threshold at such a high level would lead to the elimination of the vast majority of individual metrics. At the same time, recent analyses[16] indicate that any variable which is populated no less than 68%—or in reverse—which has less than 32% of its values missing can still be "repaired" without significantly affecting its basic distributional properties. This means that causal variables which have more than roughly one-third of their values missing should be excluded from further analysis.

The basic distributional properties of the standard normal distribution also offer value replacement hints. First and foremost, the practice of replacing all missing values with a single value (usually one of the measures of central tendency, typically either the mean

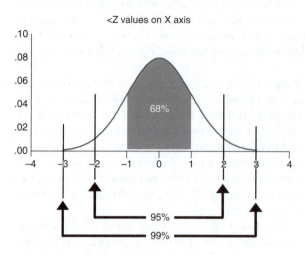

Figure 7.6 Properties of Standard Normal Distribution

or the median) should be avoided as it tends to diminish the variability in the data, which can in turn lead to bias, unreliable effect estimates, ultimately undermining the robustness of the resultant information. A somewhat better value replacement strategy used by database analysts involves mimicking the generalized normal distribution proportions, which means randomly assigning either mean or median values to some, while mean/median ±1 or 2 standard deviations to others, in a proportion depicted in Figure 7.6 above. In a number of instances, however, particularly when missing values are not randomly distributed deletion of incomplete records might be a safer road to take.

Missing Data Imputation

In instances where the deletion of missing values containing records is not a viable option, the most effective method of dealing with missing values is *value imputation*, which is the process of estimating the most likely missing value by using a non-missing value in the sample. The imputation process can either result in physically replacing the missing value—i.e., substituting an actual value in place of the missing one—or just imputing the distributional characteristics, such as means and standard deviations, or relationships from the available data without actually physically replacing the missing values. Although this discussion is concerned primarily with the former, i.e., the physical value replacement, both approaches will be discussed to paint a complete picture of the available replacement options.

PHYSICAL REPLACEMENT OPTIONS: COLD DECK IMPUTATION

Perhaps the simplest approach to missing value imputation is to replace them with an externally derived constant. However, because a single value is imputed into numerous cases, this approach will lead to an artificial reduction in the variability of data, which is likely to bias coefficient estimates, ultimately diminishing the explanatory or predictive validity of findings.

Mean Imputation.   Missing values are replaced with the commonly used measures of central tendency, such as the mean, estimated with non-missing values. Its main advantage is the conceptual and operational ease (SAS and SPSS have built-in functions to carry out this operation). The disadvantages, however, are numerous. First of all, as stated earlier, the true variance in the data will be understated, which will reduce the reliability of subsequent analyses. Secondly, the actual distribution of values is likely to be distorted. Thirdly, cross-variable relationships will be depressed because of a constant value being imputed into numerous cases. Although commonly used, this method produces results inferior to regression or model-based methods discussed below.

Regression-Based Imputation.   Regression analysis, a multivariate statistical technique described in Chapter 6, finds the best-fitting substitute for the particular missing value based on the relationship of the missing value variable with other variables in the dataset. Obviously, a multivariate-regression-based approach makes a better use of the available data, hence intuitively it should be more efficient (efficiency is a function of the algorithm's ability to yield unbiased coefficient estimates while also being easy to implement), which is indeed the conclusion of the investigative research.[17] This particular method, however, also has several distinct disadvantages. First of all, it is considerably more complex as it requires the calibration of a multivariate statistical model. Secondly, it reinforces the relationships already in the data, potentially diminishing the validity of future findings. Thirdly, the variance of the distribution will likely be diminished, unless stochastic values are added to the estimated values, which will further increase the level of complexity. Lastly, it makes an assumption that the missing value variable is highly correlated with other variables. Ultimately, empirical comparisons of the efficacy of this method found it to be less efficient than the two probabilistic approaches described next.

Probabilistic (Also Called Model-Based) Approaches.   Sometimes the simplest solutions are the most effective ones. That truism does not seem to hold in the context of missing data imputation, as the most methodologically complex methods have also been found to yield the most robust replacement values in general, while at the same time also being most efficient. There are two distinct model-based missing value replacement methods. The first is the *maximum likelihood estimation* which uses all available data to generate the correct likelihood for the unknown parameters. Although there are numerous maximum likelihood computational methods, in general, they are all based on the assumption that the marginal distribution of the available data provides the closest approximation of the unknown parameters. The good news is that the main statistical analysis systems already implemented the maximum likelihood methods for missing data (e.g., SPSS Missing Value Analysis). The bad news is these methods are quite computationally intensive, which translates into higher processing power requirements.

The second of the probabilistic approaches is *Bayesian imputation*, which represents a probability-based way to estimate the conditional and marginal distribution for missing data. Computationally, it is based on a joint posterior distribution of parameters and missing data, conditioned on modeling assumptions and the available data.

NON-REPLACEMENT OPTIONS: ALL-AVAILABLE INFORMATION APPROACH

By expressly taking into account all non-missing data, this approach estimates the cross-variable relationships, i.e., correlations discussed in the next chapter, and maximizes the pairwise information available in the sample. Each correlation is based on a unique set of observations and each correlation is computed with a potentially different number of observations. The resultant correlations are representative of the entire sample and are used (in subsequent analyses) in lieu of the raw sample. Naturally, unless the missing values are truly randomly distributed, the correlations will be biased. However, even if the missing values are random, any of the correlations between X and Y can be inconsistent with other so-computed correlations due to dataset-wide interrelationships among all variables.[18] In other words, the range of values for any X–Y correlation is constrained by the correlation of X and/or Y to a third variable, Z, as shown below (based on Pearson's product-moment correlation coefficient *r*—see Chapter 5 for more details):

$$Range\ of\ r_{xy} = r_{xz}\,r_{yz} \pm \sqrt{(1 - r_{xz}^2)(1- r_{yz}^2)}$$

Missing value imputation is an important consideration, likely to have a considerable impact on the robustness of analytic results; hence it demands careful deliberation, particularly when choosing an approach. The first step in the data engineering process should always entail deciding between the outright elimination of the incomplete metrics and imputing the missing values. In many situations, particularly those involving large transactional databases that can easily absorb sample size reductions, eliminating poorly populated data might be the most appropriate corrective step to take, provided that the missing value case deletion would not be biased (i.e., systematically eliminate certain types of records, while keeping others). Empirical research almost universally found pairwise deletion (another term for missing value case elimination) to be the most efficient approach to missing values, and certainly the safest one from the standpoint of result validity.

If, however, throwing out missing value cases is not appropriate or feasible, the probabilistic methods—namely maximum likelihood estimation or Bayesian imputation—should be employed as, again, empirical analyses found those methods to be the most efficient. The conceptually and operationally easier to tackle—and more frequently used—mean or median substitution should be avoided as much as possible. By artificially deflating the amount of variability contained in the dataset and distorting the distribution of values, these methods can introduce a considerable bias into the analysis, ultimately diminishing the validity of the results.

Lastly, to further enhance the robustness of missing value imputations, an iterative approach should be used, paralleling the process developed by Rubin[19]:

1. Impute missing values using an appropriate model.
2. Repeat the above process, n-number of times (usually, 3–5) to produce n-complete datasets.
3. Perform the desired analysis on each dataset using complete-data methods.
4. Average the resultant parameter estimates across the individual datasets to arrive at a single point estimate.
5. Compute the standard errors of the estimates as follows:

$$SE_m = \frac{s}{\sqrt{n}}$$

where,

   s is the standard deviation
   n is the number of observations

Although obviously more laborious, the multiple imputation process has distinct advantages, especially:

• Repeated re-estimation is the only valid method of generating standard error estimates, which in turn makes it possible to get approximately unbiased estimates of parameters.
• Multiple imputation is relatively straightforward to implement, thus yields an attractive cost–benefit trade-off.

Data Repairing: Derivative Value Substitution

A *derivative value* is a result of data transformation aiming to correct for undesirable distributional characteristics of the original, or raw, value. Examples include a log of weekly sales or a square root of cumulative purchases. Derivative values are usually computed with a specific application in mind, such as a regression model, and are used in place of the original values. Results based on these values should not be interpreted prior to coefficients being "translated" into their original forms. For instance, before they can be interpreted as elasticities, regression coefficients based on a logarithmic transformation must be re-expressed in the original, non-logarithmic form, which requires computing anti-logs for all coefficients stemming from previously transformed variables.

Transforming data does not guarantee that the desired distributional properties will be indeed attained, hence it is critical to assess the results of it in the context of the sought-after end objectives. It is always possible that some of the metrics will fail to take on the methodology-mandated characteristics; however, empirical evidence suggests that certain types of continuous data transformations can be highly effective at reaching the stated variable distributional goals. The vast majority of data transformations are geared toward bringing about the normality of the distribution, in effect correcting for varying degrees of the previously discussed skewness, kurtosis or both. Figure 7.7 shows some of the more commonly seen data normality deviations, along with the recommended fixes.

It is important to keep in mind that the above-recommended transformations, as well as all data transformations in general are univariate distributional fixes—i.e., their goal is to correct for a single variable's lack of normality. As previously pointed out, even if all individual metrics are normally distributed, that does not guarantee multivariate normal distribution, which takes on special importance in the context of segmentation (Chapter 9) as well as targeting and behavioral-predictions (Chapter 10) focused analytical initiatives. However, unlike the univariate variable distributions which are manifest data qualities, multivariate normality is a situational characteristic, which is a function of the variate[20] and a statistical technique selection, which are obviously highly situational. These considerations will be discussed in more detail in the ensuing chapters.

Metadata

Somewhat tautologically defined, *metadata* is data about data. Operationally, it is a summary view of the individual variables contained in the dataset expressed in terms of the key statistical descriptors, such as value ranges and the corresponding central tendencies, the average amount of variability, as well as the assessment of coverage and accuracy. Although historically more familiar to academicians than to practitioners, the concept of

Approximate Shape   **Recommended Transformation**

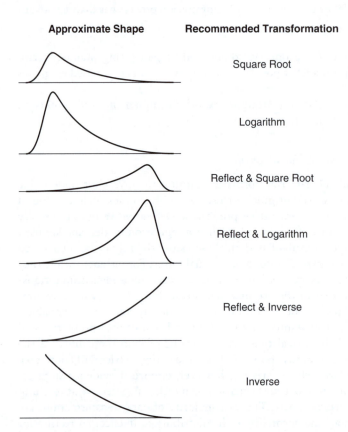

Square Root

Logarithm

Reflect & Square Root

Reflect & Logarithm

Reflect & Inverse

Inverse

Figure 7.7 Common Normality Departures and Recommended Fixes

metadata is gaining popularity among the latter as the amount and diversity of data contained in corporate repositories continues to grow to the point of becoming overwhelming. In the world of corporate databases, even the well-annotated ones, i.e., those accompanied by clear data model descriptions and comprehensive data dictionaries, are often just a hodgepodge of some well and some sparsely populated variables or discontinued or definitionally amended metrics, with little indication as to what is good and what is not.

The primary value of metadata is the time savings it can deliver. For an analyst to have an a priori knowledge of the dataset means being able to take the right data engineering steps, which in turn enables one to focus on specific statistical techniques that can be supported by the available data. When the metadata information is not available, database analyses can become riddled with time-consuming and confidence-shaking corrective re-work, largely due to the underlying data challenges not having been discovered, and corrected, in a timely fashion.

Metadata Template

Although the type and the number of specific variables can differ considerably across datasets, the informational foundation of the metadata associated with each dataset is relatively constant. A general outline of a metadata template is shown below:

	Metrics								
	Mean	Median	St. Deviation	Skewness	Kurtosis	Min	Max	% Missing	Coding*
Behaviors Transactions									
Promotional responses									
Customer-initiated actions									
Causes Demographic descriptors									
Lifestyle indicators									
Purchase propensities									
Transactional channels									
Financial indicators									

* quantitative vs. qualitative

Figure 7.8 Sample Metadata Template

The sample template is shown at a relatively aggregate level, i.e., it illustrates variable types, rather than listing specific variables which are likely to differ across datasets. The focus of the metadata is on a comprehensive overview of the key characteristics of datasets as it relates to using the data contained therein as a foundation for the development of unique, competitively advantageous knowledge. The data evaluation embedded inside of a metadata template needs to differentiate between the two key data types discussed earlier: the behavioral core (i.e., "behaviors") and the augmenting causal drivers (i.e., "causes") to aid in specific statistical technique selection.[21] In practice, behavioral metrics, especially transactions, have the highest likelihood of outlying observations. For example, the UPC-scanner data captured by virtually all retailers utilizing electronic point-of-sales systems and barcoding usually contains outlying negative values, commonly due to refunds and/or exchanges. Unless removed, these values will not only skew the basic transactional characteristics, but may also confuse subsequent sales explanatory analytics.

As shown in the outline in Figure 7.8, the main focus of metadata is on the description of the basic distributional properties of the dataset with the help of measures of central tendency (mean and median), variability (standard deviation), distributional shape (skewness and kurtosis) and extremity (minimum and maximum). Combined, these evaluative statistics clearly describe the usefulness of individual variables as inputs into specific types of statistical analyses.

Further adding to that assessment are the remaining two variables: coverage (% missing) and data type (coding). The former captures the degree of missing values, while the latter qualifies variables' informational content as either qualitative (i.e., nominal or ordinal) or quantitative (i.e., interval or ratio). High incidence of missing values can make an individual variable—particularly, a behavioral one—not analytically suitable. On the other hand, qualitatively coded values, including 0–1 indicators (often called "dummy" codes) or category labels (such as "male–female" gender classification, "under-18, 18–44, 45–65, 66+" age group categorization or "high–medium–low" spending groupings) will limit the analytic usability of such-coded variables.[22] For instance, a qualitatively coded lifetime value (e.g., high–medium–low) will disqualify such variables from being employed as a dependent variable in linear regression.

Using Metadata

Metadata is compiled—what next? Evaluate the usefulness of the individual dataset variables in the context of the analytic plan, discussed in Chapter 3. Is the available data of sufficient quality to support the knowledge creation goals laid out in the analytic

Figure 7.9 Using Metadata to Assess Analytic Preparedness

roadmap? In short, the main benefit of clear and concise metadata information is to evaluate the availability and quality of raw materials (i.e., data) prior to launching data analysis/model building efforts. Doing so entails working backwards from the desired informational outcomes, as shown in Figure 7.9.

In order to bring about the desired informational end state—i.e., the sought after knowledge—data needs to exhibit the desired quality and statistical characteristics in order to be analyzable in a valid and reliable fashion, which underscores the importance of an a priori preparation of an explicit analytic roadmap. The *data quality and appropriateness evaluation* is a process of contrasting the informational needs-dictated analytic requirements and the realities of the available data. Hence, the distribution, quality and coding constraints characterizing the available data (Metadata) are compared to Statistical Techniques' requirements, where the latter stem from Informational Needs-driven Analytic Requirements. In a sense, this is the assessment of the feasibility of the stated informational goals and metadata is the key enabler of this process.

Mini-Case 7.1: My Know-How and Your Data

Predictive analytics is a hot topic in database marketing. Broadly defined, it is the use of statistical modeling techniques for estimating the probability of future occurrences of outcomes of interest and/or magnitude of those outcomes. Its primary appeal is that it allows marketers to "cherry pick" consumers to be targeted with specific offers, by systematically assessing consumers' propensity to respond and then selecting those exhibiting the highest probability. Predictive analytics is particularly attractive to direct marketers, because of significant (on average, $1 to $10 per piece) variable costs associated with that marketing channel—it has been shown that the ability to focus direct mail campaigns on only the most prone-to-respond consumers can increase the response rate by 300% or more, which would have a multiplicative impact on the campaign ROI.

However, predictive analytics is a technically involved undertaking and given the often considerable amount of highly specialized expertise required to build and validate statistical models, many organizations opt to use outside suppliers, rather than relying on in-house capabilities. The outside suppliers, which can range from consulting firms to large global service organizations, contribute the analytic know-how, while the clients provide raw data. Given that, even those (suppliers) with a significant amount of experience in a particular industry need to invest at times considerable amount of time and effort in data due diligence to understand and fully account for any client-specific data peculiarities. However, even before any unique characteristics of data can be considered, the data needs to be properly structured as an analytical dataset—let's take a closer look at a typical transaction data file sourced from grocery store infrared bar code scanners. Here are a few data records:

6|2011–10–15|1780012631|BENEFUL   PLYFL   LFE15.5LB|3000054|DOG FOOD DRY MOIST|4054007|PREMIUM|1|15.99|015636070|2614|21110161 2513725|2011–10–15|1113252147|ALPO PRM SL BEEF 13.2Z|3000055|DOG FOOD WET|4055002|PREMIUM NUTRITION|6|4.50|-.30

115766510|2604|21110161859092|2011–10–15|1780013462|BENEFUL HEALTHY WT 7LB|3000054|DOG FOOD DRY MOIST|4054007|PREMIUM| 1|10.29|0555200|726|211102116861808|2011–10–16|3810013871|MST MTY RISE SHINE 72OZ|3000054|DOG FOOD DRY MOIST|4054001|NON PREMIUM|1|5.99|016025700|31|211032014379373|2011–03–19|1780040523 |PUR PUPPY CHOW 17.6LB|3000054|DOG FOOD DRY MOIST|4054007 |PREMIUM|1|13.99|018742990|38|211032014315270|2011–03–19|17800134 68|BENEFUL HLTH RAD 15.5LB|3000054|DOG FOOD DRY MOIST| 4054007|PREMIUM|1|15.99|0

The data shown above captures sales of dry and wet pet food. Although it is sourced from individual stores (ultimately, single check-out terminals), it is typically aggregated to a pre-determined level of geography, such as a region, and covers an agreed upon stretch of time, such as a year (the resultant file is almost always very voluminous, typically containing several hundred thousand or several million records). The raw data file exemplified above is formatted as a pipe (|) delimited text file with no column breaks and contains no column headers—those are usually made available separately and have to be matched with appropriate fields. Content-wise, there are 13 distinct variables (e.g., store ID, transaction ID, transaction date, UPC ID, product category ID, item price, markdowns, etc.), some of which are numeric (such as item price), others are alphanumeric (i.e., comprised of both letters and digits, such as store ID) and still others are formatted as dates. When the above exemplified data is read into an appropriate data analytical system, typically SAS, SPSS or R, the individual variable names need to be associated with the appropriate columns of data, so that the original pipe-delimited, heading-less file (where rows demark individual records but columns do not delimit individual variables) is transformed into a data matrix where row = records and columns = variables.

8 Exploratory Data Analyses

Broadly defined, the analysis of data can be considered in terms of two, largely non-overlapping aspects: *exploratory* and *confirmatory*. The former is usually an open-ended undertaking, focused on uncovering previously unknown insights, relationships or dependencies. The latter is focused primarily on hypothesis testing, or validating theoretically or otherwise derived beliefs. Typically, data exploration precedes confirmatory analysis—in fact, the initial exploratory analysis might give rise to hypothesis, to be tested within the realm of confirmatory analysis.

The *exploratory* → *confirmatory* progression is bound in the context of a particular informational need; furthermore, there are a number of methodologically distinct analytic options. More specifically, the combination of the nature of the business question and the characteristics of the available data will jointly determine the scope and the character of the initial data exploration, as discussed in this chapter.

Initiating Data Analyses

In a conceptual sense, the analysis of data has a very straightforward meaning in the context of the database analytical process: *The conversion of informationally meaningless raw inputs into useful and specific knowledge.* Implied in this conceptualization is the reliance on appropriate statistical techniques, the choice of which is determined by the end objectives of the data analytical process. In an operational sense, this means choosing from among an array of methods that, though similar in some regards, tend to be quite dissimilar in terms of their applicability limits.

As pointed out earlier, data analysis is often equated with summarization, tabulation and reporting. And though there certainly is value in keeping current on business-related outcomes and emerging trends, this type of information rarely, if ever, gives rise to informational advantage, for reasons detailed in Chapter 1 (i.e., the proliferation of generic data capture and reporting systems). Organizations that effectively use data to out-smart their competitors are those that found the way to systematically translate it into decision-aiding and competitively unique insights. And although the analytically proficient universe of organizations is growing, many firms nonetheless struggle to reap the benefits of their often considerable database infrastructure investments. One of the more frequently encountered reasons is the lack of methodological sophistication, not necessarily in the sense of academic knowledge.

There are a number of significant differences between the theory-building-focused academic research and the competitive-edge-oriented practical marketing analytics. First and foremost, the former seeks universally true generalizations, while the latter pursues entity (i.e., an organization) and situation (i.e., a specific business context at a point in time) unique insights. Hence the most important methodological considerations surrounding theory-building research pertain to sample-to-universe generalizability, which is in sharp contrast to future replicability demands of applied business analyses. Though seemingly of more philosophical than practical importance, these differences have a profound impact on the applicability limits of some of the more commonly used statistical techniques, as detailed later. The degree to which otherwise (i.e., academically) proficient analysts do not recognize these fundamental incongruities will diminish the quality of their results.

Subsumed under the global considerations of applicability limits of broadly defined methodological approaches is the selection of specific techniques, or computational algorithms. It is intuitively obvious that a given dataset can be analyzed in a variety of ways, particularly in the sense of specific statistical formulations. For instance, the goal of identifying segments of the customer base can be reached with the help of cluster analysis, perceptual mapping, classification trees or latent class models, to name a few distinctly different grouping formulations (see Chapter 6 for details). The proliferation of choices is, as expected, a direct consequence of progress. The availability of comprehensive and computationally powerful statistical software packages, such as SAS, SPSS or R, offering a relatively easy access to a wide array of purpose-similar techniques, eases the task of physically "crunching the data," but adds a layer of complexity to choosing the "right" data crunching technique. This underscores the importance of thorough and well-thought-out analytical planning (and a plan) described earlier.

In a more prescriptive sense, the success of virtually all data analytical endeavors hinges on structuring the knowledge creation efforts around a clear *informational needs–available data–analytic approaches and tools* rationale. As pointed out earlier, the nucleus of this process is an in-depth comparison of the stated informational needs with the informational content of the available data. Assuming the presence of clearly delineated informational objectives, this chapter offers a comprehensive overview of a process of systematically exploring the data as the first step in a much broader undertaking of extracting edge-producing knowledge.

Exploration vs. Hypothesis Testing

To a statistician, all data analytical endeavors can be categorized as either *exploratory* or *confirmatory* (also called *hypothesis testing*). Before delving into specifics of data exploration, which is the focus of this section, we should establish definitional clarity of this notion, as it relates to the goals of database analytics.

According to Wikipedia, *exploratory data analysis (EDA) is that part of data analysis concerned with reviewing, communicating and using data where there is a low level of knowledge about its cause system*. It is also sometimes referred to as "data mining," in recognition of the fact that a common objective of initial data explorations is the identification of not-yet-known patterns and/or relationships in the data. Exploratory investigations may exhibit varying degrees of complexity and sophistication and generally make use of various numeric/statistical tests as bases for establishing the validity and reliability of its conclusions. Traditionally, analysts "manually" sifted through datasets in search of (numeric test-supported and thus statistically) significant relationships and patterns. For example, a correlation matrix of appropriately selected variables in conjunction with statistical significance tests can be used as the starting point in evaluating relationships among a number of metrics, based upon which, an analyst can uncover not-yet-known relationships.

Over the last couple of decades, certain aspects of "manual" data explorations began to benefit from the explosive wave of innovations sweeping across virtually all corners of the IT sector. Of most interest to marketing analytics have been two particular sets of developments: *Automated data mining* and *data visualization*. The former represents an attempt at leveraging the advancements in data processing and software technologies to develop stand-alone, self-operating automated data mining systems. These complex applications governed by sophisticated algorithms with smart-sounding names, such as genetic algorithms of neural networks, and are intended to perform the job of an analyst by exploring data for hints of noteworthy patterns and relationships.

A related, albeit substantively quite different is a family of data processing tools focused on data visualization. Like the aforementioned automated data mining, these too are stand-alone software applications, but in contrast to data mining tools, data visualization systems require an active participation of the part of the analyst. Their goal is to replace some of the obtuse and frequently misinterpreted (and misunderstood) numeric tests with visual representations of the relationships found in data, all with the goal of making the results easier to consume by non-technical users. It follows that, although not all relationships can be depicted visually, a number of simpler, basic reporting functions can be handled quite effectively and elegantly in that format. After all, a picture is worth a thousand words (or numbers). . .

In contrast to the "let's see what's there" goal of exploratory data analyses, *confirmatory analyses* are primarily concerned with the assessment of the viability of specific knowledge claims, or stated more formally, with the testing of specific hypotheses. Among the more common database analytical applications of confirmatory data analyses are analyses aimed at *confirming* average \$\$ spend-based customer value categorization (testing the hypothesis[1] that all customers are equally valuable), or cross-customer segment promotional-response elasticity estimation (testing the null hypothesis that all targets are equally likely to repurchase). In general, these types of analyses start from the premise that certain patterns or relationships exist though ongoing validation is necessary, in part to rationalize investment allocations.

Figure 8.1 captures the different faces of exploratory data analysis.

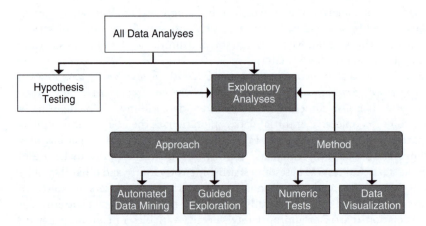

Figure 8.1 Exploratory Data Analyses

The difference between exploratory and confirmatory categories of analyses is best illustrated by customer segmentation methodologies discussed in Chapter 9. While some types of segmentation methodologies are focused on the description of an underlying structure of the customer base (i.e., are exploratory in nature), others are directed at predicting expected future behaviors (i.e., are built around difference hypotheses positing that some customer segments will outperform others). As detailed in subsequent chapters, the two entail sharp methodological and procedural differences. The remaining part of this chapter will be focused on an in-depth discussion of the exploratory dimension of the database analytical process.

Database Analytics and Data Exploration

Data exploration can take many forms, but in the broadest sense, it can entail either self-directed, open-ended data mining, or an analyst-driven, specific informational objective-focused analysis. Unfortunately, these two philosophically and methodologically distinct approaches are at times used—at least name-wise—synonymously, which is problematic, considering that, as mentioned earlier, the two can yield substantially different results: The outcomes of automated data mining are in practice highly unpredictable, simply because this type of database exploration tends to entail the widest possible scope of searching for *any* (statistically significant) patterns or systematic associations. On the other hand, analyst-directed exploratory database analyses are, from the very beginning, focused on testing the viability and reliability of a-priori-identified potential relationships, which in the context of the knowledge creation process outlined in this book would typically stem from the stated informational objectives. In other words, the former is usually driven by the question of "what's there?," while the latter is directed by the question of "what's there, that is related to those particular goals?" Not surprisingly, when it comes to data exploration, approach/methodological clarity is the key.

First and foremost: Automated pattern and/or relationship discovery certainly has its place in applied analytics, but it is not appropriate for the database analytical process outlined here, particularly when large, transactional databases come into play. As noted earlier, as a mode of insight discovery, this particular approach to database exploration is generally informationally unconstrained, in the sense of being limited to only a subset of all potential relationships. In practice, it leads to a "lumping together" of all statistically significant relationships, without regard for their business value.[2] Considering the typically large volumes of data (record counts are almost always in millions and quite frequently billions of individual records), coupled with a large number of available metrics, it is easy to see that any automated data mining tools,[3] designed to sift through the contents of these voluminous data repositories in search of any relationships that might be "hidden" there, are likely to generate an overwhelming number of "significant" relationships. Given the practical limitations of statistical significance tests (see the *Beware of Statistical Significance Tests* section later in this chapter), which offer the only objective means of identifying patterns and relationships in the data, there is oftentimes very little separating true informational nuggets from practically trivial informational tidbits. Quite commonly, an analyst will more-or-less arbitrarily pare down the list of all statistically significant relationships to a smaller, more manageable set of practically significant ones, which though understandable on a practical level, is hard to defend on the methodological level.

Automated data mining is also philosophically incongruent with the goal of organizational objectives-driven knowledge creation process, as it represents an *inductive* (or *bottom-up*, to use a business vernacular) approach to the creation of knowledge. Directed exploratory analyses, on the other hand, represent a *deductive* (also called *top-down*) insight-discovery mechanism. Although seemingly trifling, this distinction is actually quite critical in view of the database analytical knowledge creation processes described in this book.

As detailed in Chapter 2, the difference between the competitive advantage-creating knowledge generation and the accumulation of assorted informational tidbits is most evident in the extent of problem solving specificity. While the former answers specific organizational strategy-related questions, the latter tends to yield an assortment of happenstance details in the hope that those will somehow spark a Eureka-like moment. Though a Eureka-like moment is certainly always a possibility, the probability of it is usually rather remote and practically nonexistent on a repeated, systematic basis. A winning business strategy is usually "90% perspiration and 10% inspiration," to use a common expression. Counting on consistently picking the "right" practically significant insight out of a sea of statistically significant ones bears the resemblance of basing one's retirement plan on hitting a jackpot in Las Vegas.

As depicted in Figure 8.1, exploratory data analysis (EDA) can also take on two distinctly different methodological directions: numerical/statistical testing-based decision rule vs. visual/spatial data interpretation. In keeping with the belief that a "picture is worth a thousand words," spatially based data exploration has steadily grown in popularity; however it is best suited for diagnostic rather than relationship-testing purposes. The main reason behind this conclusion is that the knowledge creation demands a relationship-testing facility that can support an ongoing and unbiased assessment of the relationships of interest. Spatial data presentation delegates the task of identifying and assessing patterns and relationships to individual analysts, which confounds conclusions with subjective opinions, all of which may ultimately bias the results. In the end, objective, properly used and interpreted numerical tests are preferred over the more subjective visual data interpretation (see the *Beware of Statistical Significance Tests* discussion presented below). Spatial data representation, however, is a potent knowledge communication tool and can be a very effective method of conveying otherwise abstract or complex relationships.

Summarizing the above discussion, it follows that in the context of database analytics, *exploratory data analysis* is defined as *a multi-step process guided by the firm's strategic goals and*

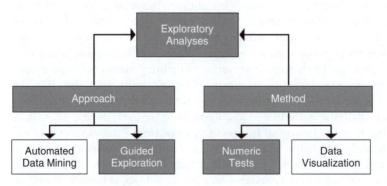

Figure 8.2 Database Analytics' EDA

Figure 8.3 EDA Guided by Strategic Goals

tasked with identifying specific informational foundations to support the development of competitively advantageous knowledge, as graphically depicted in Figure 8.2.

Data Exploration Process

To yield the desired outcomes, data exploration should follow a well-defined process. Here, the seminal work of Tukey[4] (who is also credited with creating the term *exploratory data analysis*) offers a good and widely accepted overall framework. However, the database-analytics-driven knowledge creation process outlined in this book imposes a new set of limitations and requirements, most of which stem from the previously discussed characteristics of many of the transactional databases. Specifically, the said analytical process limits the conventional data exploration process to the identification and quantification of specific data elements, as dictated by the specific informational needs stemming from the stated organizational objectives, shown in Figure 8.3 below. At the same time, it extends the said process to also include the creation of summary and index variables. Hence it is appropriate to differentiate between the general, open-ended *exploratory data analysis* and the *exploratory database analysis* guided by specific goals. In the case of the latter, the term "exploration" is taken to mean assessing the informational value of the currently available data assets, rather than identifying any significant patterns or relationships.

The so-defined EDA process can be broken down into a number of distinct steps, with each geared toward a specific end objective (see Table 8.1).

The Exploratory Data Analysis Process

The general EDA process detailed in Figure 8.1 is comprised of eight distinct stages grouped into three aggregate categories: 1. Review of previous findings; 2. Examination

Table 8.1 The EDA Process and End Objectives

EDA Process Steps	End Objectives
Step 1: List the states informational needs. Step 2: Revisit the Meta Analysis.	Review of previous findings
Step 3: Assess the sustainability of the available date. • Analytic usefulness (variability) Step 4: Graphically examine key variables	Examine data's informational quality
Step 5: Univariate exploration: Describe the dataset. Step 6: Bivariate exploration: Assess the strength of relationships. Step 7: Multivariate exploration. Step 8: Identify indexing and summary measures.	Describe–Assess–Explain

of the informational quality of the available data; and 3. Analyses of data (describe–assess–explain). The first of the three phases—the review of previous findings—offers an opportunity to "take inventory" of previous findings and assess their potential contributions to the current informational needs. The second phase—assessment of the informational quality of the available data—calls for a critical and thorough examination of the value of the data assets vis-à-vis the stated analytical objectives. The third and the final phase of the EDA process—analyses of data—encompasses a broad array of exploration-minded, informational needs-driven and analyst-directed investigations. As stated earlier, the overriding objective of the EDA process detailed below is the identification of data insights that can be expected to give rise to informational and ultimately, competitive advantage.

Placing exploratory data analyses detailed below in the context of the knowledge creation analytical framework presented in this book, it can be shown that both the scope and the direction of the initial database exploration are shaped by a couple of process steps discussed earlier (see Figure 8.3 above). First, specific informational objectives, the delineation of which was discussed in Chapter 3, gives the ensuing analyses a clear focus by directing attention to specific relationships. Secondly, Meta Analysis detailed in Chapter 7 offers a convenient method of assessing the potential applicability of some of the already-on-hand to the stated informational goals. Hence the remainder of this chapter will be devoted to the discussion of key considerations surrounding the reconciliation of earlier identified informational needs of the organization and the informational content of the available data. Doing so entails the bridging of the "level of aggregation" divide separating the highly operationally specific evaluations of the available data (i.e., the results of Meta Analysis) and the (relatively) more loosely defined informational need-dictated data requirements. In other words, *what are the stated informational needs-implied data requirements vs. the informational content of the available data?*

I should emphasize that in this case, both the robustness of the aforementioned comparison and its timing are quite important. That is because being able to complete a thorough "available data" vs. "stated informational goals" comparison at the onset, as opposed to somewhere in the mid-stream of data analyses will speed up the availability of important insights, while keeping the data-analyses-related costs down.

EDA Part I: Review Previous Findings

Knowledge creation is a cumulative process. Even the most eye-opening and revolutionary insights ultimately exist within the realm of other, previously created knowledge. This is particularly important when an organization intends to build a comprehensive reservoir of decision-aiding knowledge. That is because unless proper steps are taken, these insight repositories can become nothing more than collections of unconnected, random tidbits of information lacking collective power. In other words, even though some of the individual pieces of information can shed insight onto specific issues, there is little-to-no informational synergy being created by their aggregate total.

The knowledge creation process outlined in this book emphasizes a purposeful and systematic accumulation of data-derived insights, which stipulates that, on the one hand, each additional insight contributes something new to the already-in-place knowledge base, while at the same time, all individual elements are connected by an underlying theme. Recalling the earlier overview of the differences between automated data mining and analyst-guided data exploration, exploratory analyses should be shaped by both the stated informational goals (see Chapter 3) and the already-on-hand information (see the Meta Analysis section in Chapter 7). However, as suggested earlier, these two quite dissimilar elements do not present a "natural" fit, thus bringing them together can benefit from an objective evaluative framework.

The MECE Framework

The MECE framework (*m*utually *e*xclusive and *c*ollectively *e*xhaustive) is the most appropriate conceptual tool that can be used to jointly evaluate the already-on-hand information in the context of the stated information gathering goals. Its basic premise is that the best way to approach an analytical (but not necessarily quantitative) problem is by identifying—within the confines of the scope of the analysis—all independent components in such a way as to provide a maximally complete coverage or an explanation, while avoiding double-counting. Hence the framework stipulates that each element of knowledge should be informationally non-overlapping with other ones, but collectively, all of them should exhaustively cover the informational demands of the organization's strategic objectives.

The use of the MECE evaluative framework can instill a certain amount of informational discipline by drawing attention to pieces of information that contribute the most, individually as well as collectively, to reaching the stated informational objectives. Since the importance or value of an individual piece of information can be highly situational—i.e., it can depend on what are the stated informational goals—it follows that individual data elements should not be treated as being universally important or universally unimportant. In addition, the MECE framework also promotes thoughtful accumulation of knowledge, by helping to differentiate between causally or otherwise related explanatory factors and spurious informational tidbits.

However, in order to yield robust results, the evaluative framework requires a high degree of definitional clarity. A definitionally clear informational element is one accompanied by an unambiguous explanation of its interpretative meaning along with the detailing of its measurement, or operational qualities. Specifically, it is important to express the already available insights as well as the planned ones in maximally operational terms, which includes measurement properties (i.e., continuous vs. discrete), the unit of analysis and the acceptable value ranges, all with the goal of diminishing potential misinterpretations of individual informational elements. The importance of operational specificity carries far beyond the exploratory analyses presented in this section and will become even more evident in the context of segmentation and behavioral predictions overviews presented in the ensuing chapters. In the sense of technical analyses of data, the definitional precision matters for reasons ranging from effect specification to methodological appropriateness (i.e., making sure that metrics meet the distributional and other requirements of specific statistical methodologies).

Given the requirements governing a robust application of the MECE framework, the ensuing process of reconciling the organization's stated informational objectives with the already-on-hand informational assets entails some specific considerations discussed next.

Reconciling Stated Needs and Meta Analytic Insights

The key to any comparison is the establishment of robust and objective evaluative thresholds. Keeping in mind the MECE evaluative framework, meaningful commonalities between the stated informational needs and the currently-on-hand insights (i.e., the results of Meta Analysis) require an a priori assessment of the *appropriateness of individual variables*, followed by the determination of *sufficiency of coverage of the combined variable set*. The purpose of these two preliminary steps is to make sure the scope and contents of the raw inputs to be used in the analysis are both appropriate.

Appropriateness of Individual Variables

An *appropriate* variable is one that exhibits the desired value availability (i.e., % of missing values), scaling (i.e., the type of measurement), distributional (i.e., the shape of the frequency distribution) and interpretational (i.e., meaning) characteristics. The intent behind this evaluative dimension is to ascertain that the individual measures are statistically as well as contextually useful in the context of the informational needs-dictated ensuing analyses.

A single variable can be deemed analytically appropriate if it meets the following criteria:

- The proportion of its values that are missing are within the objectively allowed limits—i.e., the previously discussed norm of not exceeding about one-third of the total number of observations.
- Its measurement scale is appropriate given its anticipated usage—specifically, the measure is continuous, if necessary (remember that continuous variables can always be re-coded into discrete values, but discrete values cannot ever be converted into continuous ones).
- Its frequency distribution meets the requirements of the statistical techniques to be used, or the desired properties can be brought about through an appropriate transformation (see Chapter 7 for details).

At the same time the said variable can be deemed informationally appropriate if it meets the following criteria:

- Its meaning falls within the general scope of the stated informational needs.
- Recency-wise, it represents the most up-to-date level of insight.

MECE CONSIDERATIONS

The individual variables deemed appropriate based on the above criteria need to contribute incrementally to the explanatory power of the entire set. Operationally, this means that individually, measures should not exhibit excessive cross-variable collinearity.[5] This is a somewhat tricky area because it imposes seemingly contradictory statistical and informational requirements. In a statistical sense, non-trivial variable correlations (usually expressed as statistically significant at a chosen confidence interval, such as 95% or 99%) are a necessary prerequisite of meaningful multivariate and cross-variable analyses, simply because absent those, the resultant models will lack any explanatory and/or predictive power. In an informational sense, however, as stipulated by the earlier discussed Occam's Razor, each individual variable is expected to make an incremental (i.e., unique) contribution to the overall explanation in order for it to not be deemed informationally redundant. In other words, while some level of variable correlation is absolutely necessary to enable explanatory analyses, too high a correlation may preclude some variables from being included in the analysis. Fortunately, steps can be taken to find an acceptable middle-ground and Chapter 10 will offer an in-depth discussion of the recommended diagnostics and remedies.

Sufficiency of Coverage of the Variable Set

The adequacy of the informational content of the entire variable set should be evaluated by considering the following two characterizations:

- The availability of multiple indicators, which translates into two or more operationally distinct but informationally related metrics. The basic idea behind this requirement is to ascertain that the underlying informational constructs are measured with multiple indicators.
- Distributional properties of specific variable subsets are aligned with individual informational needs. For instance, if the stated informational needs are focused on high value customers, the individual metrics should encompass a robust number of high-value customers-attributable values and the overall distribution of values should adhere to the requirements of statistical techniques that are to be used.

The availability of multiple metrics for each of the individual informational dimensions is important for a number of reasons. First of all, it is necessary for explaining or predicting a particular phenomenon, since any such analyses are multivariate in nature (e.g., regression analyses require two or more variables, one to be the target and one or more to be predictors). In other situations, multiple metrics are required to ascertain the construct's convergent validity, which is the degree to which multiple indicators produce similar results, lending credence to subsequent interpretations.

Assessing distributional properties of individual variable cohorts is important primarily from the standpoint of technical data analysis. Many of the commonly used statistical techniques, such as Pearson's product-moment correlation, regression or analysis of variance, require at least some of the input variables to be continuous and normally distributed. Hence it is important that the metrics available to support individual informational needs exhibit properties required by statistical techniques that are best suited to generate the desired insights.

MECE CONSIDERATIONS

As is the case with other aggregate evaluative schemas, such as SWAT analysis, there is a certain subjectivity that is inherent to the MECE framework. It is another way of saying that effort should be taken to minimize any potential analyst bias. An obvious step that can be taken in that regard is the cross-analyst triangulation, akin to the Delphi method. Multiple analysts should each come up with an independent assessment, following which they should be shown the results of other analysts' conclusions and given an opportunity to revise their own. Several iterations should produce convergence or near-convergence and in case of the latter, an open forum discussion can be used as the mean of reaching the final solution.

EDA Part II: Assess the Informational Quality of Data

It is important to look beyond "what are the available metrics," to "what would be the ideal metrics," given the demands of the informational needs at hand. In other words, how adequate is the currently available variable set?

In practice it is rare for the data currently-on-hand to leave nothing to be desired. More often than not, the informational needs pose questions that go beyond the currently available metrics, implying other data. For instance, customer acquisition and retention rates of the firm's competitors, or competing brands' production costs or sales margins are rarely, if ever, obtainable. However, other types of insights may be embedded in the currently available raw data, though not expressly listed among the current metrics. Instead, it may be derived from the already-on-hand data either by *indexing* or *combinatorial* means. In other words, some of the already available raw metrics can be used to create new raw metrics, which then can be added into the currently-on-hand dataset. In effect, the amount of data, in terms of the raw metric count as well as the informational scope that is available at any given time can be increased with the help of some carefully thought-out steps. As a matter of fact, as shown in Figure 8.4, the gap separating the current and the ideal variable sets can be narrowed through intelligent harvesting of the not-immediately-evident informational content of the available raw data.

Current variable indexing is a process of re-expressing raw metrics in more immediately usable descriptive qualities, as exemplified by value indicators (e.g., high, medium, low) derived from numeric sales data or campaign response "flags" (e.g., yes vs. no) inferred from treatment-attributable sales metrics. It is important to keep in mind that indexing frequently takes the form of discrete indicators, thus to the degree to which it might be possible, the appropriateness of the qualitative measurement scale should be considered in the context of the contemplated analyses prior to committing to a particular measurement scale.

On the other hand, as implied by its name, *new variable combination* simply refers to creating brand new measures through the joining of two or more of the existing ones. In the informational sense this amounts to developing higher-order insights from more disaggregate raw components, as exemplified by combining individual Likert-type survey statements (usually expressed as observable indicators of the underlying latent construct) into construct-level measures. Alternatively, somewhat dissimilar metrics can

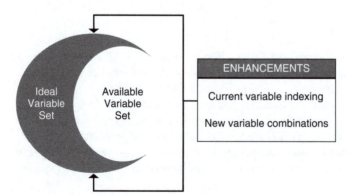

Figure 8.4 Desired vs. Available Data

be combined into new measures yielding different insights. For instance, buyer- or household-level price elasticity measure can be computed by combining the purchase and pricing details. In contrast to the previously discussed indexing, newly created variables are typically more likely to be continually distributed, leading to fewer usage restrictions.

Graphical Examination of Data

It is important to not lose sight of the fact that not all variables in a particular dataset are equally important from the informational content standpoint. In a more technical sense, some metrics that are informationally important could lack statistical robustness. Specifically, they could manifest poor measurement precision or inadequate amount of variability, both in univariate and multivariate contexts. Thus any dataset evaluation should be guided by a dual objective: First, to differentiate between theoretically critical and the lesser theoretically impactful metrics; and second, to assess the statistical quality of the crucial pieces of data.

Always a good time-saving idea, this type of pre-analysis due diligence may be a necessity when dealing with transactional databases, often populated by a staggering number and variety of metrics. The determinants of what constitutes an "important" vs. "less important" metric are obviously highly situational, though in general any data element deemed essential to understanding behavioral or attitudinal outcomes, such as drivers of purchase/repurchase or influencers of attitudes, or those explaining cross-group differences will almost always be of critical importance. On the other hand, variables offering primarily profiling or descriptive insights, such demographics, are usually less important, largely because—as shown in later chapters—their explanatory and predictive power tends to be considerably lower.

Again, the key reason for differentiating between the more and less critical metrics is to focus the attention on the former to enable an efficient assessment of their basic statistical qualities. In other words, do these important variables exhibit the desired statistical properties, given the informational needs at hand and the contemplated analytical methodologies? The quickest and perhaps the easiest method of answering such questions is through graphical examination of the data. Made possible (and quite easy) by the proliferation of powerful statistical analysis packages designed for personal computers, carefully selected data graphs can lead to a quick "thumbs up" or "thumbs down" assessment of the individual metrics. I should point out that graphical description of data is certainly not limited to univariate (i.e., single variable) depictions, but it is arguably most potent in those cases, as higher-order contrasts (i.e., multivariable relationships) are more effectively evaluated with the help of mathematical tests.

The starting point in assessment of any variable should be the characterization of the shape of its distribution, because as discussed later, many key statistical procedures are built around certain distributional assumptions, most frequently, the ubiquitous standard normal distribution. The easiest approach to assessing univariate distribution is to simply graph it. The cleanest (and likely the easiest) way of doing so is through the use of a histogram, which represents the frequencies of occurrences of data values within categories. Figure 8.5 shows an example of a histogram. The individual bars represent frequency counts, thus the taller the bar, the higher the count of that particular value.

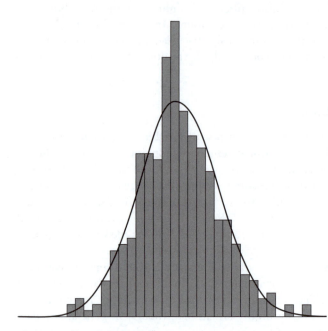

Figure 8.5 Sample Histogram

To aid in the assessment of the "normality" of a particular univariate distribution, it is helpful to add to the barred histogram an outline of the normal distribution, shown as the darker-colored bell-shape curve in Figure 8.5. Technically, the normal curve represents the expected distribution, to be contrasted with observed valued depicted by the individual bars.[7] In the above example, the distribution appears to be approximately normal. The operative term here is "approximately." It is rare to come across a distribution that has exactly the shape shown by the aforementioned bell curve and, more importantly, it is not statistically necessary. Most of the commonly used techniques, such as regression and other GLM[8] methods discussed in subsequent chapters are relatively robust with regard to some departure from normality.

Of course, as the difference between the ideal and actual distributions grows, the robustness of the analytic results will tend to diminish, which means that it is important to single out a relatively "hard" threshold beyond which a particular variable should be no longer considered normally distributed. Unfortunately, a histogram-based visual distributional assessment leaves that determination to the more-or-less qualitative judgment of an analyst. However, given the importance of accurately discerning the distributional qualities of at least the key database metrics, if a particular distribution raises doubts regarding its shape, one of the available numeric goodness-of-fit tests should be used to assess its level of normality. The x^2 (chi squared) test is among the easiest to implement univariate normality diagnostics.

The chi squared test measures the goodness-of-fit between the *observed* and *expected* (under the normal distribution) frequencies, as depicted in Figure 8.5. In other words, for every bar (observed), which represents a single data category, and line (expected) intersection, the test determines if any differences represent persistent dissimilarity or are mere random, non-systematic fluctuations. The tests requires the ability to compute the cumulative distribution function, which is the probability that the variable takes on a value that is less than or equal to the expected value. Its computation, however, is relatively straightforward:

$$x^2 = \sum_{i=1}^{\kappa} \frac{(O_i - E_i)^2}{E_i}$$

where,

O_i is the observed frequency for category $_i$
E_i is the expected frequency for category $_i$

The *observed* frequency reflects the actual counts contained in the data: On the other hand, the *expected* frequency is computed as follows:

$$E_i = N(F(Y_u) - F(Y_l))$$

where,

F is the cumulative distribution function for the distribution being tested
Y_u is the upper limit for class $_i$
Y_l is the lower limit for class $_i$
N is the sample size

The results of the χ^2 test are interpreted in the familiar *p*-value expressed significance test format, as the test is defined for the following general hypotheses:

H$_o$: The data follow normal distribution.
H$_a$: The data do not follow normal distribution.

A statistically significant result leads to the rejection of the null (H$_o$) hypothesis and a corresponding acceptance of the alternative (H$_a$) hypothesis, which ultimately leads to the conclusion that the variable of interest is not normally distributed.

It should be noted that there are multiple other tests that have been developed and used to detect departures from normality, the best known of which include the Kolmogorov-Smirnov and Anderson-Darling operationalizations. In general, though, these tests adhere to a more-or-less similar evaluative logic. In a statistical sense, the latter, which is used frequently in the financial sector, is a modification of the former, giving more weight to the tail-end of the distribution than its Kolmogorov-Smirnov parent. Unlike the chi squared test discussed above, however, these two tests are restricted to continuous distributions, thus not appropriate to use as a numerical extension of histogram-based univariate distribution evaluation.

EDA Part III: Describe–Assess–Explain

Although data visualization is gaining in popularity, the bulk of the more in-depth data exploration and virtually all of the more complex hypotheses testing remains numeric. All too often, however, the numerical data analyses do not go far enough in translating the usually somewhat abstract results into more meaningful insights. Many analysts find it difficult to look beyond *how* a particular analysis was carried out to *what* the results mean to the organization. The appropriateness and robustness of employed method-ologies will certainly always be of critical importance, but to users, the clarity of results in terms of business implications will carry a lot more meaning. In short, in order for results of analyses to yield highly impactful and advantageous knowledge, analytic findings cannot be confounded with analytic methodologies in a way that impedes users' understanding.

These considerations are particularly important in the context of the actual (exploratory) data analytical continuum of *describe–assess–explain* described next. Although throughout this section, as well as the rest of this book, a number of computational formulas are presented, the overall objective is to develop an intuitive level of understanding of the subject matter being discussed, to enable one to move beyond technical details in presenting their findings. Hence the scattering of technical details is geared toward the identification of the most effective methods of solving a particular problem, with the ultimate goal of bringing to bear the most insightful and advantageous knowledge. An added benefit of this approach is that the ensuing discussion will not get bogged down in an encyclopedic delineation of every conceivable approach available, but instead will be focused on the few that have been shown (in practical business applications) to generate the most valid and reliable outcomes.

Unlike the previously discussed (two) steps of the EDA process which focused on preparatory steps, this part of the EDA process is concerned with the exploration of the available data. In terms of the *describe–assess–explain* continuum: The *describe* part is focused on revealing the basic facts about the data, such as the average customer spending level or the frequency of store visit. The second element, *assess*, captures the goal of developing a fundamental understanding of patterns of relationship in the data. Stated in different terms, it conveys more informationally meaningful insights as it represents the first step of evolving beyond merely detailing of *what-is,* toward *why-it-is.* For instance, does promotional spending coincide with sales gains? Or, is the customer spending related to geography or household characteristics?

Lastly, the *explain* part of the continuum is the informationally richest source of insights as it brings to bear the final building blocks that are needed to transform the more-or-less generic information into unique and thus far more valuable knowledge. In practical business terms, it objectively addresses the reasons behind either the observed failure or the success of a particular action, which fosters a more effective future deployment of organizational resources.

Describe: Univariate Distributional Properties

A part of the Data Compilation and Evaluation process discussed in Chapter 7 was examining—and correcting when appropriate—individual variables' *skewness* and *kurtosis*. Additionally, the initial preparation steps also involved filling-in missing values, as necessary. The end objective of these steps was to arrive at a fully populated (i.e., no missing values) dataset, which also exhibits desired distributional properties.

Data exploration necessitates examining the resultant cleansed data in the context of their informational content. Doing so entails computing several basic univariate descriptors, all of which is necessary to validly describe the informational content and analytic usability of the individual metrics. The choice of the descriptive metrics is primarily a function of the individual variable's measurement scale, specifically, whether it is discrete or continuous.

Discretely coded data, often referred to as *categorical* or *qualitative* (the latter not to be confused with qualitative research or conclusions) assumes only values that represent distinct categories, such as integers, as exemplified by the number of children in a household, the number of UPCs making up a brand, or the number of brand purchases. For instance, a person can have any integer-expressed number of children including 0, but cannot have 2.5 or 4.1 children, just as a brand can have a varying number of specific UPCs (e.g., individual size/flavoring soft-drink alternatives), so long as that number is not fractional. In the vast majority of applied business situations, discrete variables have a finite number of values, as implied by the above examples (although that is not theoretically required).

On the other hand, a *continuous variable* is one that takes on an infinite number of possible values, usually bounded by two extremes.[9] Thus in contrast to categorical metrics where only integer-based values are permissible, here, any value is possible, so long as it falls between the range-defining end points, usually referred to as the maximum and minimum values. Common examples include sale revenues; individuals' age, weight or wealth; or even derived metrics, such as a product repurchase propensity or offer response likelihood. In a practical sense, these otherwise advantageous (from the standpoint of data analyses) basic properties of continuous variables can potentially complicate the interpretation of results, particularly in the sense of differentiating between statistically and practically significant findings (an in-depth discussion of this topic is presented below in the *Beware of Significance Tests* section).

In view of the differences between their respective distributional properties, it is intuitively obvious that the two cannot be subjected to the same types of mathematical manipulations, such as division or multiplication. As a result, the discretely coded data presents far fewer analytic options than does its continuously coded counterpart, which naturally limits its informational value. (Keep in mind that, as previously mentioned, continuous metrics can always be re-coded into categorical ones, but the reverse is not possible. It is important to remember, however, that any continuous-to-categorical conversion will lead to an irreversible loss of information as a direct result of diminished variability of the resultant data.) The practical consequences of the impermissibility of some basic algebraic operations, such as division required to compute average values, can be a source of significant impediments to knowledge creation. That said, careful due diligence is urged when contemplating data capture or variable coding and when possible, preference should be given to continuous measurement.

In view of this fundamental computational schism separating the discretely and continuously coded metrics, different statistical procedures are available to analyze descriptive characteristics. In general, discrete variables are described in terms of *counts* and *frequencies*, while continuous variables are best characterized with the help of measures of *central tendency*, a departure from the average and the range, which measures the spread between the smallest and the largest values.

Discrete Variables

Considering that discrete variables are comprised of a finite—and usually manageable— number of distinct categories, the most effective univariate analytical method involves numeric or graphical (such as the histogram depicted in Figure 8.5) frequency distribution review. However, just because the number of categories is finite, does not mean that it is small. For instance, a brand is typically a categorical (specifically, nominal) metric, yet in many instances, the number of brands in a dataset could be quite large (e.g., ready-to-eat breakfast cereal). Either numeric or graphical frequency distribution will yield a large number of categories making the output somewhat difficult to digest.

An easy corrective step to take is to create groupings of categories. Using the breakfast cereal example cited above, it would be advisable to lump a number of the smaller brands into somewhat homogenous categories, while keeping the largest (i.e., biggest-selling) brands as separate entities. An added benefit of taking that step is that it will help to limit the amount of noise in the data, since low frequency categories contribute disproportionately more to the unexplained variability in the dataset then they do to the explanatory power of most statistical models. In addition, as discussed in Chapters 6 and 7, some statistical techniques may require that the categorical variables be re-coded into *dummy variables*, which in effect converts a single, multi-category metric into multiple binary ones, where the number of resultant metrics is equal to the original number of categories. It is not only tedious, but likely will diminish the parsimony of the resultant statistical model.

Continuous Variables

Continuous variables, being informationally richer, offer more univariate analytical depth. However, the most important insights can be gleaned from the analysis of their central tendencies, variability and dispersion.

MEASURES OF CENTRAL TENDENCY

There are three commonly used categories of measures of univariate central tendency: the average, the median and the mode.[10]

The *average* depicts a typical value in a particular distribution. Computationally, there are multiple ways of calculating averages, with the *mean* being the most commonly used one. Technically, mean can be arithmetic, geometric, harmonic or weighted. The *arithmetic mean*, also referred to as a "straight" or a "simple" mean, is obtained by summing two or more values and dividing the resultant by the number of items. The *geometric mean* is defined as the nth root of the product of all values in a set of numerical data, where n is the number of values in the dataset. Although somewhat more computationally involved, the geometric mean is more resistant to extreme values than the more interpretationally straightforward arithmetic mean. The *harmonic mean* is yet another method of computing the average while minimizing the influence of extreme values and it is defined as the quotient of n divided by the sum of the reciprocals of all the values in a set of numerical data, where n is the number of values in the dataset.

Most statistical applications rely on a simple arithmetic mean, computed as follows:

$$\bar{x} = \frac{\sum_{i=1}^{n} x_i}{n}$$

where,

x_i = an individual observation
n = number of cases

Median and *mode* are the two alternatives to the mean as the measure of average or typical values. A *median* is the middle number in a set of ordered data, usually found with a simple formula:

(n + 1) / 2

where,

n = number of records

In the event a sample contains an odd number of records, the median of that sample will be one of the actual values contained herein; otherwise, if there happens to be an even number of records in a particular sample, the resultant median will be computed as the mean of the two middle values.

The last of the three measures of central tendencies is the *mode*, which is simply the actually observed value that happens to appear in the largest number of records, or put differently, it is an observed value with the highest frequency of occurrence. In contrast to both the mean and the median, the mode is likely to not be unique.

MEASURES OF VARIABILITY

In a statistical sense, the best way to think about any central tendency metric is to consider it to be the expected value of a random variable. A particular variable will, theoretically, at random take on different values and if one were to guess the most likely value that is to be assumed by a random variable, the "best guess" would be the previously discussed measure of central tendency—the mean (hence in statistical analyses, the mean is often characterized as the expected value of a random variable). Given that, if one were to compute the difference between the mean of a particular variable (i.e., the expected value) and each actual value, the difference (or the residual, expressed as actual value-mean value), aggregated across all records would yield the measure of variability contained in the data, in relation to the variable of interest. Hence, the amount of variability in the data can be simply expressed as:

$$\text{Variability} = \sum_{i=1}^{n} (observed - mean)$$

However, there is a caveat here: Given that the mean will fall more-or-less in the middle of the distribution, roughly half the values will be larger than it and half smaller, thus if added, the positive and negative deviations from the mean will cancel each other out, all of which would result in zero (0) variability (or a very small value close to 0). Simply squaring both the positive and negative values will eliminate the canceling effect and lead to a real number-based variability estimate, which offers a convenient way of circumventing the apparent computational flaw. The resultant measure is called *variance*, which is denoted as s^2 and computed as follows[11]:

$$s^2 = \frac{\sum_{i=1}^{n} (x_i - \bar{x})^2}{n - 1}$$

where,

x_i = an individual observation

$\bar{x}$ = mean
n = number of cases

The most practically compelling interpretation of variance is that it is indicative of the explanatory power of a particular variable: The larger the variance, the more likely is the variable to contribute to the resultant explanation. That is because large variance is indicative of significant cross-record differences, which is a necessary prerequisite for any metric to have strong predictive power. In addition, variance also gives rise to another useful statistic—the *standard deviation*—which is a more effective way of comparing the levels of variability across variables. Methodologically, standard deviation is simply the square root of variance, denoted by s[9] and computed as follows[12]:

$$s = \sqrt{\frac{\sum_{i=1}^{n}(x_i - \bar{x})^2}{n-1}}$$

where,

x_i = an individual observation
$\bar{x}$ = mean
n = number of cases

Standard deviation is an important metric because it illustrates the amount of variability contained in a particular variable—the larger the standard deviation, the more variance there is in a particular variable, across cases. Variables with very small standard deviation are informationally poor because they contribute little to the cross case differentiation (this is in contrast to parameter estimates, where small standard deviation is desirable as it is an indication of stable estimates). As was shown in Chapter 7, the low amount of variance can significantly reduce the predictive or explanatory power of otherwise intuitively important metrics. However, because its computation involves squaring of the residual $(x_i - \bar{x})$, both the standard deviation as well as its "parent," the variance is particularly affected by extreme values, which can be a cause for concern, but also underscores the importance of solid data due diligence efforts.

MEASURES OF DISPERSION

The last key univariate distributional characteristic is the range, which is simply the spread between the smallest and largest values. Again, because it measures the absolute distance between the extremes, it can be more informative to use an interval range, such as the frequently used quartiles. Quartiles are points that divide an ordered distribution into four parts, each containing one quarter of all scores. Examining the percentage of all cases falling into each of the four quartiles sheds additional light on the magnitude of spread depicted by the range. A large range accompanied by a condensed quartile distribution (i.e., very few cases falling into quartiles 1 and 4) is informationally poorer than an equally large range accompanied by a more evenly balanced quartile distribution. Any univariate analysis usually requires a relatively tedious variable-by-variable examination of the descriptive characteristics of data, such as the average or the range of values, which tends to narrow the focus to a relatively small subset of all available data. As previously suggested the choice of variables to be included in the analysis subset is largely subjective and driven by the analyst's level of experience. When it comes to transactional databases, there tends to be a short list of candidate metrics, including current customers' spending levels or profitability, product mix, price and promotional elasticity and repurchase frequency. The good news is that most of the important metrics will usually be included in the analysis. The bad news, however, is that it is difficult to come across new, competitively advantageous insights with everyone glued to the same set of metrics.

Even more importantly, univariate data analysis is outcome-oriented, which means it can lead to a virtual avalanche of status quo tidbits while offering little-to-no explanatory diagnostics. As a matter of fact, its implicit assumption of individual metric orthogonality, or independence, means that cross-variable comparisons can be potentially misleading as otherwise spurious associations are interpreted as cause and effect. For instance, a side-by-side comparison of seemingly related factors, such as promotional spending and sales, can suggest that an increase in the latter was caused by the former, where in fact sales gains could have been driven by a different—and unaccounted for—set of factors, such as pricing or distribution changes. This means that while univariate analysis can shed light on *what-is*, it contributes relatively little to the creation of a competitively advantageous knowledge base because it cannot offer reliable insights into the reasons behind the observed outcomes.

Assess: Bivariate Relationships

Potential relationships first suggested by univariate profiling should be initially investigated with the help of bivariate analyses, which assess the persistence and generalizability of pairwise relationships. For instance, a concurrent increase in the levels of sales and promotional spending may be indicative of certain promotions' sales impact, or the observed increase in the frequency of product repurchase seemingly accompanying coupon usage may be indicative of an apparent relationship between the two. In other words, analyses of individual variables may reveal apparent relationships between pairs of variables.

Although methodologically straightforward, analyses of associations can be riddled with hidden traps, such as the *Simpson's paradox*, according to which the direction or strength of the relationship changes when data is aggregated across natural groupings that should otherwise be treated separately. In other words, one should be cautious when searching for "globally valid" relationships—it might be better to assess multiple associations framed in the context of a more homogenized population. Furthermore, few if any databases offer anything other than a subset of all possible data that might be related to a particular phenomenon, in addition to which, the available data may vary in terms of its accuracy. Furthermore, a threat that is particularly potent in the context of bivariate analyses is the potential presence of *intervening* or *moderating factors*, where an outside variable moderates a particular bivariate or conditional relationship (where the strength or direction of the relationship changes across the values of a third variable).

Keeping an eye on these and other potential traps, there are two general approaches to quantifying bivariate relationships:

1. Simple cross-tabulation.
2. Correlation analysis.

When both variables are discrete, cross tabulation—or cross tab for short—is usually the easiest method of assessing the relationship between the two. On the other hand, when both measures are continuous, quantifying their correlation is the most effective method of assessing their relationship. In fact, a correlation coefficient can be computed for virtually all random variables, regardless of their scaling properties. However, even with the proliferation of powerful analytic software applications, correlating discrete variables can be tricky, in view of the multiplicity of esoteric and rarely used tests, so much so that a robust cross tabulation can be quite a viable alternative.

Cross Tabulating Discrete Variables

Bivariate χ^2 (chi square) analysis is the simplest approach to quantifying bivariate relationships with the help of cross tabulation. Since cross tabs involve the construction of matrices, where variables are usually expressed as columns and individual categories as rows, it is obviously advantageous to keep the number of categories relatively low[13] (at this point, we are only concerned with bivariate, or 2 × 2 designs, thus the number of variables would obviously always remain low). The goal of the test is simple: To determine if there are non-spurious associations between the specified variables. It is important to point out that the test is binary—i.e., it can confirm or reject the presence of relationships, but it yields no information regarding the strength of the association. However, as shown below, there are supplemental methods of discerning that information.

In a statistical sense, χ^2 is a nonparametric test, which means that it places no distributional requirements on the sample data. That said, however, in order to yield unbiased estimates, the test requires the sample to be random, the data to be reported as raw frequencies (not percentages), the individual categories to be mutually exclusive and exhaustive and the observed frequencies cannot be too small (the often-cited rule of thumb calls for a minimum cell[14] size of 5 frequencies—in practice, however, a minimum sample size of 50 is more reasonable to assure the robustness of business analyses). The test itself is relatively simple—it compares the difference between the observed and expected frequencies in each cell to determine if significant patterns of similarities (i.e., a relationship) exist between the two variables; it is computed as follows:

$$x^2 = \sum \frac{(O - E)^2}{E}$$

where,

O is the observed value
E is the expected value

The χ^2 test will determine if any two variables are related—however, it is not indicative of the strength of the relationship. A separate measure—Cramer's V—was developed for cross tabulations larger than 2 × 2 to quantify the strength of χ^2-significant relationships. That measure is computed as follows:

$$\text{Cramer's V} = \sqrt{\frac{x^2}{N(\kappa - 1)}}$$

where,

χ^2 is the value of the previously computed chi square statistic
N is the total number of observations
κ is the smaller of the number of rows or columns

Thus in situations where there are more than five cells (i.e., at least one of the variables has more than two categories) the strength of the relationship can be computed. The resultant Cramer's V coefficient is interpreted the same way as the commonly used Pearson's product-moment correlation coefficient, discussed next. Of course, since its computation involves the taking of a square root, the phi values will always be positive, ranging from 0 to +1.

Bivariate Analyses of Mixed Variables

As detailed above, the informationally richer continuous data yields more breadth of bivariate analytical insights. A somewhat more methodologically challenging situation is when one of the variables is continuous while the other is discrete. There are different methods available for assessing bivariate relationships of continuously measured and mixed (continuous + discrete) pairwise variable comparisons, all of which fall under the general umbrella of *correlation analysis* (not to be confused with the earlier mentioned Pearson product moment correlation, which is a special case of bivariate correlation where both variables are continuous).

The term "correlation" has a rather broad usage. Aside from bivariate correlation mentioned above, there are several other expressions of correlation-based associations. Regression analysis, discussed in Chapter 8, produces a measure of *multiple correlations*, which is the correlation of multiple independent variables with a single dependent variable. In addition, there is the *partial correlation*, which is the measure of association of two variables controlling for the impact of other variables; there is also a similarly named *part correlation*, which is similar to partial correlation except that the impact of other variables is only controlled for one of the two correlation measures. Lastly, there is also the *canonical correlation*, discussed in more detail below. All of these are special purpose variants of the general bivariate correlation and will be discussed throughout this book as appropriate. However, in this chapter the focus is on the general discussion of the bivariate correlation.

Technically, *correlation* is a concurrent change in value of two numeric variables, which represents the degree of relationship between those variables. As it is intuitively obvious, the correlation-expressed relationship can be either positive, when an increase in one is accompanied by an increase in the other, or negative, which is when an increase in one is accompanied by a decrease in the other. A numeric result of correlation analyses is a correlation coefficient, which is a metric expressing the strength of the relationship between the two variables of interest, ranging from +1 (perfectly positive correlation) to −1 (perfectly negative correlation) and centered on 0, which denotes a lack of relationship. In the context of knowledge creation, correlation represents an informational improvement over univariate analyses because it begins to explain the phenomenon of interest, which goes a step beyond just summarizing the observed status quo.

In spite of its widespread usage, there is a healthy amount of confusion surrounding the notion of correlation analysis. The bulk of the misunderstanding centers on the scope, or more specifically, the number of items being correlated; a close second is the choice of a specific formulation—i.e., a correlation coefficient.

Overall, correlation is bivariate, which means that it can only be computed for two entities at a time, as a simultaneous assessment of multivariable (i.e., 2+) relationships would be methodologically complex and practically limiting, primarily because it would necessitate the use of conditional expressions and/or interaction terms.[15] That said, it is important to point out that correlations can be computed for a set of two individual variables, as well as for two sets of variables (i.e., for correlation purposes, an entity can have very specific operationalization or it can represent a summary). Both cases, conceptually speaking, will result in bivariate relationships as there are ultimately only two entities involved, yet in the methodological sense there are two distinctly different approaches that need to be employed.

In the case of two individual variables being correlated, an approach generally described as the *bivariate correlation* should be used, while a different methodology known as the *canonical correlation* should be employed with summary-based (i.e., the previously mentioned sets of metrics) operationalizations. It should be noted, however, that in practice the use of canonical correlations is relatively infrequent in business analyses and virtually non-existent in analyses of large transactional databases. The reason for that is that since the canonical correlation is primarily of value in quantifying relationships between two sets of metrics, where each set is intended to measure the same underlying (and usually unobservable, in and of itself) construct,[16] this type of analysis will obviously be of little value to database analytics focused primarily on transactional data. Thus beyond this brief mention, canonical correlation will not be discussed here any further and the term "bivariate correlation" will denote a relationship between two individual variables only.

In terms of specific formulations there are multiple methods of computing correlation coefficients, the bulk of which were devised to address specific data requirements. Table 8.2 offers an enumeration of the different coefficient types.

Largely due to computational convenience, bivariate correlation coefficients are typically computed for multiple pairs of relationships and presented in a matrix format, yielding an efficient and succinct presentation format and one that encourages further explorations and comparisons. In addition, unlike covariances, which are expressed in the original units of measurement, correlations are standardized, i.e., the original units of measurement are replaced with mean = 0 and standard deviation = 1, which makes coefficients directly comparable in spite of any original scale differences.[17]

Figure 8.6 shows an example of a simple correlation matrix. The intersection of a specific row and a column pinpoints a correlation coefficient computed for that particular pair of variables. For instance, the value for factor_3 and factor_4 is 0.535, which is a moderately strong positive correlation. As noted above, the same variables appear in the rows and columns of the matrix, which means that the diagonal values represent correlations of individual variables with themselves, which will always be equal to 1 since a variable is perfectly correlated with itself.[18] However, this means that a half of the matrix shown in Figure 8.6 is redundant because correlations are non-directional, i.e., factor_1–factor_2 correlation is functionally the same as factor_2–factor_1 correlation. In other words, it would suffice to only show values above or below the diagonal, as depicted in Figure 8.7, which makes the matrix appear less busy thus making it easier to visually examine it, particularly when a larger number of variables are included.

However, as pointed out earlier, there is more to computing a correlation coefficient than choosing between a bivariate and a canonical correlation. The proliferation of the "point and click" computing capabilities has the unfortunate side effect of fuzzying the

Table 8.2 Coefficients of Correlation

Correlation Measure	Description	Application
Pearson's product-moment (r)	Both variables are continuous and normally distributed; relationship is linear	The most commonly used formulation
Spearman's rank (rho)	Both variables ordinal or one ordinal and one interval	The most commonly used substitute for Pearson's r
Kendall's rank (tau)	Both variables ordinal or one ordinal and one interval	A less frequently used alternative to Spearman's rho
Polyserial	Interval and ordinal variables (3+ categories) and the latter reflects underlying continuum; bivariate normality required	The preferred method used to correlate interval and multichotomous ordinal variables
Polychoric	Both variables are dichotomous or ordinal, but reflect underlying continuous variables; bivariate normality required	The preferred method to correlte two dichotomous or ordinal variables
Biserial	Same as polyserial, but the discrete variable is dichotomous	Mostly in theoretical research employing structural equation modeling
Rank biserial	An ordinal variable is related to a truly dichotomous variable (no underlying continuity)	Rarely used in practical research
Point biserial	An interval is correlated with a truly dichotomous (no underlying continuity)	Can use Pearson's r formular
Phi	Both variables are dichotomous	A substitute for Pearson's r used with dichotomies

	factor_1	factor_2	factor_3	factor_4	factor_5	factor_6	factor_7
factor_1	1	.987	−.166	−.260	−.072	−.312	.797
factor_2	.987	1	−.153	−.242	−.054	−.329	.798
factor_3	−.166	−.153	1	.535	.199	−.139	−.113
factor_4	−.260	−.242	.535	1	.268	−.142	−.213
factor_5	−.072	−.054	.199	.268	1	−.022	.013
factor_6	−.312	−.329	−.139	−.142	−.022	1	−.362
factor_7	.797	.798	−.113	−.213	.013	−.362	1

Figure 8.6 A Correlation Matrix

distinctiveness among the different correlation coefficient formulations. By far the most commonly used formulation—Person's product-moment correlation coefficient—tends to be the default in popular statistical packages, such as SAS or SPSS, but it is certainly not the only formulation and even more importantly, it carries specific data distributional (normal vs. non-normal) and relationship type (i.e., linear vs. non-linear) requirements, the violation of which will significantly limit the reliability of the resultant statistic. The

	factor_1	factor_2	factor_3	factor_4	factor_5	factor_6	factor_7
factor_1	1						
factor_2	.987	1					
factor_3	−.166	−.153	1				
factor_4	−.260	−.242	.535	1			
factor_5	−.072	−.054	.199	.268	1		
factor_6	−.312	−.329	−.139	−.142	−.022	1	
factor_7	.797	.798	−.113	−.213	.013	−.362	1

Figure 8.7 A Correlation Matrix: Non-Redundant Elements Only

two other bivariate correlation coefficients—Spearman's and Kendall's rank correlations—do not make specific data or relationship type requirements, which makes them suitable substitutes under certain circumstances.

Somewhat complicating the picture are the mixed-scale correlations, particularly where one variable is measured on a metric scale (i.e., interval or ratio) while the other one is measured on a non-metric scale (i.e., nominal or ordinal). There are two approaches to dealing with such situations:

1. Re-code the metric into a non-metric variable and use Spearman's rank correlation coefficient if the result is an ordinally scaled variable and use the polychoric correlation with dichotomies (see Table 8.2). This takes advantage of the fact that continuously measured variables are informationally richer, which means they can always be reduced into categorical ones, simply by breaking out their continuous values into discrete ranges. Of course, the re-coding process tends to be arbitrary since most continuous scales do not have natural discrete break points.
2. The second approach is to replace the product-moment correlation with amended formulations which account for scale differences. As shown in Table 8.2, there are multiple coefficients available: the *biserial, polyserial, polychoric, point biserial, phi,* etc. In general, the choice of the appropriate formulation is primarily a function of the type of measurement scale and its constancy between the variables being correlated. Specifically, different computational methods should be used when both variables have the same scale characteristics—such as both are ordinal or nominal—versus when their measurement scales are different, such as one is ordinal and the other is nominal. Figure 8.8 below offers a simple decision rule to be used when choosing among the available correlation formulations.

To select an appropriate formulation, start out by identifying the measurement scale of each of the variables to be correlated. As discussed earlier, a random variable can be nominal, ordinal, interval or ratio. Nominally scaled variables carry no ordering or magnitudinal information whatsoever—they are simply labels intended primarily for convenience. Although their informational value is quite limited, the biserial correlation coefficient can be used to quantify their relations to a metrically measured variable. An ordinal scale is informationally richer as here data points are rank-ordered, although it is still limited insofar as it contains no information about the cross-category spacing (i.e., spacing is not assumed to be equal or have any other numerical properties). An even richer source of information is the interval ratio, which in addition to being rank-ordered is also assumed to be equally spaced (i.e., the distance between adjoining pairs of values

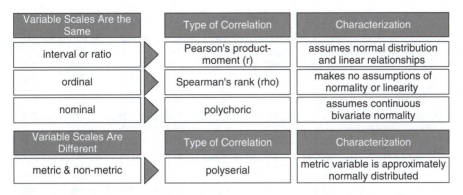

Figure 8.8 Correlation Coefficient Types

is constant across the entire value continuum, which means that the measurement distance between values 1 and 2 is the same as the distance between values 2 and 3, 4 and 5, etc.). Lastly, the ratio scale contains all of the informational characteristics of the other three scales, in addition to which it also has a rational point of origin, such as age or income.

If both variables are measured with either an interval or a ratio scale (they could both be the same, or one interval *and* the other ratio) and their distributions are approximately normal *and* their relationship is assumed to be more-or-less linear, Pearson's product-moment correlation will yield the most robust estimate of the their relationship. If, on the other hand, either of those conditions is not met—i.e., the variables are not either interval or ratio, at least one is not normally distributed or their relationship is believed to not be linear—Spearman's rank correlation is the appropriate choice.[19] An example of a typical output (generated with the help of SPSS) depicting a correlation matrix, using Pearson's product-moment method is shown below.

As shown in Figure 8.9, aside from the correlation coefficient itself there are several other pieces of information included in the output, all playing a distinct though somewhat different role in the evaluation of the correlation results.

The first is the effective sample size. An *effective sample size* is the actual number of cases used in the particular analysis, which is contrasted with a *nominal sample size*, which is the total number of cases in the dataset. Under certain circumstances, most notably a persistent missing value problem, the effective sample size can be quite smaller than the nominal one, which at some point may diminish the robustness of the findings. What then is the minimum acceptable sample size? There is no single concrete minimum, as that is usually dependent on multiple factors, most importantly the amount of variation in the data. That said, the best general guideline to minimum sample sizing can be derived from the Central Limit Theorem, which states that whenever a random sample is taken from any distribution, the sample means will be approximately normally distributed, which seems to imply that beyond a certain point, sample size expansion may not be necessary. The proverbial $64,000 question is, of course, what is that threshold? As a general rule of thumb, it is believed that fewer than about 30 observations calls for nonparametric analysis, while more than 30 but fewer than 50 observations should be treated with caution. In other words, a sample size of as few as 50 records may be sufficient. As previously discussed, normal distribution is a requirement of Pearson's

Correlations

		factor_1	factor_2	factor_3	factor_4	factor_5	factor_6	factor_7
factor_1	Pearson Correlation	1	.987**	-.166*	-.260**	-.072	-.312**	.797**
	Sig. (2-tailed)		.000	.011	.000	.272	.000	.000
	N	235	235	235	235	235	235	235
factor_2	Pearson Correlation	.987**	1	-.153*	-.242**	-.054	-.329**	.798**
	Sig. (2-tailed)	.000		.019	.000	.408	.000	.000
	N	235	235	235	235	235	235	235
factor_3	Pearson Correlation	-.166*	-.153*	1	.535**	.199**	-.139*	-.113
	Sig. (2-tailed)	.011	.019		.000	.002	.033	.084
	N	235	235	235	235	235	235	235
factor_4	Pearson Correlation	-.260**	-.242**	.535**	1	.268**	-.142*	-.213**
	Sig. (2-tailed)	.000	.000	.000		.000	.029	.001
	N	235	235	235	235	235	235	235
factor_5	Pearson Correlation	-.072	-.054	.199**	.268**	1	-.022	.013
	Sig. (2-tailed)	.272	.408	.002	.000		.737	.839
	N	235	235	235	235	235	235	235
factor_6	Pearson Correlation	-.312**	-.329**	-.139*	-.142*	-.022	1	-.362**
	Sig. (2-tailed)	.000	.000	.033	.029	.737		.000
	N	235	235	235	235	235	235	235
factor_7	Pearson Correlation	.797**	.798**	-.113	-.213**	.013	-.362**	1
	Sig. (2-tailed)	.000	.000	.084	.001	.839	.000	
	N	235	235	235	235	235	235	235

**Correlation is significant at the 0.01 level (2-tailed).
*Correlation is significant at the 0.05 level (2-tailed).

Figure 8.9 Pearson's Two-Tailed Correlations with Significance Tests

product-moment correlation; hence attaining an appropriately sized sample is important to the validity of the statistic.

In practice, however, prohibitively small sample sizes are rare in database analytics, given the size of most databases. Interestingly, the sample size "over-abundance" is a more likely challenge as too large a sample size can lead to an artificial inflation of statistical significance, a commonly used though controversial measure of the non-spuriousness of correlation and other coefficients. This is an important consideration and as such is discussed in more detail in the subsequent section.

Lastly, a proper assessment of a correlation coefficient also involves a choice between a one- and a two-tail test. A *one-tail test* is used to identify events that are different only in one direction in reference to the average—such as customer spending levels that are considerably above the average. In that sense, a one-tail test would not differentiate between the average and extremely small values, as it is focused on detecting only abnormally large values. A *two-tail test*, on the other hand, can be used to identify values that are either significantly greater or smaller than the expected or average values. Naturally, the two-tail test is informationally richer because it can detect unexpected events on both ends of the continuum—those significantly larger as well as significantly smaller than the average or expected values.

In the past, it was also necessary to specify the so-called level of *statistical significance*. Technically, the significance level of a test is the maximum probability of incorrectly rejecting a true null hypothesis, which is also known as the Type I error.[20] Since the null hypothesis typically stipulates that there are no differences between the entities being tested, such as two mean product repurchase rates, the concept of statistical significance is in fact a measure of the amount of risk an analyst is willing to accept in concluding that noteworthy differences exist where in fact there are none. In the context of correlation analyses, significance testing is used to assess the degree to which the reported bivariate correlations are manifestations of enduring relationships or a mere product of random chance. However, statistical significance testing suffers from some severe deficiencies, which are particularly evident in the context of database analytics. Given the pivotal role of significance testing in virtually all sample-based analyses, the limitations of significance testing deserve a more exhaustive treatment, presented in the next section.

Beware of Significance Tests!

Statistical significance testing (SST) is a hypothesis testing tool, the purpose of which is to identify universally true effects. SST's secondary and closely related objective is that of generalizing sample-based insights onto a larger population. Although principally a theory development method, significance testing has in recent years been adopted to promotional program measurement where it gained quick acceptance as the impact validation standard.

Operationally, SST utilizes any of the known distribution statistical difference tests, such as F, t, or χ^2 to compare observed effects to expected effects with the purpose of distinguishing between spurious and persistent relationships, as shown below in Figure 8.10.

While the statistics utilized in significance testing (i.e., the above referenced F, t, or χ^2) are themselves methodologically sound, their program measurement applications tend to outstretch their usability limits leading to misapplications and misinterpretations. Some of it is due to simple user error, but a considerable share of SSTs misuse can be attributed to fundamental lack of fit between *theory testing* and typical *business objectives.*

Although rarely compared "side-by-side," theory testing and applied knowledge creation processes differ on some very important dimensions. Perhaps most importantly, theory testing aims to uncover universally true knowledge claims, while marketing analytics focus on the identification of sustainable competitive advantage. It follows that

Significance Tests	Definition	What Does the Result Mean?
Chi-square test	A test of statistical significance based on a comparison of the observed cell frequencies of cross-tabulation of two variables that would be expected under the null hypothesis of no relationship .	❖ If p-value is less than the chosen threshold (for example, $\alpha = 0.05$), conclude that there is a relationship between two variables with 95% statistical significance .
t-test	A test of significance for continuous variables where the population variance is unknown and the sample is assumed to have been drawn from a normally distributed population.	❖ If p-value is less than the chosen threshold (for example, $\alpha = 0.05$), conclude that there is a relationship between two variables with 95% statistical significance .
F-test	A statistical test of the difference of means for two or more groups **(Analysis of variance:** Sample is distributed normally).	❖ If p-value is less than the chosen threshold (for example, $\alpha l= 0.05$), conclude that the means of two or more populations we test are different with 95% statistical significance ❖ If the test result is significant, perform post hoc test to determine specific differences.

Figure 8.10 Types of Statistical Significance Tests

significance testing is used as a *sample-to-population* generalization tool for scientific theory building purposes, and as a *now-to-future* or longitudinal replicability tool for applied knowledge creation. This is a critical distinction as it gives rise to one of the more common SST application errors discussed later in this text.

Another common SST misapplication stems from its dependence on sample size. Sample size and the likelihood of detecting statistical significance are highly correlated, so much so that at a moderately large sample size even inordinately trivial differences can become statistically significant, while not being statistically significant at a smaller sample size (everything else being the same). For a variety of reasons that are not important at this moment, theory testing research typically utilizes small sample sizes leading to limited sample size distortion. The opposite, however, is true for most applied business endeavors which depend on large scale (i.e., large sample size) for business viability, resulting in a considerable sample size distortion.

Expected precision of estimates is yet another (albeit more subtle) theory testing vs. applied business knowledge-creation distinction. In short, while theory development is primarily concerned with the identification of universally true relationships and less so with the exact quantification of the magnitude of effects, business analyses are almost single-mindedly focused on quantifying program-specific incrementality. It is a matter of pragmatism: The goal of business actions, such as promotions, is to benefit a particular organization only; hence it is of little concern to business analyses if a particular relationship is not generalizable to other users. In fact, from the standpoint of a particular organization, the lack of cross-user generalizability is actually a preferred outcome.

Putting the above pieces together suggests that when applied to a large-scale database analytical initiatives, statistical significance testing is of questionable value for three key reasons: First, extremely small treated vs. control differences are likely to be found statistically significant even if their magnitude renders them practically inconsequential, which will then give rise to the previously discussed statistical vs. practical significance divergence, ultimately leading to SST misapplication. Second, significance testing does not support future replicability generalizations, which means that we cannot use the results from today's test as basis for forming expectations regarding tomorrow's rollout; again, an issue of central importance to promotional program measurement. Third, treatment attributable incrementality cannot be expressed as an exact quantity, which although not a show-stopper is still less than ideal, particularly when the range of effects encompasses both positive and negative values.

Those are not trivial differences. Significance tests are computationally relatively straightforward and highly suggestive of normative applicability limits. At the same time, the goals of the theory building and practical applications-focused analyses are oftentimes quite different. The interaction between the significance tests' applicability limits and the different (i.e., theoretical vs. practical) applications of those tests are sufficient to question the wisdom of unqualified significance testing usage in business applications. SST's sample size dependence (i.e., the likelihood of a given relationship being deemed "statistically" significant increases as the sample size gets larger, everything else being the same), inability to support longitudinal conclusions (i.e., offering an objective quantification of the probability of future replicability of current relationships) or the basic incommensurability of scientific and business objectives (i.e., seeking universally true generalizations vs. future replicability) all highlight the dangers of blind SST reliance by business analysts.

Faced with these shortcomings of an otherwise key methodological element, analysts grew accustomed to drawing a line of demarcation between the *statistical* and practical *significance*. In effect, it has become a commonplace in applied marketing analytics to expressly differentiate between the "statistically significant results we accept" (i.e., the results that are deemed both statistical and practically significant) and the "statistically significant result we do not accept" (i.e., the results that are statistically significant but at the same time are assumed to be practically insignificant).

Let's pause for a minute: Isn't there something unsettling about the manifestly *quantitative* statistical significance tests having to be *qualified* in order to become of value to business analyses? By extension, isn't it equally unsettling that the task of differentiating between "important" and "not important" statistically significant results—for those who believe in the validity of such split—be a matter of a subjective judgment? And finally, if significance testing is indeed a robust and objective program impact validation tool, why is there even a need to arbitrarily accept some of its "significant" findings while rejecting other equally statistically "significant" findings?

In view of these and other application question marks surrounding statistical significance testing, it is recommended that the reliance on using this statistic as an objective importance threshold be kept to a minimum, to avoid the introduction of a subjective bias and even more importantly, of reaching an incorrect conclusion. Recommended strategies for how and when to use it to minimize the aforementioned dangers, as well as some plausible alternatives are discussed later.

Explain: Multivariate Analyses

Although potentially insightful, bivariate correlation is, well, only bivariate. In many business contexts the development of true understanding requires the assessment of an interplay of multiple factors, which in tech talk translates into multivariate (i.e., multi-variable) analyses. Oftentimes, even making more sense out of the observed correlations requires a broader, multivariable analyses as it is common for two key variables to be correlated due to being jointly driven by a third factor. Furthermore, as previously noted, correlation is non-directional, as reflected in an often-cited adage of "correlation is not causation." Promotional spending and sales level might be correlated, but from a business standpoint a more pertinent question is: Do promotions *cause* sales to product sales to rise? Consider Figure 8.11 below.

The four quadrants depicted in Figure 8.11 suggest that aside from the presence of either a positive (Quadrant 1) or a negative (Quadrant 2) relationships, the correlation analysis can also reveal that there is no linear relationship between the variables of interest (Quadrant 3), but what it cannot detect is a non-linear relationship suggesting a *dependence* of one variable on the other (Quadrant 4). Overall, the bivariate correlation illustrate above can be quite helpful in shedding light on the existence of a potential X–Y relationship, but it falls short of offering even a minimal amount of *causal* explanation—in other words, is X causing Y, or is Y causing X?

Generally, the type of relationship depicted in Quadrant 4 is reflective of curvilinear effects, which are most effectively explored—in a causal sense—with the help of multiple regression analyses and more specifically, by computing a squared term (technically, capturing a second-order interaction effect). Only focusing on the two variables X and Y, where X is assumed to be dependent on Y, the X–Y dependence can be tested as shown below:

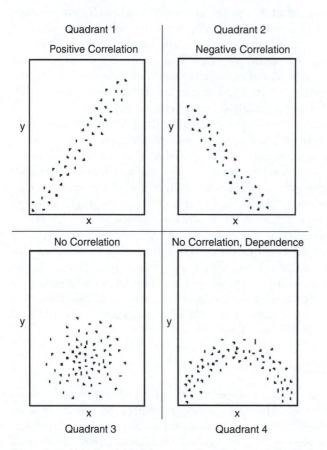

Figure 8.11 Distinguishing between Correlation and Dependence

$$y = \alpha + \beta x_1 + \beta x_1^2 + \varepsilon$$

where,

α is an intercept term (practically interpretable only when the _ terms equal 0)
βx_1 is a test of linear dependence of X on Y
βx_1^2 is a test of curvilinear dependence of X on Y
ε is an error term, or the unexplained residual

Another common analytical data exploratory challenge involves describing interactions taking place in the context of dependence analysis. As mentioned earlier, a correlation between X and Y can be a result of both X and Y being impacted by yet another factor, Z. For instance, product sales (Y) can be dependent to some degree on promotions (X), as well as specific pricing decisions (Z). Assessing an interaction between two predictors (X and Z) involves computing a new variable that is a multiplicative combination of X and Z. As a result, to test the dependence of Y on X and Z, as well as any potential interactions between X and Z, we can again use a multiple regression model to specify the following set of dependencies:

$$y = \alpha + \beta_1 x_1 + \beta_2 x_2 + \beta_{12} x_1 x_2 + \varepsilon$$

where,

α is an intercept term (practically interpretable only when the _ term equals 0)
$\beta_1 x_1$ is linear dependence of X on Y
$\beta_2 x_2$ is linear dependence of Z on Y
$\beta_{12} x_1 x_2$ is multiplicative dependence of X and Z on Y (X–Z interaction)
ε is an error term, or the unexplained residual

The above assumes that X and Z, as well Y, are all continuous (i.e., measured with either interval or ratio scales describe earlier) variables. In fact, however, these or any other metrics could be discrete. For instance, promotional spending could be dichotomously coded as "high" or "low" and product pricing could be coded as "regular" and "discounted."

Factorial analysis of variance (ANOVA), a special case of regression analysis, is the best exploratory analytical tool for tackling that problem. The inner-working of ANOVA is somewhat different from that of the above outlined regression. In essence, ANOVA carries out a number of tests, where the means of the dependent variable, such as product sales, are compared across a number of different factors (individual independent variables, such as the discretely coded promotional spending and product price) and their levels (the individual values of independent variables, such as "high" promotional spending, or "regular" pricing). The end objective is to pinpoint statistically significant[21] interactions between specific factor-level conjoints and the dependent variable of interest.

The so-operationalized pursuit of maximally complete explanation typically brings to the forefront the notion of informational domain specification. In other words, is the available data sufficient to generate a complete explanation of the phenomenon of interest?

The *informational domain specification* (IDS) is a relatively complex—and in the opinion of some—an overly academic consideration. In the most general sense, it is a conceptual "blueprint" of the entire explanatory model, spelling out indicator-construct assignments as well as the entire web of the dependence and interdependence relationships. It can certainly take on that appearance, but at the same time, it is crucially important to the creation of competitively advantageous knowledge. IDS is the only objective way of assessing the adequacy of the available raw data to support the stated informational objectives, as tackled with the above outlined statistical methodologies. Conceptually and methodologically, it is a more general form of what is commonly known as *model specification*, which is a critical component of sound theory testing research.[22] Given all that, IDS is discussed in more depth in the next section.

Informational Domain Specification

Throughout the database analytical process exemplified in Figure 1.4, there are several "transitions" where the objective, well-codified science of data analyses intersects the subjective and rarely codified art—or perhaps more correctly stated, intuition—of the analyst. Correctly specifying the informational domain is likely the pinnacle of that intersection.

In everyday terms, informational domain specification is the process by means of which analysts select and arrange specific (raw) data elements to form a conceptual model, based upon which specific (statistical) analyses and tests will be carried out, all with the goal of answering the questions posed by the stated informational needs. *Informational domain specification* represents an intersection of several competing considerations: First, the scope, in terms of the selected variables, needs to be sufficient. At the same time, or second, the selected variable list needs to be non-redundant and operationally comparable (i.e., variables that are to be related to each other on the same plain of abstraction need to expressed at a comparable level of aggregation). Third, the model needs to exhibit a certain level of parsimony—in other words, throwing every conceivable metric into the mix is undesirable from both the statistical (introduction of numerous, albeit spurious correlations tends to detract from finding a clear solution) and interpretational (describing an outcome in terms of an excessively large number of "important" factors in some way defeats the purpose of conducting the analysis) points of view.

In terms of the outcomes of the IDS process, the informational domain can be just-, over- or under-specified. Ideally, an informational domain is *just-specified*, which is accomplished when a sufficient number of non-trivial explanatory variables are available. Of course, knowing whether or not that is the case is in many regards "half the battle." First of all, no single, objective appropriate number of variables-type benchmark exists, largely because the number of metrics is not important per se, so long as the resultant solution is manageable and maximally explanatory. In other words, the number of explanatory variables is sufficiently but not excessively large when it yields a statistically exhaustive explanation, i.e., the model explains the vast majority of the variability in the data, while at the same time it is small enough to be parsimonious[23] and practically actionable. Given the obvious difficulty of balancing the number of variables and the amount of explanation contained in the model, more often than not a domain is either under- or over-specified.

An *under-specified informational domain* is one that yields too few non-trivial explanatory variables, which translates into an insufficiently small amount of the variability in the data being explained by the model (which means that any predictions made based on such a model are likely to be unstable as well as inaccurate). On the other hand, an *over-specified domain* is one that depends on an excessively large number of trivial, yet correlated explanatory factors, for the explanation of the variability in the data. This is typically an indication of either a relative scarcity of truly explanatory data, or a poor data management strategy, such as making use of too many disaggregate metrics.

In practice, informational under-specification diminishes the explanatory power and reliability of information, simply because under-specified explanations are spurious, or chance-driven. Over-specified explanations, on the other hand, are interpretationally cumbersome because they employ an excessively large number of practically unimportant factors. Under-specification is most often a function of data scarcity, which in many instances is hard to remedy. Over-specification is usually a function of flawed variable retention rationale, such as the use of too many disaggregate metrics or over-reliance on statistical significance testing (SST),[24] which is used frequently as a variable inclusion or retention standard. Excessive dependence on statistical significance tests increases the likelihood that variables of negligible importance will be included alongside highly explanatory factors, particularly as the sample size increases. As large sample size analyses are becoming a commonplace due to the proliferation of large databases coupled with rapid gains in data processing technologies, the frequency of the significance-testing-induced informational over-specification increases, so much so that a more in-depth discussion of the, well, significant limitations of SST seems warranted.

Although much of the informational domain specification is situational, as it depends of the specific characteristics of data, there are a number of general steps that can be taken to increase the likelihood of the informational domain being just-specified. These include metric aggregation, indexing and variable transformations.

METRIC AGGREGATION

Transactional and other databases usually are made up of variables exhibiting various degrees of aggregation, or specificity. As detailed in the *Data Basics* chapter, some of the marketing data is a by-product of operations (e.g., point-of-sales), other data is purposefully acquired (e.g., consumer satisfaction surveys), and still other represent third-party estimates (e.g., geodemographics), resulting in considerable amount of informational properties invariance. Homogenizing the individual metrics' levels of aggregation can be a relatively complex task, as it may entail computing summary measures for detailed, indicator-level metrics (usually with the help of factor analysis discussed in the next chapter), as well as householding of more disaggregate purchase details. Nonetheless, combining detailed metrics into more aggregate, summary-level variables will have the desirable effect of reducing the number of explanatory variables while retaining the bulk of the original metrics' informational content.

INDEXING

As it is used in the database analytical process outlined in this book, *indexing* refers to the assigning of predetermined labels to database records with the goal of delineating distinct and non-overlapping categories of database records (e.g., households, customers, etc.). In some regards, indexing leads to the creation of "shadow" variables, which are typically used as the basis for record grouping and homogenization of analytical subsets, such as identifying and subsequently selecting (for analysis) only high-value customers. The resultant metrics are almost always categorical which, on the one hand may limit the usability of such metrics in certain contexts, while at the same time may expand the data file's informational domain by creating new predictors.

TRANSFORMATIONS

The *Analytic File Creation* chapter outlined a number of potential data transformations that can be used to correct undesirable distributional properties, such as skewness or kurtosis. Data transformations can also be a useful informational domain specification tool—specifically, the underlying measurement characteristics of data can be re-coded by reversing negatively coded consumer opinions into positively coding ones, or by standardizing items measured on magnitudinally dissimilar scales. Carefully transforming selected metrics will increase the availability of "eligible" variables, thus diminishing the possibility of under-specification.

Data Reduction

The last general area of the data exploration involves possible data reduction steps. In contrast to the previously described data exploration process, which is an integral part of any database exploratory analytical endeavor, data reduction may be a desired component of that process, but not necessarily a required one. Whether or not it should be considered depends on the type of data, which is meant in both an informational as well as a technical sense.

Informationally, a database can contain a number of disaggregate metrics, many of which might be indicators of a more general (and meaningful) higher-order construct. For instance, consumer survey data might contain a number of substantively similar, yet distinct variables, simply because the psychometric measurement theory dictates that latent constructs (such as product interest or brand attitude) should be assessed with multiple indicators, because a single (observable) indicator is rarely, if ever, a perfect predictor of the underlying (unobservable) construct. In the end, a database housing the results of consumer or other surveys is likely to contain a number of metrics which in a singular form are informationally trivial and which should be combined into more meaningful, higher-order aggregates.

At the same time, it is important to consider the technical aspects of such metrics, most notably, their measurement scales. Ideally, these disaggregate metrics are continuous (i.e., measured with either an interval or ratio scales), as that would offer the maximum amount of analytical flexibility. As previously noted, continuous variables are informationally richer than their discrete counterparts, making them analyzable with a wide array of statistical techniques. This is important in the context of data reduction considerations because the most commonly used data reduction technique—*factor* or *principal component analysis*[25]—requires the input variables to be continuously distributed.

However, data reduction is not limited to surveys. Some databases are "cluttered" with so many metrics that basic exploratory analyses or even simple reporting become very cumbersome. Should that be the case, it might be worthwhile to consider extracting the most usable subset of the data into a more easily analyzable sub-environment—in effect setting aside a smaller *data mart*, while keeping everything else in a larger *data warehouse* (see the *Data Basics* chapter for a more in-depth discussion of the differences between data marts and data warehouses). In doing so, it is important to keep in mind that *what is being done* is as important as *how it is being done*. In that sense, selecting a subset of a large database can be a daunting task and making arbitrary choices between what to keep vs. what not to keep would obviously be counterproductive. Hence, at least in some instances, rather than selecting a smaller subset of data, it might be more desirable to compress large quantities of detailed (and individually informationally trivial) metrics into a far smaller number of more aggregate variables. In analytical jargon, this amounts to data reduction analyses.

In general, there are two distinctly different statistical approaches to data reduction:

1. Factor analysis.
2. Correspondence analysis.

Factor Analysis

Although sometimes used to denote a single statistical technique, *factor analysis* is in fact a generic name referring to a class of multivariate statistical methodologies tasked with defining the underlying structure of the data and extracting sets of common underlying dimensions, known as factors. In essence, the analysis evaluates the pattern of cross-variable correlations and identifies interrelationships in a way that pinpoints the inherent variable groupings, giving rise to an objective summing up of multiple disaggregate metrics into a single higher-order variable.[26] Since the underlying analyses are based on inter-variable product-moment correlations, factor analysis requires the input data to be continuous.

Perhaps more than most other multivariate techniques, factor analysis is an iterative method that is built around the loop of *input–analysis–outcome evaluation–input changes–analysis*, etc. The basic reason for the repetitive iteration is the weeding out of specific metrics that may only be spuriously correlated with others—i.e., could not be included in a robust higher-order metric aggregation. Again, because the method simultaneously considers the entire correlation matrix (i.e., all inter-variable correlations), finding a robust, reliable solution requires the identification and elimination of random distractions.

Aside from the data, it is also important to make several analysis-related decisions, as discussed below. The first two—the extraction and rotation methods—are input decisions, while the third consideration—retention criteria—is the output consideration.

Extraction Method

There are several different approaches to identifying the underlying variable groupings, including the principle component analysis, generalized least squares, maximum likelihood, alpha factoring, etc. Naturally, these decisions should be made in the context of data specifics, but in general, the *principal component analysis* was found to yield stable and valid results, across situations. However, given its inner-workings (i.e., it is built around the extraction of a single factor—the principal component—followed by a redistribution of factor membership), this extraction method necessitates a careful selection of a factor rotation method, discussed next. It is important to keep in mind that the extraction order is important, as the amount of the total variance explained by individual factors is a function of their extraction order. Thus the first factor will always explain more variability than the second, which in turn will always explain more than the third, etc.[27] It is also important to keep in mind that the resultant factors are based on an assumed linearity—in other words; non-linear cross-variable interrelationships are likely to go unrecognized.

Rotation Method

Since factor analysis essentially leads to a grouping of variables in a multidimensional space typically represented by the axes of Cartesian coordinates, a decision needs to be made regarding the stipulated interrelationship among those classifying axes. In general, that relationship can either allow for some factor correlations (a provision statistically known as *oblique* rotation) or it can assume full factor independence (statistically known as *orthogonal* rotation). Once that decision is made, the axes themselves need to be mathematically rotated to find the best fit for the previously extracted variable groupings. Although there are a number of specific axis rotation algorithms that have been developed, they can all be categorized as either *orthogonal* or *oblique*, since the underlying factors can either be assumed to be correlated or uncorrelated. Orthogonal extraction methods include varimax, equimax and quartimax, while the oblique extraction methods include oblimin, promax and orthoblique techniques. Although subtle computational differences separate the individual orthogonal and oblique rotation algorithms, in practice they tend to produce results that are not interpretationally different.

Retention Criteria

The key output consideration is how many factors to retain. In that sense, factor analysis could be viewed on a continuum ranging from the *number of factors = the number of input variables*, to the *number of factors = 1* (i.e., all input data is summarized into a single factor). Clearly, neither of the two extremes is particularly appealing or usable, which is why it is important to identify an objective decision rule. There are typically two options: 1. a pre-existing knowledge of the number of factors that are to be expected, or 2. eigenvalue[28] = 1 rule. Although an analyst might certainly have an expectation of the number of factors based on previous research or theoretical considerations, it is far more common for that not to be the case. The frequently used "eigenvalue = 1" rule of thumb simply postulates that a combination of several variables (i.e., a factor) that cannot explain the amount of variance that is an equivalent of a single variable has trivial informational value and should be treated as a set of spurious correlations, rather than enduring cross-variable relationships.

The end result of the three-part consideration set outlined above should be a rotated factor matrix, exemplified in Figure 8.12.

As shown in the figure, there were 5 separate factors extracted in this particular analysis. The intersection of rows and columns identify variable-factor memberships and the individual coefficients spell out factor loadings, which represent the strength of the relationship (i.e., correlation) between the underlying factor and its individual components. The factor loadings are standardized, ranging from −1 to +1 and the coefficients smaller than .4 were not shown to make the visual output interpretation easier. It is worth pointing out that several variables, not shown, were excluded from the analysis during earlier iterations due to being split-loaded, which is a condition of a variable exhibiting strong correlation to more than a single factor (typically, it exhibits itself in two or more approximately equal-sized loadings).

The end result of the analysis depicted in Figure 8.12 was the compression of a set of 15 disaggregate input variables into 5 higher-order factors, which represents a 3-to-1 reduction in a number of variables—a rather moderate reduction. Depending on the type of data, an average ratio of 10-to-1 or so may be plausible.

To account for cross-factor differences in the number of constituent variables (as previously implied, the first extracted factor typically pulls the highest number of input variables, followed by the second extracted factor, etc.), the resultant factor composites are also weighted by the number of inputs variables, as shown below:

$$factor_{\kappa} = (variable_1 + variable_2 + variablen)/_n$$

The resultant summed and weighted factor scores are themselves continuously distributed metrics that can be used as inputs into subsequent analysis, such as cluster analysis discussed in the *Segmentation* chapter, or regression analysis outlined in the *Behavioral Predictions* chapter.

Beyond the factor structure shown above, it is also important to consider the amount of the total input dataset's variance explained by the analysis. Figure 8.13 shows the typical evaluative output.

As shown above, the 5 factors (called *components* above, due to the *principal component analysis* being used as the extraction method) cumulatively explain nearly three-quarters

Rotated Component Matrix[a]

	Component				
	1	2	3	4	5
CompanyAge_ Transformed					.831
NumberofEmployees_ Transformed	.854				
AuditFeesOther_ Transformed	.556				
AuditFeesTax_ Transformed	.591				
NumberofBoard MeetingsLastYear_ Transformed				-.781	
DominantShareholder Percentage_Transformed			.897		
InsiderControl Percentage_Transformed			.801		
InsidersPlus5Owners Percentage_Transformed			.791		
SharePrice52WkHi_ Transformed		.979			
SharePrice52WkLo_ Transformed		.939			
SharePriceCurrent_ Transformed		.971			
SharesOutstanding_ Transformed	.828				
Revenues_Transformed	.880				
PreviousCEOTenure_ Transformed				.697	
CEOAllOtherComp_ Transformed					.504

Extraction Method: Principal Component Analysis.
Rotation Method: Varimax with Kaiser Normalization.

a. Rotation converged in 5 iterations.

Figure 8.12 Rotated Factor Matrix

Total Variance Explained

	Rotation Sums of Squared Loadings		
Component	Total	% of Variance	Cumulative %
1	3.137	20.911	20.911
2	3.073	20.484	41.396
3	2.291	15.272	56.668
4	1.307	8.714	65.382
5	1.242	8.280	73.662

Extraction Method: Principal Component Analysis.

Figure 8.13
Explained Variance

of all variability in the input dataset, which reflects a good fit of the final factor structure to the data. It means that the initial set of 15 variables could be replaced with a much smaller set of 5 factors, an 80% reduction in the number of variables achieved at the cost of loss of only about 24% of the potential explanatory power, which can be a very attractive tradeoff, particularly when the starting point is a dataset containing several hundreds or even thousands of individual metrics.

An important, yet often overlooked constraint placed on factor analysis is the ratio of the number of records to the number of variables. It is usually recommended that, at minimum, the input data matrix has at least 4-to-5 times as many usable records as it has variables; e.g., a 100 variable dataset should have at least 400–500 usable observations. Significant departures from this number of records-to-number of variables ratio can make factor loading estimates unstable.

Correspondence Analysis

Unlike factor analysis, the use of which is relatively widespread, particularly in survey and academic research, correspondence analysis (CA) is a relatively little-known technique, at least in the U.S. The general goal of this methodology, as implied by its name, is to describe the relationships between discrete (nominal or ordinal) variables in a low-dimensional space (i.e., a relatively small number of categories), while at the same time describing the relationships between each variable's categories. Similar to cross-tabulation contrasts, χ^2 tests are used as bases for making conclusive determinations, but CA decomposes the χ^2 measures of association into components, in a manner resembling the above-described factor analysis (specifically, the principal component extraction). Thus in a way, correspondence analysis accomplishes the goal of factor analysis for categorical data, effectively offering a complementary methodology for non-continuous data reduction. In a methodological sense, CA projects estimates for one variable on an underlying "factor" to a category estimate for the other variable, thus making possible the arranging of the individual metrics based on their similarity to each other and relative to axes in multidimensional space. Ultimately, it makes possible the conversion of frequency table data into graphical displays.

A simple illustration of the correspondence analysis process steps is illustrated in Figure 8.14.

Shown in part (A) are two categorical variables: one with categories A through F and the other one with categories 1 through 5. By rearranging first the column values A–F for (variable1), as shown in part (B), followed by rearranging of the row values 1–5 (variable2), a clear pattern emerges, as shown in part (C).

	A	B	C	D	E	F
1		X	X	X		X
2	X	X			X	X
3	X	X	X			X
4			X	X		X
5	X	X				X

(a)

	A	B	C	D	E	F
5	X	X			X	
2	X	X			X	X
3	X	X	X			X
1		X	X	X		X
4			X	X		X

(b)

	D	C	F	B	A	E
5				X	X	X
2			X	X	X	X
3		X	X	X	X	
1	X	X	X	X		
4	X	X	X			

(c)

Figure 8.14 The Process of Correspondence Analysis

The two key questions typically raised in conjunction with the assessment of the results of correspondence analysis are those of external and internal stability. *External stability* is of most interest in the context of theory-testing-oriented research, as it points to the concepts of statistical significance and confidence interval estimation. In other words, are the sample-based results indeed representative of a larger population? Depending on the specific goal of the data analytical endeavor, external stability of CA results may be of varying concern to the analyst. Quite often, in applied analysis, the goal is to quantify effects that are true only of the particular sample only. For instance, when investigating purchase trends of a particular brand's buyers, an analyst is in fact only interested in effects that are attributable just to that particular sample of shoppers, as generalizing those results to all shoppers would be of no practical value. Should that be the case, external stability of CA results would not be of great concern.

On the other hand, *internal stability*, which is a reflection of the degree to which specific results provide a good summary of the dataset on which they are based, will always be of keen interest to analysts. In other words, how valid or robust (in a statistical sense) are the results vis-à-vis the underlying dataset? In terms of the underlying data, internal validity is about determining if results were unduly influenced by outlying observations or overly influential variable categories, so much so that the shown results are not likely to be replicated with another dataset.

Both external and internal stability of correspondence analysis can be assessed with *bootstrapping*, which is a technique of sequential simulated re-sampling with replacement from the dataset at hand. The effect of bootstrapping is an empirical examination of the replicability of CA solution by comparing results across multiple, simulated "new" samples.

The plot in Figure 8.15 shows a clustering of two discrete metrics: the *number of board (of directors) meetings last year* and *the overall board effectiveness grade*.[29] The former is

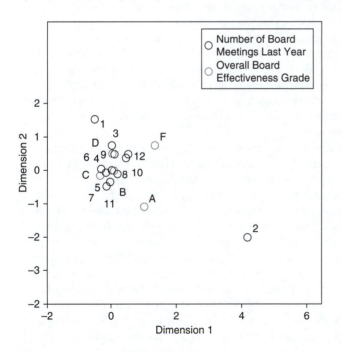

Figure 8.15 Correspondence Analysis

measured on a scale ranging from monthly (12) to once a year (1), while the latter is measured on a traditional school scale of A–F. The scatterplot reveals close interactions between the two factors as well as the individual factor levels.

Although visually compelling, the results of correspondence analysis are considerably more subjective than outputs of factor analysis. Nonetheless, this technique offers a tool that could be quite helpful in compressing the otherwise hard-to-manage number of non-continuous metrics.

Mini-Case 8.1: New Insights or Spurious Associations?

The proliferation, ubiquity and the ever-expanding processing power of computer technologies have dramatically increased the quantity of data captured by business organizations, which in turn brought to the forefront the idea of automated data processing. As an abstract concept, *automated pattern recognition*, the conceptual predecessor of today's data mining applications, existed long before the rise of modern computing infrastructure—however, it was not until the introduction of cluster analysis and neural networks (which enabled machine algorithm-based classification) in the mid-1950s that the idea started to assume a somewhat tangible form. Still, it took four more decades and another noteworthy discovery— the introduction of first *support vector machines* in the 1990s—that the idea of automated (i.e., unsupervised) mining began to develop into commercially viable solutions. Interestingly, in spite of their name, support vector machines are not really "machines" in a sense of mechanical devices—in fact, they are nothing more than concepts that combine select statistical and computer science notions, the function of which is to enable humans to "teach" machines the logic of pattern recognition. As such, support vector machines made it possible to move beyond the bounds of the "traditional," fairly limited data mining techniques, such as cluster or factor analysis (which require a considerable amount of human input throughout the pattern discovery process). Those advancements notwithstanding, key challenges remain, with one of the most nagging also being the most fundamental: How to differentiate between meaningful and spurious associations, especially in the context of vast transactional datasets, which can potentially yield a staggering number of associative linkages?

One of the more commonly used (in business and otherwise) tools to differentiate between spurious and material associations are statistical significance tests (discussed at length earlier in this chapter). In general, relationships that are deemed to be statistically significant are accepted as being material, or at least investigation-worthy; those that are not statistically significant are discarded. Subject to various influences, such as those related to sample size (the larger the sample size, the greater the chances of a particular relationship being deemed statistically significant), significance tests are far from being foolproof. However, it is not just the significance testing that can lead to confusing of non-informative data artifacts with noteworthy discoveries—explanatory analyses themselves can paint a confusing picture, as illustrated by the charted comparison of the monthly Consumer Price Index (CPI) for wireless services and cross-carrier subscriber migration (subscribers abandoning one carrier in favor of another) in Figure 8.16.

Correlation	
	Carrier Migration
CPI Wireless Svcs.	−0.867
p-value	0.000

— CPIWirelessSvcs — Carrier Migration

Figure 8.16 Price Index vs. Wireless Subscription

As suggested by the correlation results (upper left corner of the graph), monthly values for *CPI Wireless Svcs* and *Carrier Migration* are very strongly (−0.867 on a −1 to 1 scale) inversely correlated—yet, when graphed, there does not appear to be a clear, if any, relationship between these two metrics. Why? In this case, it is a combination of two, very different reasons: First, what appears to be an essentially flat trend for CPI Wireless Svcs is not at all flat once the scale-compressing effects of Carrier Migration are removed, as shown in the second graph (Figure 8.17). In fact, the CPI Wireless Svcs trend is clearly downward-sloping (as opposed to the strongly positive Carrier Migration trend), which is in keeping with the afore-mentioned correlation results.

However, in order to see the now-clearly negative trend of CPI Wireless Svcs, the granularity of the measurement scale had to be increased 50-fold (the combined chart's y-axis scale is 0–500, while the scale of the chart showing only CPI Wireless Svcs is only 0–10), which means that relative to Carrier Migration, CPI Wireless Svcs' trend is very tepid. And therein lies the problem: Correlation does not take into account magnitudes—it only considers pattern similarities, regardless of how pronounced or meager the underlying movements.

There is yet another possible, albeit probably not as profound, source of the numeric vs. graphical interpretational divergence: As shown in Figure 8.18, the distributions of both variables show significant departures from normality, which could potentially pose a problem in view of the "default" use of Pearson's *r* as a

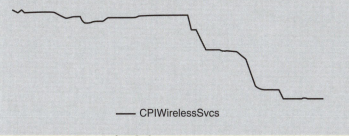

— CPIWirelessSvcs

Figure 8.17 Price Index Only

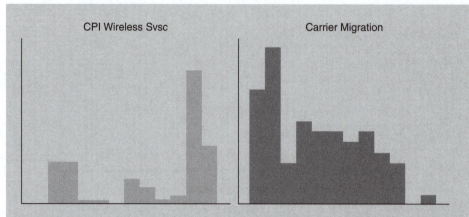

Figure 8.18 Price Index–Carrier Migration Relationship

measure of correlation.[30] More specifically, although there are numerous types of correlation coefficients, the Pearson's *r* is by far the most widely used in applied business analyses, so much so that it is used as a default setting by applications such as SPSS or SAS. Given that there are reasons to believe that Pearson's correlation measure is not robust with regard to departures from normality, it is possible that some of the presumed strength of the relationship shown by the CPI Wireless Svcs–Carrier Migration correlation (−.867) could be a mathematical artifact.

What would a machine do in view of the above conflicts? The answer is suggested by the nature of machine learning: The more subtle the issue under consideration—the less likely it is that an automated data mining application will be able to mimic or replicate human thinking, which means it will default to more tangible decision rules, which in this case is the fairly "yes vs. no" statistical significance testing. Hence, under most circumstances, an automated data mining application would single out the relationship between CPI Wireless Svcs. and Carrier Migration as "significant."

9 Segmentation

The design and execution of marketing communications needs to balance the demands of customer-centricity with promotional economics. On the one hand, tailoring promotional programs to customers' needs, wants and preferences is believed to increase the effectiveness of those programs, while on the other hand, it tends to increase their costs. Not surprisingly, much effort is put into finding that often elusive point where the program customization and the return on marketing investment are both maximized.

Identification of economically actionable customer segments is an important part of that endeavor, as it offers a middle-ground-type solution to the continuum demarked by no differentiation on the one end, which is often deemed to be ineffective, and the so-called "one-to-one" marketing on the other end, which is rarely economically or operationally plausible. That said, though conceptually quite straightforward, customer segmentation can be a relatively complex and involved undertaking, particularly when "squeezed" within the demands of informational needs governing the scope and the direction of the marketing database analytics process discussed in this book.

Simple Yet Complex

Segmentation is perhaps one of the most intuitively obvious as well as the most misused concepts in marketing analytics. In the most general sense, *segmentation* is the process of grouping together entities based on shared similarities. It is used extensively by both consumer- and business-oriented organizations, where it enables the identification and differential treatment of distinctly different segments. Although its most visible applications involve product and service marketing, or more generally, demand generation, segmentation is also used extensively in the front-end product and service design as the basis for tailoring product functionality or service attributes to buyers needs and tastes.

However, anything that is used by many tends to be misused by some. In general, segmentation misuse stems from a complex web of segmentation types, usage situations and statistical methodology decisions hidden behind the veil of simplicity. Sounding intuitively straightforward and operationally uniform (i.e., how many ways could there be of grouping customers?), segmentation is actually very situational as well as method-dependent and desired-outcome-dependent. In fact, a single customer dataset can yield vastly different segmentation outcomes, depending on how it is approached. Avoiding the many potential pitfalls associated with investing time and resources in segmentation-related analyses requires a robust segmentation selection process combining the anticipated goals and usability, the available data and its limitations, the already

Figure 9.1 Segmentation Choice-Influencing Factors

developed yet differently purposed conceptual approaches and the competing method-ological grouping techniques, as shown in Figure 9.1.

One of the most important truisms about segmentation analyses is that there is no such thing as a "one size fits all" solution. Even the most methodologically advanced and informationally robust models have a limited applicability scope. For instance, as detailed below, descriptive solutions can be an excellent tool for depicting the structure of the marketplace, but as a rule are equally ineffective as treatment differentiators or new buyer classification tools. This means that more likely than not, an organization will need more than a single segmentation schema, but even more importantly, the segmentation building process should involve clearly mapping out specific segmentation-related needs, identifying the most appropriate methodologies and prioritizing any subsequent development efforts. In other words, it is important to view segmentation as a process rather than an event, which is marked by a basic customer-base structure description at the onset, gradually evolving into an adaptive, forward-looking predictive schema. The many segmentation options notwithstanding, it is important to remember that the goal of any and all data analysis described in this book is the creation of competitively advantageous knowledge. Thus, choosing the right approach should not only reflect the intersection of all relevant constraints, but should also offer a reasonable chance of reaching the competitive informational goals.

Segmentation Types

Segmentation comes in many shapes and sizes, from the generically used descriptive customer-base structure mapping or lifetime value analysis (LTV) to many proprietary scoring and classification algorithms. Yet at their core, most if not all of these overtly different approaches can themselves be grouped into a handful of general categories based on *what they try to do* (purpose) and *how they do it* (approach). The conjoint of these two broad considerations leads to a 3-way dichotomomization of segmentation approaches:

1. Strategic vs. tactical.
2. Descriptive vs. predictive.
3. Factual vs. ascribed.

Strategic vs. Tactical

The purpose of a *strategic segmentation* is to establish a broad and general informational base, primarily with the goal of informing business planning efforts. In many regards, the strategic segmentation is the least immediately actionable form of customer group-ing, as it yields a general overview of the underlying structure of the marketplace. In a broad sense, it yields a general overview of the structure of the customer base—in other words, it helps to determine what to do, although it rarely points to the most effective means. A strategic segmentation is likely to suggest the most plausible segment or customer differentiation strategy, including segment sizing, all of which is intended to map out the most effective customer promotional strategy.

A *tactical segmentation*, on the other hand, will typically contribute the "how to do it" part of the puzzle. In other words, its goal is to identify the most effective means of carrying out the strategic segmentation recommendations. For instance, should the organization decide, based on the initial strategic segmentation, to pursue the strategy of differentiated customer treatment, it will then need to operationalize that strategy by specifying the most effective cross-segment differential spending allocation and the within-segment customer value and/or response propensity deciling. In that sense, the tactical segmentation is intended to pick up where the strategic segmentation left off and identify the most productive (i.e., resulting in the greatest impact at the lowest possible cost) means of the stated strategic goals. Table 9.1 highlights the key differences between strategic and tactical segmentation approaches.

It follows that the strategic–tactical continuum does not represent an either-or choice, but rather a decision of what to do and when. As such, the strategic segmentation tends to be *descriptive* in nature, as its goal is to identify and describe the structure of the underlying customer base. On the other hand, tactical segmentation is usually *predictive* in nature, as it offers an "educated guess" about customers' propensities to engage in certain behaviors in the future. Conceptually, this distinction closely parallels a different way of categorizing segmentation approaches, which tackles that task from a methodological point of view.

Descriptive vs. Predictive

Functionally, segmentation can be either descriptive or predictive. The former is somewhat akin to the strategic form discussed above, as its goal is to identify and describe the underlying structure of the customer base. Operationally, this entails grouping of the individual customer base records and the subsequent detailing of within-group similarities as well as between-groups dissimilarities. Methodologically, a *descriptive segmentation* most commonly uses physical-distance-based clustering algorithms, such as cluster analysis, which groups individual records into segments built around random or analyst-supplied starting points called seeds. A commonly used alternative to clustering algorithms are the so-called decision trees, which derive their name from a tree resembling graphical structure wherein leaves represent individual record classifications and branches represent conjunctions of attributes that lead to those classifications.[1] Whether based on clustering algorithms or decision trees, a classificatory segmentation

Table 9.1 Strategic vs. Tactical Segmentation

Segmentation Type	Purpose	Functionality
Strategic	To guide promotional planning	Structure of customer base Segment-treatment strategy Segment sizing
Tactical	To guide resource allocation	Segment spending allocation Value & propensity deciling Cost–benefit of differentiation

is retrospective insofar as it yields an interpretation of past outcomes captured in the database.

In contrast, a *predictive segmentation* approach is prospective in its character, as its main objective is to pinpoint future events that are most likely to occur, which parallels the objective of the previously discussed tactical segmentation. Methodologically, predictive segmentation is distinctly different from a descriptive one, as it most commonly entails a predictive model calibrated to estimate individual-record-level probabilities of a certain outcome, such as product repurchase or promotional response. The most commonly used tools are regression models, although predictive regression trees, such as MARS (Multivariate Adaptive Regression Splines) have been slowly gaining ground, since their initial introduction a decade or so ago.

Factual vs. Ascribed

Thirdly, segmentation can be either factual vs. ascribed. The former uses observed, concrete outcomes, such as demonstrated purchase behaviors, while the latter relies on attributed characteristics, such as attitudes or derived demographics.[2] As discussed in Chapter 6, factual, observed behaviors are the most informationally rich and accurate source of database insights, simply because they represent objective manifestations of critically important outcomes, such as product purchases. That said, attitudes and other ascribed data—such as geodemographics, lifestyles or even generalized behavioral propensities—often contain important insights into the drivers of the observed behaviors.

Unlike the just-discussed descriptive–predictive continuum, the factual vs. ascribed segmentation distinction does not lend itself to an easy methodological categorization. A *factual segmentation*, such as a behavioral one, can as easily be descriptive—if its goal is a mere discovery of an underlying structure of the customer base—as it can be predictive—if its goal is the estimation of customer record level repurchase propensities: The underlying methodology is as likely to be a classificatory clustering or a decision tree as it is a predictive regression model. Although in principle an *ascribed segmentation*, such as an attitudinal one, could either be descriptive or predictive in nature, in practice it ends up being more heavily skewed toward the former. The reasons for that typically point to data sourcing, as ascribed database characteristics are often externally sourced (i.e., acquired from outside data vendors), which translates into imperfect coverage at the aggregate database level and a diminished level of precision at the individual record level. The former stems from a combination of cross-database coverage differences, household mobility, householding rules and name/address inconsistencies. The latter, on the other hand, are usually a consequence of the elusive nature of the ascribed database qualities, which in contrast to the objectively factual behavior tend to be either less accessible to organizations (such as individual level demographics, which though captured by the U.S. Census Bureau are not available for use by commercial entities) or have a lower informational reliability, as tends to be the case with attitudinal characteristics.[3]

A Multidimensional Perspective

Although the three ways of approaching segmentation have definitive overlaps, each of the three dichotomies also contributes some uniquely distinct aspects of categorizing the different ways of approaching database segmentation, as shown below in Figure 9.2.

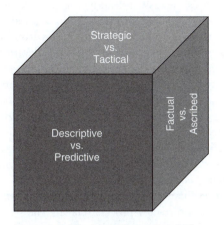

Figure 9.2 The Multidimensional Nature of Segmentation

One of the key, yet common, mistakes made during the segmentation selection process is not expressly recognizing the inherent differences among the above three segmentation classification dichotomies. These are not just different ways of thinking about grouping of customer database records—each of these three dichotomies is a manifestation of fundamentally dissimilar business process and each addresses a somewhat distinct aspect of the overall process.

Strategic vs. tactical dichotomy is a usage-focused dimension of segmentation categorization, which in essence addresses the *anticipated usage* of the resultant solution: Is the segmentation solution to be used to form the basis for a general promotional strategy, such as mass vs. differentiated treatment strategy, or is it to be used to guide specific customer treatment decisions, such as the type and the number of treatments or spending allocation?

Descriptive vs. predictive categorization captures the *desired usability* of the segmentation solution: Is it to be just a snapshot-in-time picture of the structure of the customer base, or is it intended to serve as a forward-looking tool for identifying customers exhibiting the highest levels of the desired outcome propensities, such as repurchase or promotional response?

And lastly, factual vs. ascribed dichotomy addresses the data-focused considerations, specifically, the customer-record-grouping bases, which are an indicator of anticipated individual *record scoring accuracy*. Factual and individual database-record-attributed data, such as product purchases, will almost always yield more precise segment groupings than the aggregate-to-record extrapolated generalizations, such as geodemographics or lifestyles. Thus to sum it up, each of the three general segmentation categorization dimensions contribute fundamentally different decision making considerations.

Thus it would be a mistake to look at segmentation as being only categorized as, let's say, strategic vs. tactical, because taking such a limited view would not resolve the fundamental methodological or even expected functionality ambiguities. In the end, the results will be very significantly influenced by the choice of a methodology, so much so that a completely different solution can be obtained by opting for a different method. A physical-distance-based clustering algorithm will in most instances "output" a different-looking structure of the customer base than, for instance, a decision-tree-based approach.

In addition, reliance on cluster analysis complicates the task of dealing with new records being added into the data (such as new customers) as this methodology does not allow for a simple scoring and categorization of new records,[4] which is not the case with most decision-tree-based approaches. As detailed later, there are multiple other considerations that need to be taken into account while contemplating a segmentation approach.

The inherent relativity of customer base segmentation can be somewhat unsettling, but in fact it merely underscores a general characteristic of most data analytic techniques, namely that there is usually some degree of method–result confounding. It highlights the importance of a well-reasoned, careful methodology selection process, much as it is important to consider side effects of an otherwise beneficial medication. As possibly the most extreme illustration of the method–result dependency, the success of segmentation analyses is particularly dependent on the pre-analysis evaluation process.

This chapter offers a segmentation selection evaluative schema, which is intended to provide a comprehensive yet thorough segmentation review process relating the stated informational objectives, intended usability and the limitations of the currently available data. Once again, the goal here is not to provide an exhaustive technical review of the individual statistical techniques, but rather to bring to light the different types of statistical methodologies and highlight how they can be employed to tackle specific database segmentation related tasks. Those interested in a more in-depth discussion of the individual techniques outlined throughout this chapter are encouraged to consult any of the large number of multivariate statistical sources that are widely available.[5]

The rationale outlined below is based on the belief that a step-by-step decision making process is the only reliable solution to the ambiguities posed by the multifaceted nature of the task at hand. The ensuing discussion starts with the delineation of key segmentation considerations, which is followed by a discussion of a stepwise approach designed to ease the alternative evaluation process.

The Evaluative Process

Given its broad scope and the multiplicity of pertinent considerations, the overall segmentation decision making process can be broken down into two distinct parts:

1. Business evaluation process.
2. Analytical selection process.

The purpose of the business evaluation process is to provide a forum for the future business users of the segmentation solution and analysts that will develop it to have a "meeting of their minds" in a structured and goal-oriented fashion. As mentioned in earlier chapters, the key difference between "information" and "knowledge" is in the level of the decision making applicability of the latter. While information encompasses all insights derived from the underlying data without regard for its decision making impact, or the level of importance, knowledge represents the further refining of the most attention-worthy subset of all information. The segmentation business evaluation process parallels the information-to-knowledge evolution logic. Its basic operational goal is to align the specifics of the analytical approach with informational expectations of its users to make sure the future "finished product" offers the right type of functionality and contributes the right types of insights. In short, the goal of the business evaluation process is to make certain that the analysts hear exactly what the future users are saying.

On the other hand, the analytical (segmentation) selection process is intended to provide the means of translating the agreed upon (in the business evaluation process) informational needs into a specific set of methodological and data related steps. This undertaking is primarily focused on the specifics of the underlying analytics, such as the selection of appropriate statistical techniques as well as data-treatment-related considerations (transformations, indicator creation, etc.). It is important to note, that the analytical selection process should always follow the above-discussed business evaluation, to make sure that the former incorporates the key decisions reached in the course of the latter process, most importantly those surrounding the expected usage and desired functionality.

Business Evaluation Process

Among the enabling factors of any consumer-oriented business strategy is an organization's ability to align customer needs with the most appealing product and/or service offerings. And as it may not always be feasible or practical to target individual consumers, due for instance to difficulties involving technological shortcomings or the nature of the product, an organization has be able to at least group consumers into somewhat homogenous segments in order to be able to create some linkages between its products' benefits and consumers' needs. Yet, no clear guidelines exist for helping managers with this important task. As a consequence, even the coarsest of segmentation decisions, such as the choice of a segmentation type, are often not well thought out. For example, decisions involving the three generalized dichotomies of segmentation types, *strategic* vs. *tactical, descriptive* vs. *predictive* and *factual* vs. *ascribed*, are routinely made without explicitly considering interdependencies among desired outcomes, available methodologies, data types and expected functionality.

It is not surprising then, that the *one size fits all* view of customer segmentation has evolved over time. So, while "customer segmentation" has a ring of familiarity, a question inviting a discussion of the task-appropriateness of "predictive," "attitudinal" or "behavioral" segmentations will draw more puzzled looks than ready, well-considered answers. Intended or not, the task of segmenting customers is often approached like that of cutting a cake, where everyone is so anxious to get a slice that little-to-no attention is paid to how the slicing is done. More often than not, the process of customer grouping is launched without establishing a connection between the organization's *promotional needs* and the most appropriate *segmentation approach*, not to mention the *available data–segmentation type* or *predictive/descriptive power–segmentation methodology* links. And although for the ensuing few weeks or months significant amounts of effort may be invested in customer segmentation, the results oftentimes fail to identify new and viable business opportunities or even increase the retention rate among current customers. When that happens, it is almost a matter of instinct to conclude that "segmentation does not work," when frequently, it was simply poorly constructed and executed.

The point here is that to design a robust segmentation solution, the decision making that drives the process has to explicitly address a number of important issues, ranging from the model's promotional objectives to its anticipated problem solving capabilities. It is so because, depending on the segmentation approach chosen, considerably different functionalities (e.g., strong classificatory power vs. revealing market structure description), outcomes (e.g., attitude-based affinity clusters vs. behavior-rooted value clusters), or usage situations (e.g., incremental revenue generation vs. loyalty building) can be built into a segmentation model.

That's the bad news—the good news is that the underlying segmentation selection process is relatively straightforward and once developed, it can be routinely re-used. Keeping in mind possible segmentation functionalities, diverse usage situations and varied promotional objectives of customer segmentation, a well-functioning segmentation solution can be crafted by systematically progressing through the following three interlinked segmentation planning steps focused on delineating the following:

1.   Segmentation business objectives.
2.   Desired functionality and expected usage situations.
3.   Data availability.

Step 1: Clearly State Segmentation Business Objectives

No segmentation solution is universally applicable. For example, customer prospect lists can be typically segmented into multiple customer opportunity segments, however, once some of the prospects have been converted into customers, that "new customer group" will require a different segmentation model. Why? Because of the models' differing objectives: A *prospect segmentation* aims to identify conversion opportunity segments for customer acquisition, while a *current customer segmentation* forms basis for loyalty and/or pinpoints cross- and up-sell opportunities. To accomplish these divergent objectives, robust prospect segmentation will likely entail one set of clustering dimensions, while a successful current customer segmentation will call for a different set (effectively reformulating the segmentation model). The two segmentation types may on occasion end up being substantively very similar, but if it happens, it is by coincidence, and not by design.

In a nutshell: *Do not think of customer segmentation as a "one size fits all" solution—in order for it to yield meaningful insights it needs to be tailored not only to a given product or service, but also to promotional objectives at hand. Think of segmentation as an answer to a business question— changing questions will call for fresh answers.*

Step 2: Identify Desired Functionality

One of the most common misunderstandings among segmentation users is that, generally speaking, attitudinal and behavioral segmentation approaches are equally well-suited for usage as customer classification and/or description mechanisms. That, coupled with the generally fuzzy understanding of differences in functionality and optimal usage situations distinguishing predictive from descriptive segmentation approaches, leads all too often to disappointing results. And in my own experience, it is usually analysts, not models, that under-deliver.

Here are some suggestions: If your goal is to better understand the structure of your market or to derive preference/affinity segments, use consumer-attitude/preference-driven descriptive segmentation; be cognizant, however, that down the road you will struggle trying to classify new customers into previously derived segments. If, on the other hand, you need to build a segmentation schema capable of driving cross- and up-sell-oriented promotional programs, consider behavior-driven predictive segmentation, which, although not as explanatory as the former, will give you a far greater scoring precision and classificatory power.

Like it or not, there is no single segmentation operationalization that can satisfy all of even the most commonly seen objectives. As is evident in the previous discussion, where attitude-based descriptive segmentation models under-perform is where behavior-centered predictive approaches excel, and vice versa. The former is a potent descriptive and a poor classificatory tool—the latter is a poor descriptive but a strong classificatory instrument. What is oftentimes not clearly understood is that a strong promotional program will call for at least two different segmentation solutions, simply because no single approach is capable of yielding desired levels of functionality (i.e., robust answers to marketing questions) across usage situations. Here is an illustration:

Utilizing a sample of its database customers, a large consumer package goods company derived several affinity segments based on respondents' expressed attitudes toward the company's key products. The results of this segmentation drove the design of a number of successful promotional programs; however, as new customers continued to be added to the database, the task of classifying and scoring them correctly proved to be very difficult. The new customer classification and scoring impasse was remedied by creation of value segments driven by customer purchase behaviors (rather than attitudes). As behaviors tend to be more tangible and hence more precisely measurable, the task of new customer classification became far less formidable, as the customer-segment assignments became more statistically accurate. It is worth noting that neither of these two different (i.e., attitudinal-descriptive vs. behavioral-predictive) segmentation approaches were used to replace the other; instead, they were rightly treated as complements to each other.

In a nutshell: *Having aligned your segmentation plans with your promotional objectives (see Segmentation Evaluation Step 1), bring into the focus your model's desired functionality and expected usage situations. Descriptive segmentation solutions can be quite successful in describing market structures, while classificatory segmentation models are robust organizational mechanisms for both current and future customers. Do not expect your segmentation to do both, as, generally speaking, it will not. Instead, carefully think through your promotional objective and desired functionality/expected usage situations and consider multiple segmentation solutions.*

Step 3: Investigate Data Availability

All too often a segmentation approach is chosen based on data availability. For instance, an organization rich in transactional data will naturally gravitate toward behavioral segmentation (i.e., one classifying customers into like groups based on metrics such as the level of spending, the frequency of purchase, loyalty, etc.); another organization may opt for attitudinal segmentation primarily because it boasts an abounding reservoir of customer likes and preferences. There is of course nothing wrong with leveraging your data assets, so long as the segmentation objectives—including those of the model's functionality—are not subsumed under data availability. For instance, an organization trying to understand consumer repurchase motivations in hopes of creating an effective loyalty program would be ill-advised to develop a behaviorally focused predictive segmentation model (rather than the far more applicable attitudinally focused one), only because of an easy access to sales data. Unfortunately, this is far more common than one would expect.

In a nutshell: *Leverage your current informational assets, but do not lose sight of the promotional need at hand. Just because a particular data type is conveniently or inexpensively available does not mean that it should be your de facto choice for segmentation input. Make your data selection focusing on the anticipated benefits and expected usability—do not put the "what's" before the "why's."*

The above three-step process is not intended to be a panacea for all segmentation analysis ills, but it is a good starting point to planning for a well-functioning solution, or to evaluate the efficacy of the current ones. As industries and organizations within and across them vary in terms of their goals and circumstances, the above process can be made better by enhancing its level of specificity to the organization, which can be readily accomplished by adding organization-specific detail under each of the three general steps.

Analytical Selection Process

Before delving into the "hows" of the segmentation analytical selection process, it might be helpful to consider why taking these extra steps is worthwhile. Outlined below are two of the most compelling reasons.

Methodological choices made by analysts can have a profound impact on the segmentation solution's level of utility, as seen by its users. Yet all too often these decisions do not involve direct or even indirect input from the latter, as in many organizations the producers and users of information tend not to look far beyond their often narrowly scoped set of responsibilities. To put it bluntly, non-technical users of data-derived knowledge, such as marketers or brand managers, tend to show little interest in getting involved in methodological considerations, which could be as much a function of self-selection (i.e., individuals tend to gravitate toward tasks that reflect their occupational comfort zone) as it is a function of the organization's inner-workings. By the same token, technical analysts tend to get immersed in the specifics of their tasks, such as statistical models calibration and validation, much to the exclusion of practical consequences of their technical decisions. As a result, potentially fruitful methodological approaches are never explored. That said, much about data analysis will most likely always remain hidden from business users' view, for obvious reasons, thus the most effective way of bridging that gap is the development and adaptation of systematic processes that can aid in what might otherwise be a difficult business–analyst dialogue.

Another important reason for instituting a robust analytical selection process is to set forth appropriate statistical decision guidelines. Of particular importance is the interpretation of statistically derived coefficient values in the context of two key statistical notions: *point* vs. *interval estimates* and *statistical significance*. The former entails expressing effect coefficients as either precise (i.e., point) or range (i.e., confidence interval) based values, while the latter is an often-used method for quantifying the level of precision of statistical-analysis-based inferences. In applied data analysis, particularly in business, it is common to see point estimates expressed in terms of statistical significance—for example, the lift attributable to treatment A = 11.5% and it is significant at the .95 confidence interval—which is an incorrect interpretation of these concepts.[6]

Although there is a tendency to dismiss the above considerations as dull and unimportant technical details, these seemingly mundane specifics can—and often do—have a highly deterministic impact on the subsequent qualitative result interpretation, shaping the information and ultimately the knowledge stemming from the analysis. This impact can be particularly pronounced in the context of database analytics, especially transactional databases, primarily due to the basic characteristics of the data, as detailed in the earlier chapters.

Detailed below is the process aimed at enhancing the validity and reliability of any segmentation-based data analysis. Its goal is twofold: First, it is to offer an all-encompassing look at segmentation-related considerations and to explicitly specify the interrelationships and interdependencies among the individual components of the segmentation process. Second, it is to provide a "discussion template" to help bridge the aforementioned analyst–knowledge-user gap. To that end, one of the goals of the process detailed below is to "strip away" much of the technical (i.e., statistical) lingo and focus instead on the more universally understandable considerations.

Segmentation Selection Step 1: Delineate Components and Dependencies

Central to any complex analytical problem is a thorough detailing of all measurable decision components and their interdependencies. A typical segmentation problem will likely entail more "moving parts" and dependencies than most other database analytical undertakings, though some of that difficulty should be lessened by the previously outlined Business Evaluation Process, particularly in the sense of clearly identifying and articulating the stated informational objectives and desired levels of the resultant solution's functionality. Figure 9.3 below captures a general template intended to convey the most typical segmentation components and their interdependencies.

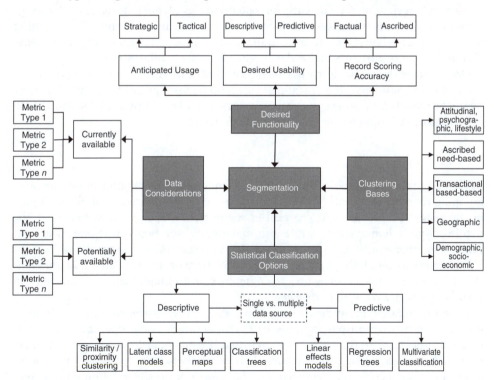

Figure 9.3 Segmentation Considerations Map

Clearly, it is a complex picture. It shows that a typical segmentation analysis entails four separate sets of decisions: 1. the identification of the desired functionality, which is one of the outcomes of the previously discussed Business Evaluation process; 2. data specification; 3. clustering bases identification; and 4. statistical classification option selection. First, each of the four sets of components will be discussed in more detail, followed by the specifics of the evaluative process highlighting the inherent tradeoffs among the said four general sets of decisions.

DESIRED FUNCTIONALITY

Segmentation functionality considerations should start with the premise that the knowledge the analysis will generate will be a tool that will be used to bring about competitive advantage to a firm. This means that segmentation should be highly utilitarian. It should be anticipatory of the most likely usage contexts, should encompass the most desired usage functionalities, both of which should also take into account the accuracy of the individual record segment classificatory power (i.e., record scoring accuracy).

At this point, the goal is to clearly identify the key aspects of the desired functionality, as defined by the Business Evaluation Process. All descriptions should be maximally operational—i.e., should point to specific components of *anticipated usage*, *desired usability* and *record scoring accuracy* (see Figure 9.3).

DATA CONSIDERATIONS

A thorough review of the currently or potentially available data is critical to segmentation planning efforts because it forms natural feasibility limits. Data planning should be descriptive of the currently available data, as well as exploratory in the sense of considering not currently on hand, yet potentially accessible sources.

Data strategy should be clearly outlined. Specifically, will other than the "currently in hand" data be considered? If so, maximally operational description of any data of interest should be provided. In any event, a definitive listing of all currently available data should be compiled, including any necessary data dictionaries.

CLUSTERING BASES

Regardless of the specific objectives or method employed, segmentation always involves grouping together of records (e.g., customers) based on manifested similarities. From a methodological point of view, the goal of segmentation analysis is to maximize the within-segment homogeneity while also maximizing the between-segments heterogeneity. In other words, segment members should be as similar as possible, while individual segments should be as different as possible from other ones. That said, different clustering bases, such as behaviors, demographics or geography will typically vary in their ability to deliver against that goal.

A clear delineation of the general segmenting bases needs to be put in place. In most instances, there are multiple grouping bases that could be pursued at any given time, thus it is important to prioritize the anticipated benefits in order to arrive at the most beneficial solution, at this point in time. It is generally helpful to consider the appropriateness of competing clustering bases in the context of the stated informational goals and the desired functionality.

STATISTICAL OPTIONS

Just as there are different informational bases for grouping of customer records, there are multiple statistical techniques available for doing that. Broadly speaking, they can be broken down into two methodological "families": 1. descriptive and 2. predictive methods. The former encompasses all methods the goal of which is to uncover and discover the underlying structure, usually with little-to-no analyst input. On the other hand, the latter includes all techniques purporting to differentiate between distinct, a priori identified groups, such as high- vs. low-value customers.

Of the four key inputs into the segmentation decision making process, this one should almost always be considered last, primarily because it is most dependent on the outcomes of the other three decisions. The stated informational goals, the available data, desired functionality and the chosen clustering bases all combine to determine the most appropriate family of statistical methodologies and in many instances, the single most appropriate technique.

Evident in the above brief description of the four broad segmentation determinants are the interdependencies among them. For instance, the interplay between the available data and the desired functionality will obviously to a large degree dictate the type of clustering bases that should be considered, which in turn will be suggestive of the type of statistical technique that should be considered. An express set of decision rules built around those considerations is discussed next.

Segmentation Selection Step 2: Identify Best Goal–Data–Method Combinations

The fundamental segmentation decision making process is built around the idea that the two factual anchors—the available data and the stated informational objectives—combine to determine the most appropriate clustering–method combinations, as previously shown in Figure 9.1. In other words, what should be the specific clustering basis employed as well as which of the multiple statistical techniques should be used are both a function of the combined effect of informational goals and the available inputs. Acceptance of that simple and intuitively obvious premise leads to a decision framework based on the planning template presented in Figure 9.3.

A couple of notes: The business evaluation process inputs (shaded in Figure 9.3) entail eight possible combinations of Anticipated Usage, Desired Usability and Record Scoring Accuracy (two options for each, or $2 \times 2 \times 2$), which can be reduced to a smaller number as some of these combinations are not practically plausible. For instance, a strategic segmentation is very unlikely to be predictive in nature, considering the demands of strategy formulation vis-à-vis the attributes of a predictive segmentation capability. By the same token, a tactical segmentation is very unlikely to be descriptive in character, for the same set of reasons. This means that the goal of developing a strategic customer-base segmentation implies descriptive functionality, while a tactical segmentation suggests a predictive usability.

In principle, both the strategic-descriptive and tactical-predictive conjoints can be developed with either factual or ascribed data, though most often ascribed data is used with the former combination and factual for the latter. The primary reason for that is that the descriptive segmentation aims to identify certain enduring commonalities, such as lifestage, lifestyle or product usage similarities, while the predictive segmentation purports to pinpoint behaviorally different patterns within those descriptive segments.

Since behavior modification, such as increasing product repurchase frequency or propensity, is usually the goal of segmentation-using business endeavors, only behavioral (i.e., factual) data should be considered for predictive segmentation. On the other hand, in view of the purpose of the more general, exploration-focused descriptive segmentation, its data focus should be either on ascribed data, such as psychographics or geodemographics, or on non-purchase factual data, such as individual/household reported demographics, lifestyles or other like descriptors. Figure 9.4 summarizes the recommended *goal–data–method* conjoints.

Segmentation Selection Step 3: Review Data Options

In general, segmentation planning efforts, falling within the domain of database analytics as defined in this book, can be focused either entirely on the currently available data or a combination of it and some addition, outside (to the database) data, as shown in Figure 9.5.

As discussed in Chapter 6, the majority of customer databases are transactional, typically comprising the individual or household purchase detail core and descriptive causal augments—most typically demographics (or geodemographics). A more complete database might also contain any available (past) promotional campaign details, such as raw promotional responses or processed generalized propensity scores. At the same time, it is rare for such databases to contain competitive or other product purchases or general propensities to purchase online, from catalogues, etc.

The delineation of the currently available data along with an overview of any outside, i.e., potentially available data is a critical step in the segmentation planning process. However, it entails not just the enumeration of individual metrics, but also a clear categorization by type (i.e., factual transaction or demographic vs. ascribed trait) and measurement scale (i.e., nominal label or ordinal rank vs. continuous), as well as data quality (see Chapter 6) and its *analytic value*. The last concept demands a more detailed description.

The analytic value of any data element is the amount of informational input it can contribute to a particular analysis (informational input is simply the amount of predictive, classificatory or explanatory power attributed to a particular metric). Naturally, a metric's

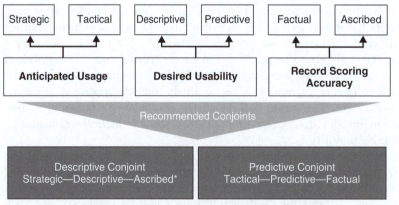

Figure 9.4 Recommended Goal–Data–Method Combinations

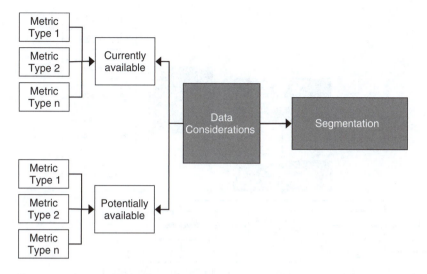

Figure 9.5 Segmentation Data Review

analytic value is somewhat context-dependent, as variables can yield differing amounts of information, depending on how they are used. However, the bulk of any metric's value is a function of its measurement scale, the metric's aggregate amount of variability and its accuracy. Everything else being equal, continuously measured[7] variables have a higher informational value than discretely measured[8] ones, simply because the former allows an infinite number of values (within a particular range), while the latter has a finite and usually relatively small number of categories. The aggregate amount of variability, which is often operationalized by summing of square deviations[9] is a convenient measure of expressing the amount of cross-record differences in values of a particular variable.[10] Lastly, the accuracy of a particular metric should pinpoint above average missing value proportion as well as outlying and unreasonable values.

Obviously, the assessment of variables' analytic value is first and foremost an empirical exercise which requires access to the data of interest. However, when considering the acquisition of any outside data, the aforementioned analytic assessment dimensions should be among the questions asked about the validity and reliability of the contemplated data source.

Segmentation Selection Step 4: Delineate the Data Analysis Approach

Arguably, this is the most technically involved part of the segmentation planning process. In terms of the four basic segmentation-shaping forces outlined earlier—i.e., the desired functionality, data considerations, clustering bases and statistical classification option—this step entails the latter two. At the same time, it is also the most impacted— and in some instances nearly fully determined—by decisions made earlier, specifically, those detailing the informational goals, the desired segmentation solution's functionality and the available or sought data. As a result, this segmentation selection step involves a myriad of specific methodological decisions, as depicted below in Figure 9.6.

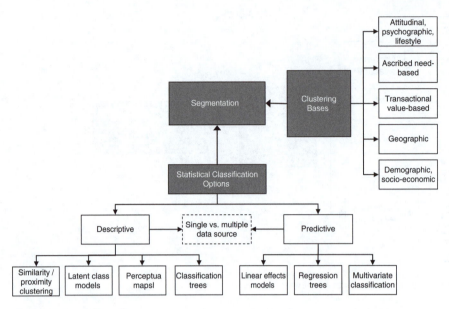

Figure 9.6 Technical Bases

CLUSTERING BASES

This consideration helps to single out the dominant grouping bases of the segmentation, pointing to a specific informational dimension around which the individual customer, or more generically, database record clusters are to be built. The selection of the basic clustering bases is a function of the stated segmentation's informational objectives and the available data. The overriding consideration is the identification of MECE-like groupings of records—mutually exclusive and collectively exhaustive. As previously listed, there are five broadly defined segmentation bases that are commonly used in conjunction with database segmentation models:

1. **Attitudinal/psychographic/lifestyle.** Uses augmented (see Chapter 6) information, frequently ascribed to database records from outside sources, focused on finding common belief or preference segments.
2. **Ascribed need based.** Built around augmented, typically externally sourced, metrics focused on uncovering generalizable, product-type-related needs.
3. **Transactional value based.** Makes use of core transactional metrics, such as product purchases, database information with the objective of grouping records into similar cumulative value (e.g., aggregate purchases over a period of time) groups.
4. **Geographic.** Built around location information, such as ZIP+4 address detail translated into latitude-longitude grid location, to identify physical-location-based clusters.
5. **Demographic/socio-economic.** Uses demographic and/or wealth indicators, frequently sourced externally, to group records into segments.

Although the *clustering bases* considerations clearly revolve around the type of data, the decision making process should be focused on prescriptive identification of the segmentation-objective-dictated ideal record-grouping commonalities. In other words, given the informational goals of the segmentation analysis, what is the most appropriate approach to identifying unique and homogenous segments? For example, if the end informational objective of the segmentation analysis is to delineate spending-level segments, the *transactional value-based* segmentation basis seems most appropriate. On the other hand, if the sought-after informational segmentation outcomes aim to pinpoint the type and the number of demographic segments among brand buyers, the *demographic/ socioeconomic* basis might be most appropriate. In that sense, the purpose of the clustering bases consideration is not to review the types of available data, but rather, it is to identify the most appropriate type of data that should be used, without regard to what might currently be available.

STATISTICAL OPTIONS

Whereas the *Clustering Bases* considerations spell out the type of metrics to be used for grouping, the Statistical Classification Options evaluate the most appropriate method-ologies that could be used to segment the database records. As shown in Figure 9.6, there are multiple techniques available, which can be grouped into *descriptive* and *predictive* tools.

The *descriptive* segmentation methodological options encompass three general types of statistical techniques, which as a group are focused on uncovering the underlying struc-ture of database records and profiling the resultant groupings. As outlined below, as a group these methods share a lot of process commonalities, among which is the relative difficulty of objectively assessing the accuracy or the "goodness of fit" of their results.

1. Similarity/Proximity Clustering. Clustering methods use relational similarity (e.g., cross-variable correlations) or physical proximity (e.g., Mahalanobis distance separating responders) as the basis for sub-dividing the total set into a small number of mutually exclusive groups. The most common application of *cluster analysis* within the confines of database analytics entails grouping of entities (e.g., customers) into unique segments utilizing measures of physical distance (often computed from correlations) to identify the optimal number of segments in an *n*-dimensional space, where the number of dimensions is in effect equal to the number of metrics[11] used as basis for grouping. The two most commonly used classes of clustering algorithms are: 1. *k-means cluster analysis*, which as implied by its name requires continuously distributed data as basis for record grouping, and 2. *hierarchical cluster analysis*, which can accommodate discrete data. The former usually requires an a priori specification of the number of clusters which often entails trial-and-error iterations to identify a solution that produces maximally dissimilar clusters while evenly distributing cases across the groups. The latter does not require an a priori number of clusters specification, but the analyst must identify the optimal solution on a continuum ranging from the *number of clusters = number of records* to *number of clusters = 1* continuum. An important characteristic of *cluster analysis* in general (*k*-means and hierarchical) is that there is no underlying data model; the resultant cluster structure cannot be evaluated in terms of its potential spuriousness or the goodness-of-fit to the underlying data. In fact, the typically used cluster allocation criterion of minimizing within-cluster variation (*k*-means cluster) may result in a somewhat arbitrary assignment of cases to groups. An important, though frequently overlooked, requirement of the *k*-means cluster analysis is the need for a priori variable standardization to avoid obtaining clusters that are dominated by variables exhibiting the most variation.

Evaluative criteria.   The most effective way to evaluate the effectiveness of cluster analytic solutions is to consider the intersection of the solution's *parsimony*, which is how manageable is the resultant number of factors; its *balance*, which is how proportional is the record distribution across clusters; *within-segment similarity and cross-segment dissimilarity*; and the solution's *stability*, which is the ability to reproduce a similar-looking structure across different samples. In general, it is undesirable for a solution to extract more than about 5–10 different segments, as it is rarely practically feasible or cost-justifiable to differentially treat more than a handful of different segments. Equally important is that each of the retained segments be maximally dissimilar from the rest, while itself being as homogenous as possible, which is usually evaluated with the help of cluster mean comparisons (see Figure 9.7) and key metrics distributions computed for individual segments. Closely related to that objective is that each individual segment meets a predetermined size requirement, which should be driven primarily by business considerations, such as what is the minimum segment size that can be differentially treated in an economically feasible fashion. Also, as noted above, cluster analysis is not a modeling approach per se; hence the resultant cluster structure cannot be evaluated in terms of the traditional model-based outcomes, such as non-spuriousness of the depicted associations or the explanatory power of the solution.

2. **Latent Class Models.** A relatively new approach to segmentation, *latent* (i.e., unobservable) classes are groupings of cases assumed to underlie observed categorical

Final Cluster Centers

	Cluster		
	1	2	3
Classifying Dimension 1	−1.23714	−.90685	.06473
Classifying Dimension 2	−.14713	−.03877	.00459
Classifying Dimension 3	−6.20023	−.07891	.12353
Classifying Dimension 4	−.44566	−.49920	.03108
Classifying Dimension 5	−1.72280	−.11595	.03855
Classifying Dimension 6	.02330	−3.90969	.17554

Figure 9.7 Three-Clusters K-Means Solution

measures, but themselves have not been measured directly. Latent classes are typically just nominal categories, but the analysis can also be used with other scales. Although their usage and interpretation are somewhat similar to the more commonly used cluster analysis outlined above, latent classes are based on an underlying model, hence the approach can be thought of as an alternative to the ad hoc, or non-model-based cluster analysis. In fact, while the cluster analysis can more-or-less arbitrarily assign records to groups with the goal of minimizing the within-group variance (the evaluative criterion of k-means clustering), latent class models, due to being based on a mixture of underlying probability distributions generated from the data, result in a mathematical model fitted to the underlying data, based on assignment of cases to groups. As such, the resultant solution can be evaluated in terms of traditional goodness-of-fit statistics. Unfortunately, in contrast to the now-standardized terminology and computational approaches associated with both k-means and hierarchical cluster analyses, latent class (LC) models are still in the early stages of reaching the same level of standardization. As it stands right now, LC models can be referred to *as mixture likelihood approach to clustering*, *model-based clustering, mixture-model clustering, Bayesian classification* or *latent class cluster analysis,* or *latent discriminant analysis,* which results in several different algorithms and stand-alone software applications that can be used to estimate their model parameters.

Evaluative criteria. As suggested above, latent class models can be assessed in terms of their classificatory accuracy as well as the goodness-of-fit of the underlying data model. In addition, LC solutions' parsimony, expressed as the appropriateness of the number of clusters (to the underlying data), can be evaluated in term of the tradition Bayesian information criteria (BIC).

3. Perceptual Maps. In general, these techniques attempt to find a visually depicted structure in a set of proximity measures between objects. More specifically, the objective is to transform responder judgments of similarity or preference (e.g., such as quality perceptions of multiple brands) into distances represented in multidimensional space. *Multidimensional scaling* is the best-known formulation within this general group of methodologies. In general, perceptual maps are most appropriate for survey data focused on trait evaluations and considerably less applicable to large, transactional databases. Figure 9.8 shows an example of a perceptual map of fishing boat brands based on consumers' evaluations of several sport fishing boat attributes, such as price, perceived quality, reliability, etc.

Evaluative criteria. Perceptual maps are among the most difficult to objectively evaluate methodologies due to the scarcity of complementary result analogs. Furthermore, it is important for these solutions to reflect any already known empirical relationships. Considering the example shown in Figure 9.8, if it has already been established (through earlier research) that traits such as durability, good value and safety tend to "cluster together," the current analysis should reflect those already established relationships, which is the first step in establishing the validity of results.

4. Classification Trees. These techniques offer a continuum-based approach to grouping database records into progressively more idiosyncratic groupings. Unlike some of the other methods, classification trees are usually bounded only by the two opposing extremes (all records = single segment vs. # of records = # of segments), leaving the

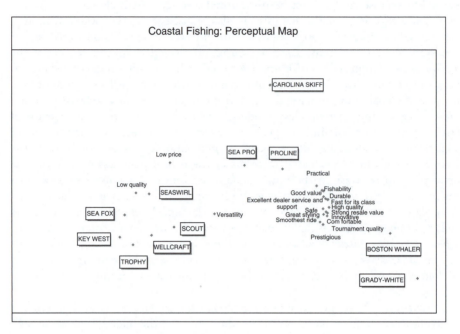

Figure 9.8 An Example of a Perceptual Map

optimal solution selection decision largely in the hands of analysts. Although conceptually similar, there are multiple algorithms that are built around sufficiently different assumptions to yield at times considerably dissimilar solutions. Of particular importance is the number of splits, which is the number of categories created by each successive variable. As a rule, classification trees can be based on either a *binary split*, in effect enforcing dichotomous classification rule, or a *multi-way split*.[12] In practice, solutions based on these different classification standards will often yield results that are substantially dissimilar from each other, which naturally raises concerns among the information end users. It has been the author's experience that the binary-split approaches generally yield more interpretationally cleaner outcomes thus their use is recommended, unless there are compelling reasons to employ a multi-way split-based approach. Figure 9.9 shows an example of a small, binary-split-based tree.

Evaluative criteria.   Similar to other descriptive methods outlined above, classification tree evaluation depends heavily on the solution's parsimony and balance. Splits that divide that sample into grossly uneven groups, such as 90%–10% are undesirable as are excessive numbers of terminal nodes and branches. Through an iterative "tree pruning," poorly discriminating variables can be eliminated giving more room for other, more robust measures to exert their impact.

The *predictive* segmentation methodologies also encompass three general families of statistical methodologies. Although considerably different in terms of their methodological approaches, these three sets of techniques share some key traits, including an objective results evaluation.

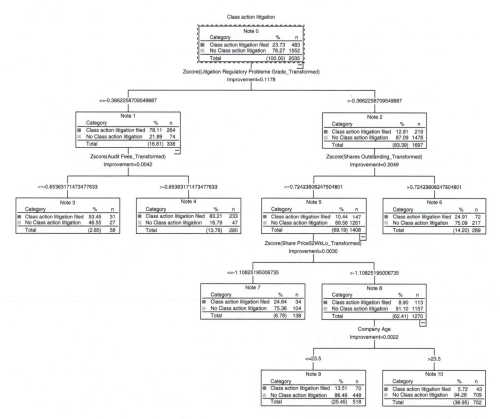

Figure 9.9 Classification Tree: Binary Splits

1. Linear Effects Models. As a class, these methods emphasize classification (into segments) through maximally complete explanation of the *cause–effect* relationships. If the overall customer base can be subdivided into multiple and distinct segments, what are the determinants of the individual segment's membership? This family of techniques encompasses conceptually similar but methodologically distinct set of dependence methodologies, including *discriminant analysis*, *logistic regression* and *multinomial logit*. The target metric in all these methods is categorical since any segmentation structure has to be summarized as an integer (i.e., there could be 2, 5 or 12 but not 2.3 segments) and in some instances, such as in the case of choosing between a logistic regression and a multinomial logit, the number of segments will be one of the key determinants of the appropriate technique (e.g., logistic regression can only be used with 2-segment classification, while the multinomial logit supports multi-segment classification). It follows that *linear effects models* are primarily predictive in character because the number of segments needs to be a priori specified (although in practice, multiple trial-and-error solutions are typically tested) and the very purpose of these technique is to quantify a function to assign new records to pre-defined groups.

Evaluative criteria. As a family of statistical techniques, the linear effects models all attempt to fit an explanatory structure to the data, thus a goodness-of-fit statistic can be computed for all three, quantifying the degree to which that structure (i.e., the predicted values) fits the data (i.e., the actual values). Since all three techniques (logistic regression, multinomial logit and discriminant analysis) have a categorical target, the goodness-of-fit estimation typically involves the interpretationally straightforward χ^2 (chi square) statistics, which simply contrasts the frequency counts of actual vs. predicted values. In addition to the goodness-of-fit, these predictive classificatory methodologies are also evaluated in terms of their classification accuracy, and the efficacy of the two regression-based techniques (logistic regression and multinomial model) is also assessed in terms of deciled gains, which is the increase in the predictive power associated with top model deciles (explained more fully in Regression Trees below). Lastly, in addition to the overall model's goodness-of-fit assessment, the individual predictors comprising it can also be assessed in a similar fashion.

2. Regression Trees. Best exemplified by the Multivariate Adaptive Regression Splines (MARS) solution, these methods try to combine the best traits of the traditional regression modeling, descriptive classification trees discussed above and the automated data processing and pattern discovery data mining algorithms, such as neural networks. The "best of breeds" in that category of analytic solutions offer a regression-like delineation and quantification of the drivers of the outcome of interest, an estimate of multi-way variable interactions, as well as an estimate of both linear and non-linear effects, all in a highly automated procedure. The regression trees in general and MARS in particular are a relative newcomer to the field of statistics—introduced in the early-to-mid 1990s—as they represent one of the growing number of methodological innovations spurred by the explosion in the size and the diversity of commercial databases and the growing difficulty of timely and effective conversion of that data into accurate and actionable information. Consequently, these methods are well adapted to the demands of database analytics.

Evaluative criteria. Consider the MARS gains chart, depicted in Figure 9.10. It represents a common method of evaluating the power of regression-based methodologies with a categorical target, which includes multinomial logit and logistic regression as well the MARS methodology outlined here. The straight diagonal line represents the average prediction, which in practical terms is the proportion of certain outcomes in the

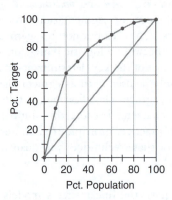

Figure 9.10 Gains Chart

overall population (e.g., if 10% of the initial product trials are followed by repurchase, the 10% would in effect be the average prediction). It could be interpreted as the "prediction without the benefit of the model." The curve represents group likelihoods for predicted values that have been rank ordered, based on their estimated probabilities (from the highest to the lowest) and grouped into deciles. The point of maximal inflection represents the maximum group probabilities, which in the above example is associated with the top 20% of the population. Hence as shown above, the top 20% of records account for about 60% of the target behavior. In addition to the decile gains estimation, the regression trees' predictive power is also assessed with the traditional goodness-of-fit statistics, as described above in the linear effects model section.

3. Multivariate Classification. This is perhaps the "least statistical" approach to segmentation, as it entails an analyst-constructed set of decision rules leveraging a priori data exploration. For instance, a behavioral multivariate classification could be established around the following rules: "*If total brand spending ≥ x and if purchase recency ≥ y and if purchase frequency ≥ z, then segment membership = Segment_A; if total brand spending < x and purchase recency < y and purchase frequency < z, then segment membership = Segment_B, if . . .*" This approach to segmentation is obviously heavily dependent on the robustness and the availability of the underlying information to group individual records into a set of clusters that are both maximally homogenous as well as maximally dissimilar from each other. The primary appeal of this approach is that it is very easy to understand by non-technical audiences, which can contribute to quicker and wider acceptance.

Evaluative criteria. Although it is in reality a simple set of grouping rules, the multivariate classification can also be assessed in term of its goodness-of-fit χ^2 statistic, as the predicted and actual value counts can be contrasted in the context of the corresponding degrees of freedom. In addition, a simple accuracy ratio can also be compiled by contrasting the rule-based classificatory accuracy with the expected average, the latter being a function of the average frequency of occurrence of the modeled outcome in the population of interest.

Keeping in mind that the above-outlined methodological options represent "families" of techniques, meaning that there are even larger numbers of actual application-coded techniques, it is clear that there are quite a few, dissimilar ways of arriving at a segmentation solution, even if there is a relatively well-focused set of informational objectives. To make things even worse, in the sense of complexity, some of the individual techniques are computationally quite dissimilar, which means that they are likely to yield fundamentally different answers. Hence the segmentation quagmire: *The same informational objectives pursued with different statistical approaches will often yield fundamentally dissimilar answers, raising the question of what is the right segmentation solution.*

Without getting tangled up in relativism vs. positivism type of an arguments (i.e., is there or is there not a single "true" answer to the question), the important lesson here is that the choice of a statistical technique should not be made independently from other segmentation-related decisions. It is generally intuitively obvious that the stated informational objectives should be embedded into the selection process, but it is far less clear that the interrelationships between the *Statistical Classification Options* discussed here and the *Clustering Bases* discussed earlier should be considered in a systematic manner. The process for doing so is discussed next.

Identifying the Most Appropriate Combinations

Consider Figure 9.11. The relatively large number of potential *statistical classification option–cluster bases* interactions implied in Figure 9.11 (which can potentially grow even larger considering that each of the *statistical classification options* listed there contains multiple specific applications) can be reduced to a far smaller set of plausible and appropriate combinations.

Some of the steps required to bring about these reductions are dictated by purely methodological considerations—e.g., perceptual maps are only applicable to data reflecting individual responder's beliefs/evaluations—but some others stem from more-or-less empirical experience, such as the assertion that regression trees applied to geodemographic data tend to produce unreliable results. The overriding consideration, however, is to focus the analytical efforts on the facets that are most likely to yield valid and reliable findings.

Of the three segmentation classificatory schemas depicted in Table 9.1 (strategic vs. tactical, ascribed vs. actual and descriptive vs. predictive), the *descriptive–predictive* distinction yields the sharpest line of demarcation in identifying the most appropriate *classification option–cluster bases* combination. That is because in contrast to the other two schemas which are almost entirely either conceptually (strategic vs. tactical) or data (factual vs. ascribed) focused, the descriptive vs. predictive continuum combines the elements of conceptual, data and methodological considerations, thus it offers the most comprehensive way of finding the most appropriate purpose–technique–data combinations.

As a general rule, predictive segmentation models require the use of dependence methodologies, since their goal is to estimate future values or states of target outcomes. *Dependence methods* include all statistical techniques that clearly distinguish between dependent (or target) and independent (or predictor) metrics for the purpose of using the latter to construct a prediction about the former. Overall, dependence techniques can be distinguished from one another based on purpose, data requirements (for dependent or predictor variables, or both) and the number of dependent variables. Altogether, the most commonly used techniques include linear and logistic regression models, multi-

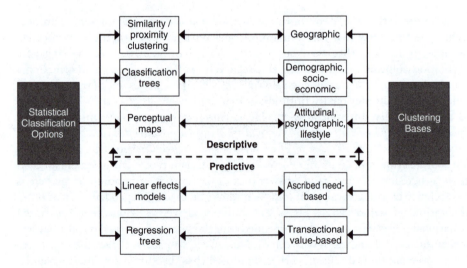

Figure 9.11 Simplifying the Selection Process

nomial logit, discriminant analysis, analysis of variance (ANOVA and MANOVA), canonical correlation, conjoint analysis and the newest addition, regression trees. Of those, *logistic regression*, *multinomial logit* and *discriminant analysis* comprise the linear effects models outlined above,[13] the purpose of which is to identify a linear combination of predictor variables that yield the most robust prediction of the target, or dependent variable. Although regression trees are also a part of the same dependence techniques family, they simultaneously automatically[14] estimate linear and non-linear effects and thus cannot be classified as linear effects models.

Predictive: Ascribed Needs–Linear Effects Models

As a group, the linear effects models are the most appropriate tools to be used with the *ascribed need* clustering data basis. Ascribed needs represent a relatively broad data category, ranging from large-volume transaction-based estimates of inferred product category purchase intensities (where category-wide purchase levels are interpreted as product needs) to relatively small sample-based self-reported needs, typically collected with the help of a survey.

In general, the stated informational objectives should focus the analysts' attention on a specific data type, which can be a function of availability, cost or reliability-related user judgment. In other words, the input data is likely to encompass a relatively narrow variety of metrics, thus making the model and effect specification relatively straight-forward. Taken a step further, this line of reasoning suggests that although a regression tree methodology, such as MARS, might also be considered to be an appropriate tool, the relative simplicity of the underlying data may not warrant its deployment, particularly if it would require the investment in the acquisition of new tools (e.g., a stand-alone regression tree statistical application). At the same time, the analysis itself might entail a more extensive data processing and preparation, such as lag and index metric creation, which at the present time are difficult and at times impossible to accomplish with the said stand-alone special purpose packages. In the end, considering a potential tradeoff between the added costs of a new tool and the anticipated *incremental* benefits associated with the expanded methodological capabilities may point away from investing in a special purpose analysis tools. Overall, any of the linear effects models (subject to the before mentioned individual techniques' application limits) will under most circumstances offer the most economical means of conducting ascribed-need-based segmentation analyses.

Predictive: Transactions–Regression Trees

Perhaps the most self-evident aspect of transactional data is its size and growth trajectory. As noted in Chapter 6, a mid-size supermarket chain of around 500 stores captures several million transactions daily, adding up to billions of transactions in a course of a single year. As a result, retail databases of several terabytes[15] and higher are quite common nowadays. To put that in perspective, the most recent available (2009) estimate of the digitized part of the collection of the Library of Congress (which itself represents about half of the 32 million books and about an eighth the Library's entire collection) is about 74 terabytes.

However, it is not just the sheer volume that could make the analysis of transactional data a daunting task—it is also the proliferation of SKUs (stock-keeping units). For instance, Coca-Cola is a single brand, but it is made up of about 100 SKUs, as it comes in different flavors, sizes, caffeine content, types of packages, etc., which combine into a large number of individual product variations. Thus it is common for retailers of all types, i.e., grocery, general merchandisers and others, to carry tens of thousands of individual SKUs, which results in even samples of transactional databases being usually quite large. That said, since regression trees combine the traits of predictive models, such as regression analysis, and automated data mining pattern recognition algorithms, such as neural nets, they are well suited for analysis of large, transactional databases. Their ability to yield at least an initial assessment of interactions and non-linear effects can be invaluable in such typical transactional data base segmentation endeavors as value or propensity buyer grouping.

Descriptive: Geographic–Proximity Clustering

One of the common ways of grouping and profiling customers contained in corporate databases is through leveraging physical proximity similarities, or geographic segmentation. For organizations that view their customer base structure through a prism of distinct sales or account management territories, the geography-based segmentation might be highly instructive of resource allocation, competitive threats or even future growth opportunities.

Cluster analysis is a commonly used technique, particularly adept at groupings of records in accordance with correlational or physical distance bases of similarity. Although in theory n-number of dimensions could be specified, where n can be any non-negative, non-zero integer, in practice a cluster solution defined in terms of more than three classificatory dimensions becomes difficult to meaningfully interpret. (The reason for that difficulty is the impossibility of graphically depicting more than three classificatory dimensions. Proximity clustering, in turn, makes heavy use of graphical group display, which is of particular value to the assessment of within-cluster homogeneity and cross-clusters distinctiveness.)

Thus in contrast to the above discussed predictive segmentation methodologies where more predictors is generally preferred to fewer (at least as inputs into the initial analysis; final explanation-wise, of course, a more parsimonious solution is typically preferred), cluster analysis will typically "force" the analyst to choose only a subset of the available metrics as the basis for classification. In other words, the cluster analytic techniques lack a facility for identifying the most appropriate clustering dimensions, in effect requiring that determination to be done by other means. Trying out different sets of metrics might be one strategy for dealing with that difficulty, but because the resultant solutions are fundamentally different, the resultant comparisons might lack objective evaluative bases, ultimately making the selection of the "best" solution a difficult one. An alternative and likely more effective strategy is to compute higher-order metric summaries, called "higher-order factors" in advance of cluster analysis and use the more globally defined metric aggregations or composites as bases for segmentation (see the *Data Reduction* discussion in the *Exploratory Data Analyses* chapter for a more exhaustive review of the appropriate methodologies).

Descriptive: Demographic–Classification Trees

Another common approach to describing a customer base is through the identification of demographic and socioeconomic groupings. A statistical technique that is generally most effective in identifying such segments is classification trees, as exemplified by AnswerTree or CART software-packaged solutions.

A unique—for a descriptive segmentation methodology—trait of classification trees is that these solutions are highly interactive (i.e., the resultant "trees" can be "pruned," which means the results can be iteratively shaped) and they produce explicit definitions of successive groupings. In other words, the segments representing different levels of aggregation—on a continuum ranging from *all records = single segment* to *1 record = 1 segment*—are expressly defined by specific variable breaks. Combined, these two key characteristics give the analyst the ability to shape the depth and the specificity of the resultant segments and profiles, respectively. This is particularly important when working with discretely measured demographics or socioeconomic metrics, such as age or income categories (given the highly personal nature of this information, it is very rarely available in other than the categorical form) because it lends insight into the efficacy of the coded categories. For instance, it might be noted that the tail categories lead to classificatory confusion via contributing to the creation of an excessive number of "dead-end" terminal nodes, which may suggest the need to combine some of the categories, in effect reducing their number, ultimately resulting in increasing classificatory and descriptive clarity. Such within-process learning and improvement is not possible with other descriptive segmentation techniques.

Descriptive: Psychographics–Perceptual Maps

The last general category of segmentation basis comprises of attitudinal, psychographic and lifestyle metrics, all of which represent somewhat different ways of depicting the more difficult-to-observe customer characteristics. While the other sources of descriptive data all point to either physically manifest or at least observable characteristics, such as recorded purchases, physical location or otherwise evident demographic or socioeconomic factors, the psychographics and related dimensions are themselves inferred or latent customer (or in a sense of data–record) characteristics.

Loyalty Segmentation

The purpose of this section is to highlight one of the several cutting-edge database analytical approaches to segmentation. The approach described below focuses on a common and important problem—the identification of the brand's most loyal and most profitable buyers, for the purpose of developing differentiated treatment strategies. The guiding principle permeating throughout the ensuing discussion is that the brand's promotional investment should be allocated in a manner that reflects the anticipated, monetary benefits. As a result, the specifics of the approach described here encapsulate not only the task of identifying "ideal" customer groupings, but also spell out a process of taking that basic information and systematically translating it into competitively advantageous actions.

Buyer Loyalty Initiatives

The proliferation of consumer databases is rapidly redefining promotional practices across industries. The influx of consumer, market and competitive insights is transforming promotional art into science, increasing its productivity through better targeting.

As a result, the "one size fits all" mass marketing is slowly giving way to data driven, segmented and differentiated promotions.

Exemplifying the new face of marketing are brand loyalty programs, a broad category of reward-based initiatives aimed at stemming customer attrition. Already common in the frequent-usage product categories such as retail, travel or hospitality, buyer loyalty programs are slowly spreading into other consumer product and service categories, including auto and entertainment. Taking advantage of rapidly advancing informational technologies, these promotional initiatives are emerging as the most effective means of finding and retaining brands' most profitable buyers.

In spite of their promise and growing popularity, many buyer loyalty programs become financial liabilities instead of self-funding business assets. Often struggling to convert initial consumer interest in the program itself into incremental product purchases, they deliver poor return on their investment. The loyalty initiatives' economic underperformance typically stems from a lack of broader strategic program rationalization, manifesting itself in technology and incentive overspending. In other words, infrastructure and incentive spending decisions are often made without the support of thorough cost–benefit analyses.

Sources of Underperformance

Dearth of sound loyalty program investment rationalization is usually a function of two, highly interrelated factors: inadequate program planning and insufficient customer insights. The former signals a lack of well-defined, robust planning frameworks, while the latter points to inadequate data-analytical supports. Absent these two key supports, loyalty program contact cadence and treatment[16] strategy decisions end being based on intuition rather than objective data. In addition, program participant recruitment tends to take the form of customer self-selection supported by open-to-all, mass communicated offers.

Treatment strategy and participant recruitment inefficiencies are typically overlooked until the effects of *adverse customer selection*[17] are felt, which usually manifest themselves through a frequently noted correlation between program registrants' price sensitivity and their propensity to register. In other words, the initial rush of program registrants is usually followed by disproportionately small increases in brand consumption. In the end, even the most technologically advanced and creatively ingenious programs end up subsidizing current customers, while only marginally contributing to sales incrementality.

Also worth mentioning is the quality of the available information, best exemplified by the choice of program performance metrics. One of the most commonly used assessment tools is the registration rate, which is a simple tally of the number of customers signing up with the program. Somewhat less evident is that this metric equates program performance with non-purchase behaviors, which can easily lead to erroneous conclusions. Although indicative of the initial program's appeal, the non-purchase-requiring customer registration is neither the end objective of loyalty initiatives, nor is it predictive of future sales gains. It is, however, easily obtainable and interpretationally simple which explains the metric's widespread popularity.

Poor choice of metrics is sometimes a result of limited data, but more often it is a product of undisciplined analytics. Inexperienced analysts, time pressures and the overwhelming quantities of data combined with the lack of clear database analytical standards often takes away from the validity of analytical efforts. Further compounding those challenges is the self-focus of individual data domains. Transactions captured through POS, consumer opinions collected with surveys or promotional program results gathered online or by mail are usually housed in separate, differently structured[18] datasets, further divided by departmental boundaries, skill sets and narrow objectives. Considerable informational synergies are lost because of the failure to convert domain-specific data into customer attributes, where a full view of buyer interactions links promotional actions with purchase outcomes.

The purpose of this section is to suggest a series of loyalty program planning and analytics related improvements to circumvent the current process limitations. The ideas presented here are rooted in hands-on loyalty program planning and measurement experience and are primarily focused on methodological improvements. The ultimate objective of these suggested enhancements is to turn good buyer loyalty ideas into valuable business assets.

Building a Profitable Loyalty Program

It is often said that success is 95% perspiration and 5% inspiration. In some sense that is true of buyer loyalty initiatives, where a kernel of a unique idea and a great deal of disciplined planning and analysis are needed for a successful program to emerge. To make the most of the "perspiration" aspect of building a robust initiative, these efforts should be focused on a few critical aspects.

First and foremost, clearly state your program's end objective—is it a net increase in the brand's revenue or profitability? If it is the former, focus on product-level price elasticity considerations, which means a broad-based program built around volume discounts and cash rebates. On the other hand, if the growth in net profitability is your objective, focus on buyer-level repurchase propensity, which translates into careful customer target selection and tailored offerings de-emphasizing price discounting. Keep in mind that a loyalty program can boost your brand's revenue if it is built around price incentives, or it can be a profit-generating tool if it is focused on identifying and attracting highest value customers. Avoid the temptation to pursue both of these goals simultaneously or you run the risk of missing both targets.

Second, select appropriate impact measurement metrics. The frequently used customer registration rate is a poor indicator of program performance because it relates the impact of the program to an activity that—by itself—delivers little-to-no economic value to the brand. Don't forget that the role of a loyalty initiative is to drive repurchase—program registration is merely a means to that end. To avoid overstating the impact of your treatment strategy, express its performance in terms of program-attributable sales gains, or comparable revenue-producing activities (e.g., re-enrollment, renewal, etc.).

Lastly, make your program's target audience strategy explicit and operationally clear. Most programs are built around open consumer self-selection, meaning that anyone can elect to participate. The alternative is to invite only a select group of customers. Due to the adverse customer selection, the "open" approach usually attracts scores of registrants but generates not nearly as many incremental purchases. On the other hand, the invitation-based approach focusing only on pre-qualified customers may generate fewer registrants but typically yields higher purchase incrementality. Buyer self-selection-based recruitment is attractive because it is easy to execute, but the added complexity of

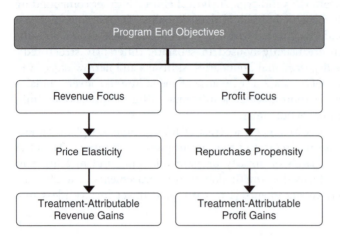

Figure 9.12 High-Level View of Loyalty Analytical Planning

differentiated treatment typically more than pays for itself in greater sales gains. It is important to note, however, that the effectiveness of the invitation-based audience strategy depends on the availability of robust customer pre-qualification[19] insights.

Figure 9.12 presents a high-level view of a program planning process of building economically sound customer loyalty initiatives.

Loyalty Analytics

The best plans are those built around objective facts and fact-supported projections. Yet few loyalty initiatives have the right information available at the right time. The first step toward changing that is to identify and prioritize the most critical analytical tasks. To that end, most programs' economic success is dependent on answering the following three (albeit loaded) questions:

1. Who are the best customers and what is their value to the franchise?
   Analytic competency needed: *customer-level value assessment and classification*
2. How much should be spent to retain those customers and what are the best incentives?
   Analytic competency needed: *treatment-level incentive type and dollar amounts*
3. How are specific campaigns and incentives performing against their stated goals?
   Analytic competency needed: *program impact measurement*

The first of the three sets of insights forms the basis for scaling and rationalizing the level of program investment. Building on its findings, *incentive and offer identification* (#2 above) pinpoints the most effective contact and offer strategy to drive loyalty programs' economic success. Lastly, *program impact measurement* (#3) supports reliable and objective assessment of sales or revenue incrementality. Jointly, these capabilities form a loyalty program support continuum that helps to steer it toward long-term profitability. As shown in Figure 9.13, they are sequentially dependent, which means that findings from #1 are used as inputs into #2 and outcomes of #1 and #2 are incorporated into #3.

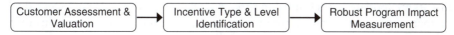

Figure 9.13 High-Level View of Loyalty Analytics Development

Methodologically, these are self-contained analytical competencies require unique statistical approaches. For that reason each will be discussed separately, starting with Customer Assessment & Valuation, followed by Incentive Type & Level Identification and Robust Program Impact Measurement.

Customer Assessment and Valuation

At its most rudimentary level, customer base assessment is primarily concerned with accurate brand buyer categorization and a meaningful segment description. With an eye toward total customer value, which is a function of a sum of purchases accumulated over a period of time (with the further back in time purchases discounted appropriately, such as by using the organization's cost of capital as a discounting factor), the overall buyer base is usually divided into *brand loyal* and *brand switching* customer groups. The basis for this categorization is typically the brand-to-category repurchase rate, expressed as *a proportion of the Brand purchases vis-à-vis total product Category purchases over a period of Time*, or:

$$\text{Brand Loyalty} = \left(\frac{b}{c}\right)_{t=i}$$

where,

b = number of purchases of the brand of interest
c = total number of purchases in the overall product category[20]
t = the period of time over which the purchases are evaluated, such as 12 or 24 months

Implicit in this quantification is the equivalence of *brand loyalty* and *repurchase exclusivity*. In other words, a truly *loyal* customer is someone who repurchases only a single brand in the category, because being 100% loyal requires that the number of brand-specific purchases be equal to the number of category-wide ones. Allowing for an occasional "straying," brands typically classify as *loyal* a customer whose share of the Brand-to-Category purchases meets or exceeds a chosen threshold, such as 70%. In more general terms, the frequently used loyalty categorization heuristic classifies brand buyers into loyalty groupings in accordance with the following logic:

if $= \left(\frac{b}{c}\right)_{t=i}$ ≥ chosen threshold (e.g., 70%), the customer is classified as "loyal,"

alternatively

if $= \left(\frac{b}{c}\right)_{t=i}$ < chosen threshold (e.g., 70%), the customer is classified as "switcher."

Although this or a similar decision rule has been used across a wide array of buyer loyalty programs, its appropriateness is limited to situations where consumers are not expected to purchase more than a single brand in the product category within a period of time. In other words, all products in the category offer functionally substitutable bundles of benefits, and consumer choices reflect their brand preferences, not different functional needs.

There are numerous situations where consumers can be expected to purchase more than a single brand in the category for reasons other than brand preference. For example, a consumer with multiple pets may need more than a single brand of pet food for nutritional or related reasons. Using the above brand loyalty categorization heuristic, that consumer's single brand loyalty could not reach the 100% upper limit. At the same time, a single pet owning consumer would not face the same loyalty classification limit. In other words, the brand loyalty categorization heuristic is biased. The key to its enhancement can be found in the closer analysis of: 1. implicit brand loyalty–repurchase exclusivity equivalence, and 2. household-level purchase aggregation.

Loyalty–Exclusivity Equivalence

In a transactional sense, the brand loyalty ratio discussed above stipulates that: to be considered loyal a brand buyer is expected to repurchase the same brand either exclusively, or least the majority of times when shopping the brand's category. In other words, it is measuring the degree of buyers' repurchase exclusivity. It also means that the line of demarcation between a loyal customer and a brand switcher is highly arbitrary for anyone other than the exclusive brand repurchasers (i.e., 100% loyal).

Household Purchase Aggregation

Also implicit in the current buyer loyalty categorization approach is that brand repurchase analyses are conducted at the transaction level, where the unit of analysis is an "individual buyer–single purchase" conjoint. However, this abstraction conflicts with observable reality. In the majority of cases involving analyses of customer databases, the effective unit of analysis is typically a household, which is defined as *"individuals living singly or together with others in a residential unit."*[21] The reasons for transaction-data householding (i.e., combining a single individual-attributable purchases into a pool of purchases attributed to a single residential unit defined by a combination of surname, address and telephone number) are involved and will not be detailed here, but they include analytically necessary data cleansing and summarizing as well as third-party appending.[22] Specific reasons notwithstanding, given that roughly three-quarters of all households are comprised of multiple individuals, the sum of category purchases used as the basis for the loyalty ratio is very likely to represent a pooling of multiple individuals' purchases.

Looking back to the loyalty ratio, it is clear that it is in need of re-thinking. Data householding is an analytical reality and it should be reflected in the ratio's computational logic. Household-level purchase data pooling alone warrants decoupling of the brand repurchase exclusivity and brand loyalty, a conclusion that is further reinforced by definitional clarity. Brand loyalty is defined as cross-time product repurchase independent of incentives. Repurchase exclusivity is a special case of brand loyalty, where only a single brand in the product category is being repurchased. As a matter of common sense, all exclusive repurchasers should be viewed as being brand loyal, but not all loyal customers should be expected to be exclusive brand repurchasers.

Enhancing the Accuracy of Buyer Loyalty Classification

Before jumping into technical details, let's take a moment to reflect on the origins of the commonly used applied business methods or metrics, such as the loyalty ratio and the classificatory heuristic. It seems that more often than not these methods come to be through accidental practices. In other words, pragmatic solutions that "make sense" are copied across organizations and industries, over time gaining acceptance to the point of unquestioned adherence, often in spite of a lack of methodological due diligence. Some of these makeshift heuristics can quickly outstretch their usability limits—and even become misleading. Whether it is due to not being able to keep up with the growing specificity of insights or heightened accuracy expectations, the once-acceptable techniques can become obsolete. This is precisely the case with the brand loyalty categorization heuristic discussed earlier.

As previously noted, the brand loyalty ratio needs to be updated to reflect the rolling up of individual-level purchases to household-level aggregates, as shown below:

$$\text{Household Brand Loyalty} = \sum_{i=m}^{n} h\left(\frac{b}{c}\right)_{t=i}$$

where,

b = number of purchases of the brand of interest
c = total number of purchases in the overall product category
t = the period of time over which the purchases are evaluated
h = household purchase pooling

The second, more involved step is to expand the brand loyalty operationalization to accommodate the cross-household variability in *category purchase requirements* (CPR), thus effectively relaxing the repurchase exclusivity assumption. The new metric capturing these effects—CPR—is defined as an estimated number of distinct product types or brands repurchased by a single household in a product category over a period of time. It enhances the heuristic's classificatory validity by differentiating between single- and multi-brand loyalty, effectively replacing the current "loyal vs. switcher" dichotomy with a 3-category classification of "single-brand loyal," "multi-brand loyal" and "switcher."

Computationally, the buyer loyalty categorization heuristic should be amended as follows:

If,

$$(\kappa = 1)_t \rightarrow \sum_{i=m}^{n} h\left(\frac{b}{c}\right)_{t=i} \geq threshold = \text{single-brand loyal, } else \; if$$

$$(\kappa > 1)_t \rightarrow \left[\sum_{i=m}^{n} h\left(\frac{b}{c}\right)_{t=i} / \kappa \right] \geq threshold = \text{multi-brand loyal, } else \; if$$

$$(\kappa = 1)_t \rightarrow \sum_{i=m}^{n} h\left(\frac{b}{c}\right)_{t=i} \; or \; (\kappa > 1)_t \rightarrow \left[\sum_{i=m}^{n} h\left(\frac{b}{c}\right)_{t=i} / \kappa \right] \; threshold = \text{switcher}$$

where,

k = household-level CPR estimate
b = number of purchases of the brand of interest

c = total number of purchases in the overall product category
t = the period of time over which the purchases are evaluated
h = household-level purchase aggregation

It should be pointed out that the classificatory validity of above categorization rule is contingent on a sufficiently large number of household-level brand purchases. The acceptable threshold will vary across product types, but in general, for frequently repurchased products, such as consumer packaged goods, a minimum of 18–24 months of past purchase history should be examined. On the other hand, infrequently repurchased products, such as automobiles or consumer electronics, may require all of the available purchase history to yield valid results. This means that in some cases there will not be sufficient amount of historical data to support robust analysis. A potential solution here is to sub-divide the buyer base into "classification-ready" and "classification-pending" groups, with the former containing all households that can be attributed with a sufficiently large number of purchases and the latter group holding households not yet meeting the number of category purchases requirements. The "classification-pending" segment can be proxy-analyzed with the help of the so-called "look-alike" analysis focusing on identification of high-potential-value customers with current high-value brand-buyers-based profile similarity.

Overall, the new, three-category loyalty classification logic better aligns loyalty analytics with data realities and it also relaxes the unrealistic repurchase exclusivity assumption. In doing so it emphasizes brand repurchase patterns over arbitrary "share of category" thresholds. It recognizes that households can be loyal to multiple brands and that continued brand repurchase is the ultimate manifestation of loyalty. Finally and probably most importantly, the expanded three-tier loyalty categorization minimizes potential buyer misclassification.

Incentive Strategy

The second of the analytical priorities is an objective assessment of the treatment strategy. Once the retention targets have been identified and profiled with the help of robust customer valuation outlined above, the focus shifts to program economics. The most important components of the incentive strategy are: 1. the monetary dimension capturing the economically valued offer; 2. frequency, which encapsulates the overall contact mix; and 3. the messaging dimension combining the content and creative aspects of the incentive strategy.

Figure 9.14 shows a treatment strategy planning framework built around the assessment of the expected impact of the individual components. Leveraging empirical results derived from a cross-section of direct (mail and email) consumer programs, the resultant 3×3 matrix spells out the expected impact of the monetary, frequency and messaging elements of the contact strategy on customer repurchase rate, program cost and the potential implementation complexity.

The monetarily valued offer has the greatest potential impact on repurchase rate, but can be expensive in terms of added cost. It can take many forms such as money-off coupons, free product sample, a fee waiver, a preferential treatment or service upgrades. For example, airlines use "bonus miles," hotels reward frequent travelers with room and service upgrades, some credit cards give their customers "cash back" and retailers rely on

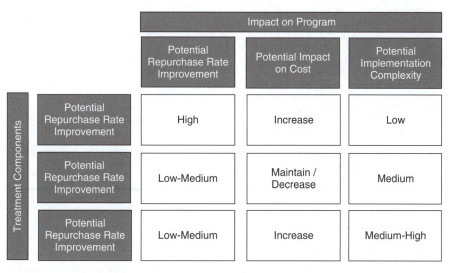

Figure 9.14 Generalized Treatment Strategy Effects

anything from "instant discounts" to free merchandise. A potentially high cost of these upgrades mandates differential treatment, to limit those offers to customers whose profit contribution warrants that level of investment (i.e., the importance of customer valuation). Ideally, the monetary value of an incentive should be based on either the current or expected future value of the customer to keep program economics on the right track.

The frequency of customer promotions is another important element of program strategy. Although it can positively impact repurchase, an even more significant benefit to optimizing the frequency of communication is the potential cost saving. For example, a major bank used to contact each new customer eight times with cross- and up-sell offers, but with the help of response pattern analyses realized that in most cases four contacts were optimal. Cutting back on the number of mailings allowed it reallocate some of the promotional funds into higher impact areas, thus increasing the overall productivity of its promotional mix. As shown in Figure 9.14, the frequency dimension has a comparatively modest impact on stimulating repurchase rates but has a considerable potential to decrease the overall program cost. It is usually more complex to implement than the monetary dimension, primarily because it may entail a more involved customer treatment matrix.

Lastly, the creative contact strategy dimension, which encapsulates the "look and feel" of the promotional materials, typically yields the least amount of directly attributable impact on loyalty initiatives' economics. That is not to say that the messaging dimension is not important—it is simply not as effective at driving sales incrementality as the other two offer strategy components. Changing it, however, can be costly primarily due to the labor-intensive nature of the redesign work; there is also a tendency to migrate from low-cost single-page direct mailers or text-only email messages to higher cost dimensional mailings (e.g., a high-quality box containing numerous promotional materials) or more interactive, design richer email options. Naturally, implementation complexities can be considerable.

Table 9.2 offers a concise summary of the expected effects and supporting justification.

Table 9.2 Behavioral Impact of the Components of Treatment Strategy

Facet	Expected Impact	Justification
Monetary	Impacts repurchase propensity by reducing acquisition costs • strongest expected impact	Demonstrated above average price elasticity of demand
Frequency	Impacts repurchased propensity by amplifying potential benefits • second strongest expected impact	Additional touches lead to additional sales
Messaging	Impacts repurchased propensity by influencing perceived cost–benefit ratio • the weakest expected impact	Requires relatively high reader involvement

Program Impact Measurement

The final of the top three analytical priorities is the development of a robust impact measurement methodology, one that is capable of quantifying treatment-attributable incrementality. Unlike the previously discussed front-end planning and incentive assessments, this is a back-end functionality intended to capture the impact of the program on an ongoing basis to support improvement recommendations.

Depending on the available data and treatment restrictions, such as the requirement of extending credit-related offers to all customers whose credit was queried, one of several impact measurement options might be selected. Table 9.3 presents a summary of the available options.

In general, the all-round most effective method of quantifying treatment-induced purchase incrementality is *experimentation*. It supports the most effective means of controlling for potentially confounding extraneous influences, thus yielding the cleanest, most reliable quantification of impact. The reason it is not always used is that it is also the most demanding, specifically in terms of the sampling frame and treatment rule requirements. The need to set aside a control group can lead to perceived opportunity loss of not promoting to a group of otherwise qualified prospects; in other instances, control groups cannot be set aside because of credit queries mandating a requirement of making a credit-related offer. Even if the organization is willing and able to set aside a control group, the treated vs. control groups' size or the overall sample composition can fall short of technical requirements, precipitating the confounding of treated with non-experimentally controlled factors. In the end, although experimentation has the potential to provide the most accurate assessment of program's effectiveness, it will not be a viable option for some organizations or situations.

Where experimentation is not an option, *statistical baseline* might be a viable alternative. As outlined above, its requirements are considerably different—in fact, somewhat complementary to those of experimentation, making it a good substitute for situations where setting up experiments is not feasible. For example, statistical baseline does not require setting aside control groups nor does it carry any treatment-related sampling requirements. On the other hand, it does require a sufficient amount of historical data and an a priori development of a statistical model. Its key advantage is the emphasis on standardization of cross-treatment effects, longitudinal consistency and low maintenance reusability.

Table 9.3 Program Impact Measurement Alternatives

	Statistical Baseline	Experimentation	Consumer Survey
General Description	• Multivariate model leveraging historical and promotional data • Models "unpromoted" level of sales to be contrasted with actual sales • Singles out multiple promotion specific effects and calibrates their respective elasticities • On-going	• Approach built around **treated** (promotional exposed) and **control** (held out from promotion) groups • Non-treatment specific differences randomized or blocked to avoid confounding • Impact of treatment: $incrementality = (treated - control)$ • Point-in-time	• A sample of consumer surveyed via phone, or email or other means • Probes product purchase intentions or reasons for purchase • Relies on consumer recall of purchase reasons rather than actual purchases • Point-in-time

Requirements	• A minimum of 18 months of past purchase and promotional data
	• A multivariate model:
	  • unpromoted base
	  • offer-specific elasticities
	• Periodic refresh of the model
		• Conceptual experimental design
		• Test plan, target-offer conjoints and sampling plan
		• Measurement plan
		• Willingness to set aside control groups
			• Recency of customer behaviors
			• Measurement instrument (i.e., a questionnaire)
			• Decision rules to translate consumer opinions into quantifiable behaviours

Strengths	• Purchase-based, objective and unbiased • Quantifies effects of multiple promotions concurrently • Ideal for cross-time comparisons and trending • Very low long term cost	• Purchase-based, measuring actual sales • Unbiased and objective • Capable of attributing incrementality to specific promotions or other actions • No responder/ measurement bias	• Does not require setting aside control groups or a priori statistical models • Can yield consumer insights • Does not require pre-program planning
Weaknesses	• Requires development of possibly complex statistical model • Too complex for one-shot programs	• Requires setting aside untreated control groups • Depends on robust pre-program launch planning • Difficult to factor-in external macro factors, such competitive activity	• relies on consumer recall to attribute purchases to specific promotions • Subject to multiple biases, such as poor recall, demand effect, biased measurement • High cost
Usage Situations	• On-going programs requiring persistent and consistent measurement of impact	• Ad hoc / one-time programs with well defined offer • Special interest elements within on-going programs	• Programs where experimentation or statistical baseline cannot be used

Lastly, in some situations a *consumer survey*-based approach has also been used. Relying on buyer recall and rarely able to account for a number of macro factors, this is by far the least accurate method of quantifying treatment-attributable incrementality. As a matter of fact, it should only be used in situations where neither experimentation nor promotional baseline can be deployed.

To deliver the hoped-for impact, database segmentation cannot be viewed as existing in isolation from the other components of the database analytical process. In many regards, engaging a more methodologically advanced segmentation schema sets higher standards for what comes next—most notably, behavioral analyses to guide targeting, and back-end impact measurement to gauge the impact of the resultant business actions. In the more positive sense, as the first comprehensive data modeling step, a well-crafted database segmentation schema will set the tone for the ensuing data modeling efforts.

Mini-Case 9.1: Segmenting the Leisure Boating Market

While quite fragmented, the leisure powerboating industry is also characterized by relatively little brand differentiation, in spite of a fairly large number of established brands and considerable price variability. The industry, as such, can be thought of as a composite of several distinct boat-type segments, defined by a combination of length and purpose, which gives rise to four broad categories: 1. *runabouts*, which hold 4–8 people, have no cabin, usually measure up to 25 feet in length and can be used for general moving about on the water; 2. *cruisers*, which typically provide cabin accommodations and range from about 25 up to about 45 feet; 3. *yachts*, which are essentially larger versions of cruisers (45+ feet in length); and 4. *coastal fishing* vessels, which are non-commercial boats meant for sport fishing. By and large, brands competing in each of those segments are primarily price-differentiated; positioning-wise, there is little-to-no customer need-based differentiation and promotion-related decision making is often based on anecdotal evidence, rather than objective research.

Given the fairly information-weak state of the industry, one of the leading U.S. leisure powerboat manufacturers commissioned a comprehensive customer segmentation study to exploit a potential opportunity for gaining competitive advantage by better aligning their promotional strategies with end-customer needs. Due to the fact that the said manufacturer's portfolio of brands cut across all of the above-delineated industry segments, the focus of the research was on the entire leisure powerboat industry, with the ultimate objective encompassing the description of the *industry's competitive structure* and the identification of *unique and actionable consumer segments*. Approach-wise, both qualitative—in the form of boat owner interviews—and quantitative—taking the form of telephone surveys—research methods were utilized, along with management interviews and the review of applicable industry research. Brand scope-wise, detailed customer data were collected for more than 40 different brands across the four leisure powerboat segments, focusing primarily on boat owner needs, attitudes and usage situations, in addition to brand perception and evaluations and demographics. Lastly, the overall research was shaped by the desire to balance two important considerations

Top 10 Attributes	Brand A	Brand B	Brand C	Brand D	Brand E	Brand F	Brand G	Brand H	Brand I	Brand J
Quality	1.12	1.43	0.87	1.34	0.99	1.00	0.91	1.31	1.07	1.20
Value	1.43	1.14	1.00	1.22	0.94	1.04	1.19	1.00	1.32	0.76
Price	1.00	1.39	0.98	1.54	0.88	1.01	1.11	1.17	1.01	0.91
Prestige	0.95	1.61	0.88	1.55	0.78	1.01	1.05	1.33	1.14	1.03
Comfort	1.01	1.41	1.04	1.37	1.01	0.87	0.99	0.89	1.16	1.35
Speed	1.11	1.48	0.88	1.44	0.79	0.91	1.00	1.22	1.08	1.31
Interior styling	1.05	1.39	1.06	1.72	1.02	0.79	1.04	1.03	1.21	1.32
Exterior styling	1.09	1.45	0.99	1.63	1.00	1.02	1.09	1.11	0.99	1.20
Interior space	1.07	1.52	1.09	1.49	0.96	1.09	1.03	0.88	0.93	1.03
Exterior space	1.13	1.46	1.01	1.43	1.04	1.04	0.95	1.01	1.03	1.02

Figure 9.15 Indexing

of *interpretational parsimony* (the smaller the number of grouping dimensions, the easier it is to "make sense" of the overall solution) and *explanatory completeness* (the resultant containing solution most of the "top of mind" considerations).

Once all the requisite data was collected, amalgamated and cleaned, the exploration of the market structure was initiated with the delineation of the most important (from the standpoint of boat owners) brand evaluation criteria, which in turn led to the assessment of the individual brands on those attributes. An abbreviated summary of findings (see Figure 9.15), showing consumer evaluations of the top 10 brands (based on sales) in terms of the top 10 most salient attributes, is shown in the brand vs. attributes matrix above (highlighted in green are the top three attributes for each brand). As is clearly evident, the analysis revealed a considerable amount of variability of owners' evaluations of the degree to which individual brands meet their needs, which suggested the need for a more explicit evaluation of relative brand positioning.

Given the combination of the task at hand and the type of data, *perceptual mapping* was deemed to be the most appropriate method of relating owners' evaluations of the key product attributes and owners' perceptions of brands on those attributes. The resultant perceptual map (again, limited to only the top ten attributes and brands) shown in Figure 9.16 suggests some natural attribute and brand groupings as well as some cross-brand and cross-attribute distinctiveness (e.g., brands B, C and F, and price and speed, respectively). Taken together, the two sets of analyses offer worthwhile insights describing the structure of the overall industry, as seen from the standpoint of 1. what are the important boat ownership related characteristics, and 2. how the individual brands stack up, relative to each other, on those attributes.

The second of the two focal research areas—the identification of unique and actionable boat owner segments—entailed a reversal of the analytical perspective: The customer brand evaluations that formed the basis of the assessment of industry competitive structure were replaced with the examination of the customer base itself. Also, the importance of the two research precepts mentioned earlier (interpretational parsimony and explanatory completeness) became particularly pronounced due to the necessity of reducing the multiplicity of need and attitude-describing attributes into a more aggregate (i.e., fewer in number but retaining the

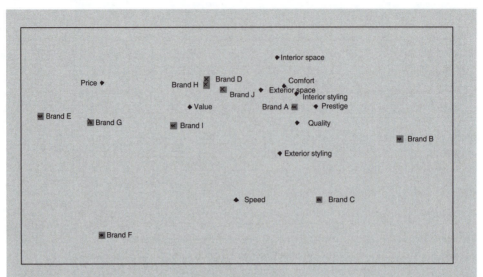

Figure 9.16 Perceptual Mapping

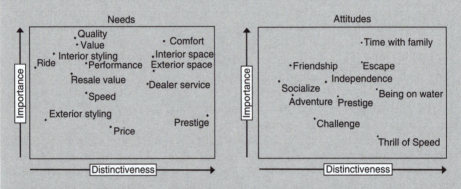

Figure 9.17 Multidimensional Scaling

detailed metrics' informational content) set of metrics. (The reason for that was that using a large number, i.e., more than about 3–4, of disaggregate measures would likely yield a segmentation solution that would be too complex to interpret and apply.) To gain initial insights into potential attribute groupings, *multidimensional scaling* (MDS), a statistical technique frequently used to explore cross-variable similarities, was utilized (see Figure 9.17). More specifically, owner-expressed evaluations of the individual "need" (tangible product attributes) and "attitude" (intangible or hedonic factors) brand attributes were statistically evaluated along the "distinctiveness" and "importance" dimensions, yielding the findings graphically displayed in the "Needs" and "Attitudes" maps. Although some natural clusters seem evident (e.g., the "comfort + interior space + exterior space + dealer service"), the solution did not overall offer clear enough grouping guidance, prompting the need for additional analysis. The next analytic step was to make use of *factor analysis* (FA), a widely used dimensional reduction technique. In contrast to MDS, FA is an iterative technique, the (ultimate) goal of which is to identify unique variable groupings, while weeding out individual variables that are either uncorrelated with other variables or are correlated with multiple other variables (and thus not uniquely related to a single, meaning-homogenous, variable set).

The results of the factor analysis (shown in Figure 9.18) point to three distinct dimensions under which most of the boat owner needs can be subsumed: 1. *utility*, comprised of internal and external space, ride and speed; 2. *value*, which includes price, resale value and performance; and 3. *prestige*, which, in addition to a disaggregate measure of "prestige" also includes interior and exterior styling. Leveraging these three summary indicators of boat owners' needs, *k-means cluster analysis* was utilized next with the goal of identifying unique customer segments, defined in terms of the individual owners' positioning relative to each of the three need dimensions (in other words, using individual boat owners' dimension-specific values, each customer was, in effect, "plotted" or positioned in the 3-dimensional space defined by utility, value and prestige; the objective of the *k*-means cluster algorithm was then to identify optimally spaced group centers so that the resultant clusters maximized both the within-group homogeneity as well as the between-group heterogeneity). Also, it is important to note that the customer segmentation was carried out separately for each of the four vessel types (runabouts, cruisers, yachts and coastal fishing), given the distinctiveness of each of the craft type's user and utility characteristics. The sample summary of the optimal solution (*k*-means cluster is an iterative technique—in this case, a different number of clusters were iteratively derived and compared, and based upon this, the 4-cluster solution shown here was deemed optimal) for the runabout vessel type, is shown here. The solution is highly statistically significant, which means that each of the three classifying dimensions—utility, value and prestige—offer effective means of cross-customer differentiation, which is also confirmed by noticeable cross-cluster means differences. Furthermore, as attested to by the "number of cases in each cluster" measure, the 763 runabout owners (i.e., survey respondents who own a boat classified as a runabout) appear to be fairly well spread out among the four segments. (An explanatory note: As it is intuitively obvious, it is not theoretically or

Classifying Dimensions	Cluster Means				Stat. Sig.
	1	2	3	4	
Utility	0.42	0.58	0.29	0.32	0.000
Value	0.30	0.20	0.42	0.28	0.000
Prestige	0.15	0.10	0.16	0.28	0.000
Number of cases in each cluster	284	121	211	147	

Figure 9.18 K-Means Clusters

Descriptor Demographics	Cluster 1	Cluster 2	Cluster 3	Cluster 4
Age	1.35	1.00	1.04	0.85
Income	1.40	1.10	1.25	1.10
Children (#)	1.20	1.30	1.10	0.95
Employ. Tenure	1.50	0.90	1.20	0.85
Education	1.00	1.20	1.10	1.40
Lifestyles				
Active	1.10	0.90	1.30	1.50
Reading	1.40	1.30	0.85	1.00
Entertainment	1.20	1.10	0.90	1.40
Sports	0.90	1.20	1.30	1.40
Media	0.95	1.30	1.20	1.50

Figure 9.19 Cluster Profiling

practically reasonable to expect an even cross-cluster respondent distribution—at the same time, in order for the resultant solution to be practically viable, each cluster needs account for a material share of the total).

Given the satisfactory quality of the *k*-means cluster-derived grouping solution, the final remaining analytic step is to profile each of the above four clusters. Among the many ways of profiling customer segments, *indexing* is perhaps the most effective method, because it emphasizes what matters the most (in this context)—distinctiveness. A sample of an index-based profile is shown in Figure 9.19. Cluster-specific values of each of the individual measures comprising the two distinct sets of descriptor—demographics and lifestyles—are operationalized using a standardized, 1- centered index, the values of which can be interpreted in the context of one of the following three, mutually exclusive categories: *value = 1* (e.g., "age" for Cluster 2) means that on that particular attribute the cluster is neither above nor below other clusters; *value < 1* (e.g., "reading" for Cluster 3) means that the cluster falls below other clusters on that particular attribute; lastly, *value > 1* (e.g., "income" for Cluster 1) means that the cluster is higher than other clusters in terms of a given attribute. Obviously, the directionality of indexed conclusions is inherently neither good nor bad, but rather offers a way of describing the overall structure of the customer base in a way that emphasizes the distinctiveness of individual segments.

10 Behavioral Predictions

Predictive analytics is a term used frequently in business, though not always in a correct manner. Oftentimes, it is invoked to describe virtually any type of data analysis relating to an outcome of interest, even basic data exploration. To a large degree, this unfortunate trend can be attributed to a relative lack of applied business analytics' definitional clarity and a considerable variability in the amount of analytic rigor across usage situations.

The goal of this chapter is to bring forth and examine some of the more important methodological considerations surrounding behavioral-prediction-focused applied marketing database analytics. Even more importantly, it is to make a series of recommendations regarding the use of prediction-focused statistical techniques in the process of creating actionable, decision-aiding knowledge. As such, the ensuing discussion does not purport to offer a comprehensive survey of all applicable statistical techniques—rather, it aims to point to specific techniques and related considerations that have demonstrated the greatest amount of data analytic utility.

Behavioral Predictions and Decision Support

What makes companies succeed? Why do some organizations prosper in the same environment where others struggle? Although specific answers may vary, as documented by Tom Peters and Robert Waterman in their well-read book *In Search of Excellence*, as well as a number of other researchers, there are certainly clear commonalities both differentiating effective from mediocre firms and uniting the former, even across industry lines. The manner in which they use information available to them and make decisions is one of the most significant determinants of their success. Using data to create sustainable competitive advantage translates into the development of a robust informational baseline with the help of various descriptive and pattern identification tools and methods described in earlier. At the same time, it also means using data in a more prescriptive fashion, most often embodied in predictive modeling capabilities, specifically, those focusing on behavioral predictions.

Model Specification Revisited: Data vs. Statistical Effects

Any discussion of behavioral predictions needs to include an explicit differentiation between *data* and *statistical effects*. The key difference between the two is that the former exists independently of any modeling endeavors, while the latter is inextricably connected with a specific analytic exercise. In other words, although some data may be collected with a specific purpose (i.e., customer base segmentation) in mind, in general, data exists whether it is being used or not, because it tends to be a by-product of business transactions.[1] A statistical effect, on the other hand, is a metric that is created with a specific analytical purpose in mind—i.e., it does not exist prior to, and often outside of, specific analytical endeavor.

Conceptually, data and statistical effects should be approached differently. Data can explored for the insights it hides, in which case little-to-no theoretical foundation is necessary. It can also be used in a prescriptive or predictive manner, in which case it is necessary to have at least a general theoretical model in mind, spelling out the presumed relationships.

Statistical effects, on the other hand, require a foundation of sound theoretical reasoning, largely due to practical considerations. Also, in contrast to data, which for most part is a manifestation of certain observable outcomes, such as product sales, statistical effects are intended to capture the intangible component of the forces shaping those outcomes, such as the interdependence of sales and promotional spending or the diminishing productivity of extra promotional spending. In short, statistical effects represent means of modeling, or replicating reality with the goal of understanding (and quantifying) the impact of specific business actions. Although in theory there can be an infinite number of statistical effects, they tend to fall within the four basic categories: *indicators, indices, interactions* and *velocitators*.

Indicators

These typically dichotomous measures are used to denote the presence or absence of an event, trait or a phenomenon of interest. Often referred to in practice as "flags" or "dummy-coded variables," they are most frequently expressed as nominal measures, which means their analytic applicability is relatively constrained (see Chapter 7 for more detail). Coding-wise, indicators can be qualitative (e.g., "yes" vs. "no," or "male" vs. "female") or quantitative (e.g., "0" vs. "1"). Although interpretation-wise it makes little difference, it is often more convenient to use quantitatively coded indicator measures as inputs into analyses.

Indices

Most types of transactional databases entail repetition, whether it is repeat purchases of a given product or by a given household, or repeat measures of certain outcomes, such as financial reports submitted to the SEC on quarterly or annual basis. Either way, this translates into a need to capture frequency counts of certain events or other occurrences. For instance, to be able to determine a household's brand loyalty, it is necessary to count the number of certain types of purchases. Indices are metrics designed especially for the purpose of providing such frequency counts. In contrast to indicators, they are almost always numerically coded and measured on either interval or ratio scales, which makes them more statistically versatile.

Interactions

What if the above mentioned indices and indicators were not sufficient to explain the variability contained in the data, yielding a statistically poor model fit and an inadequate amount of predictive power? One of the tactics that can be used to improve the model's performance, without dramatically increasing the number of variables (which would take away from the model's parsimony, discussed earlier) is to introduce measures of cross-variable interactions and nonlinear effects.

In general, dependence-methodologies-based behavioral models, such as regression, are based on the assumption of predictor independence. For the most part, this is of course a sound idea, as its goal is to eliminate redundancy among the individual metrics, which ultimately leads to greater parsimony. Unfortunately, sometimes it results in relatively weak (prediction-wise) models, simply because the assumption that the outcome of interest, such as brand sales, is largely shaped by a set of mutually independent factors simply does not reflect reality. Interaction terms, which represent the combined effect of two or more factors,[2] can be introduced to enhance the predictive power of a behavioral model. However, since an interaction term can employ measures that are already included in the model as stand-alone predictors, the inclusion of these terms will typically violate the assumption of predictor independence mentioned earlier.[3] (In a technical sense, behavioral models meeting the assumption of predictor independence are "additive," which allows for an assessment of cumulative power of the otherwise singularly measured metrics; adding-in interaction terms will often result in "non-additive" models.)

Methodological considerations aside, interaction effects can yield informationally invaluable insights, simply because they capture what are often quite pronounced real-life interdependencies. For instance, a consumer's decision to repurchase a particular brand could be expressed as a function of that brand's price level and prices of suitable alternatives, each expressed as a singular effect. The resultant predictive score would then be comprised of the sum of stand-alone impacts of the individual brands' prices. What the score would not capture would be any potential interactions among the different brands' prices. In other words, what exactly is the benefit of quickly matching competitors' prices vs. adhering to a more-or-less self-dictating pricing tactic? How about promotional "pulsing-stacking"—is it more beneficial from the standpoint of incremental revenue or profitability to run multiple promotions concurrently (followed by a period of no promotions), or to run individual promotions sequentially, without a significant overlap? Such knowledge is what gives an organization sustainable competitive advantage, which is why at least testing of the interaction effects should always be considered an important part of behavioral model development.

In terms of model specification, interaction terms introduce an added level of complexity for a couple of distinct reasons. First, their inclusion changes the character of the model from the conceptually more straightforward additive formulation to the more involved multiplicative formulation. Additive models tend to be easier to evaluate—in terms of the statistically expressed goodness-of-fit—and to interpret. Second, the addition of interaction terms increases the level of difficulty of the previously discussed model specification. However, the additional specification complexity will then tend to diminish the model specification error. Specifically, inclusion of interaction, or product[4] (as they are also called) terms will generally diminish the model under-specification by lessening of the omitted variable bias.

As suggested earlier, the inclusion of interaction terms can draw criticisms from some methodologists because it tends to increase collinearity (inter-correlations among predictor variables) in the resultant model, though there is no evidence suggesting that it reduces the robustness or validity of the model. That said, when considered from the standpoint of developing a knowledge base of competitively advantageous insights, the trade-off between a more realistic (i.e., all-encompassing) explanation vs. greater collinearity, when there is no compelling evidence suggesting that the latter diminishes the robustness, seems to point to the appropriateness of erring on the side of including interaction terms.

Velocitators

Many statistical models used in the industry are built around the idea of linear or constant effect of predictors on outcomes of interest. For instance, a promotional mix model will often estimate a household's product purchase/repurchase propensity to be a function of a slew of factors, including past purchases, prices, various promotional vehicles, etc. The resultant effect estimates are commonly linear in nature, which is in direct contradiction to the frequently observed law of diminishing marginal returns.[5] Although such an oversimplification can be "tolerable" from the standpoint of exploratory, descriptive analyses, it can yield dubious recommendations in the context of promotional mix allocation and related business planning.

Operationally, linear relationships hold certain effects to be constant across the range of values, which in practice can lead to some hard-to-believe outcomes. For instance, when expressed linearly, the presence of a single coupon might increases the brand repurchase likelihood by 5%, which would then lead to the conclusion that the presence of 10 such coupons would increase the repurchase likelihood by 50%; similarly, if the promotional budget of X produces Y incremental gains, a linear extrapolation will lead to the conclusion that increasing the said promotional budget, say 10-fold will produce a corresponding 10-fold increase in the incremental gain. Clearly, no good business purpose can be served by making decisions rooted in such unrealistic extrapolations.

At the same time, it is important to note that the linear-effect-induced interpretational error does not necessarily need to be inflationary in nature, as just as easily it can lead to the understanding of certain propensities. For instance, in the context of securities class action[6] mitigation, the initially small impact of a relatively (monetarily) small net income restatement might increase exponentially as the value of the said restatement grows. Here, expressing the initially computed class action probability linearly would lead to the understating of the potential consequences of net income restatements.

In view of the significant shortcomings of only considering linearly expressed relationships, yet another category of statistical effects is necessary to capture any nonlinear effects that might better describe the interrelationships embedded in the data. Velocitators are a type of statistical effect designed expressly to capture the degree to which certain measures have a non-constant or nonlinear impact on the outcomes of interest. Similar to the previously discussed interaction terms, the inclusion of velocitators will add to the analytical complexity of behavioral models, but the added complexity will be outweighed by the resultant informational gains.

The Role of Effect Types

Capturing and correctly coding the statistical effects of real life business interactions are critically important to the ensuing behavioral analyses. The degree to which any model can capture—and henceforth, explain—reality is highly contingent on the sufficiency of model specification. Of particular importance is the efficacy of the business-relationship-to-statistical-effect translation and the adequacy of the scope of model coverage.

The efficacy of the *business-relationship-to-statistical-effect translation* is a reflection of the accuracy with which individual variables and cross-variable interrelationships are both operationalized adequately. As pointed out in the Informational Domain Specification discussion, a model can be over-, under- or just-specified. An inadequate operationalization of individual variables and/or cross-variable interrelationships can lead to model under-specification. Such models will be characterized by poor explanatory and classificatory power. In other words, they will demonstrate poor goodness-of-fit statistics (i.e., low amounts of explained variance, such as relatively small R^2 in linear or pseudo-R^2 in logistic regression models) and will yield low predictive accuracy power (i.e., low correct classification rate, such as correctly classifying as "high-value" buyers who indeed turn out to exhibit above-average spending levels).

The adequacy of the *scope of model coverage* is a reflection of the model's inclusion logic—which variables and relationships are explicitly embodied in the model? Simply put, it is a measure of the degree to which what is included within the scope of the model provides enough "raw materials" to answer the questions posed by the stated informational objectives. In the context of the Informational Domain Specification, inadequate scope of coverage can manifest itself either in the form of model under-specification or over-specification (although in practice, under-specification is far more common). Outcome-wise, the evidence of an inadequate scope of model coverage is a bit less self-evident than is the evidence of the above-discussed efficacy of the business-relationship-to-statistical-effect translation. Primarily, it is made visible by a potential gap separating the informational content of the model's "take-aways" and the stated informational objectives: If the results of the model do not provide sufficient information to objectively answer the stated business questions, it is likely that the underlying model's scope is not sufficiently broad, in an operational sense.

Some Practical Considerations

Recall the earlier discussion of *Informational Domain Specification* (Chapter 8). As noted there, the inclusion of statistical effects requires the foundation of a solid theoretical reasoning, primarily for the very practical reason of containing a possible effect proliferation. An average transactional database contains hundreds of raw metrics, which potentially could give rise to thousands of potential statistical effects (indicators, indices, interactions and velocitators). For instance, let's estimate the number of potential interaction effects for a database containing 100 individual metrics. To do so, we can use the following factorial formula:

$$\text{Number of Potential Interactions} = \frac{n!}{\kappa!(n - \kappa)!}$$

where,

κ = number of 2-way interactions
n = number of raw metrics

Solving the above equation for $k = 2$ (2-way interaction) and $n = 100$ (100 individual raw variables), we arrive at 4,950 potential interaction terms! Needless to say, that number does not include indicators, indices or velocitators and for that matter, it only accounts for 2-way interactions. Clearly, without an a priori rationale focusing the attention on a specific subset of all of the potentially available statistical effects, even a moderately sized (in terms of the number of raw metrics) data file might result in an overwhelming number of analyzable measures.

Predictive Reliability of Indicators

Chapter 8 contains a warning against over-reliance on statistical significance testing (SST), particularly when constructing longitudinal generalizations. SST has been frequently—and incorrectly—used to "validate" numerous promotional decisions, such as making forward projections from small-scale promotional campaign pilots, which at times has led to the blurring of the line between "statistical" and "practical" significance. That said, the computational mechanics of these tests (such as t-tests of means or χ^2 tests of proportions) can support sample-to-population generalizations that form the foundation to the derivation of a wide range of inferential statistical models. This is particularly the case in the calibration of sample-based predictive models geared toward the delineation of specific drivers of the phenomenon of interest, such as a class of predictive models falling under the umbrella of response propensity models.

A *response propensity model* is a statistical solution quantifying the probability of occurrence of specific events, such as the probability of a consumer purchasing a particular product, following his/her exposure to purchase-incentivizing promotional stimuli. In general, promotional response propensities capture the inclination of potential brand purchasers to respond to promotional offers targeted at them. As such, these models play a dual role: First, they offer a unit-of-analysis-specific (i.e., a prospective buyer) assessment of response likelihood, which usually forms the basis for focusing promotional efforts and dollars on the most-likely-to-respond subset of all prospective targets (a practice commonly referred to as "differential treatment"). Second, propensity models also tend to bring to light the most pronounced drivers of respondents' inclination to respond, which, in database analytical terms, constitutes the delineation of indicators of the phenomenon of interest. It is here that statistical significance tests can be of considerable value, if used properly.

As detailed in Chapter 8, SST quantifies the probability that an observed relationship could be a result of a mere chance, rather than an indication of an enduring association. In other words, significance testing offers the means of attesting to the generalizability of sample-based findings and/or conclusions. Since these tests are based on inferences, their conclusions will always be probabilistic—i.e., based on the degree of confidence, rather than absolute certainty. Over the years, a three-tiered significance level became widely accepted: $\alpha = 0.01$, which corresponds to 1% probability of the observed relationship arising purely out of random chance; $\alpha = 0.05$, which corresponds to 5% probability of the observed relationship arising purely out of random chance; and $\alpha = 0.10$, which corresponds to 10% probability of the observed relationship arising purely out of random chance.[7] Stated differently, a conclusion of statistically significant relationship can have 1-in-100 (p = 0.01), 1-in-20 (p = 0.05) or 1-in-10 (p = 0.10%) chance of being incorrect. This means that in the context of a large, multivariate model, different metrics can be significant at varying numerical levels. A common practice is to choose one of the three thresholds (p = 0.05 being the most commonly used) and evaluate all potentially explanatory indicators in relation to that singular threshold. In the academic-theory-building sense this is a very rational and an appropriate approach, but it is not necessarily so in the context of applied business analyses. Here is why:

Let's say that a response propensity model resulted in singling out a dozen of the individual drivers of response. Let us further assume that some of those indicators are highly significant, i.e., $p \leq 1\%$ (telling the analyst that the likelihood of those relationships being spurious is less than 1-in-100), some others are somewhat weaker, but nonetheless still significant, i.e., $1\% > p \leq 5\%$ (again, telling the analyst that the likelihood of those relationships being spurious is approximately 1-in-20), with the remaining group registering as statistically significant, but at the lowest of the three previously mentioned levels, i.e., $5\% < p \leq 10\%$ (telling the analyst that the likelihood of those relationships being spurious is about 1-in-10). Let us then say that only a single significance threshold is used, which is quite typical. Unless the most restrictive of the three significance cut-off values is used (i.e., $p \leq 1\%$), metrics manifesting considerably dissimilar levels of reliability will be lumped together into a single category, which in turn may lead to equal reliance (in the business decision making process) on metrics exhibiting otherwise distinctly differently levels of reliability.

Imagine confronting a choice of following two potential courses of action: Option 1 has a 1-in-100 chance of leading to damaging consequences; Option 2 has a 1-in-10 chance of leading to damaging consequence. Assuming that no other differences exist between Options 1 and 2, which one would you choose? Clearly, this is a rhetorical question, since no rational person would pick Option 2. Why then treat quantitatively quite dissimilar insights as equally reliable?

There is an obvious alternative to the fuzzying of the otherwise important cross-indicator reliability differences: Construct a 3-tier *indicator reliability* table, as illustrated in Table 10.1.

As seen in Table 10.1, statistically significant metrics are grouped into 3 tiers, corresponding to the three generally accepted thresholds of $p \leq 0.01$ (1-in-100 "false positive" chance), $p \leq 0.05$ (1-in-20 "false positive" chance) and $p \leq 0.10$ (1-in-10 "false positive" chance). In addition, standardized estimate of each metric's contribution to the explained variability (e.g., partial R^2 for linear regression) is also provided to round off the overall assessment of all statistically significant metrics' predictive power.

Once again, the importance of this step lies in increasing the business efficacy of the otherwise abstract statistical findings. To the degree to which individual predictors vary in terms of SST-related reliability, their usefulness as, for instance, target population selection tools will also vary accordingly. For example, a propensity-to-repurchase indicator falling into Tier I (1-in-100 "false positive" chance) offers considerably higher levels of targeting utility than indicators falling into Tiers II or III.

Model Building vs. Behavioral Predictions

There is a tendency to embrace the "model-building" mindset, which is especially true in the context of predictive analyses. The unfortunate consequence of that trend is the subsequent confounding of the organizational knowledge goals with the (usually) highly abstract statistical models. Perhaps more than any other aspect of the database analytical process described in this book, behavioral predictions tends to be more about the underlying statistical infrastructure than about the end user functionality, due to their heavy reliance on multivariate statistical modeling techniques. Arguably, this is among the key explanations for why, in spite of a considerable amount of effort and technical talent often deployed against predictive analytical endeavors, their ultimate impact may at times seem disproportionately small. Circumventing of that apparent shortcoming

Table 10.1 Three-Tier Indicator Reliability Assessment

| Metrics | Predictive Reliability | | | Explanatory Power |
	Tier I: 1-in-100 "false positive" chance	Tier II: 1-in-20 "false positive" chance	Tier III: 1-in-10 "false positive" chance	Standardized Estimate of Contribution
Metric A				
Metric B				
Metric C				
Metric D				
Metric n				

requires looking at predictive analytics more from the standpoint of end user functionality, or desired informational benefits and "backing" into the appropriate techniques. This can be a surprisingly simple endeavor, given that the most common informational goals of behavioral analyses can be grouped into the following three categories:

1. **Threat Anticipation.** Encompassing the means of identifying weaknesses in the current customer base, this dimension of behavioral prediction is usually associated with questions such as, *what are the "early signs" of attrition, the drivers of the likelihood to attrite and the most at-risk customers*, etc. The analytical focus here is limited to the current customers only, which in effect expands, often considerably, the universe of usable data.

2. **Opportunity Identification.** Focused on the identification of near- and longer-term growth opportunities, this aspect of behavioral predictions is often evident in questions such as *what are the most effective and efficient ways of growing customer base and revenues; what are the drivers of new customer acquisition, current customer repurchase and/or value growth*, etc. The analytical focus of opportunity identification is the point of differentiation between "good" and "bad" acquisition targets, usually accomplished via scoring of all available prospects on the probability of certain outcomes, such as brand purchase. Informationally, this limits the data universe to the subset that is available for all targets.

3. **Mix Assortment and Optimization.** This particular area represents the analytically most challenging aspect of behavioral predictions, and consequently its least developed one. Informationally and analytically, the focus of mix assortment and optimization is considerably different from the previous two areas; it encompasses a relatively wide array of business issues ranging from the identification of the most productive promotional mix assortment to what-if resource allocation scenarios. In particular, whereas *threat anticipation* and *opportunity identification* are primarily concerned with prospective and current customers, respectively, *mix assortment and optimization* is focused on the aggregate performance of distinct promotional vehicles. In analytical sense, rather than modeling individual- or household-level propensities, this particular area of the targeting and behavioral predictions part of the overall database analytical process aims to model aggregate macroeconomic effects. Furthermore, while both threat anticipation and opportunity identification are analytically static—i.e., they quantify individual- or household-level probabilities at distinct points in time—mix assortment and optimization is intended to be a dynamic tool used for an ongoing "what-if" scenario planning.

A brief conceptual overview of each of the three behavioral analyses areas is presented next, followed by an in-depth discussion of the methodological considerations.

Threat Anticipation

Over time, some of the current customers will increase their purchase levels while others will diminish their spending; new buyers will be acquired, while some of the current ones will be lost. Virtually all customer/prospect databases are fluid over time and thus one of the key goals of database-focused promotional efforts is to make sure that the said fluidity results in a net gain to the organization. That said, some downward value migration and/or customer attrition—to use the business jargon—are usually inescapable as those changes reflect the dynamic nature of the customer base, as it is influenced by forces such as lifestage and lifecycle, economic conditions or competitive activities. However, an *excessive* loss of customers or customer base value, i.e., average purchase levels, is preventable.

Although what constitutes an "excessive" loss is usually open to an interpretation. Objectively it can be said that an excessive customer base loss is that portion of the total loss which can be deemed *preventable*. In other words, while some loss to any customer base is inescapable due to "natural" factors—including value migration (e.g., "trading-up" to a more upscale product category) and customer attrition (e.g., no longer in need of a particular product type, death)—customers can also abandon a particular brand in favor of its competitor, which is generally the controllable part of the customer base loss. Overall, if a brand's customer base is steadily declining over time, either in customer count or in aggregate customer value (i.e., revenue or profitability), it is more than likely due to inadequate customer retention measures. This assertion is particularly true if during the time in question the overall population grew at a steady rate, as did the average household income—under those circumstances, most brands' customer databases should not exhibit persistent, downward customer count or value trends. Those that do are usually losing the competitive struggle by not taking adequate steps to minimize the preventable customer base attrition.

Hence, the focus of the discussion surrounding customer base threat anticipation is on the analytic means of pinpointing the "most at risk of attrition" customers, coupled with the identification of the most effective means of reducing that risk. It should be pointed out that the recommended approaches are guided by what might be called an "ROI-centric" philosophy. In short, it amounts to saying that the goal of the customer base threat identification analytics is not a mere singling out of the customers who are most likely to attrite, but rather it is also to expressly differentiate between the two key categories of such customers: the (retention) investment-worthy group and the low-value switchers (i.e., customers not warranting a comparable level of retention spending).

Opportunity Identification

Of all goals shared by organizations, growth is probably the most universal one. Publicly traded companies' stock valuations and their analyst ratings are both strongly influenced by a given company's growth prospects. Insofar as customer/prospect databases are concerned, to continue to grow, an organization needs to be able to relatively accurately pinpoint the most effective ways of attracting new buyers and encouraging existing ones to increase their spending levels.

Growth can be either acquisition-driven or organic. The former is a result of acquiring assets previously owned by other organizations. It follows that in the vast majority of instances, acquisition-based growth strategy can be pursued at the level of an organization, rather than an individual brand. Organic growth, on the other hand, can be pursued at the more disaggregate level, such as an individual brand. In terms of database-related applications, the notion of growth is operationally quite similar for acquisition as well as organic expansion. Acquisition of new customers typically entails "taking over" of an existing customer base, while organic growth entails "working more effectively" with the existing customer base. In either case, it translates into being able to accurately project future behaviors onto the current set of customers and prospects. Specifically, it calls for robust differentiation between the identification of the ways—and means—of attracting new buyers to an existing set of brands or increasing the repurchase levels/frequencies among the current customer base. To deliver sufficient incremental gains, both of these endeavors require robust and well-thought-out analytical insights.

Perhaps one of the most puzzling features of that aspect of customer base analytics is the commonly seen lack of recognition of the inherent interdependencies between, on the one hand, the retention of current customers and the acquisition of new ones, on the other. Although in the business sense the two might be perceived as sufficiently different and thus are often pursued with separate strategic planning efforts and tactical initiatives, not to mention different teams, the persistent lack of recognition between current customer retention and new customer acquisition frequently manifests itself in sub-par results of both. As a result, the emphasis in the ensuing discussion of the analytics of customer opportunity identification will be on exploring and subsequently leveraging these interdependencies.

Mix Assortment and Optimization

Consider the well-known hierarchy of needs, first postulated by Abraham Maslow.[8] In that context, the earlier outlined *threat anticipation* and *opportunity identification* aspects of predictive database analytics could be categorized as the fundamental or basic food-and-shelter type of business needs, the *mix assortment and optimization* aspect of behavioral predictions should be viewed as the top of the business need pyramid—the informational self-actualization, of sorts.

Organizations with well-grounded basic behavioral predictive capabilities should naturally progress toward evolving those functionalities into more interactive and more encompassing scenario-planning capabilities. The static insights yielded by opportunity identification and threat anticipation methods can be molded into dynamic, "what-if" scenario-planning assets capable of yielding cross-scenario comparative decision making inputs. This is particularly pertinent to promotional mix optimization problems, where the challenge lies in the identification of the most effective—given the stated promotional objectives—combination of promotional tools, such as direct mail, general advertising or online promotions. Since there are usually multiple plausible cross-promotional channel resource allocation scenarios, the ability to conduct objective and reliable side-by-side comparisons of competing allocation scenarios will be of considerable benefit to the decision makers.

Threat Anticipation

In many regards, current customer retention is both the least challenging from the analytical point of view and the most overlooked from the business standpoint aspect of the customer base strategy. It is often perplexing why so many organizations with both the resources and data/methodological means continue to disregard the obvious benefits of more robust customer retention efforts. According to the often repeated business factoid, it costs an average organization about four times less to retain a current customer than it does to acquire a new one, yet so many pursue new customer acquisition with a lot more vigor—and resources—than they invest in retaining their current customers.

Over the years, entire industries embarked on often hard-to-understand (business rationale-wise) new customer acquisition "wars." Cellular service providers, for instance, became infamous for offering prospective subscribers rates that were considerably more favorable to those made available to their current subscribers, creating (current) customer resentment that ultimately (i.e., upon the contract expiration) translated either into defection or considerable profit decreases stemming from retention subsidies made necessary by new customer acquisition offers. In some regard, the reason organizations tend to be so focused on new customer acquisition is often their lackluster or halfhearted current customer retention efforts. And although some of the blame may rest with organizational policies and reward structures (i.e., offering new customer acquisition bonuses, but no corresponding retention incentives), many organizations also lack robust current customer valuation and related retention analytic supports.

Still, even some of the organizations that make heavy use of data to support current customer retention efforts do so in a way that does not yield sustainable competitive advantage. Specifically, they tend to identify and pursue all at-risk-of-attrition customers, allocating the same amount of resources and effort to all customer types. However, as detailed in the previous chapter's *Loyalty Segmentation* discussion, not only are not all customers equally valuable to the organization, the retention of some can be unprofitable, i.e., it is better to let those customers attrite. In that sense, the reason the otherwise well-intended customer retention efforts may not always enhance the firm's competitive advantage is because these efforts are oftentimes operationally indiscriminant. This is a direct consequence of being "targeted" at retaining a cross-section of the customer base universe, as opposed to being expressly focused on higher-value buyers only. It follows that a competitively advantageous customer retention approach is one that enables the organization to retain a disproportionately high proportion (i.e., an "unfair share") of high-value customers, while expressly de-emphasizing the retention of lower-value customers. The reason this line of thinking offers the most direct road to gaining and sustaining competitive advantage is that, over time, it will systematically boost the proportion of "high category spenders" in the organization's customer base mix. Business planning-wise, however, it requires that retention goals be governed by profit-related considerations, rather than the frequently seen raw retention counts (i.e., an unqualified number of retained customers).

Consequently, the customer retention approach outlined here is built around the philosophy of differential customer treatment and resource allocation, according to which, the amount of retention effort should be proportional to the value of the customer to the organization. The value of the customer, on the other hand, should be expressed as a function of that customer's cumulative profit contribution, adjusted for promotional response likelihood, where possible. Transactional frequency, often used as a customer value proxy, should only be implicitly incorporated into that assessment. This means that, everything else being equal, a frequent but subsidy-intensive buyer will likely be deemed less valuable than a less frequent but also less subsidy-intensive one. It also means that retention resource allocation will be skewed toward high-value customers, so much so that in some instances no resources will be allocated against the lowest value customer tier.

The key to developing effective customer retention analytical supports lies in the *customer value nesting* rationale depicted in Figure 10.1. As shown in this visualization, nested within the universe of "all consumers" is the sub-universe of "high category value" buyers, and then nested within the latter grouping is the segment of "brand high-value" consumers.

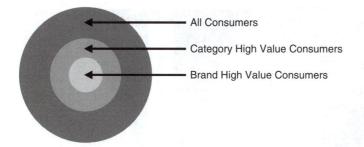

Figure 10.1 Current Customer Categories: Retention View

Analytically, the customer value nesting rationale suggests that the *all current customers* universe should be the sampling frame for the identification of *all at-risk current customers,* which in turn should be the sampling frame for the identification of all *high-value at-risk current customers*.

The sequencing implied above, where the at-risk segment is delineated ahead of the high-value one, is critical. In general, the results of any statistical modeling endeavor are at least in part contingent on the characteristics of the sample on which the model's coefficients were calibrated, since the model merely reflects any relationships that are "hidden" in the data. Flagging of all at-risk customers first defines the total universe of potential defectors[9] in a way that gives rise to a quantitative assessment of the aggregate amount of attrition-related risk, at a given point in time. In other words, it gives the organization a clear picture of the potential cost of customer attrition, which should be used as the basis for resource planning. This is best expressed through a couple of "share" metrics: *the at-risk share of the overall customer base*, and the *at-risk share of total profit*.

$$\text{At-risk share of customer base} = \sum_{t=\kappa} \frac{C_r}{C_a}$$

where,

c_a = all current customers
c_r = all at-risk current customers
t = time period

$$\text{At-risk share of total profit} = \sum_{t=\kappa} \frac{P_r}{P_a}$$

where,

p_a = total profit
p_r = profit attributable to all at-risk customers
t = time period

The intersection of the *at-risk of attrition share of customer base* and the *at-risk customers' share of profit* metrics forms the basis for guiding the differential retention resource allocation in a way leading to sustainable competitive advantage. In essence, it highlights the fact that since not all customers contribute equally to the organization's profitability, the cost

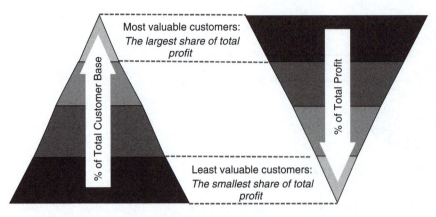

Figure 10.2 Customer Segment-Profit Relationship

of current customer attrition will vary, often quite considerably, across the at-risk customer universe, as illustrated in Figure 10.2.

Hence the initially identified sub-universe of all at-risk current customers should be rank-ordered based on their respective value to the organization. In most instances, the bulk of the firm's profit is generated by a relatively small subset of all customers—e.g., the frequently cited "80–20," where 80% of the brand's or organization's profit is concentrated in the top 20% of all customers. Of course, the flip side of that statistic is that the bottom 20% or 30% of the customer base account for a very small proportion of the total profit, often as low as 2%–5%. The relationship depicted in Figure 10.2 makes clear both the perils of the "one-size-fits-all" retention strategy implicitly assigning equal value to all customers, as well as the potential for sustainable competitive advantage associated with more intelligent, differential retention efforts. Thus quantifying the customer-specific (i.e., database record) cumulative value, in relation to the attrition expectancy will enable the decision makers to prioritize any retention efforts and differentially allocate retention resources, in a manner that best reflects the expectancy of risk-adjusted customer value.

As expected, however, a differential retention strategy is more information-intensive. Specifically, as implied by the *at-risk of attrition share of customer base* and the *at-risk customers' share of profit* metrics discussed earlier, differential retention strategy requires historical-spending-based assessment of customer value as well as the forward-looking projections. In addition, it requires a thoughtful interpretative step to "translate" numerical probabilities into clear business action recommendations. In other words, it entails two separate analytical steps:

1. **Identification.** Up-to-date customer value quantification and behavioral likelihood estimation.
2. **Categorization.** Development of action-suggestive categories.

Classification

As suggested by the customer value nesting discussed above and depicted in Figure 10.1, current customer value classification requires the identification of all at-risk customers followed by the delineation of all high-value at-risk customers, as defined below:

- Step 1: Identification of all at-risk customers as a sub-population of all current customers.
- Step 2: Delineation of all high-value customers as a sub-population of the at-risk group defined in Step 1 above.

Step 1: At-Risk Customer Identification

To some degree, every customer has a certain intrinsic probability of opting for a different brand while repurchasing within a given category of products or services[10] for reasons ranging from competitive promotions to evolving needs, tastes or preferences. This suggests that the task of at-risk of attrition customer identification calls for a probabilistic approach, capable of estimating that likelihood for all current customers. In an operational sense, the end objective here is to assign a unique, numerical probability to each current customer (i.e., database record, which might describe a single individual, a household or a business), in a way that best reflects that customer's likelihood of not repurchasing the same brand (which is obviously a reciprocal of the likelihood same brand repurchase).

Although this could be accomplished by a variety of means, the most effective of the field-tested methodologies is the "look-alike" application of logistic regression. This particular application entails two important considerations: First, two distributionally similar samples of customers need to be selected, where one sample is comprised of current customers who did not attrite and the other is made up of former customers (i.e., those who switched to another brand). It is important to note that being distributionally similar does not mean that the two samples should be identical or even similar in terms of their characteristics,[11] rather it requires that distributions of at least the defining characteristics be similar in term of the basic properties.

The second part of that process involves the calibrating of a logistic regression model, with the goal of quantifying the odds of individual customers not repurchasing the current brand. In essence, this particular application of logistic regression estimates the degree to which individual database records look like (hence the name of this particular analytical approach—the "look-alike" analysis) the target group, commonly referred to as *brand defectors*. That is why the aforementioned cross-sample distributional similarity is so important—the predictive and classificatory accuracy of the resultant solution is highly dependent on key metric mean differences between the two samples, which requires similar proportions across the continuum of responder types.

It is important to keep in mind that even the most robust logistic "look-alike" models just quantify record-level attrition probabilities, which though critically important, in and of itself does not solve the problem of objectively demarking "high" from "low" attrition probability customers. As is usually the case, the tail ends of the resultant distribution—e.g., the 5% attrition probability or 90% attrition probability cases—will carry with them self-evident interpretation, while it will be the objective line of demarcation drawn to separate the high and low likelihood groups that will be most puzzling. Nonetheless, a set of relatively objective decision rules can be used with an eye toward a consistent application of the same rationale to bring about cross-sectional and longitudinal result comparability. The recommended process is detailed in Table 10.2.

Table 10.2 The Look-Alike Modelling Process

Process Step	Description	Decision
	Select the representative samples of current and attrited customers (2 samples)	The sample sizes should be at least 50% higher than required to allow for future pruning.
Modeling samples selection		<u>Weak test</u>: Prepare side-by-side histograms (for the two samples), showing actual value labels and conduct visuals, qualitative inspection of pairwise degrees of similarity. *Although not ideal, the weak test provides a "quick and dirty" look at the two samples and can be used effectively to identify metrics on which samples are grossly dissimilar*
	Quantify distributional similarity between the two samples	<u>Strong test</u>: The logistic regression based "look-alike" modeling requires the predictor metrics to be either normally distributed or dummy-coded (for categorical variables). Hence a more robust alternative to a direct-side-by-side distributional comparison is a normative contrast, where both samples' distributional properties are assessed in terms of their normality, which as detailed in Chapter 7 involves assessment od swewness and kurtosis. If both samples are deemed "normal" in accordance with a priori established criteria, then they should be considered functionally identical. *A more objective and methodologically robust approach, the strong test should be used whever possible.*
Look-alike modeling	Identify appropriate set of predictors	• Assess metric collinearity • Consider metrics' level of aggregation (see *Data Reduction* discussed in Chapter 5) • Review input data requirements, such as indicator/dummy variable coding for discrete variables
	Fit the model / calibrate coefficients	• Review model's classificatory accuracy—confusion matrix for logistic regression • Assess model'sgoodness-of-fit indicators—pseudo R^2 statistic • Assess model's explanatory parsimony—review the predictive variate for nnumber of predictors and assess the individual predictor'sincrement explanatory contribution.

Step 2: High-Value At-Risk Customer Identification

In an analytical sense, the task of delineating the high-value subset of all at-risk customers is considerably less taxing than the at-risk customer identification, as it simply entails summing up of purchases over a predetermined period of time and, delineating the number of value-based customer groupings and drawing a line of demarcation between those predefined categories. Simpler on the one hand, it is also less objective insofar as it leaves a lot more open to subjective analyst interpretation. That said, it is both possible and beneficial to construct a set of simple a priori rules to guide the value category creation and individual customer valuation steps.

It is helpful to think of value groupings as deviation from the average—i.e., customers can be classified as exhibiting the average levels of spending and those falling below as well as above it, which suggests three distinct customer value categories: *the average value*; *below-average* value and *above-average value*. Possibly the most objective benchmark for determining group boundaries is to simply divide the entire universe into three more-or-less equally sized groups, with each of the three value groupings accounting for approximately 33% of the total.

Another approach that is a bit more subjective is to count as average the "middle" 50% of customers, with the remaining 50% being divided up into two equal groups of above and below average. This approach is intuitively appealing because it parallels the frequently used quartile approach, where the total is divided into 4 equally sized grouping, or quartiles. In this case, the middle two quartiles are collapsed into a single category—the average-value customers—while the remaining two quartiles correspond to the above- and below-average customer value categories. Graphically, this could be illustrated in the context of the standard normal distribution discussed earlier (see Figure 10.3).

One of the key advantages that the quartile-based approach enjoys over the equal group sized one (where each group accounts for about a third of all customers) is that it constrains the definition of high- and low-value customers, while grouping a larger section of customers as "average." Empirically speaking, a "typical" customer base has far fewer "extreme" customers than it does "average" ones and the ratio of high-to-average or low-to-average value customers is usually 1-to-2 (for every 1 high-value customer, there are 2 average-value customers) or 1-to-3, or even lower.

Yet another often-used value grouping approach utilizes decile-based customer value groupings. The decile approach, where the total customer universe is broken down into 10 equally sized groups is illustrated in Figure 10.4.

The hypothetical decile-probability distribution depicted in Figure 10.4 results in the identification of four *above average probability* segments as well as the five *below average probability* groups, separated by a single *average probability* segment. In a statistical sense, the "look-alike" analysis exemplified above yielded the maximum degree of cross-customer behavioral outcome likelihood differentiation, thus effectively pulling apart the most likely from the least likely to defect (in this case) customers.

Although frequently used and intuitively straightforward, the decile-based grouping suffers from some practical shortcomings, the most pronounced of which is a thin line of demarcation separating adjoining deciles. Representing different categories, the

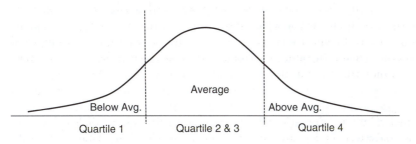

Figure 10.3 Quartile-Based Value Grouping

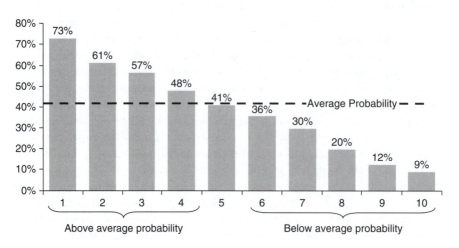

Figure 10.4 Statistical Outcomes of Look-Alike Modeling

deciles 2 and 3 or 7 and 8, for instance, both lend themselves to fundamentally the same interpretation and as a result—the same business action. Hence in practice, two or more adjoining deciles are typically more-or-less arbitrarily (i.e., subjectively) collapsed into a smaller set of more aggregate clusters, which not only seems contradictory to the original purpose of delineating a higher number of those segments, but it also introduces difficult to replicate (cross-sectionally as well as longitudinally) subjectivity into the process, ultimately taking away from the robustness of the process. Thus it is highly advisable to thoroughly consider the desired functionality prior to selecting a grouping schema to minimize the infusion of the potentially biasing subjective decisions.

Categorization

The drafting of the a priori customer value groupings is obviously only the first step toward the high-value at-risk customer identification. Once created, the value groupings need to be populated which brings to light the *mechanics of value computation*, which usually involves objective selling price and profit metric determinations. Depending on the type of data— i.e., consumer vs. business purchases, scanner vs. invoice-based, etc.— selling price and profit quantification might be somewhat tricky. In some instances, transactions may at times not be attributed correctly or may altogether not be captured[12]; the actual selling price will differ from the list or stated price due to on-the-spot or otherwise-not-recorded incentives; or the cost of goods or services sold might be difficult to determine (thus complicating accurate profit calculations). An important consideration to keep in mind is that of consistency. Customer value determination is a somewhat relative exercise, which means that the absolute value accuracy is not nearly as important as is the consistent and unbiased method of arriving at it. The primary goal of customer value grouping is to differentiate between the more and less retention-worthy customer segments, thus it might even be worthwhile to use standard metrics in place of actual values. Computationally, metric standardization parallels the z-score creation discussed earlier:

$$z = \frac{x - \mu}{\sigma}$$

where,

x = an observed value
μ = mean
σ = standard deviation

Standardizing customer value metrics helps to re-direct the focus away from the actual value, which as mentioned earlier may not necessarily encompass all database record-attributable transactions, and toward relative customer comparisons. A less obvious benefit might also be a potential rebuffing of some intuitively derived yet treated-as-facts customer base descriptions.

Also, although past behaviors are usually a good indicator of future ones, it is important to keep in mind that they are typically just one of a number of potential influencers of the next purchase. Factors such as macro-economic conditions, competitive offerings, pricing or changing lifestyles can also mitigate the current customer's decision to repurchase the same brand. Due to that, a simple extrapolation of the past behaviors into the future will rarely yield robust predictions, particularly over longer time horizons.

As suggested by the preceding discussion, the goal of behavioral predictions is to understand to what degree the past behavioral patterns will repeat themselves, as well as to estimate expected attrition-related losses. Specifically: *What is the probability of attrition for each of the current customers?* and, *What is the expected revenue/profit loss associated with individual customers?*

To be of value, the answer to this question needs to encompass unambiguous action recommendations, the derivation of which requires the development of a cohesive categorization schema outlined in Figure 10.5.

The schema in Figure 10.5 is based on a simple 2×2 example, to enhance the instructional clarity of the explanation, but the number of either one or both of the

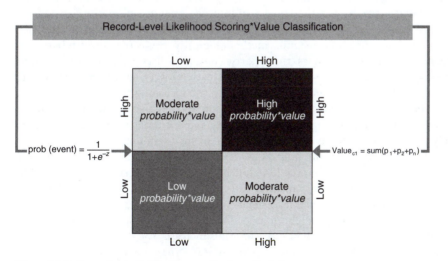

Figure 10.5 From Analytic Findings to Business Insights

classificatory dimensions can be increased as needed without substantively changing the rationale presented above. In short, the two previously discussed analytic steps—the identification of the at-risk customer subset of the entire customer base and the assessment of the cumulative value of the individual customers—are amalgamated into a single categorization schema to yield a small (in a sense of being manageable) number (4 in the above example) of mutually exclusive and action-suggestive current customer segments. This is in keeping with the earlier discussed customer retention philosophy, according to which customer retention-worthiness is a function of their profitability to the organization as well as their attrition likelihood.

Opportunity Identification

The topic discussed in this section is the most effective generalized approach to translating quantitative transactional and related data into competitively advantageous knowledge focused on new customer acquisition. As stated earlier, this approach is built around the philosophy that new customer acquisition should be guided by the long-term customer base value maximization, which is a function of identifying potential acquisition targets defined by the interaction between long-term retention likelihood and incremental brand profitability. In other words, it is focused on finding the highest future-value, retainable brand buyers, as opposed to merely attracting new buyers to the franchise.

The recommended database analytical approach is rooted in a conceptual discussion surrounding the notion of customer mix optimization. Furthermore, it expressly delineates between the notions of customer *retainability* and *value*, positing that the most effective—from the standpoint of long-term customer base value maximization—approach to new buyer acquisition necessitates finding the optimal trade-off between these two key dimensions.

Some General Remarks

New customer acquisition tops the marketing agendas of most organizations. After all, the ever-present attrition and the equally ubiquitous growth expectations make customer recruitment a virtual necessity. Yet in spite of its apparent importance, acquisition as a marketing practice area remains methodologically neglected. Over-reliance on convenience populations such as third-party consumer lists coupled with generic purchase incentives and off-the-shelf consumer valuation/targeting schemes continue to handicap its effectiveness. Even more importantly, the focus on the near-term program response "head count" as the de facto acquisition success metric and the resultant inattentiveness to longer-term product repurchase and customer retention continue to adversely impact the productivity of customer recruitment efforts.

Many of the acquisition shortcomings are encapsulated in its most common tool, a discount-based open (i.e., one available to all consumers) offer, best exemplified by the "cash back" in the auto industry or manufacturers' coupons in consumer goods. Not only are these offers weighing down transactional profitability, but can also contribute to longer-term attrition through heightening of consumer price sensitivity. Overall, tying new customer acquisition to ongoing discounting increases the dependence of brands' sales volume on price reductions thus negatively impacting the overall customer base profitability.

Yet many organizations seem undeterred by high costs and low yields, as they continue to pour significant resources into ineffective customer recruitment efforts. Impact measurement-wise, acquisition managers rarely look past the initial brand trial, typically operationalized by "promotional response rate." For one reason or another, marketers tend to endure in their belief that the initially discounted brand samplings will spark full price repurchase on a large enough scale to warrant the often hefty acquisition investments.

Working with organizations in the consumer/packaged goods, automotive, retail, financial services and other industries, I found limited support for that rationale. In fact, the few instances where I encountered supporting evidence involved relatively specific, well-defined consumer segments. More often than not, the net sum of program-attributable incremental sales gains did not justify the overall program expenditures.

Adverse customer self-selection, which is the tendency of the least desirable consumer types to show the highest brand interest, bears much of the blame. The name itself may sound new, but the trend of price-sensitive brand switchers exhibiting the strongest propensity to respond to a discount-based brand trial offer is well known to many. Equally familiar is the frequently seen consequence of adverse selection, which is that the initially attractive near-term promotional response and brand trial rates are often followed by low full-price repurchase, which is illustrative of brand switchers not sticking around without continued subsidies. In the end, considerable up-front acquisition program expenditures routinely deliver unacceptably poor longer-term returns, leaving in their wake no more than a handful of brand repurchasers acquired at an excessively high per customer cost.

The poor performance of new customer acquisition programs can be traced back to a couple of interrelated factors: 1. the practice of approaching acquisition as a stand-alone promotional function, and 2. over-reliance on open offer discounting. Starting with the former, when treated as a self-contained effort, new customer recruitment takes on a near-term focus, as evident in the initial brand trial being the primary success metric. The longer-term brand benefits, such as the overall customer base profitability are not fully considered. As a consequence, random customer self-selection takes the place of systematic customer base value replenishment as a means of combating the ongoing attrition. This is of pivotal importance to the overall customer base and will be covered in more detail later.

The second key cause of acquisition ineffectiveness is the proliferation of price-discounting-based incentives. As briefly mentioned above, open discounts not only take away from transactional profitability but can also bring about the heightening of consumer price sensitivity. Although perhaps less immediately, that can lead to a further exacerbating of the customer attrition problems initially created by adverse customer selection. In the end, acquisition programs built around generic discounting have limited longer-term benefit. This is not to say that temporary price discounting should be abandoned—it should, however, be used in a more targeted fashion.

Taking a bigger picture view, any increases in acquisition productivity are contingent on the re-casting of its objectives in the context of longer-term customer base growth and profitability rather than a mere near-term brand trial. Of course, it is not an easy task simply because it requires a considerable philosophical and methodological mind shift away from the "mass marketed" acquisition and toward information-driven, targeted and differentiated programs. In other words, the acquisition paradigm needs to evolve from a generic discount focus to consumer-type centeredness.

Naturally, a change of that magnitude can only happen in a stepwise manner, with the first step being an explicit recognition of the crucial acquisition–retention link. With that as a foundation, other, more operationally minded steps should follow, involving consumer targeting and offer differentiation considerations. The notions of *transaction-* and *customer-base-level profitability*, *customer base replenishment* as well as those of *strategic alignment* and *methodological parity* will all play a pivotal role in the development of an acquisition-transitioning roadmap. The overall process, as well as its individual components, are outlined in the ensuing sections, starting with an in-depth overview of the retention–acquisition link.

The Retention–Acquisition Link

As previously suggested, the most striking trait of new customer acquisition programs is their lack of emphasis on repurchase and transaction-level profitability. Most are designed to drive brand trials through unsustainable discounts, drawing customers to discounts, not the brand itself. Not surprisingly, many of the initially "successful" acquisition programs turn out to perform quite poorly when evaluated in the context of longer-term repurchase or profitability. It seems obvious that it is nearsighted to equate acquisition success with discounted product trials as it does not account for post-trial repurchase nor does it reflect transaction-level profit contribution. To be worth the investment made in it, new customer acquisition needs to generate acceptably high numbers of near-term product trials as well as acceptably high longer-term, full-price repurchase rates. In short, acquisition needs to be closely integrated with retention.

The key to seamless acquisition–retention integration is the notion of *customer attrition loss replenishment*. This concept reflects the ubiquitous nature of customer attrition—an ongoing customer loss due either to competitors or "natural" causes such as customer lifecycle. In other words, some level of attrition is unavoidable, which precipitates the following questions: How effective are the current new customer acquisition efforts in replenishing customer base losses? More specifically, if disproportionately large numbers of high-value customers are leaving the franchise, are their replacements of equally high quality? These questions highlight an important dimension of new customer acquisition, namely attrition replacement and the importance of attracting well chosen, not just any customers.

Let us not forget the widely used acquisition objective, which is that of driving near-term initial brand trials. Joining these two objectives together, namely the customer attrition loss replenishment and initial brand trials, the value of avoiding the trap of initially strong promotional response followed by dismal repurchase rates becomes even more pronounced. In short, acquisition and retention need to be treated as two related parts of the same process, rather than two separate processes. In analytical terms, the two should jointly contribute to the optimization of the customer mix through strategic alignment and methodological parity, as graphically shown in Figure 10.6.

Figure 10.6 depicts a couple of acquisition "musts." First and foremost, program requirements need to be stated in terms of customer base objectives. Brand trial should not be viewed as the end objective of acquisition, as the often subsidized initial purchase is rarely profitable or for that matter even indicative of future full-price repurchase. A stable and profitable customer base, not just a one-time brand trial, should be the ultimate goal of new customer acquisition. That goal, however, cannot be realized if acquisition continues to be treated as a stand-alone process. To be effective as a business

Figure 10.6 Customer Mix Optimization

tool, it needs to be thought of as means of attracting tomorrow's high-value loyal buyers, which in turn necessitates the retention–acquisition integration. As shown in Figure 10.6, the means to that end are the notions of *strategic alignment* and *methodological parity*.

Given their importance, *strategic alignment* and *methodological parity* warrant deeper explanation. The former is a two-pronged requirement: First, it calls for an explicit delineation of the current customer base structure, attrition trends and velocity as well as the most effective retention magnets. At a more global level, it requires a retention and acquisition shared brand positioning vision, clearly communicated in the respective programs' targeting decisions and messaging themes. In other words, strategic alignment is a manifestation of acquisition and retention programs' shared level of customer base understanding and goal coordination.

The more operationally minded *methodological parity* encapsulates communality of buyer-type segmentation schemas and the basic analytical structure of differential treatment and investment allocation guidelines. Acquisition and retention should be two branches of the same methodological tree, sharing common segmentation and treatment methodologies. The benefits of it include maximizing the potential of the customer based, ultimately manifesting itself in higher customer base profitability.

At least to some of the readers, acquisition–retention strategic alignment and methodological parity may sound alarmingly complex. When contrasted with "one size fits all" programs built around generic discounts, integrated acquisition programs are indeed more complex to design and execute, especially since their end objective goes far beyond initial brand trials. Some of the otherwise nonexistent obstacles include data modeling requirements, the development of multiple differentiated offers, consumer-segment-specific investment reallocation, or impact measurement expectations. On the other hand, these programs deliver superior results, ranging from higher initial response rates (twofold and higher increases are common), to higher long-term repurchase rates (i.e., 2x–4x increases in the automotive or financial services industries) to encouraging program ROI (usually, highly positive). The reason behind their success and higher level of difficulty is the information-driven customer mix development.

Customer Mix Optimization

Approaching acquisition as a customer base optimization process forces a brand to look beyond the number of initial product trials (i.e., the possibly misleading "head count") and consider the long-term revenue stream as the ultimate goal of new customer acquisition. In doing so, customer acquisition planning evolves beyond offer-centricity and customer self-selection and into targeted high-potential value buyer recruitment. Generic, open offers built around temporary price reductions are replaced with offers tailed to specific consumer types and targeted at "pre-qualified" consumers only.

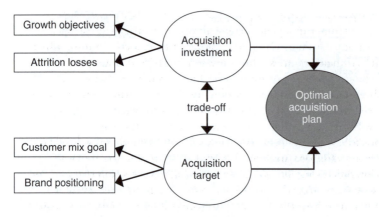

Figure 10.7 Optimal Customer Acquisition Logic

Instrumental in this transition is an explicit delineation of the key acquisition drivers of targeting and investment allocation, which in turn requires clearly stated growth objectives, attrition loss accounting, future customer mix goals and an operational level of brand positioning understanding. Figure 10.7 outlines the individual components as well as their interdependencies.

Acquisition investment represents the desired *quantity* of the net expected customer base increase, expressed as a function of growth objectives adjusted for attrition losses. Acquisition target on the other hand embodies the desired *quality* of recruited customers, which is a function of customer mix objectives and brand positioning. The trade-off between acquisition investment and acquisition target reflects the "give and take" between the required level of investment and the stated acquisition target objectives.

The customer acquisition process outlined above goes beyond mere replenishment of *quantities* as it explicitly addresses *quality* considerations—in doing so, the ineffective *discount orientation* is replaced with *customer type orientation*.

For example, if during a given time period buyer loss is skewed toward high-value customers, the customer-type-focused acquisition takes into account both the raw replenishment needs and customer-type-specific goals, thus balancing near-term "head counts" with longer-term retention and customer base profitability. Its impact, particularly when contrasted with an open-offer-based acquisition, can be substantial, as illustrated by the following hypothetical case.

Offer-Centric Acquisition Scenario

An open offer program's likelihood of acquiring a high-value customer is approximately equal to the overall proportion of those buyers in the product category. Given that, on average, high-value customers account for 10% or less of all buyers, an open offer program's likelihood of attracting a high-value customer is 10% or less. That means that if a given brand is losing its high-value customers at a rate higher than 10%, open-offer-based new customer acquisition will not be able to keep up with high-value customer attrition, leading to a gradual erosion of the overall customer base profitability. All that while, in the near term, it may generate sufficient offer response "head counts."

Customer-Type-Centric Acquisition

The above scenario is exactly what the customer-type-centric acquisition is trying to circumvent. It does so by bringing to bear current attrition trends and other related inputs to set specific customer type acquisition targets (see Figure 10.7 above), to be followed by differential treatment (discussed later in more detail). For instance, high-value customer attrition of 10% translates into a clear replenishment goal, which is supported by consumer profiles and targeted/differentiated messaging and offer strategies. Adverse consumer selection is minimized and sustained or growing customer base profitability is a matter of working known means toward clearly stated objectives. Customer-type-centric acquisition replaces uncertainty and guesswork with factual information supporting well-defined promotional actions, all without increasing the overall cost.

The remainder of the Opportunity Identification section outlines the process for migrating from the open-offer-acquisition approach to the customer-type-focused one. For comparative purposes, a brief summary of the former is presented first, followed by a more detailed discussion of the latter. The emphasis of the ensuing overview is funneling the above-discussed rationale into a competitively advantageous new customer acquisition database framework.

Pitfalls of Open-Offer-Based Customer Acquisition

A widely used mass acquisition approach, open product trial offers rely on temporary price discounts to pull consumers to the brand. Trying to appeal to generic many consumers rather than select few consumers, those programs are relatively easy to execute but yield poor ROI. They rarely include explicit retention considerations, which inhibits their ability to stem longer-term customer base profitability erosion. Consequently, customer acquisition built around open offer programs will suffer from the following:

1. **Inflated Per Acquired Customer Costs.** Large prospect pools, multiple channels, over-reliance on price incentives and low response rates all add up to a considerable financial outlay made in every newly acquired customer.
2. **Poor Repurchase And Retention Rates.** As outlined previously, self-selected brand switchers comprising the majority of the open-offer-attracted new customer pool are very likely to defect without ongoing considerable price discounts.
3. **Poor Transactional Value.** High per customer acquisition costs coupled with high attrition propensity make this mode of acquisition relatively unprofitable in both the near and long terms.
4. **Heightened Likelihood Of Long-Term Customer Base Profitability Erosion.** As exemplified above, open-offer-based acquisition is a game of odds, but one where the odds are stacked against it to begin with, as the high-value customer recruitment rates associated with those programs are usually lower than most brands' high-value customer attrition rates.

Customer-Type-Centric Acquisition

Price discount habituation, low transaction-level profitability, poor retention, potential customer base profitability decay are all sufficient reasons to consider an alternative to an open-offer-based customer acquisition. The previously outlined customer-type-centric methodology is one such alternative: fundamentally different from the open-offer-based acquisition, this approach takes a broader view of the customer recruitment process by expressly relating near-term incentive-based product trial, longer-term post-trial repurchase and the overall customer base profitability. Built around the notions of strategic alignment and methodological parity between customer acquisition and retention (see Figure 10.6), the customer-type-centric acquisition approach expands upon the key acquisition considerations depicted in Figure 10.7, by operationalizing consumer value in a way that supports explicit differentiation between category-wide spending levels and brand-specific conversion propensity. The alternative acquisition methodology is outlined in Figure 10.8.

The acquisition methodology shown in Figure 10.8 is rooted in several key considerations. First of all, it promotes the belief that to be efficient and economically sound, acquisition should be focused on targeting the right—not all—high-value consumers. A common error is to define an acquisition prospect's value in terms of category-wide purchase levels, thus implicitly assuming that all high-category spenders have the same brand conversion propensity. From the standpoint of a given brand, a consumer's value should be considered high only if that consumer's category spending levels *and* brand conversion likelihood are both high. For example: In a category where $500 in annual spending delimits a high-value consumer, a $1,000/year consumer with a 60% probability to convert to a given brand is a high-value prospect to that brand, with the opposite being true of another $1,000/year consumer with only 10% brand conversion likelihood. It follows that from the brand's point of view, a $2,000/year consumer with only 10% conversion likelihood is worth less a $1,000/year consumer with a 50% conversion probability.

Recall the three-tier (current) customer categorization first presented in Figure 10.1. In a fashion similar to the customer retention rationale presented then, new customer acquisition can be focused on all consumers, a subset of all consumers comprised of only "high category value" consumers, or even a more homogenous subset of "high brand value" consumers, as depicted below in Figure 10.9.

Intuitively, the Brand High-Value Consumers seem most appealing, as an acquisition target, which is not without a reason: Those "pre-qualified" consumers convert at a

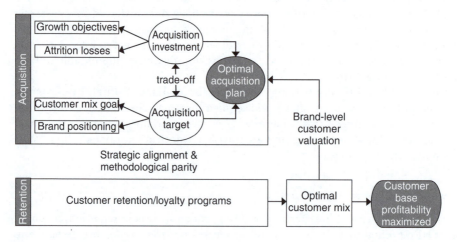

Figure 10.8 Customer-Type-Centric Acquisition

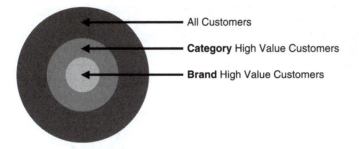

All Customers

Category High Value Customers

Brand High Value Customers

Figure 10.9 Customer Value Categories: Acquisition View

higher rate, are more profitable and can be retained more easily. Refocusing the brand's acquisition on brand high-value consumers requires a couple of steps. First, an appropriate *analytic frame of reference* and decision metrics need to be identified. Start out by defining consumer value at the brand, not the category level. Chances are you will not be able to recruit every heavy category spender, so focus on identifying those heavy spenders you can recruit. As a rule of thumb, the bulk of the promotional dollars should be invested in the middle of the consumer conversion continuum with lower per capita investments allocated against both the least and most likely to convert prospects. That's because investing heavily in the most likely to convert group represents unnecessary profit reduction as those consumers are willing to buy the brand without much "extra help," while spending heavily on the least likely to convert will do little to combat their loyalty to other brands or a lack of *product–lifestage* fit.

The second step needed to refocus the brand on brand high-value consumers entails the development of an explicit *investment matrix*. The starting point of this process is analytics-intensive, entailing consumer segmentation and valuation to uncover conversion-likelihood-based consumer segments (see Chapter 9 for an in-depth discussion). Next, each of the conversion segments needs to be profiled to support differential treatment strategies, which in turn involves varying investment level and promotional tactics across segments. Of particular importance is the segment-by-segment spending allocation. In general, the spending should be allocated keeping anticipated returns in mind, but proportional allotments should be avoided. In other words, the attractiveness of the high-value segment should not be translated into overinvestment into that segment. In fact, as previously suggested, the mid-range conversion likelihood segment is the most appropriate overinvestment target, as those consumers will likely show the highest incremental return on the additional spending. A general rule of thumb to help with setting the optimum selection threshold level is to pick a level where the relationship between total acquisition costs and the total consumer value is maximized. A sample Investment Matrix is shown in Figure 10.10:

Figure 10.10 depicts a continuum of brand purchase propensity reduced to three action-suggestive categories placed in the context of two key sets of decisions: promotional spending allocation across the three consumer value groupings and thematic messaging considerations. Within the investment allocation dimension it is important to differentiate between two separate considerations: offer-specific promotional spend allocation vs. delivery-specific allocation. Offer spending refers to the cost of any purchase incentives, while delivery expenditures capture the cost of promotional materials,

Figure 10.10 Sample Investment Matrix

both on per piece basis as well as in total (i.e., the number of touches _ per piece cost). As shown above in Figure 10.10, this distinction is important particularly for *high brand purchase propensity* prospects, who do not require significant purchase incentives to convert, but whose interest in the brand should be reinforced with high quality materials and more frequent touches.

Summary of the Customer-Type-Centric Acquisition Benefits

The various advantages of the customer-type-centric acquisition framework have already been described throughout the previous discussion; Figure 10.11 below offers a concise summary.

As illustrated in Figure 10.11, decreasing per responder costs and increasing response rates are the most tangible benefits of the proposed acquisition framework. The per responder costs decline as a result of lower number of targeted consumers, after the "low category value" and then the "low brand value" consumers are eliminated from the target acquisition set. At the same time, the response rates climb, as more consumers react favorably to the offer, on percentage basis.

The following simple illustration serves to quantify potential savings. Let's say that for every 1,000 high category value consumers targeted, Brand A succeeds at converting 20 of them, all at the cost of $5 per targeted consumer. This translates into a 2% conversion rate and a total cost of $5,000, or $250 per converted consumer.

Brand B, on the other hand, is frustrated with high costs and relatively low return on its acquisition efforts and so decides to only target those high-value consumers who

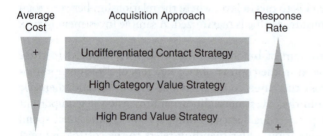
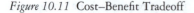

Figure 10.11 Cost–Benefit Tradeoff

exhibit the highest conversion likelihood. Rather than targeting all of the 1,000 high category spenders, Brand B decides to only focus on consumers whose conversion likelihood is greater than 50%, which leads to a drop of 300 consumers from the original 1,000 (a very conservative estimate). Since the eliminated consumers were only those who were least likely to react positively, Brand B also converts 20 consumers, the same as Brand A, but there is a significant difference in the acquisition costs. Brand B's expenditures are considerably lower in terms of: total costs ($3,500 for Brand B vs. $5,000 for Brand A), per acquired customer costs ($175 for Brand B vs. $250 for Brand A) and the conversion rate (2.9% for Brand B vs. 2% for Brand A).

But that's not all. A less (immediately) visible and more difficult to quantify benefit of the consumer-centric acquisition approach is a higher long-term customer retention rate. As this might seem a bit less intuitive, a brief explanation might help.

As implied throughout this discussion, an initial product trial may be brought about by price incentives or a perceived fit between prospect needs and product benefits. It follows that the former will attract mostly price-sensitive brand switchers while the latter will net a higher proportion of loyal repurchasers.

Considering their deal-seeking orientation, switchers are easier to entice into price-discounted product trials, but absent continued price incentives they are also very likely to attrite. Overall, they have low per transaction profitability and dismal future value. Open-offer-based acquisition programs attract a higher proportion of those buyers than the customer-type-centric approach. Adding to that the inherently more attractive profit and retention characteristics of prospects targeted by the latter, a clear picture emerges of a decisively better method. According to least one well-known source (Fred Reichheld, *The Loyalty Effect: The Hidden Force Behind Growth, Profits and Lasting Value*[13]), a 5% increase in customer retention may lead to as much as 75% increase in long-term profits.

Mix Assortment and Optimization

Identifying the most productive combination of business promotional mix components is undoubtedly the most challenging aspect of predictive analytics. As detailed later, the data availability across domains is uneven, the depth and robustness of domain-specific metrics is highly variable and methodological challenges surrounding the amalgamation of the relatively diverse data sources into a single and informationally robust capability are considerable. Yet the potential benefits, expressed both in terms of cost savings as well as efficiency and efficacy gains, are considerable.

To yield an adequate level of informational precision, a (promotional) mix assortment and optimization methodological framework must exhibit an in-depth "understanding" of the most likely components of promotional assortments being optimized, from the business as well as data perspective. Hence the ensuing overview begins with a brief outline of component areas—the most commonly available data types—and lastly, a review of specific informational challenges stemming from the interaction between the overall optimization purpose and data idiosyncrasies. The resultant template presented below is intended to be used as a general guide that can be applied to situations where dissimilar data sources need to be molded into a single-purposed capability. As is the case with the previously discussed aspects of behavioral analyses, the goal of the mix assortment and optimization approach, discussed here, is the development of competitively advantageous knowledge base.

Promotional Mix

Today, marketing is about "more"—more promotional vehicles, more choices, more clutter. Nowhere is that trend, well, more evident than it is in the general TV media. Not only did the available programming and channel venues explode in numbers, but the long-standing dominance of the three major networks has all but disappeared as the broadcast television has been forced to take the back seat to cable and satellite as the mode of household delivery. Direct response TV (DRTV) and the web-enabled inter-active programming are an early indication of even more fundamental changes reshaping that channel as a consumer utility and a promotional tool.

But it is not just the television media that is undergoing radical transformations—the promotional mix as a whole is being reshaped. A couple of decades ago the Internet was an esoteric, limited-purpose tool of negligible value to advertisers, while today is a critically important communications channel. As a result, the direct-to-consumer promotions are no longer limited to the high-cost direct sales force or the high-waste direct mail, but can also leverage the low cost of email and tap into the visually impactful online interactive product demonstrations.

Yet more promotional choices do not always result in greater impact. In fact, the proliferation of promotional alternatives has led to greater overlap and duplication, ultimately resulting in higher promotional waste. At the same time, the target audience for many brands is becoming more fragmented and harder to reach with any single promotional vehicle. In a word, the need to find a robust and objective means of identifying and integrating the most impactful mix of promotional tools is now more pronounced than ever before. Marketing as an applied discipline is quickly approaching a point where no significant productivity gains can be expected without a true integration of the individual elements of the promotional mix.

The idea of integrating and optimizing the entire promotional mix is certainly not new, as it dates back to the late 1940s and the introduction of the *simplex method*. Currently, some well-known marketing texts, such as the one authored by Belch and Belch[14] offer a conceptual overview of this topic, while on the applied side, various marketing consulting firms (e.g., Peppers and Rogers Group; Marketing Analytics, Inc. and others) offer applied marketing mix integration services. The former tend to yield limited practical applicability, largely because they lack adequate operationalization. The solutions offered by consulting firms, on the other hand, fall into two distinct categories: There are those making lofty promises, while providing surprisingly little operational support for their lofty claims (e.g., one firm talks of combining the "right" channels, timing and objectives with the "right" customers, which certainly sounds good, but how will the determination of what constitutes "right" channel–timing–objective be made? No details here . . .). Then there is a different grouping of consultants offering extensive operationalization, but virtually devoid of a compelling theoretical foundation. The latter might seem like a reasonable practical approach—after all, why should theory matter in practical applications? Well, it does in this case, as the absence of a sound theoretical rationale makes the impact validation process quite difficult. In a way, embracing heuristics that lack a robust conceptual foundation can be likened to validating a model's predictive accuracy by pointing to the level of sophistication of the model's classificatory algorithms. Aside from being intellectually troubling, such a self-validating way of thinking does not address one of the most nagging problems facing media analytics, which is the availability and accuracy of promotional data.

All said, the label of promotional mix integration has a ring of familiarity, but operationally much remains to be done before this promising idea yields equally robust results. Viewed as an analytic endeavor, promotional mix integration and optimization-related knowledge is tremendously important from the standpoint of creating and sustaining a competitive advantage.

A recent study sponsored by Microsoft and conducted by a consortium comprised of Procter and Gamble, Nestle and Kraft found that online advertising can lead to significant branding and offline sales gains.[15] This finding appears to be collaborated by another industry source, Dieringer Research Group. Based on a survey of 3,000 consumers, Dieringer concluded that online product research helped to drive over $180 billion of offline purchases in addition to over $100 billion in online transactions, all in the course of a single year.[16] In other words, there is a growing amount of empirical evidence substantiating the commonsensical belief that there is much to be gained by finding a way to more closely integrate the individual promotional mix components.

Still, making it happen is far from simple. Individual promotional mix components, such as advertising, direct marketing, interactive or sales promotions are functionally and executionally different and all have a long-standing history of self-defined planning and measurement processes. For example, TV advertising emphasizes branding, defined as a process of systematically associating positive attributes with goods or services,[17] in hopes of creating long-term, sustainable brand distinctiveness. As a result, advertising is usually measured with the help of consumer brand awareness increases, but rarely attributed to quantifiable sales increases. In contrast to that, direct marketing which focuses on stimulating near-term purchases is measured by quantifying treatment-attributable sales increases. In other words, the impact of the former is measured with coarsely-defined attitudinal changes taking place over long periods of time while the latter is evaluated on near-term, relatively precisely estimated behavioral outcomes. To make this picture even more complex, the sales impact of other components of the media mix, such as public relations, is rarely quantified[18] at all.

Yet even though the individual mix components are operationally different, they all share a common end objective: to positively impact the consumer decision making process.[19] Shown in Figure 10.12 is the frequently used depiction of that process, the *purchase funnel*.[20]

Figure 10.12 Purchase Funnel

The basic rationale embedded in the purchase funnel postulates that consumer decision making progresses along a fairly predictable path, starting with brand awareness, followed by purchase consideration, trial and finally purchase. The successive funnel stages are attritive in nature, as consumer self-select to consider the brand or not, to try it or not and ultimately to purchase or not. Considered in the context of a measurable (i.e., analyzable in the database analytical sense) consumer decision making progression, the role of the promotional mix can be described as a stage-to-stage consumer conversion maximization tool, as it serves to increase the amount of brand awareness, the frequency of its inclusion in the consideration set and ultimately, the brand's purchase rate. As is intuitively obvious, the upper funnel functions of awareness and consideration are most effectively influenced with the help of general media,[21] which includes broadcast and cable TV advertising, radio, public relations and certain print communications.[22] On the other hand, the lower funnel functions of trial and purchase are most impacted by direct media, which encompasses mail, personal selling and sales incentives.[23]

The purchase funnel is a tool frequently used by marketing firms, such as Minneapolis-based Carlson Marketing or Boston-based Digitas, to illustrate the need for a closer integration of the individual elements of the marketing. But in practice, most of the applications of the purchase funnel tend to be limited tothe linking of direct mail, email and online interactive capabilities, while excluding the harder-to-quantify general advertising and public relations. Part of the reason is highly pragmatic (i.e., marketing service organizations' usage of the purchase funnel reflects their scope of service offerings), but some of the reasons are of more methodological nature, namely, to-date, no single all-promotional-media encompassing framework offering business rationalization and operational clarity has been proposed and peer reviewed.

Components of the Promotional Mix

In its comprehensive report discussing the media spending outlook, eMarketer points out that there is no agreement among the major research providers as to what constitutes "total promotional media." Although the major research suppliers, such as J. P Morgan, McCann, Myers Group, Jupiter or Veronis Suhler agree that the big four of TV, radio, magazine and newspapers should all be counted, no such uniformity exists with regard to the other elements of the media mix, as some do not count the Internet or even direct mail.[24]

One authoritative source[25] defined promotional mix to be comprised of advertising, sales promotion, public relations, personal selling and direct marketing. The recent emergence of Internet adds another heavily used and important channel, bringing the total to six distinct promotional mix components.

Advertising

In many cases accounting for the lion's share of total promotional expenditures, historically this has been the primary branding tool, used to build brand awareness and establish positive, desired brand associations. TV advertising is the icon of general media, although it also includes print (newspapers and magazines), internet advertising, billboards, directories (e.g., the Yellow Pages), point of purchase displays, brochures, inserts, etc.

Direct Marketing

Best exemplified by direct mail and telemarketing, historically this has been the most effective means of communicating and distributing specific purchase-related offers to targeted households or individuals. In recent years, email-based direct marketing efforts grew in popularity, primarily due to considerable cost efficiencies. Other examples include catalogs, electronic shopping and fax promotions.

Sales Promotions

Price has traditionally been one of the most effective, though not necessarily the most efficient, promotional tools, and price promotions tend to take on many forms, which often reflect industry-specific channel dynamics brands' objectives. For example, packaged goods firms rely heavily on trade promotions to manipulate sales levels, while the automobile makers prefer "manufacturer cash back" as a means to effect volume. In a general sense, sales incentives can take the form of trade promotions, where a manufacturer lowers wholesale prices, which usually triggers retail price reductions, or consumer-direct promotions, where a manufacturer offers rebates directly to consumers. Specific examples include coupons, rebates, free product samples, sweepstakes, exhibits, trade-in allowances and others.

Personal Selling

Complex products, such as pharmaceuticals or commercial equipment need a highly personalized, consultative selling approach to accurately convey the extent of their capabilities. A dedicated team of (typically) company-trained professionals, offering face-to-face product benefit demonstration is an expensive but also an effective method of promoting the unique value proposition of complex products.

Interactive

The emergence of the Internet as a communication channel led to the emergence of real-life-emulating product experience capabilities. A dynamic medium gives consumers the ability to conduct in-depth product evaluations and simulated trials at their home and their convenience. Although principally a mass medium, interactive is also highly customizable, in contrast to other mass media, thus bridging the gap between mass and direct promotional capabilities. Examples include online product demonstrations, Web seminars and online shops.

Public Relations

PR is the most frequently overlooked component of the promotional mix. Charged with "...*help{ing} an organization and its publics mutually adapt to each other*," PR is focused on an organization as a whole, rather than individual brands or products.[26] Yet in the same way as general advertising is aiming to create associations between brands and desirable attributes, PR can have a positive halo effect by creating positive associations with the organization as a whole.

From the standpoint of their impact on sales, the above six distinct components of the promotional mix can be categorized as either *direct* or *indirect* influencers. The difference between the two is best understood in the context of the purchase funnel shown above in Figure 10.12 and the notion of action-attributable incrementality, discussed in more detail later.

The purchase funnel stipulates that the process of selecting a "new" (i.e., not previously evaluated) product entails a progression of several evaluative steps of *awareness–consideration–trial–purchase*. At the same time, the efficacy of the database analytical process detailed in this book requires that the productivity of specific promotional initiatives is assessed in terms of its contribution to increasing the sales of a particular product—i.e., action-attributable incrementality. It follows that some of the aforementioned six elements of the promotional mix will primarily influence "higher funnel" functions, such as awareness or consideration, while other promotional mix components will impact the "lower funnel" functions, such as trial or purchase. Consequently, the former are categorized as indirect influencers, while the latter fall under the umbrella of direct influencers.

The line of demarcation separating the direct and indirect influencers is, to a large degree, intuitively obvious. An individual watching a product TV advertisement has no compelling reason to "run out and buy" the product following the exposure to its ad, simply because general advertising (an indirect influencer) rarely if ever contains behavioral "calls to action," such as a time-sensitive price discount. On the other hand, a coupon (sales promotion) offering a price discount if redeemed within a pre-determined time frame clearly contains the requisite incentive, or the "call to action" offering a reason to purchase the product. In that sense, sales promotions have direct influence on sales.

In terms of data availability and quality, there are considerable differences among the above summarized elements of the promotional mix. Of the six distinct promotional vehicle types, only three—direct mail, sales promotions and interactive—"automatically" generate robust data trails. Yet given the importance of the remaining three channels, especially advertising, no meaningful integration and optimization insights can be created without expressly and objectively assessing the impact of the entire promotional "set" on the overall customer base revenue and/or profitability. Uncovering the means of doing so, inclusive of the not readily available data, requires a solid understanding of the economics and some of the inner-workings of the promotional mix "industry."

The Promotional Mix "Industry"

From automobiles to cereal, from television programming to telecommunication options, from banking alternatives to coffee varieties, the number of functionally substitutable product alternatives has grown at a rapid pace. At the same time, so did the number of promotional communication vehicles. Television channels are numbered in high hundreds, radio broadcasts offer a choice of the "traditional" vs. advertisements-free services and direct-to-consumer mail is delivered through a combination of physical and electronic means. In addition, an entirely new dimension of product information and experience has come into existence in the form of interactive online capabilities. In short, a rapidly expanding brand set is being communicated via an equally rapidly proliferating web of promotional alternatives.

Taken as a whole, the amorphous promotional mix "industry" is responsible for over $350 billion[27] of annual expenditures in the U.S., with the bulk of it going to general advertising. The broadest of all promotional mix elements, general advertising is composed of television (broadcast and cable, national and local markets), radio and print ads (newspaper, magazine, yellow pages and outdoor media), individually accounting for roughly $55 billion, $19 billion and $78 billion,[28] respectively, of total marketing expenditures. General advertising is also the most fragmented of all six promotional mix components, as illustrated by the magazine category which offers roughly 24,000 periodicals published annually across some 280 groupings.[29]

In terms of the overall expenditures, the sales promotions component comes in second with total expenditures of more than $80 billion in 2002. In contrast to general advertising, however, sales promotion spending is driven primarily by packaged goods manufacturers, who allocate to it on average a whopping 17% of their gross annual sales.[30]

During the same timeframe, direct mail accounted for about $47 billion in overall marketing expenditures, while online interactive came in at about $6 billion, although the latter is still considered to be in its infancy and it is expected to grow significantly in the near future.

Aggregate annual expenditures for the two remaining promotional mix components, personal selling and public relations are difficult to quantify for a number of reasons. Most importantly, although direct sales is an easily identifiable activity (e.g., the U.S. Labor Department reports there are about 14 million persons employed in sales positions in the U.S.), the direct sales process often involves significant amounts of time of those not otherwise classified as salespersons. In addition, in contrast to advertising or direct mail where the bulk of the cost is accounted for by media buying (i.e., "air time"), production or printing and delivery expenses, much of the direct-sales-related expenditures is the personnel cost, which is not readily available in publicly published sources.

Even more difficult to quantify is the total marketing-attributable cost of public relations. In most organizations it is a shared function spreading far beyond building awareness and goodwill to also include investor, community, government and employee communications. As a result, its cost is often considered to be a part of the overall corporate overhead making the marketing share of it difficult to estimate.

The aggregate spending on the elements of the promotional mix yielding an indirect impact on sales, most notably general advertising, underscores the importance of capturing its impact, as one of the key prerequisites to comprehensive promotional mix optimization. In that sense, the impact of those elements of the mix ought to be assessed with the help of indirect measures, such as attitudinal changes. On the other hand, the impact of direct promotional mix elements (i.e., those that can be clearly linked to product purchases) needs to be assessed with the help of action-attributable incrementality. Aligning the type of impact with proper measurement outcomes will lead to a more truthful assessment of the individual components' sales contributions, which will ultimately enable more robust promotional mix spending allocations.

The Value of Better Mix Allocations

A proverbial "chicken and egg" issue, it can be debated whether large promotional spending drives proportionately large sales gains. Far easier to determine are the promotional spending levels of large, public organizations (publicly traded firms are required to disclose a relatively detailed breakdown of their overall expenditures). The biggest spender of all, General Motors, poured a total of over $3.3 billion into marketing-related initiatives in 2002, followed by Procter and Gamble with $2.5 billion and Ford in close third with about $2.4 billion in total marketing expenditures. In total, the top 10 of the largest U.S. advertisers spent nearly $22 billion in 2002.[31]

An obvious question comes to mind: Did these organizations reap $22 billion worth of business benefits? The joke-phrased conventional wisdom suggests that a half of all ad spending is wasted, though no one knows which half. . . On a more serious note, according to the Advertising Research Foundation,[31] the estimated media waste is closer to 90%. Considering the combination of the venue proliferation and a virtual explosion in the number of functionally substitutable brands brought by deregulation and globalization, the ARF estimate does not seem all that far-fetched. Obviously, as the promotional clutter continues to increases, it is ever more difficult to get through to the "right" consumers. Whatever the actual level of the aggregate promotional waste, it is highly illustrative of the potential cost savings associated with injecting robust rationalization into the promotional planning processes.

However, a more cost-effective integration of the individual promotional mix components is not just about waste reduction. Many brands, particularly the growth-minded ones, are more interested in enhancing their promotional impact than they are in cost savings. They will be encouraged to learn that promotional mix integration has the potential of being a tremendously potent productivity growth stimulant. According to a survey of 3,000 consumers conducted by Dieringer Research Group, online product research helped to drive over $180 billion of offline purchases, in addition to over $100 billion in online transactions, in the course of a single year. In an operational sense, these benefits were realized from just a 2-way interaction between the online media and product choice. On the other hand, a full promotional mix integration implies a 6-way interaction (advertising * sales promotions * direct mail * personal selling * online interactive * public relations), which has the potential to deliver even more significant impact magnification.

The integration-sourced promotional productivity gains stem from the following general benefits of better mix synchronization:

BRAND POSITIONING UNIFORMITY ACROSS THE COMMUNICATION MIX

Integrated communications tell a single story, in effect forcing a brand to choose a message and convey consistent positioning and brand associations. That is in contrast to a common practice of each promotional vehicle being given the creative and messaging freedom to craft its own positioning and messaging strategy. For instance, general advertising can be seen trying to build an image of quality or exclusivity while direct marketing is flooding the marketplace with gimmicks and heavily discounted purchase offers, effectively undermining the efforts of the former.

MAGNIFIED IMPACT OF THE BRAND'S MESSAGE

Repetition is the key to learning. A consistent brand message steadily communicated through a variety of channels and vehicles has stronger impact than an assortment of multiple, potentially contradictory themes.

PROMOTIONAL WASTE REDUCTION

Whether ARF is right in its conclusion that close to 90% of advertising spending is wasted, or even if it is "only" 50% as suggested by conventional wisdom, the amount of waste across the entire promotional mix is considerable. By rationalizing its promotional allocations, an organization can increase the productivity of its promotional investments.

But none of those benefits are likely to materialize without a comprehensive integration framework. The remainder of this chapter is focused on the description of such a framework, built around the analysis of the theoretical and operational considerations, key computational recommendations and an overarching process of relating the individual promotional vehicles and ongoing performance fine-tuning.

Integration Considerations

To be generalizable across industries and usage situations, promotional mix integration framework needs a sound theoretical foundation. At the same time, to be operationally feasible, it also needs a solid grounding in the realities of data availability. A discussion of both follows.

Theoretical Foundations

The theoretical foundation of a comprehensive promotional mix integration framework rests on two well-known conceptualizations: the *persuasion theory*[32] and the *equimarginal principle*.[33] The former yields insights into consumer-level impact of different mix components, while the latter rationalizes promotional mix assortment decisions.

In the most general terms, the *persuasion theory* postulates that beliefs plus values and/or motives combine to produce attitudes which in turn influence consumer behavior, as shown below:

Beliefs + Values/Motives = Attitudes → Behavior

The notion of marketing promotions as means of (potential) buyer persuasion is closely related to the purchase funnel shown in Figure 8.12. Successfully migrating a prospective brand buyer from developing brand awareness to actually considering the brand and finally to making the purchase is, in the promotional sense predicated upon presenting the "right" arguments through the "right" means. In other words, converting a prospect into a customer requires a compelling—i.e., highly persuasive—argument.

When approached as a persuasion tool, a promotional strategy will be more effective at focusing consumers' attention on brands' most desired attributes, thus increasing the likelihood of brand purchase. An impactful strategy is one that acknowledges the progressive, multi-step nature of consumer decision making depicted by the purchase funnel, by correctly aligning promotional vehicles with individual stages in the consumer decision process. For instance, general advertising is usually an effective awareness-building vehicle, which makes it an appropriate "upper funnel" promotional tool. A different mix vehicle, direct mail, is most productive when used against "lower funnel" goals of product trial and purchase, simply because it is a highly targeted, efficient mean of delivering purchase incentives. In general, all of the six promotional

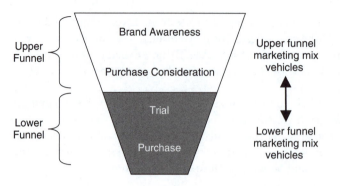

Figure 10.13 Promotional Mix, Purchase Funnel and Persuasion

mix vehicles can be categorized as either upper or a lower funnel tools when considered in the context of the persuasion theory, as depicted in Figure 10.13.

Approaching promotional mix integration as a potential brand buyer persuasion endeavor underscores the desirability of creating a single "promotional voice" repeated via different means to continually impact successive stages of the decision making process. The brand's sales increase as a result, as heightened brand awareness is converted into higher consideration and ultimately, higher sales through cross-vehicle consistency. Integrating individual promotional vehicles around the notion of prospective brand buyer persuasion not only creates promotional synergies, but also leads to promotional waste reduction, further increasing promotional productivity.

These insights are further extended by the *equimarginal principle*, a key economic conceptualization that can offer operational means of identifying and quantifying waste reduction opportunities. Building on the law of *diminishing marginal utility*, this notion stipulates that the economic output of promotional communications is maximized when the return on the last dollar spent is the same in all areas, as shown below:

(Sales Lift of A) / (Cost of A) = (Sales Lift of B) / (Cost of B) = … (Sales Lift of n) / (Cost of n)

From a more tactical point of view, the equimarginal principle underscores the importance of relying on vehicle-type-attributable sales incrementality as a measure of promotional impact. In an analytical sense, the utility of the explanatory power of the equimarginal principle is maximized when the sales lift is ascribed to a single treatment, rather than a more aggregate program. It also implies promotional-mix-wide impact measurement standardization.

The level of measurement rigor called for by the equimarginal principle is on a par with leading-edge direct mail programs, but is rarely if ever associated with other promotional vehicles. As a matter of fact, it has been commonly argued[34] that an adequate level of measurement precision is not feasible for the "upper funnel" promotional vehicles, such as general advertising. Such claims, however, are slowly losing their validity. The rapid growth in business process digitalization coupled with transaction tracking capabilities are now making available response and transactional data that, just as short as a decade ago, simply did not exist outside of rare experiments. As detailed later in this discussion, promotional vehicle-to-sales attribution is rapidly becoming feasible across the entire spectrum of the promotional mix.

Taken together, the persuasion theory and the equimarginal principle offer a rich theoretical basis to support drafting of a generalizable promotional mix integration process. The former helps to explain why message integration yields promotional synergies and increases the impact of the entire mix, while the latter contributes analytical means of optimizing promotional-vehicle-specific resource-level allocations. Combined with the purchase funnel, these conceptualizations form the theoretical bases for the mix rationalization analytical framework discussed below.

Methodological Considerations

No matter how compelling a rationale is offered by the persuasion theory and the equimarginal principle, these abstract notions require robust operationalization before they can deliver tangible informational gains. In fact, the most significant obstacle to theory-to-practice transfer is the lack of appropriate data and/or a robust analytical methodology.

To the degree to which some of the requisite data has been available for some time (i.e., direct mail tracking, sales promotion redemptions, etc.), the earlier promotional mix integration attempts failed to deliver solid results because they were attempting to leverage generic methodologies, such as "standard" regression models. These operationalizations did not deliver satisfactory results for a number of reasons, including:

- High degree of predictor intercorrelations leading to inflated promotional vehicle specific effect sizes.
- Inability of a single mathematical formulation to adequately accommodate pooling of diverse promotional effects measured with considerably different levels of granularity and accuracy.
- The necessity to express media effects in terms of confidence intervals (as opposed to point estimates) resulting in overlapping coefficient ranges and spurring interpretational ambiguity.

An even more fundamental explanation of the methodological difficulties derailing earlier promotional mix integration analytics points to a broadly defined analytical approach. A "typical" promotional mix modeling initiative (such as the aforementioned regression-based promotional mix models) focuses on modeling the absolute changes in the dependent variable (such as sales or revenue), rather than the more appropriate relative promotional vehicle assortment sets comparisons. In other words, the analyses of promotional mix integration are typically carried out by means of the end outcome (i.e., sales) forecasting, which is inherently more inaccurate than comparing the efficacies of differently assorted promotional mix sets.

Replacing *sales-level prediction* focus with *relative media mix efficacy* not only reduces the methodological burden but it is philosophically more appropriate, since the goal of integration is to identify the most effective combination of promotional vehicles, not forecasting anticipated sales gains. Models based on sales forecasts demand a higher degree of accuracy across all promotional mix metrics because they require relatively tight elasticity estimates, which poses significant measurement challenges, particularly for the "upper purchase funnel" vehicles, such as general advertising. On the other hand, relative mix comparison operationalizations built around side-by-side assortment set efficacy contrasts have less stringent measurement requirements, expecting only directional rather than absolute accuracy. And perhaps most importantly, the relative effect coefficient estimates are more germane to the objective of marketing mix integration.

To be valid, however, relative mix comparisons need to expressly acknowledge the inherent time-decay associated with all marketing promotions. Analytically expressed as nonlinearity of promotional effects, this modeling characteristic is further complicated by the necessity to differentiate between two statistically dissimilar types of effects: First, the promotional-vehicle-type-specific effects reflecting the cross-situation generalizable impact of a particular promotional vehicle. In other words, the expected sales contribution of a singular vehicle, generalized across applications. The second type of effect captures situation-dependent interactions reflecting the combined effects of different promotional vehicles under a specific set of circumstances.

Overall, the following are the key analytical challenges facing relative mix comparisons:

- Reconciling promotional-vehicle-type-specific main effects with an assortment-set-specific (i.e., a particular promotional mix) interaction term estimates, where both are expressed as standardized sales lift or elasticities. In other words, the generalizable main effects, such as average direct mail response rates, are kept constant across the individual scenarios, while specific interaction effects, such as a combination of online interactive and TV advertising that is unique to a particular scenario, are estimated independently for each individual scenario. In a statistical sense, a relative mix assortment independent variate consists of a constant representing the aforementioned generalizable media type wide estimates and scenario-dependent specific interaction terms. In other words,

$$\text{Scenario}_n = [\textit{constant} \ (\Sigma \ \text{Main Effects})] + [\textit{variable} \ (\text{Interaction Effects})].$$

As a result, cross-scenario comparisons can be carried out in terms of marginal lift attributable to the unique nature of individual scenarios, as stipulated by the equimarginal principle discussed earlier.

- Diminishing returns to scale are inherently nonlinear, which requires either an estimation of a complex set of nonlinear effects or the identification of multiple "proxy-linear" response range intervals.
- Data-related differences among individual media mix variables need to be accounted for, which means that no single mathematical formulation is likely to fit (equally well) all data across the mix.

Steps can be taken to at least diminish the potential impact of the above considerations. Some might be viewed as final, i.e., satisfactory solutions, while some others as first steps toward optimal solution identification. Initial suggestions are outlined in the next section.

Tackling the Methodological Challenges

The analytics of promotional mix integration will continue to be an evolving science, progressing from the initially rough approximations to gradually increasing levels of accuracy. Outlined below is a 3-step process intended to serve as the point of departure.

STEP 1: ESTIMATE MEDIUM-SPECIFIC AND TIME-DEPENDENT RESPONSE CURVES

It is generally believed that certain branding-focused media, such as general advertising, have a cumulative effect, where each subsequent treatment or exposure adds incrementally to the previous one, as illustrated in Figure 10.14A. As a result, these "upper funnel" promotional vehicles emphasize reach and frequency as the means of creating and sustaining the cumulative branding effect, which in turn has some important impact measurement considerations, fully explored in Step 2.

In contrast to the "upper funnel" promotional vehicles, the "lower funnel" tools, such as direct mail are not generally credited with discernible longer-term branding effects, which is not surprising given their transactional focus. That said, the lower funnel vehicles are an effective means of bringing about near-term sales increases, as illustrated in Figure 10.14B.

As visually depicted by Figures 10.14A and 10.14B, there is quite a bit of impact variability across the different promotional vehicles. The sales impact of the "upper funnel" functions of general advertising and public relations is less direct than the "lower funnel" tools of direct mail, sales promotions and direct sales. In the analytical sense, these effect differences translate into lift measurement invariance with consequences

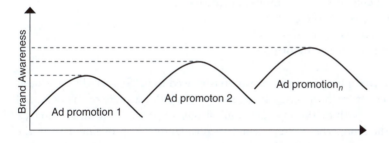

Figure 10.14A Cumulative Branding Impact of the Upper Funnel Media

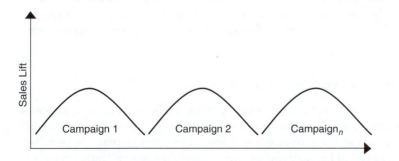

Figure 10.14B Transactional Impact of the Lower Funnel Media

ranging from method and metric idiosyncrasies to sampling and impact timing. Some of the specific measurement recommendations addressing those challenges are discussed next; others are outlined later.

STEP 2: ESTIMATE RELATIONSHIPS AND CALIBRATE COEFFICIENTS

This step consists of both a qualitative as well as a quantitative aspect. First of all, the specific media mix components to be included need to be identified and the effective historical time horizon defined. A somewhat arbitrary step, it is nonetheless important in deciding how far back to look to estimate the response functions outlined in Step 1, and which of the promotional vehicles should be included in the relative scenario comparisons.

The next part of this process step is considerably more objective and methodologically rigorous—it involves the estimation of the main and interaction effects. At least initially, this task can be simplified by averaging vehicle type specific elasticities (i.e., lift attributable to specific treatment types) for near, medium and long term response impact, as shown below:

$$\left[\left(\frac{\Sigma_{M_1}L}{n}\right)...+...\left(\frac{\Sigma_{M_n}L}{n}\right)\right]_{t_{near}} \quad +\left[\left(\frac{\Sigma_{M_1}L}{n}\right)...+...\left(\frac{\Sigma_{M_n}L}{n}\right)\right]_{t_{med}} \quad +\left[\left(\frac{\Sigma_{M_1}L}{n}\right)...+...\left(\frac{\Sigma_{M_n}L}{n}\right)\right]_{t_{long}}$$

w*here,*

L = elasticity, or main effect attributable to a media type
M_1 and M_n = promotional vehicle designators (e.g., advertising, direct mail, etc.)
n = promotional vehicle specific number of treatments
near = near-term effects (<6 months)
med = mid-term effects (6–12 months)
long = long-term effects (12 months+)

In a similar fashion, the appropriate interaction terms need to be estimated for the *near*, *medium* and *longer* term time horizons. Although only a rough estimate of the potential nonlinearity associated with marketing communications' impact on consumer purchase behavior, this method nonetheless represents a considerable improvement over the commonly used linear effect model estimation. At the same time, it is obviously not as methodologically robust as a full-fledged nonlinear effects model, but it is considerably more operationally manageable while still capturing the key aspects of the diminishing returns to scale on the one hand and the cumulative branding effects on the other. And it is, after all, merely a point of departure for this aspect of analytics of the promotional mix integration.

STEP 3: DEFINE INTERVALS AND SIGNIFICANCE LEVELS

Regardless of the computational method employed, main effect elasticities and cross-media interaction effects represent sample-based inferences made with regard to the probability of population-wide representativeness. This means that the resultant coefficient estimates need to be expressed in terms of *confidence intervals* rather than *point estimates* (i.e., mean values), which might lead to some interpretational ambiguities, particularly for smaller magnitude effects. In other words, a small mean coefficient estimate, such as .03 could have a confidence interval-expressed range of .00 to .05 (particularly if more confidence is sought through higher significance levels), which qualitatively translates into "no effect" vs. "some effect" interpretation. Should that be the case, it is prudent to err on the side of caution by putting forth the more conservative end of the confidence interval.

The actual significance level notwithstanding, converting mean coefficient values into confidence intervals is necessary but can also give rise to interpretive challenges, particularly when choosing among competing mix scenarios. To correct that, the desired significance level could be lowered (e.g., the initial threshold of α = .05 could be reduced to α = .10), though that may not always be acceptable. Under some circumstances, the sample size used in calculating *standard errors* (a measure of average error in mean estimates used in computing confidence intervals) could be increased leading to smaller standard errors and tighter confidence interval ranges.

Naturally, each of these steps can be further refined and frankly, it is assumed it will be. The response curves can increase in specificity, evolving from vehicle-wide generalizations shown above to more idiosyncratically defined sets, such as direct mail treatment curves that model individual effects of treatments on a one-by-one basis. Similarly, effect coefficients can be calibrated for increasingly more homogenous populations as well as narrower time horizons. In short, the analytical steps outlined above should be viewed as a general point of departure for which the next step is to be adapted to the needs and data idiosyncrasies of specific industries. The key to this ongoing evolution of promotional mix integration analytics is a robust and generalizable integration framework to guide the future enhancements. The proposed comprehensive mix integration framework is outlined below.

Generalizable Promotional Mix Integration Framework

The previous discussion brought to light two of the biggest obstacles standing in the way of promotional mix allocation rationalization: cross (promotional) vehicle goal differences and the sheer number of promotional alternatives. In regard to the former, the goal of advertising is to increase brand awareness through the use of mass media; direct sales and direct mail aim to increase near-term sales volume with the help of targeted purchase offers, while sales promotions rely on the general media to also bring about near-term sales increases; online interactive product demonstrations try to build brand interest with the help of mass but potentially customizable media, while public relations usually looks past the brand itself and toward larger organization-wide goodwill considerations. Due in a large part to the variability in their respective goals and methods, each of the promotional mix vehicles over the years developed idiosyncratic planning processes and performance assessment standards tailored to their specific needs, but less applicable to others. It all leads to, seemingly, irreconcilable data and ultimately, informational differences separating individual promotional vehicles.

The second of the aforementioned mix rationalization obstacles is the (typically large) number of promotional options. In the not-too-distant past, all of television was broadcast-based with three major networks each offering a handful of channels. No cable, no satellite, no DRTV. Email and online interactive capabilities did not exist (and database marketing, for that matter, was just an idea). In short, by today's standards, promotional vehicles were relatively few and the potential promotional means redundancy comparatively low. Under those circumstances, content fine-tuning probably was the most effective way of increasing the productivity of the promotional mix.

Needless to say, today's promotional landscape is vastly different. The number of alternatives is large as is the overlap among them, and consumers are increasingly harder to reach as a result of media type and within-media-type option proliferation and technological (i.e., TIVO, DVR) and regulatory/legislative developments (i.e., the Shelby Act, anti-spamming provisions, etc.). As the promotional clutter intensified manyfold, the effectiveness of individual promotional vehicles' has eroded, which carries a profound implication for how the impact of the individual elements of the promotional mix ought to be evaluated. It also implies that even the biggest promotional spenders simply cannot have a dominant voice across all of the promotional mix vehicles. Thus, making better-informed promotional decisions has become a key contributor to firms' competitive advantage.

The following is the first step in the direction of establishing of an objective, ongoing promotional mix rationalization database analytical functionality.

As shown in Figure 10.15, the initial promotional mix assortment should be guided by the brand's end objectives, which in the context of the database analytical process detailed in this book are captured in the form of stated organizational goals discussed earlier, the accumulated experience or the knowledge base of the organization and results of past promotions. Then, the efficacy of the initial promotional mix assortment and allocations should then be periodically assessed, based upon which changes should be made geared at productivity improvements.

The macro process outlined above can be broken down into two separate sets of activities: 1. *the initial promotional mix integration* and 2. *ongoing improvements*. The former involves compiling the initially available information to thematically align individual mix elements, while the latter calls for continual fine-tuning of the initial mix decisions to increase impact and eliminate waste.

Initial Promotional Mix Integration

The logical starting point in amalgamating the components of the promotional mix is to relate the (previously) stated organizational objectives to the individual promotional vehicles. Next, the brand goals ought to be contrasted with the brand's own market charac-

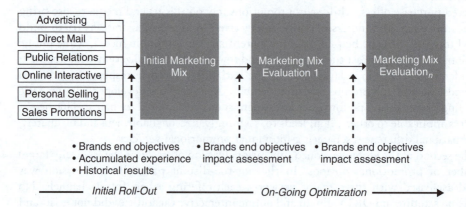

Figure 10.15 Ongoing Promotional Mix Rationalization

teristics, such as new-to-market vs. an established player or high volume vs. niche positioning, as well as in the context of the earlier discussed purchase funnel (see Figure 10.12).

The purchase funnel model suggests that general media (TV, radio and print advertising, online interactive and public relations) are the most impactful means of enhancing brands' awareness and other upper funnel functions, often referred to as *branding*. On the other hand, the lower funnel modalities, which are direct mail, sales promotions and personal selling, are the most effective tool for stimulating near-term product purchases. The purpose of contrasting the brand's goals with the individual promotional mix vehicles in the context of the purchase funnel is to identify maximally persuasive promotional strategies.

Let's say the stated objective is that of market share capture. Growing sales for a new-to-market brand means increasing brand awareness by emphasizing upper funnel activities accompanied by purchase incentives delivered by lower funnel modalities. In contrast to that, the goal of stimulating sales for a mature, established brand may call for stepping up lower funnel promotional efforts and cutting back on upper funnel spending. In terms of specific mix components, the former would translate into more GRPs for TV advertising accompanied by wide-scoped sales promotions support, while the latter should be driven by more insightful targeting (e.g., segmentation, propensity scoring and profiling) and tailored purchase incentive offers delivered via direct channels.

Also important in setting up the initial promotional mix is the within-funnel-stage redundancy minimization. For example, both the direct mail and sales promotion are potent near-term purchase stimulants: Should both be deployed at the same time, or would using just one of the two be sufficient to reach stated objectives? Rationalizing promotional vehicle selection and spending allocation in this manner leads to curtailing promotional waste, as stipulated by the equimarginal principle. Figure 10.16 offers a visual representation of the initial promotional mix integration process.

As shown in Figure 10.16, the overall process centers on a modified purchase funnel, where individual funnel stages are linked with their respective highest anticipated

Impacting Medium	Purchase Funnel	Integration Focus
Advertising Public Relations	**Awareness** *To create/enhance brand familiarity*	Brand positioning Creative & message themes
Advertising Direct Mail Interactive Personal Selling	**Consideration & Trial** *To enhance interest in brand*	Promotional focus Channel & treatment strategy
Direct Mail Personal Selling Trade Promotions	**Purchase** *To select brand*	Treatment tactics Treatment mix
Brand Experience Loyalty Programs	**Repurchase**	Loyalty incentive strategy

Customer base value growth

Figure 10.16 Promotional Mix Integration: Initial Rollout

impact promotional components. There are two modifications to the "generic" purchase funnel model depicted in Figure 10.12: The first one entails combining the previously distinct *consideration* and *trial* stages; the second modification adds the *repurchase* stage as the follow-up to *purchase*. These modifications are important for two reasons: First of all, they expressly acknowledge that the goal of product/service promotion is to win customers (i.e., ongoing brand repurchase) rather than merely bringing about a single transaction (i.e., a purchase), which is intuitively obvious though not expressly incorporated into the aforementioned "generic" purchase funnel conceptualization.

The second purchase funnel model enhancement that is evident in Figure 10.16 involves combining the "trial" and "consideration" processes stages. The rationale behind this amendment is a bit more methodological in nature—in essence, it stems from the fundamental lack of generalizable discriminant validity separating these two process components. In other words, while virtually all product and service purchase processes entail distinctly separate "awareness," "consideration" and "purchase" steps, some do not include equally distinctly separate "consideration" and "trial" stages. For example, a car purchase process nearly always involves a selection of a handful of brands of interest from a much larger set and a subsequent trial (i.e., test drive); on the other hand, a new breakfast cereal purchase hardly ever involves product trial (in the sense of a car test drive) prior to repurchase. Although this might be a relatively trivial consideration in the context of the overall purchase process conceptualization, it is operationally quite important, as shown later.

Another defining characteristic of the initial integration rollout process depicted in Figure 10.16 is its singular focus on maximizing the growth in size and value of the customer base. In a sense, the purchase funnel, promotional mix and the strategy as well as the tactics linking all these pieces together are all merely a means to an end, which is increasing the value of the current customers and acquiring more high-value brand buyers. This is accomplished by focusing on process-wide as well as stage-specific vehicle and investment allocation decision. The former involves the identification of the most impactful funnel stage—promotional media alignments, summarized under Impacting Medium. The latter calls for a stage-by-stage explicit differentiation between a message reinforcing repetition and an unnecessary overlap with the goal of lowering promotional waste while making vehicle selection and investment allocation decisions, which is captured under Integration Focus.

For example, from the purchase funnel point of view a range of promotional vehicles, including advertising, direct mail and interactive can be deployed against the task of stimulating brand consideration and trial. However, depending on the characteristics of the brand, such as its lifecycle (new vs. mature), penetration (common vs. special need), distribution (national vs. regional) and the general product category, as well as the past promotional history, all or only a subset of those vehicles should be used to get the maximum benefit without the wasteful and unnecessary overlap. The selected consideration and trial-specific promotional mix should be closely linked by a common promotional and treatment strategy as the means of maximizing its persuasive effectiveness.

Setting the Stage for Ongoing Optimization

A high-level view of the integration optimization process depicted in Figure 10.16 implies the need for an ongoing impact quantification methodology. Objectively assessing the efficacy of the initial promotional mix decisions and any subsequent productivity fine-tuning requires the ability to measure the contribution of each promotional vehicle on the individual funnel stage as well as the end goal of the entire promotional process, which once again is increasing the size and value of the customer base.

The latter requirement is the key measurement difference between fully integrated promotional mix and one that is not, as well as one of the key integration obstacles. Traditionally, performance of individual promotional mix vehicles has been assessed with the help of multiple idiosyncratic metrics, such as advertising exposure, online click-thru rate, coupon redemption or direct mail response rates. Not only are these metrics not directly comparable (i.e., they are not standardized), but even more importantly, most are not linked to the brand purchase. Thus it is rarely known whether the upper funnel general advertising efforts can be attributed to higher brand sales or not—it is assumed that increased brand awareness and consideration ultimately translate into sales gains, but these assumptions are not systematically tested. It is simply not good enough.

Since there are no economic benefits to the brand in consumers just knowing about it, just as it is of equally little benefit to count non-purchase program responses, the impact of all promotional initiatives needs to be expressed in terms of attributable sales incrementality. Given that virtually all marketing programs require monetary outlays, the only rational way of quantifying program productivity is to isolate program-induced monetary inflows. Furthermore, implementing a purchase-funnel-wide standard impact measurement methodology is necessary to optimizing promotional mix decisions on an ongoing basis. In general, there are three distinct program impact measurement methods that could be used for that purpose, each requiring somewhat different levels of measurement sophistication and yielding varying degrees of accuracy,[35] as summarized in Table 10.3.

Overall, the all-round most effective method of quantifying treatment-induced purchase incrementality is *experimentation*. It supports the most effective means of controlling for potentially confounding extraneous influences, thus yielding the cleanest, most reliable quantification of impact. The reason it is not always used is that it is also the most demanding, specifically in terms of the sampling frame and treatment rule requirements. The need to set aside a control group can lead to perceived opportunity loss of not promoting to a group of otherwise qualified prospects; in other instances, control groups cannot be set aside because of credit queries mandating a requirement of making a credit-related offer. Even if an organization is willing and able to set aside a control group, the treated vs. control groups' size or the overall sample composition can fall short of technical requirements, precipitating the confounding of treated with non-experimentally controlled factors. In the end, although experimentation has the potential to provide the most accurate assessment of program's effectiveness, it will not be a viable option for some organizations or situations.

Where experimentation is not an option, promotional baseline might be a viable alternative. As outlined above, its requirements are considerably different, somewhat complementary to those of experimentation, making it a good substitute for situations where setting up experiments is not feasible. For example, promotional baseline does not require setting aside control groups nor does it carry any treatment-related sampling requirements. On the other hand, it does require a sufficient amount of historical data and an a priori development of a statistical model. Its key advantage is the emphasis on standardization of cross-treatment effects, longitudinal consistency and low maintenance re-usability.

Table 10.3 Treatment-Attributable Lift Quantification Approaches

	Experimentation	Statistical Baseline	Consumer Survey
Type	Snapshot in time	Ongoing	Snapshot in time
Focus	Fact-based, objective	Fact-based, objective	Consumer recall
General Description	• Approach built around treated (promotion exposed) and control (held out from promotion) groups. • Non-treatment-specific differences randomized or blocked to avoid confounding. • Impact of treatment: *incrementality* = (*treated − control*).	• Multivariate statistical model leveraging historical purchases and promotional data. • Models "unpromoted" level of sales to be contrasted with actual sales. • Singles out multiple promotion specific effects and calibrates their respective elasticities.	• A sample of consumers surveyed via phone, or email or other means. • Probes product purchase intentions or reasons for purchase. • Relies on consumer recall of purchase reasons rather than actual purchases.
Strengths	• Purchase-based, measuring actual sales. • Unbiased and objective. • Capable of attributing incrementality to specific promotions or other actions. • No responder bias / measurement bias.	• Purchase-based, objective and unbiased. • Quantifies effects of multiple promotions concurrently. • Ideal for cross-time comparisons and trending. • Very low long-term cost. • No measurement bias.	• Does not require setting aside control groups or a priori statistical models. • Can yield consumer insights. • Does not require pre-program planning.
Weaknesses	• Requires setting aside untreated control groups. • Depends on robust pre-program launch planning. • Difficult to factor-in external macro factors, such competitive activity.	• Requires development of possibly complex statistical model. • Too complex for one-shot programs.	• Relies on consumer recall to attribute purchases to specific promotions. • Subject to multiple biases, such as poor recall, demand effect, biased measurement, etc. • Difficult to factor-in external macro factors.

Lastly, in some situations a consumer-survey-based approach has also been used. Relying on buyer recall and rarely able to account for a number of macro factors, this is by far the least accurate method of quantifying treatment-attributable incrementality. As a matter of fact, it should only be used in situations where neither experimentation nor promotional baseline can be deployed.

Ongoing Optimization

The long-term success of the initially integrated promotional mix is to a large degree dependent on setting up ongoing, systematic impact measurement capabilities. The previously described experimentation and statistical baseline lift quantification methodologies offer different means of objectively tackling this important challenge. Further operationalizing the measurement task and enabling ongoing fine-tuning of the initial vehicle assortment and spending allocation decision are the selection of funnel stage appropriate evaluative metrics, a funnel-wide sampling plan and spelling out specific comparative contrasts relating each of the medium-stage combinations[36] to the final objective of customer base value growth, all of which are detailed in Figure 10.17 below.

As shown in Figure 10.17, the key to ongoing integrated promotional mix improvements can be found in connecting individual purchase funnel stages to the most effective promotional vehicles as well as setting up a robust impact measurement around delineating funnel stage specific evaluative metrics, sampling rationale and the evaluative logic. For example, the upper funnel is about generating or increasing brand awareness, most effectively assessed with brand recall and recognition. In general, in-market experimentation contrasting treated to holdout groups' brand awareness levels offers the most robust means of quantifying lift, induced by specific advertising or PR activities. Although not expressly captured in the above process representation, it is important to express the incremental awareness gains in terms of confidence interval ranges to account for sampling error. In the same vein, in view of statistical significance tests' interpretation limitations,[37] their results should be interpreted carefully.

An important consideration deserving a more detailed discussion is sampling. As is well known, to give rise to valid inferences, a sample needs to be representative of the population from which it was drawn. When measuring the impact of promotional programs, the widely used random sampling is not always the best approach to take for two reasons: First of all, oftentimes what is labeled as "random" is in fact a "convenience"

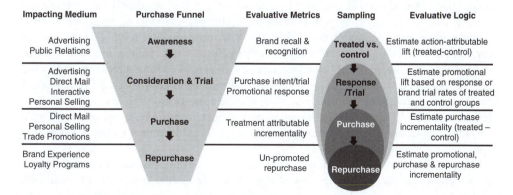

Figure 10.17 Promotional Mix Integration: Ongoing Improvement

sample, simply because selecting a truly random sample—defined as all elements comprising a sampling frame having a known and equal probability of being selected—can be prohibitively difficult in practice. In addition, even when the definitional random sampling requirements have been met, a randomly selected sample may under-represent quantitatively small but interpretationally important consumer segments. In the end, sampling decisions should strike a balance between definitional accuracy and inter-pretational expectations, which will often require looking beyond random and toward more involved sampling schemas, such as stratification.

An equally important sample selection consideration is its sizing. In the context of the purchase funnel, sample size decisions need to be made in a bottom-up fashion, which means starting with the final purchase funnel contrast effective sample size and moving up the funnel by factoring actual (based on historical results) or expected sample size drop off rates. In a technical sense, the purchase funnel focused impact measurement requires a nested sampling frame because the downward funnel carryover effects' quantification (i.e., increased brand awareness translating into heightened brand consi-deration ultimately spurring higher purchase rates) requires a single, static consumer sample. Depending on the consumer fallout associated with downward funnel move-ment, the initial (i.e., associated with the first funnel stage) sample size may need to be considerably larger than the effective (i.e., associated with the final funnel stage) one. For example, to end up with an effective sample size of 200 consumers in the repurchase stage and assuming 50% drop off along each of the preceding funnel stages calls for an initial sample of 1,600 consumers.

Looking beyond sampling considerations, the overall level of difficulty increases as the focus shifts down the purchase funnel, mostly due to impact additivity. In other words, in addition to quantifying funnel stage–promotional vehicle specific effects (i.e., the lift attributable to the impact of a particular promotional vehicle on an individual purchase funnel stage), it is also necessary to capture the carry-over effects in keeping with the overall measurement goal of estimating the promotional mix productivity in terms of its sales incrementality. In an operational sense, the initial process stage—awareness—only calls for the measurement of its own main effect with no carry-over effects. However the next stage—consideration and trial—requires both its own main effect estimation as well as an assessment of the awareness–consideration carry-over effects. The measure-ment bar is raised even higher at the purchase stage, where a three-way carryover effect of awareness–consideration–purchase needs to be estimated on top of the stage-specific main effect. An additional complicating factor might be introduced by promotional vehicle data differences, which may require the deployment of multiple impact quantification methodologies (see Table 10.3). In other words, relying on in-market experimentation is not always feasible, mostly because setting aside appropriate control groups may not be plausible (for instance, all consumers whose credit records were queried need to be subsequently made a credit offer), just as constructing a promotional baseline may prove to be prohibitively complex and time-consuming in other situations. It follows that the task of putting in place a robust measurement process requires a considerable amount of up-front preparation and the willingness to deploy multiple approaches contemporaneously.

On a more positive note, the potential benefits of a more rigorous program impact measurement are compelling in view of the previously discussed impact enhancements and cost savings associated with trimming of unnecessary promotional expenditures. In addition, the availability of robust and standardized program or treatment attributable lift estimates can form the basis for the development of comprehensive planning and simulation capabilities. A "what-if" promotional mix scenario planning tool can be invaluable in terms of the obvious planning efficiencies it could provide as well as its impact on transforming the decision making culture away from the subjective "gut-feeling" and toward the far more effective "fact-based" paradigm. Figure 10.18 offers additional analytic granularity in the form of the required contrasts.

The aspects of the funnel measurement depicted in Figure 10.18 are only limited to capturing the integration-attributable lift. This means that any single medium-specific effects are not captured here, as they are not indicative of the effectiveness of the integrated mix.

As shown in Figure 10.18, the initial brand awareness, assessed by contrasting treated and control consumer samples, is further added-onto by the consideration and trial enhancing mix elements of additional advertising, direct mail, online interactive and personal selling. Assessment-wise, the initial treated vs. control awareness contrast is expanded to take into account consideration effects by means of contrasting the consideration rate of heightened brand awareness consumers with those whose awareness was not enhanced by advertising exposure. The same cumulative logic is applied to the *purchase* and *repurchase* stages. It is also important to note that throughout the funnel measurement process appropriate steps need to be taken to ascertain the statistical validity of the individual contrasts.

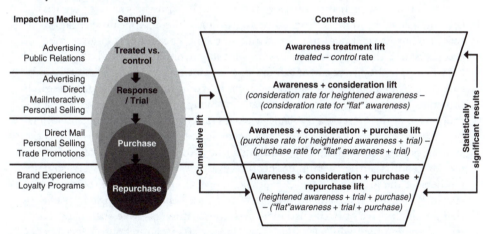

Figure 10.18 Funnel Impact Measurement

Mini-Case 10.1: Consumer Coupons and Look-Alike Modeling

Mass media-distributed product or service coupons are among the most commonly used purchase incentives, particularly popular among consumer package goods companies. Although primarily a brand-level promotional tool, coupons are also used as a mean of expanding category-wide sales (think of ready-to-eat breakfast cereals where an individual company, such as Kellogg or Post, owns multiple brands within a single category). Yet in spite of its widespread usage, this promotional tactic is often viewed as a "necessary evil"—necessary because large chunks of the customer base have grown to expect coupons and evil, in a manner of speaking, because it erodes the profitability of individual brands. Stated differently, although the intent behind issuing coupons is typically to attract new customers, the lion's share of coupon redemptions represent repurchases of existing customers.

It is fairly obvious that the key reason behind couponing's inefficacy (the bulk of redemptions representing de facto purchase subsidies for existing customers rather than an enticement to non-customers) is the reliance on mass distribution. Setting aside the (some might argue) unnecessary price subsidies offered to current customers, the new customers acquired that way tend to be the price-sensitive *brand switchers,* who are generally the least profitable customer segment. In a more general sense, the Achilles heel of mass-distributed coupons is *self-selection,* or more specifically, *adverse self-selection.* When a business organization issues a purchase price discount-based "open invitation," those who exhibit the greatest propensity to take advantage of such an offer are the same category buyers who also exhibit the greatest probability of taking advantage of similar offers made by other organizations.

An almost intuitive solution to the problem of adverse self-selection is to forgo the open invitation of mass distribution in favor of targeting a thoughtfully selected audience, such as prospective buyers that exhibit the greatest potential of becoming loyal customers. Conceptually it sounds like an appealing idea, but in practice, how is the brand to know which of the potentially very large number of prospects has the potential to become loyal customers? By and large, while customers' purchasing behavior is knowable for consumer (and many other) brands, that is not the case for non-customers. (I should point out that syndicated research providers, such as the Nielsen Company or SymphonyIRI capture a very large proportion of the *all commodity volume* via data purchase agreements with retailers, but that data is product—not purchaser-centric because UPC scanners record the "what," not the "who" of individual transactions. To get the latter attached to the former requires either a retailer-specific loyalty card, which is rarely sold by retailers, or the so-called "reverse credit card append," which is both imperfect and currently illegal). There are, however, non-purchase behavior-based sources of data that are descriptive of both customers and non-customers—one such data source is geodemographics, which are block-level (about 20–30 households) aggregates of individual-level demographic details derived from the U.S. Census data (the U.S. law prohibits the Bureau from selling individual-level data to commercial interests); psychographics is another widely used and available descriptive data source. It follows that a brand could use its customer purchase data to identify its most valuable customer segments and then use descriptive data sources, such as the aforementioned geodemographics and psychographics, to profile those segments. The resultant profiles could then be used as the basis for finding "similar" looking individuals within the universe of non-customers. The underlying analytical approach is known as "look-alike modeling"; it is a widely used tool for targeting marketing promotions, such as coupons, at pre-screened subsets of prospects. The example that follows describes some of the key operational details.

The starting point in look-alike modeling is the delineation of value-based customer segments, which can be thought of as focused (on very specific classificatory dimensions) segmentation. Let's take a widely used consumer product, such as ready-to-eat (RTE) breakfast cereal. As suggested above, purchase history offers by far the best basis for differentiating between high- and low-value customer (the number of value groupings varies across usage situations, but between two and four is the most commonly seen number). An important consideration here is the length of time to be used in the analysis—usually, the higher the average repurchase frequency, the shorter the length of time (measured as the difference between the most recent data and a point in the past). For a relatively high repurchase frequency RTE breakfast cereal, 18–24 months would generally be deemed sufficient.

The next step is the selection of an appropriate grouping approach—here, a commonly used framework is the so-called "RFM," which stands for *recency, frequency* and *monetary*, where *recency* captures the timing (relative to current) of the most recent purchase, *frequency* is a measure of the total number of purchases (commonly expressed as a number of purchases per unit of time) and *monetary* is the total spending. The product of frequency and monetary dimensions (frequency _ monetary) forms the basis for quantifying *customer value*, while recency is commonly used as the basis for identifying *lapsed buyers*. (Customer-specific "time since the last purchase" is contrasted with "average category repurchase cycle"—for example, if Customer A's time since the last purchase of Brand X is 4 weeks and the category-wide RTE breakfast cereal repurchase average repurchase cycle is 2 weeks, then that customer would be considered lapsed, from the point of view of Brand X.)

Value Groupings		Avg. Purchase Frequency	Avg. Spend ($) Level	Avg. Estimated Profitability
High Value	N		106,874	
	Mean	46	$142.08	$28.42
	Median	45	$140.18	$28.04
	Maximum	96	$254.65	$50.93
Mid-High	N		121,115	
	Mean	26	$61.19	$12.24
	Median	22	$59.75	$11.95
	Maximum	52	$176.18	$35.24
Mid-Low	N		124,177	
	Mean	21	$50.48	$10.10
	Median	20	$49.01	$9.80
	Maximum	43	$122.18	$24.44
Low Value	N		124,149	
	Mean	12	$37.86	$7.57
	Median	14	$30.90	$6.18
	Maximum	31	$98.74	$19.75
All values were annualized				

Figure 10.19 RFM Segmentation

Lastly, mutually exclusive value categories are established based upon the aggregate distribution of individually determined customer value estimates. Assuming a simple binary classification heuristic—i.e., high- vs. low-value—the results commonly adhere to Pareto's principle, where a fairly small proportion of buyers account for the bulk of purchases—e.g., 20% and 80%, respectively. A sample, four-group RFM-based customer value categorization is shown in Figure 10.19. The four frequency- and monetary-based value categories—High-Value, Mid-High, Mid-Low & Low-Value—exhibit considerable differences in *average annualized purchase frequency, average annualized spending level* and *average estimated profitability*. As predicted by Pareto's Principle, the bulk of the brand's profitability is concentrated in about 20% of its customers, which is fairly typical of consumer brands—hence it follows that, ideally, the brand's couponing efforts should be directed toward prospective customers who look like the high-value current customers. However, since, as noted earlier, non-customers' purchase behavior is generally not knowable, we need to find a way of using what is knowable (most notably, the widely available geodemographics and psychographics) as a predictor of customer value. Analytically speaking, having leveraged past purchase behavior as the means of identifying distinct value-based customer segments, we now turn to the available descriptive data to construct a customer value prediction mechanism. Depending on the number of dependent variable categories (i.e., the number of value groupings or segments), the most reliable statistical technique that is used for that purpose is either *logistic regression* (2 categories only, such as high- vs. low-value) or *multinomial logit* (for 3+ categories). In practice, even if the number of initial value groupings is greater than two, as is the case in this example, value-predicting modeling tends to use only two categories (high- vs. low-value) simply because the ultimate goal of the analysis is to estimate the probability of individual non-customers becoming high-value customers.

The starting point in the predictive model development was the creation of a two-group indicator, where Group 1 = high-value customers and Group 2 = remaining three categories (mid-high, mid-low and low-value groupings). Coding-wise, Group 1 was coded as "1" and Group 2 as "0," with "1" being the reference variable, which is the predictive focus (i.e., the outcome or state the probability of which is being predicted) of the analysis; outcome-wise, the goal of the logistic regression outlined here was to single out individual (geodemographic and/or psychographic) variables that maximize the *distinctiveness* of high-value customers. In other words, given that the purpose of the analysis is to estimate the probability of a customer boasting a particular set of traits being a high-value customer (the near-term goal of a logistic regression model should not be confused with the longer-term goal of estimating the probability of individual non-customers becoming high-value customers), which specific of geodemographic and psychographic factors out of several dozens of available measures are most predictive of that outcome?

The first step in interpreting the results of logistic regression (see Figure 10.20) is to assess the key statistical goodness-of-fit measures, most notably the estimates of the amount of variability in the dependent variable that has been collectively explained by the predictors exhibiting statistically significant association with the

Model Summary

-2 Log likelihood	Cox & Snell R^2	Nagelkerke R^2
541.093[a]	.505	.679

Hosmer and Lemeshow Test

Chi-square	df	Sig.
9.816	8	.278

Figure 10.20 Goodness-of-Fit

outcome of interest (i.e., the probability of being a high-value customer). The two widely used metrics, which can be likened to the R^2 statistics used in linear regression, Cox & Snell R^2 and Nagelkerke R^2, suggest a reasonably strong predictive power characterizing the predictors comprising the final model. The Hosmer and Lemeshow test, which compares the model's prediction to known (i.e., actual) outcomes, also suggests a well-fitting model (the sig. estimate of .288 indicates that the number of model-generated "high-value" group memberships is not statistically different from the actual number).

Further complementing the model assessment is the two-way classification table (see Figure 10.21), which shows the actual vs. predicted comparison shown as actual counts and percentages, rather than somewhat abstruse statistics. The overall correct classification rate of 83.7% should not be taken literally, as it is unlikely that the application of the model outlined here would indeed yield such fairly high predictive accuracy—that said, the assessment of the model is indeed indicative of a fairly robust performance, though likely somewhat below the validation threshold (there are numerous reasons for that, one of the main ones being that the model calibration and validation samples are subsets of the same, larger customer sample, while the future application will be against a completely different sample of non-customers).

Satisfied with the goodness-of-fit, we can now turn to examining the model itself, which is a set of statistically significant predictors, along with their coefficients, as shown in Figure 10.22. Although developed with a predictive purpose in mind, the logistic regression model shown here can also be looked at as an explanatory mechanism. Staying with the predictive functionality first, the model-delineated predictor metrics (i.e., "Predictors") along with their respective weights

Classification Tablea

Actual		Predicted		
		High Value		Percentage Correct
		0	1	
High Value	0	1,277	710	79.6%
	1	630	4,100	86.7%
Overall Percentage				83.7%

Figure 10.21 Confusion Matrix

Predictors	B	S.E.	Wald	df	Sig.	Exp(B)
Age_35-44	.022	.007	10.816	1	.001	1.022
Age_65-74	−.061	.017	12.979	1	.000	.941
LOR_2-5Yrs	.057	.015	14.190	1	.000	1.058
LOR_10Yrs	−.312	.046	44.912	1	.000	.732
Gender_F	−.319	.091	12.373	1	.000	.727
Gender_M	.313	.136	5.280	1	.022	1.367
Children_2-3	−.273	.047	34.386	1	.000	.761
Lifestyle_Fitness	.037	.015	5.782	1	.016	1.038
Constant	34.086	4.372	60.797	1	.000	636.000

Figure 10.22 Model Variables

(i.e., "B," or betas) will comprise the *scoring algorithm* to be applied against the available universe of non-customers with the purpose of computing individual-level probabilities of becoming a high-value customer. A more in-depth discussion of the mechanics involved in that process are discussed in the *Database Scoring* chapter and the scoring part of this example will be continued there.

Let's turn to the explanatory aspect of the regression discussed above. Knowing which specific geodemographic or psychographic attributes are associated with heightened likelihood of a current non-customer becoming a future one can be very helpful when designing the content of marketing communications—however, the results of statistical models can be sometimes hard to grasp and appreciate by non-technical audiences. In other words, in order to enhance the usability of the explanatory aspect of this and other logistic regression models it is worthwhile to "translate" the esoteric techno-talk into more universally understandable outcomes. Consider Figure 10.23 above. The first step in doing so is to recognize that—from the standpoint of promotional planning—the numerically expressed conclusions can and should be reduced into qualitative and directional insights. Consider the sample segment profile shown here: High-value customers of the RTE breakfast cereal brand used in this analysis are considerably younger (i.e., the largest number of those customers falling within the "35–44 Years Old" grouping) than the brand's low-value customers (who fall primarily within the "65–74 Years Old" grouping), which obviously is worthwhile information for those crafting the brand's promotional strategy. Knowing that the mean age of the high-value customers is 39.4 years while the mean of the low-value segment is 66.1 years of age would not have a material impact on promotional strategy considerations, hence there is no compelling reason to communicate exactness-conveying statistics—sometimes, less is indeed more. . .

Metrics	Customer Value			
	High	Mid-High	Mid-Low	Low
Age Range				
25-34 Years				
35-44 Years				
45-54 Years				
65 -74 Years				
Length of Residence				
2 - 5 Years				
6 - 10 Years				
10+ Years				
Marital Status				
Married				
Single				
Gender				
Female				
Male				
Occupation				
Professional				
Executive				
Homemaker				
Retired				
Sales				
Number of Children				
None				
1 Child				
2 or 3 Children				
Lifestyle & Interests				
Outdoors				
Athletic				
Fitness				
Domestic				
Cultural				
Technology				
Reading				
Only difference-conveying metrics are shown here				

Figure 10.23 Model Visualization

11 Action-Attributable Incrementality

One of the most common and most significant shortcomings of marketing analytics is the reliance on raw response rate, or similar metrics, as the basis for estimating the impact of promotional activities. The raw response rate to a marketing promotion is perhaps the easiest "assessment" to carry out, hence its popularity, but it is also potentially one of the most misleading ones: It reflects the attractiveness of the promotional stimulus, while offering no insights into the incrementality of responders' actions.

The goal of marketing promotions is to either attract new buyers to the brand or to convince current customers to increase their spending—unfortunately, many promotions end up subsidizing existing customers or attracting the usually unprofitable "brand switchers." Hence, what might appear to be a successful marketing campaign from the standpoint of its response rate, could be quite unprofitable when looked at in terms of return on marketing investment. Thus it follows that the effective measurement of the "true"—or incremental—impact of marketing promotions is an essential component of an effective marketing management system.

Incrementality Measurement

One of the key challenges of database marketing is an objective determination of the impact of individual actions or decisions. Typically, this entails an assessment of how much—if at all—a particular promotional action increased the overall sales, revenue or profit levels.

The most often employed and potentially the most misleading approach to impact measurement is a simple quantification of *gross incidence rates*, such as the frequency of promotional responses (i.e., a response rate) or the proportion of product/service purchasers who were also included in a particular promotion (i.e., a purchase rate). Operationally, these measures generally involve tallying of product purchases during the qualifying times (i.e., promotional periods) and for qualifying targets (i.e., targeted potential buyers) to arrive at a total promotional purchase rate, as illustrated in Figure 11.1.

The reason the above approach is both frequently used as well as potentially misleading is that it is based on an implicit assumption that the action of interest—typically, a specific promotion—is the sole reason for the observed sales increases (assuming that there indeed has been an observable sales upswing). In reality, a single promotion or other actions geared at stimulating purchase rates is usually only one of several factors potentially influencing sales. Other promotions, competitive actions and macro market forces, such as new regulations or interest rates are all potential moderators of the

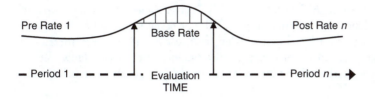

Figure 11.1 Cross-Purchase Rate Approach

promotion–purchase rate relationship. In other words, attributing all of the observed sales increases to a single business action without controlling for (i.e., factoring-out) other potential contributors can lead to, at times, significant overstating of the effectiveness of the said promotion.

Secondly, a simple count of "qualifying" purchases does not take into account the frequently observed phenomenon of "pantry-loading," whereby buyers buy in larger quantities and/or ahead of the actual need manifestly to take advantage of the offered savings, which in effect cannibalizes future sales. Consider Figure 11.1 above. Even though *Period 1–Promotion Purchase* levels may increase, the subsequent rate may drop below the pre-promotion (i.e., pre-Period 1) levels.

Overall, a gross incidence-rate-based approach potentially confounds effects attributable to actions of interest with factors falling outside of the consideration set. And because it is not known what other factors may have impacted the gross promotional purchase rate of interest (and to what degree), it is impossible to tell the true magnitude of the action–response relationship.

In addition, these methods tend to measure success in terms of easily manipulated outcomes, such as revenue, rather than the more objective profitability. Considering that a vast majority of products and services exhibit some level of *price elasticity* (i.e., price-change-driven changes in demand), it is easy to see how near-term purchase rates can be relatively easily manipulated. Gross revenue-measured promotions tend not to differentiate between profitable (i.e., revenue > cost) and unprofitable (i.e., revenue < cost) sales, even if the impact of other, potentially confounding factors has been adequately controlled. Of course, no brand or organization can remain viable, over the long run, unless it can earn a profit. It is easy to see that seemingly "successful" promotional campaigns can be total flops in terms of longer-term customer base productivity: The near-term (i.e., the "promotion" time period, as shown in Figure 11.1 above) revenue lift can quickly disappear, once the timeframe of analysis is widened. Or, once adjusted to fully account for all costs, the apparent revenue gains turn out to yield a net loss. Or, still, the "double whammy": no long-term sales lift coupled with a net loss. Given the often loose standards for how the impact measurement of promotions and other business actions tends to be carried out, it is easy to find success where the opposite might be true. . .

An obvious question comes to mind: Why are gross incidence rates used so often? The answer is quite simple: These measures are easy to compute and require little-to-no a priori preparation. A purchase rate computed for a time period demarked by the beginning and the end of a particular promotion is contrasted with a pre-promotion rate, and the difference is often attributed to the action of interest—it is both easy to execute and to understand. It also lends itself to easy cross-campaign comparisons—for instance, 2% response rate to Campaign A denotes noticeably "better" outcome than Campaign B's 1% response rate. Hence, the reliance on gross sales or revenue as the key evaluative metric further lessens the computational burden, as the capture of these metrics is typically a part of many organizations' day-to-day business practices.[1] However, as pointed out earlier, it can lead to either unwarranted or altogether untrue conclusions.

Impact Assessment

As is the case throughout the database analytical process, the combination of the availability of disaggregate data and robust statistical techniques gives rise to unique and precise insights, previously beyond reach of most managers. In that sense, continued reliance on the "rough" impact measurement approaches outlined seems irresponsible and in a practical sense, diminishes the quality of data insights and ultimately, the firm's competitiveness.

The notion of action-attributable incrementality was first introduced in Chapter 1 and further discussed in a variety of contexts in subsequent chapters. It is of central importance to the database analytics-driven knowledge creation process outlined in this book because it offers the means of identifying competitively advantageous business actions.

Operationally, the logic of the action-attributed incrementality impact measurement is built around two key elements:

1.   Estimation of the action–result effect
2.   Determination of the profit impact of the action–result effect

Action–result effect estimation captures the methodological considerations and process steps that are required to objectively and reliably quantify the incremental impact of a specific business action, such as a marketing promotion. The determination of the profit impact of the action–result effect represents the business assessment of a specific business action. Combined, these two complementary steps enable a robust side-by-side comparison of otherwise dissimilar business actions.

Action–Result Effect Estimation

The delineation of action-attributable *incrementality* or *lift*[2] forms the basis for expressly and objectively differentiating between effective and ineffective business actions. Simply put, it answers the question of "How many additional sales were realized due to the specific activity of interest?" Conceptually it is a relatively straightforward task, but operationally it can be quite complex. First and foremost, it requires the untangling of the effects of multiple promotional and other actions that might be working concurrently, in such a way as to support the apportionment of their combined effect to the individual components. Second, to yield a comprehensive picture, the quantification of action-attributable incrementality calls for estimation of both the *main effects*—or singularly attributable impact of the action of interest—as well as any *interaction effects*—or synergy stemming from combining the action of interest and other actions.

As outlined in Chapter 10, there are two general approaches to capturing the amount of lift attributable to a specific activity: *experimentation* and *statistical baseline* (the third, survey-based approach, is usually too coarse to support robust lift estimation). The two approaches differ markedly in terms of the demands they place on business users, such as marketing managers implementing specific activities, and analysts who capture and analyze the results.

Experimentation

Experiments are one of two primary means of gathering empirical information (observation is the other one) to serve as bases for hypothesis testing. They entail willful and purposeful manipulation of factors of interests while controlling for potential influences and disturbances. Experiments require a clear delineation of the factors to be studied and their interactions, as well as the means and the scope of the control mechanisms. Operationally, this translates into separate, appropriately sized and selected (i.e., assigned to specific groupings, or cells, as discussed later) *test* and *control* groups and putting in place appropriate *control mechanisms*, or means of preventing the emergence of competing explanations.

Under most circumstances, experimentation is the most effective method of quantifying action-attributable lift. It is the only method offering a methodologically clean and interpretationally robust means of separating effects of the action of interest from other concurrent and possibly confounding actions. Considered from the standpoint of hypothesis testing, *action–result* effect estimation usually involves directional hypothesis tests[3] as the end objective of a test is to ascertain whether the action of interest had a positive impact on the focal outcome, such as sales level.

However, experimentation is also most demanding of the business user and under some circumstances—most notably, when prospects' credit is queried—it may be impossible to implement.[4] Yet in the majority of database applications, where it is indeed feasible to deploy this approach to incrementality quantification, the quality of the resultant insights is certainly worth the extra effort.

Setting up a robust test involves several distinct steps outlined below.

Experimental Design Development

This is the conceptual process of developing a test plan. It is at this stage that a marketing plan is "translated" into a testable and measurable entity. Arguably, it is the most difficult part of the measurement process. The outcome of it is a testing/measurement blueprint.

Sampling Requirements Assessment

The overall process of explicitly contrasting the design-mandated sampling/sample requirements with available data. The outcome of this process is a set of explicit sample selection guidelines, and experimental design amendments, if its requirements cannot be met by existing data.

Effect Analysis

It entails an explicit, numerical assessment of the impact, if any, of experimental stimuli on the population of interest. It can take two forms:

1. INCREMENTALITY ASSESSMENT

Quantification of lift determined by contrasting the impact of experimental stimuli on test and control response groups. Ideal for ROI and absolute lift determination; requires sufficient response sample sizes.

2. RANK-ORDERED EFFECT ASSESSMENT

Directional, analysis of variance (ANOVA)-based insights. Ideal for response effect rank-ordering; considerably smaller sample size requirements.

Experimental Design Development

There are a large number of potential test designs depending on the number of factors, type of comparisons and sampling constraints. In the context of experimental test design, a *factor* is defined as a stimulus the impact of which is being investigated, while a *factor level* is a specific value or a range of values for the said stimulus. A simple, single factor experiment may test the impact of the age of a product purchaser on price elasticity by grouping test subjects into several non-overlapping age groups. In that example, age would be the factor while age groups would represent the individual factor levels.

For the purposes of the *action–result effect estimation*, however, the otherwise diverse experimental variety can be grouped into three general types of designs summarized in Figure 11.2.

The first category of test designs is the *Single Factor Randomized* group, exemplified by test designs such as Completely Random, Randomized Block or Incomplete Block. The common link connecting all of these test types is that their goal is to assess the impact of only a single action—i.e., a factor and the experimental subjects are randomly assigned to individual test cells. In business terms, the Single Factor Randomized family of test designs only allows the manipulation of a single promotional component, such as either frequency or the type of an offer, but not both. Also, as illustrated below, this group of

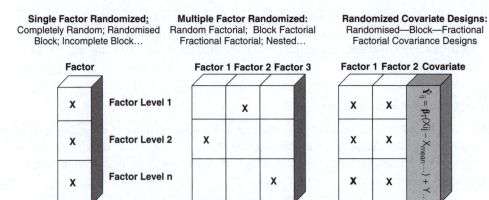

Figure 11.2 Experimental Test Designs

test designs is complete, meaning that each cell representing a factor level has subjects assigned to it (denoted by "X").

Overall, a single factor test is usually appropriate in situations calling for very specific, narrowly defined insights, which means these types of designs will be overly restrictive for broader questions (i.e., ones requiring the assessment of several different elements) as they would require separate experiments for each factor, which is both impractical and does not allow for the assessment of cross-factor interactions. One final and important characteristic of this family of test designs is that the task of controlling for extraneous sources of variability, which is critical in eliminating undesirable competing explanations for any potentially significant relationships, is handled outside of the test itself by either the previously mentioned random subject assignment or by *blocking* of said influences. The latter is typically accomplished by holding constant, across all cells, the values of the variable to be blocked. Computationally, the Single Factor Randomized designs are analyzed with the help of analysis of variance, or ANOVA procedures readily available in most statistical packages.

A natural extension of the single-factor designs is the *Multiple Treatment Randomized* group of experimental designs. Exemplified by Random Factorial, Block Factorial or Fractional Factorial (the last one depicted in Figure 11.2), this family of test designs allows the simultaneous assessment of multiple factors and factor levels. Constraints on the resultant number of cells are more practical then theoretical in nature, as increasing the number of cells has to be accompanied by a proportional increase in the overall sample size, not to mention the increasing treatment and tracking costs and difficulty. At the same time, being able to assess the impact of multiple factors simultaneously is attractive both from the standpoint of timeliness and efficiency, as well as the possibility of quantifying cross-factor interaction effects or synergies.

A possible solution to the potentially large number of cells associated with a multi-factor design can be offered by a *Fractional Factorial* design, illustrated in Figure 11.2 (center), which allows the investigator to reduce the number of cells by selecting only a representative sample of all cells. Depending on the specifics of the design, as little as 10% or 20% of all cells can be used to generate learnings that can be generalized to the full test matrix. However, as is usually the case, this gain too comes at a price: Cross-factor interaction effects cannot be computed with a Fractional Factorial design, which means that a more manageable design will prevent the investigator from uncovering potential synergies. In a fashion similar to single-cell designs, the potentially confounding influence of extraneous factors is controlled for outside of the test itself, by means of either randomization or blocking, or both. Computationally, the Multiple Factor Randomized designs are analyzed with the help of multiple analysis of variance, or MANOVA procedures.

The final and the most methodologically complex type of an experimental test design are the *Randomized Covariate* designs. These are multi-factor, complete (i.e., all delineated factor levels have experimental subjects assigned to them) designs that offer additional means of dealing with extraneous influences. In addition to the outside-the-experiment blocking and randomization, the Randomized Covariate designs enable the analyst to eliminate (or at least diminish) any undesirable outside influences by means of regressing their effects prior to carrying out the planned test contrasts. Computationally, Randomized Covariate designs are analyzed with analysis of covariance, or ANCOVA for single-factor studies or multiple analysis of covariance, or MANCOVA for multi-factor designs.

Sampling Requirements Assessment

Sample adequacy is a critically important area that often receives insufficient levels of consideration. The general process describing selecting of an analysis sample from a data repository (i.e., data warehouse) has been outlined in Chapter 6. In the realm of experimental test design, a more micro view of sampling comes into play, as subsets of the overall analysis sample need to be assigned to individual experimental cells. In this context, the two considerations of most importance are sample composition and sample sizing.

In general, the impact of *sample composition* is primarily felt in the context of result utilization and/or application as well as the proper attribution of the test effects. Hence it is important both from the standpoint of generalizing the findings as well as containing the sources of extraneous variation. The former impacts the usability of results, as it usually arises when the population of interest is comprised of two or more *analytically-distinct* segments.[5] If such segments are not properly recognized, i.e., the analysis sample under- or over-represents some vis-à-vis the others, the results of the analysis might not be equally applicable to all, in other words, might not be generalizable.

The latter of the sample composition-related considerations, the containment of the sources of extraneous variation, impacts the robustness of the analysis itself. Specifically, it helps to eliminate alternative explanations to which the observed effects might be attributable. It addresses the critical part of any experimental design, which is that the goal of subsequent analysis is not only to quantify the magnitude of effects, i.e., sales lift or incrementality, but also to precisely identify the source of sales lift, which is to attribute results to a particular business action.

The importance of s*ample sizing* is a bit more straightforward, insofar as it reflects the adequacy of the available sample size to arrive at statistically sound conclusions. The primary concern here is, once again, twofold: First of all, to delineate the *effective sample size*, which is the estimation of the minimum required number of subjects/responses at the most disaggregate level of analysis. Secondly, it is to identify an objective *record-to-group assignment method*.

The *effective sample size* is the actual number of records used as inputs into analyses, in contrast to the *nominal sample size* which is the number of records available for analyses. The former is almost always smaller that the latter, which is due primarily to missing values, as many commonly used statistical techniques exclude records containing missing values. Thus it is possible that an initially robust sample size may be reduced to a prohibitively small effective sample size in a context of a specific statistical technique, which in turn may lead to unstable, biased effect estimates. When determining the minimum required effective sample size, attention should be focused on the ratio of the number of usable records (i.e., those without any missing values) to the number of variables. A minimum ratio of 4:1, i.e., 4 usable records for every 1 variable, is recommended. It is important to keep in mind that the sample size determinations should be made at the most disaggregate level of analysis, which in the context of incrementality quantification means the most narrowly-defined *business action–outcome* contrasts. Of course, this is a situational determination as the type (and thus a number) of metrics used will obviously vary across different analyses.

Devising an objective *record-to-group assignment method* is considerably more complex than identifying the minimum acceptable effective sample size. Record-to-group allocations have to be carried out in a way that will support an unambiguous effect interpretation, operationalized as attributing the observed effects to specific stimuli. The task may be further complicated by the presence of multiple response groups or two distinct sets of stimuli, or both. In other words, the goal of incremental impact quantification is often to contrast the productivity of two of more in-market programs and/or to assess the impact on two or more types of consumers. The following generalized example outlines the recommended approach to determining an objective *record-to-group assignment*.

Generalized Example: Record-to-Group Assignment Method for 2+ Groups

This example outlines a sample selection logic for a large manufacturer operating two lead generation programs, for two product groups (Group 1 and Group 2), concurrently. The objective of the logic outlined below is to quantify the contribution of individual programs (i.e., action-attributable incrementality) to the overall lead capture endeavor.

Upon the completion of each monthly lead capture cycle, all qualifying leads are divided into two groups, Group 1 and Group 2, with each group receiving approximately 50% of the total. The "lead-to-group" assignment of the aforementioned leads is to be carried out in accordance with the stratified sampling logic, outlined below. The purpose of the stratification is to ascertain between-group invariance with regard to the two key lead characteristics: 1. the number of entities requested, and 2. the expected purchase horizon. Within each of the resultant strata (i.e., a unique combination of the *number of entities requested* and *expected purchase horizon*), leads are to be randomly assigned to Groups 1 and 2. The total number of sampling strata should be equal to the [*number of entities requested*] × [number of distinct *expected purchase horizon* categories]. If the resultant number of cells is too high, a *fractional factorial test design* (see Figure 11.2) can be employed to reduce it, or some of the categories of either or both of the classifying dimensions can be collapsed. However, since the fractional factorial design would make the assessment of cross-factor interactions (a highly desired insight, in this example) impossible, the latter of the two alternatives will be pursued. Thus to simplify the overall structure, the number of entities requested and expected purchase horizon categories will be collapsed into 3, which will result in the total of 9 experimental cells.

The following are the sample selection steps referenced above:

Step 1: Define the "number of entities requested" and "expected purchase horizon" groupings:

Number of Entities Requested groupings:

```
if # entities requested < 3, then Group = 1
if # entities requested ≥ 3 and < 6, then Group = 2
if # entities requested ≥ 6, then Group = 3
```

Expected Purchase Horizon groupings:

```
if purchase timing < 1, then Group = 1
if purchase timing ≥ 1 and < 3, then Group = 2
if purchase timing ≥ 3, then Group = 3
```

Step 2: Determine the share of each grouping of the overall total, where the sum of all groupings is equal to 100%. Grouping specific distributions must add up to 100%, as shown below:

 # Entities Requested groupings:

> Group1_Request = x1%
> Group2_Request = x2%
> Group3_Request = x3%
> **Group_Request_Total** = 100%

Purchase Timing groupings:

> Group1_Timing = y1%
> Group2_Timing = y2%
> Group3_Timing = y3%
> **Group_Timing_Total** = 100%

Step 3: Derive Group 1 and Group 2 samples in accordance with the following logic:

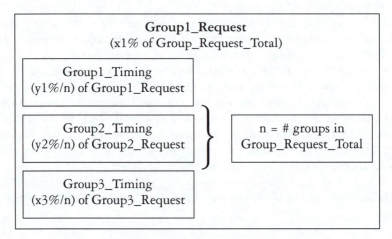

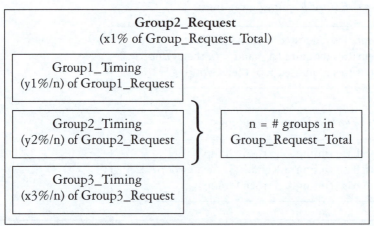

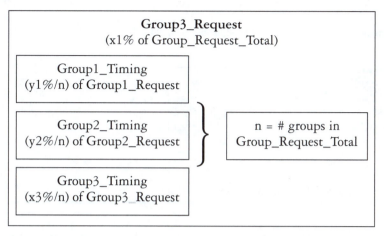

Effect Analysis

There are several ways of quantifying the magnitude of action-attributable incrementality in the context of an experiment. These methods can, however, be grouped into two general categories: *cross-sectional* and *longitudinal contrasts*.

The preferred *cross-sectional* method, offering the "cleanest read" or the most accurate assessment of net impact (assuming the presence of sufficient extraneous variability controlling mechanisms) entails contrasting of treatment and control groups. The resultant difference, or lift to use statistical jargon, captures the action-attributable incrementality and it can be either null (lift = 0) or positive (lift > 0).[6] Here, *positive incrementality* represents a quantitative estimate of the net benefit associated with the business action (such as fielding of a particular promotion) being measured.

If for some reason setting aside a control group is not possible (e.g., credit issuers are required by law to make a credit offer to any consumer whose credit worthiness has been queried), an alternative to the above "test vs. control" cross-section impact measurement entails contrasting specific action cells with the experiment-wide average (excluding the action cells of interest). Conceptually, this type of contrast may yield a somewhat diminished accuracy, simply because the random error of the overall mean will tend to be larger than the random error of the control group mean. Hence, the most significant disadvantage to this approach is that effects of smaller magnitudes might be somewhat harder to detect. However, as pointed out earlier, under some circumstances setting aside a control group may simply not be viable and when that is the case, the "treated vs. overall mean" type contrasts will yield an objective and an unbiased estimate of the incremental effect of the business action of interest. It is also worth mentioning that neither of the two types of cross-sectional contrasts considers the impact of time, thus it is important to properly time-align any treated vs. not treated comparisons.

Longitudinal contrasts, on the other hand, are all about time. Their basic design calls for comparing pre-action and post-action levels, such as sales rates prior to the action of interest (such as a specific promotion) and sales rates following the introduction of the action of interest. In many instances, an important consideration entails factoring-in any post-action or post-treatment effects, such as promotion-induced stocking up—e.g., "pantry loading"—and the subsequent dampening of the sales level. In other words, to yield a true picture of the net impact of the action of interest, a longitudinal pre-post

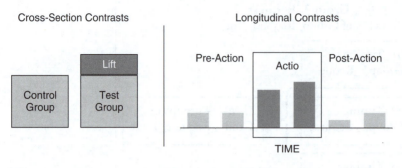

Figure 11.3 Cross-Sectional and Longitudinal Lift Quantification

incrementality quantification method needs to adjust any initial gains (e.g., "no promotion" vs. "promotion in effect") by any subsequent action-driven decreases (e.g., "promotion in effect" vs. "no promotion"). Not doing so, which is surprisingly common, will lead to an overestimation of the potential net benefit of the action of interest in the near term and disappointing results in the long run.

Visually, cross-sectional and longitudinal impact quantification approaches are depicted in Figure 11.3.

Analyses of experimental effects touch upon two important, though frequently misapplied notions of *point vs. interval estimation* and *statistical significance*. As discussed in Chapter 8, statistical significance tests are often used in conjunction with point estimates to "attest" to the tangibility of measured effects. All too often, these two concepts are used erroneously.

The Impact of Statistical Significance Testing

One of the most common misapplications of the statistical significance testing in program measurement, focused around program treatment incrementality attributions, is exemplified and discussed below.

EXAMPLE 1: REPORTING SALES LIFT LACKING STATISTICAL SIGNIFICANCE

Treated* buy rate:	2.5%
Control** buy rate:	2.0%
Incremental buy rate:	0.5% → Lift: 25%
Desired confidence:	$\alpha = 0.05$ (95%)
Significance level***:	0.60

Consumers who received a particular offer/mailing
**Consumers who were held out of a particular mailing for comparison purposes*
*** Levels below 90% considered not statistically significant in accordance with a common convention ($\alpha = .10$). Although not recommended, levels as low as 80% ($\alpha = .20$) are sometimes deemed statistically significant.*

As shown in the above example, the *treated* appears to have outperformed the *control* group by 0.5%, suggesting an incremental sales lift of 25%. The level of significance of the reported lift is only 60%, which is considerably below the expected 95% level and in general considered "not statistically significant."

The example presented above highlights a common program measurement practice of quantifying and reporting as "real" results lacking statistical significance, despite their ostensibly spurious nature. Specifically, I am referring to the above shown *Incremental Buy Rate = 0.5* and *Lift = 25%* metrics, which are both quantified even though they lack statistical significance. The dependence of sales incrementality (and thus lift) on statistical significance is not acknowledged as evidenced by presenting the two as independent insights, leading some into believing that the treatment had an incremental impact, just not statistically significant one. Interpretations like that are self-refuting, as there simply are no instances of sales lift being both "real" in the sense of representing a genuine increase in sales, while at the same time not being statistically significant. Incremental buy rates, sales lift or any other impact metric that lacks statistical significance should be reported as zero and only as zero. Reporting actual effect magnitudes for not statistically significant results—such as the above incremental buy rate of 0.5% with the level of significance of 0.60—can lead to erroneous conclusions as it is easy to look past the abstract *level of significance* detail and focus instead on the reported impact of the program, which after all is of far more interest to program managers. That said, whether one agrees with the logic of SST or not, using it to validate the impact of the program necessitates its correct application, which centers on inseparability of program impact metrics and their level of significance. Thus only statistically significant effects should be quantified and reported as real gains (or losses); all not statistically significance results should be reported as 0.

A Quick Methodological Note.   The above reasoning is reflective of the hypothesis testing logic, which is SST's scientific parent. Whether it is explicitly stated or merely implied, virtually all business action measurement tasks are about testing of some type of test–control equality hypotheses.[7] In other words, we start out by assuming that the treatment had no noticeable effect (this is the so-called "null hypothesis"), but we are ultimately hoping that we can find evidence to the contrary, which would enable us to reject the null and accept the alternative hypothesis.[8] Statistical significance tests are a mechanism used as the basis for making the "reject" vs. "accept" decisions, thus they play a central role in the hypothesis testing process. (It is worth pointing out here that the hypothesis testing logic itself is not beyond reproach as it is built around the assertion that any two sample means are expected to be equal, which is hard to reconcile with such basic statistical concepts as random error; this topic, however, falls outside the scope of the present discussion.)

The basic decision rule governing hypothesis testing is quite simple: If the treated rate the control rate and the difference between the two is statistically significant the null hypothesis is rejected; otherwise it is accepted. If the two response rates are different but the difference is not statistically significant the null hypothesis is accepted as true. In that case observed treated vs. control response rate difference is disregarded as a random anomaly and the sales lift is assumed to be zero. That is why the above exemplified treated and control buy rates should be presented as statistically equal to each other and

Table 11.1 Hypothesis Testing Logic

Treated = Control	Statistical Significance	Incremental Lift
Yes	n/a	0
No	No	0
No	Yes	Exact: No Range: Yes

the sales lift should be reported as zero. Overall and as applied to program measurement, the hypothesis testing logic can be summarized as follows:

In the above table a distinction is made between "exact" and "range" based incremental lift, which represents yet another common SST misinterpretation. This distinction is the focus of Example 2 shown below.

EXAMPLE 2: ASCRIBING STATISTICAL SIGNIFICANCE TO EXACT VALUES

Treated buy rate:	2.5%
Control buy rate:	2.0%
Incremental buy rate:	25%
Desired confidence:	$\alpha = 0.5$ (95%)
Significance level:	0.01

In contrast to Example 1, depicted above is a clearly statistically significant (at 99% or $\alpha = 0.01$) incremental buy rate of 0.5%. Much like before, however, this too illustrates a misapplication of significance testing, albeit more subtle one centering on interpreting SST in the context of exact values, technically referred to as *point estimates*.

In short, statistical significance can only be ascribed to a range of values (technically known as a *confidence interval*) and never to a specific value (i.e., a *point estimate*). This is a manifestation of the impact of data noise, known as *random error*, on statistical techniques in general and significance testing in particular. Simply put, SST is not precise enough to substantiate the validity of an exact value, such as an incremental buy rate of 15%. Turning to Example 2, to correctly interpret the information contained in it the exactly stated incremental buy rate of 25% should be restated as a range. Assuming the lower end of the range (i.e., lower confidence limit) of 23% and the upper end of the range (i.e., upper confidence limit) of 27%,[9] the correct interpretation of the Example 2 data would state that we can be 99% *confident that the buy rate increase was in the range of 23% to 27%*. This is in contrast to what appears in Example 2, which states that we can be 99% *confident that the satisfaction increased by 25%*, which is incorrect.

The above examples highlight an interesting interplay between significance testing and impact measurement objectives: SST application and interpretation limits at times run counter to business informational needs. Typically, the ultimate metric of success is the business action's return on investment (ROI), which requires SST-validated action-attributable incrementality quantification. For obvious reasons, decision makers are interested in an exact ROI estimate, rather than a range of values. Nonetheless, only range-based estimates are permissible within the context of significance testing, which imposes a stringent and at times difficult to accept limitation.

Promotional Baseline

In contrast to experimentation's broad theoretical foundation and a wide diversity of usage situations, *promotional baseline* is a narrowly defined, specific application focused on (and stemming from) practical business applications. Its origins can be traced to the emergence of promotional mix modeling, which is a general set of statistical approaches to estimating the share of individual components of the promotional mix on the overall marketing efforts attributed gains. Promotional baseline extends the point-in-time view taken by promotional mix modeling to a continuous, ongoing measurement.

Promotional baseline is a methodology designed to isolate and quantify any incremental sales contribution that can be attributed to specific promotions. Enabling it to do that is a multivariate statistical model calibrated to compute the base, or "un-promoted" level of sales, which is simply the level of sales that could be expected in the absence of specific promotions. Treatment (e.g., a campaign) attributable sales increases are quantified with the help of *sales elasticities* (promotional coefficients in the multivariate model), which constitutes the core of the Baseline's statistical engine. The other critical part of that engine is the operationalization of *confidence intervals* that assure a conservative effect size estimates by explicitly factoring in the variability in the above coefficient estimates. The Baseline is built around lower confidence bound estimates of predicted un-promoted level of sales contrasted with the actual sales level, with the difference attributed to specific promotional treatments based on their respective elasticities, as exemplified below.

The "actual" to the "predicted" sales level comparisons are carried out longitudinally to enable point-in-time as well as cross-time comparisons. Overall, promotional baseline can be characterized by the following traits:

- Uses regression models to determine the elasticity of each promotion.
- Tracks multiple programs on a continuous, monthly basis.
- Builds in competitive and general advertising context.
- Breaks out total repurchase levels into un-promoted level of sales and program specific incremental sales.

The above outlined baseline characteristics spell out several important benefits:

- Understanding of program performance at any individual point in time, as well as the cumulative effect (time specific effects are additive).
- Differentiation between *offer* and *treatment* effects—i.e., point-in-time treatment impact vs. cumulative program impact.
- Assessment of the impact of successive treatments within the program.
- The ability to evaluate program performance in a wider context.
- Potentially, the assessment of promotional synergies.

Example and Validation

Figure 11.4 shows an example of promotional baseline.

Interpretation

The baseline generated information can be interpreted along program treatment and time dimensions.

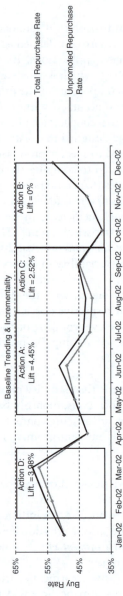

2012 Baseline	Jan-02	Feb-02	Mar-02	Apr-02	May-02	Jun-02	Jul-02	Aug-02	Sep-02	Oct-02	Nov-02	Dec-02	12-Month Summary	
						Monthly Incrementality								
Unpromoted Repurchase Rate	49.78%	53.53%	57.65%	42.46%	46.37%	48.82%	41.51%	40.77%	44.78%	37.58%	42.33%	52.99%	46.55%	Monthly Avg.
Lift attributed to:														
Action A					0.00%	2.36%	2.09%						4.45%	Cumulative Lift
Action B										0.00%	0.00%	0.00%	0.00%	Cumulative Lift
Action C								2.07%	0.45%				2.52%	Cumulative Lift
Action D		1.88%	2.10%										3.98%	Cumulative Lift
Total Repurchase Rate	49.78%	55.41%	59.75%	42.46%	46.37%	51.18%	43.60%	42.84%	45.23%	37.58%	42.33%	52.99%	47.46%	Monthly Avg.

Attributable-Spending Insights:

Action-specific lift ranges from 0% to 4.45% (cumulative) and 0% to 2.36% (monthly)

	Jan-02	Feb-02	Mar-02	Apr-02	May-02	Jun-02	Jul-02	Aug-02	Sep-02	Oct-02	Nov-02	Dec-02
Non-Attributable Spending	Parity	Parity	Disadv.	Disadv.	Disadv.	Parity	Advant.	Advant.	Parity	Parity	Disadv.	Disadv.

Non-Attributable Insights

Promotional spending parity effects other programs

Figure 11.4 Promotional Baseline

TREATMENT INSIGHTS

Program incrementality is quantified for each month the offer is in effect; monthly and total incrementality estimates are available.

MONTHLY INSIGHTS

For each month, a total level of promotional incrementality can also be estimated.

EFFECT MAGNITUDE

Due to reliance on the upper confidence interval limit, baseline-derived incrementality estimates are conservative in terms of reported magnitudes.

Validity

Baseline utilizes a multiple linear regression model, which relies on the amount of variability explained (R^2) for goodness-of-fit. In the above actual example, the model's *goodness-of-fit* metric, which ranges from 0 (no fit) to 1 (perfect fit), is 0.77, which is very strong for this class of models. The 0.77, or 77% of all variability explained suggests that model predictions, i.e., period based un-promoted repurchase rates, should be framed in the context of confidence interval to account for the 0.23 potential error of prediction. Thus, the initially derived mean un-promoted repurchase rates were expressed as 95% confidence intervals, with upper limits of those confidence intervals being used as conservative estimates of un-promoted repurchase rates.

Graphically, this can be expressed as seen in Figure 11.5.

Usage and Requirements

The most visible and impactful of promotional baseline's benefits include the following:

- Answers the question *"how is the program performing?"* across time.
- Quantifies incrementality at the treatment level (vs. offer level), producing more precise program assessment.
- The lack of control group requirements makes it unobtrusive and economical.
- Continuous cross-time base and incremental measurement.
- Examines multiple factors simultaneously, including competition.
- Can be automated as a database tool.

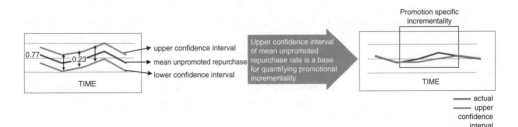

Figure 11.5 Effect Validation

As with any analytic application, the development of promotional baseline is contingent on several important steps:

- The availability of 18–24 months of immediate historical transactional history (ideal), with 12 months constituting the minimum acceptable level.
- All promotions to be explicitly "called out" in the analysis have to have distinct periods of *on* and *off*.

Profit Impact

The second key aspect of estimating business action-attributable incrementality entails translating the somewhat abstract statistical effect estimates into directly interpretable business insights. Central to these considerations is the choice of metrics. In other words, what is the outcome that should be used to evaluate the magnitude of observed effects?

To a large degree, the choice of the assessment metrics should reflect the stated business objectives delineated in the first part of the database analytical process described here (see Chapter 2). For instance, the (stated) goal of increasing the current customers' brand loyalty will result in *brand repurchase rate* being the key evaluative metric, while the goal of increasing the brand's overall market penetration will lead to the *number of new brand buyers* or *the brand's market share increase* as the most appropriate metrics.

Although conceptually these are all appropriate impact measurement targets, operationally they are somewhat ambiguous. As shown earlier, there are multiple (some more robust than others) approaches to quantifying brand loyalty or even new brand buyers and the robustness of the resultant insights is highly dependent on the soundness of a particular end outcome quantification. Considering the overall goal of the database analytical process (i.e., the development of unique and competitively advantageous knowledge), it is very important to select both the "right" metric and the "right" computational methodology.

With that in mind, the most appropriate evaluative criterion is the *profit contribution* that can be attributed to specific business actions. As it is intuitively obvious and expressly discussed below, the ability of the organization to effectively differentiate between more and less profitable actions—such as choosing among different types of promotional campaigns or unique combinations of offers—is one of the most pronounced determinants of the success of its database initiatives. In short, the organization's ability to establish a source of competitively advantageous knowledge will ultimately manifest itself in its ability to robustly quantify the profit impact of different business actions. For instance, if a particular action—such as a promotion—has led to an increase in the number of new (i.e., incremental) brand buyers, the resultant net increase in the number of customers' needs to be expressed in terms of its attributable profit contribution. After all, the long term well-being of the business requires a positive cashflow and the "interim" metrics, such as the number of customers counts, are only important to the degree to which they translate into better financial outcomes. In other words, the ultimate assessment of the impact or productivity of a particular *action–outcome* relationship should not merely count, for instance, the number of new, action-attributable product buyers, but rather should focus on quantifying the number of new, action-attributable *and profitable* product buyers.

This is an important distinction because, simply put, given sufficiently deep discounts or other profit-reducing incentives virtually any brand can register at least a temporary up-tick in its demand, as the vast majority of products and services exhibit some level of price elasticity (i.e., as the price falls, the demand increases). Of course, in some instances, price decreases that are necessary to generate worthwhile demand gains are not sustainable over longer runs, which is one of the reasons why a new buyer-acquisition strategy driven primarily by discounts rarely, if ever, leads to a longer-term customer base growth (a lesson learned the hard way by the Detroit's "Big Three" automakers). To make matters even worse, many discount-based business initiatives also suffer from *adverse customer selection*, which is the phenomenon of the least attractive (from the standpoint of customer base value) buyers[10] exhibiting the strongest propensity to participate in discount-based initiatives. In other words, a money-losing initiative can look very successful if the focus is on the wrong end outcomes. Obviously, a brand cannot sustain itself over a longer run unless it can generate profit, regardless of how many new buyers its various initiatives might claim.[11] This means that the true measure of promotional actions should be the profit impact of the end outcomes of interest, such as the above-mentioned product repurchase or market share growth. Incidentally, assessing the business impact of the earlier described action-attributable incrementality in this fashion also offers the only objective means of systematically "removing" action-unique idiosyncrasies (such as the hard to quantify cross-program design differences, etc.), which is a necessary prerequisite to robust cross-action comparisons.

This line of thinking also discourages excessive discounting as the means of propping up near-term sales. Not only is it a game that, once started, does not have an easy or a logical end in sight (e.g., consider the plight of the U.S automakers following their introduction of ever-deeper discounts), but it also rarely leads to a long-term strengthening of the firm's customer base or balance sheet gains. In the knowledge creation sense, it establishes a clear linkage between a stimulus—which is a business action being evaluated—and its association response—which is the return earned with the investment made in the action of interest. The immediate results of business actions, such as the number of new product purchasers, that are so often incorrectly used as the yardstick for measuring the efficacy of programs, are treated here as the means-to-an-end, as shown below:

Clearly, an organization that possesses the ability to distil individual promotions and other business actions geared at increasing either the base or the productivity of the customer base will be in a competitively advantageous position, vis-à-vis its competitors who are forced to guess.

Competitively Advantageous Set

Needless to say, an objective assessment of results of business actions can lead to sobering conclusions. An action initially deemed to be highly successful, such as a promotional program using attractive price discounts to spur an encouraging number of new brand trials may ultimately turn out to have a negative profit impact. The assessment of other actions may lead to opposite conclusions, where initially modest results may give rise to

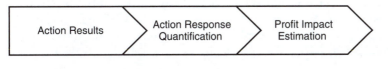

Figure 11.6 Understanding Impact

enduring, longer-term benefits. Focused on the pursuit of sources of sustainable competitive advantage, the action–result impact incrementality assessment ultimately takes on a comparative character, where multiple actions are contrasted with the goal of identifying the most beneficial courses of action. Ultimately, it is difficult to categorize a particular outcome as being "strong" or "weak" without framing it in a comparative context (e.g., does a 5% profit increase represent a strong or a weak performance?). Furthermore, the goal is rarely to pinpoint the single most effective promotion or an offer type, but rather to identify the most effective cohort of promotional alternatives, simply because different means might be suitable to different end objectives.

Hence in practice, the goal of impact measurement is to identify a mix of the most effective actions. Here, the *equimarginal principle* outlined earlier can be used as a conceptual framework. Building on the law of diminishing marginal utility, the principle stipulates that the economic output is maximized when the return on the last dollar spent is the same across all actions, as shown below:

$$\frac{lift_A}{cost_A} = \frac{lift_B}{cost_B} = \dots \frac{lift_n}{cost_n}$$

In effect, the equimarginal-principle-based impact comparisons reduce the effects of individual actions to their corresponding returns on investment (ROI), which makes it possible to make comparisons across the otherwise dissimilar actions. It also makes it possible to "assemble" the most productive set of differently-purposed actions, giving rise to a competitively advantageous set, or an assortment of business actions that have proven to yield the most advantageous results. As a result, the organization can make the best use of its resources.

Mini-Case 11.1: Estimating the Efficacy of Wireless Carriers' Advertising

In the 1880s, a prominent Philadelphia merchant, John Wanamaker famously remarked that he knew that *half of his advertising budget was wasted, he just did not know which half*. That sentiment, which has been echoed by a number of distinguished industry figures throughout the decades, including J.C Penney, Henry Ford, Lord Lever (of Unilever fame) and many others, poses an interesting question: If 50% of advertising-related spending is indeed wasted, is the impact of the other 50% worth the price?

The U.S Wireless industry is one of the largest and most competitive segments of the economy. It is also one of the largest, revenue-wise, industries, boasting aggregate revenues approaching the $200 billion mark. The industry's *ecosystem* (illustrated in Figure 11.7) is an interesting one, insofar as it is comprised of three, somewhat distinct competitive tiers: Tier 1 is occupied by two leading national carriers, Verizon and AT&T, accounting for about 60% of the total subscriber base; Tier 2 are the two "runner-up" carriers, Spring Nextel and T-Mobile, also national in scope but lagging behind the leaders in terms of coverage and market share (about 35% combined); lastly, Tier 3 accounts for the remaining 5% of the

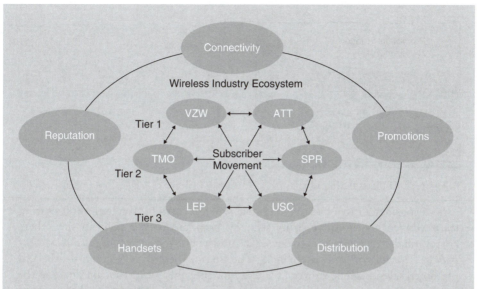

Figure 11.7 Competitive Ecosystem

subscriber base and is comprised of a fairly large number of regional carriers, with Leap and US Cellular being the largest two of that group. In spite of this rather distinct competitive pecking order, the wireless industry is highly commoditized, with just a handful of attributes, including connectivity, distribution, handsets, promotions and reputation determining subscriber carrier choices. Not surprisingly, the leading carriers are among the biggest advertising spenders, with their aggregate ad spend fast approaching the $10 billion mark. The two largest national carriers—Verizon and AT&T—each spend between $2 billion and $2.5 billion annually on advertising, while Sprint Nextel, the third largest U.S wireless carrier, recently surpassed the $1 billion mark (in 2009, Sprint's ad spending jumped from about $950 million to $1.265 billion). If Wanamaker was right and 50% of advertising expenditures are indeed wasted, the wireless industry wastes billions of dollars each year. . .

A lot has changed since the days of Wanamaker (or Henry Ford, J.C Penney and Lord Lever)—most notably, advances in information technology are making it possible to shed light on previously unknowable questions. Is John Wanamaker's supposition one of those questions? The pervasive and ever-expanding behavioral tracking mechanisms are making it possible to objectively link consumer exposures to promotional messages with subsequent behaviors—of course, not all types of promotional activities can be linked to behaviors simply because not all promotional activities are built around calls to actions. General advertising is the case in point here: Commonly tasked with strengthening of brand awareness and familiarity, it rarely—if ever—is expected to yield immediate behavioral actions on the part of its target audience, which makes the measurement of its impact quite elusive. However, just because its effect is not directly measurable, does not mean that its impact cannot be estimated at all.

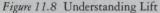

Figure 11.8 Understanding Lift

Let's consider a case of a large, national wireless carrier interested in estimating the effectiveness of its advertising strategy. From an analytic point of view, there are several distinct elements to consider, most notably, *un-promoted sales*, *promotion-induced incrementality* and *actual sales*. The first of these three elements—the un-promoted sales—can be viewed as a proxy for the inherent utility contained in the product or service, to the degree to which it captures the sales level that could reasonably be expected in the absence of any promotional activities. The second element, broadly described as promotion-induced incrementality, reflects the benefit of the totality of marketing activities insofar as it is measure of additional sales realized because of the various promotional activities. The third and final element—actual sales—is, as the term implies, the realized sales volume as of a point in time. Information-wise, actual sales is a "hard" (i.e., tangible and objective) metric, while both un-promoted sales and promotion-induced incrementality have to be analytically estimated. Let's start with un-promoted sales.

As noted above, un-promoted sales can be operationalized as actual sales less any promotion-induced incrementality. Conceptually it seems quite straightforward, but analytically it is akin to trying to solve an equation with two unknowns, which is practically problematic due to a lack of a single, unique solution. In order to remedy that situation, un-promoted sales need to be individually and independently estimated, which can be accomplished with the help of one of two general approaches: 1. fitting a time-dependent regression line (i.e., regressing of sales against time), or 2. estimating of *prior moving average* (use the mean of *n* periods' sales prior to current as the estimate of current). Both methods have merit, but given the wireless carrier's substantial sales variability (see Figure 11.9), the latter of the two techniques is deemed more appropriate. Furthermore, it is important to not overlook the fact that prior moving average-estimated un-promoted sales level is a mean-based approximation, which means it is necessary to factor-in the expected variability in the computed mean, to account for relative imprecision of the estimation process. That is accomplished by computing upper and lower confidence limits (shown as Upper CL and Lower CL in the Sample Baseline graph); effectively, the point-based mean estimate was transformed into a range-based estimate, with the areas falling outside of that range representing an increase or a decrease in sales volume that represented a statistically significant departure from the expected level. Given the purpose at hand—i.e., to estimate the efficacy of the

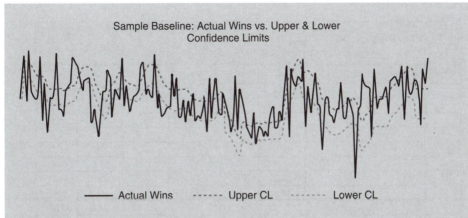

Sample Baseline: Actual Wins vs. Upper & Lower
Confidence Limits

——— Actual Wins ----- Upper CL ------- Lower CL

Figure 11.9 Moving Average

wireless carrier's advertising strategy—the positive upside deviation from the upper confidence limit can be taken as an estimate of promotion-induced incrementality.

Now, it is time to consider the totality of promotion-induced incrementality. In the case of the wireless carrier, it is a product of a mix of diverse marketing activities, including price incentives, direct mail, as well as print and general (most notably, television) advertising. The first two of those promotional tools—price incentives (e.g., free or discounted handsets) and direct mail offers—are geared toward stimulating purchase behaviors, which means their impact should manifest itself in terms of sales, which is not the case for the second pair of general and print advertising. Furthermore, general and print advertising are also more operationally ambiguous, as there are multiple ways of capturing their effects. The former can be operationalized in terms of several "absolute" measures, such as the number of (typically) 30-second spots per unit of time or aggregate expenditures per unit of time, or it can be expressed in terms of relative metrics, such as *share of voice* (company-specific absolute / peer group or industry-wide aggregate absolute); the latter, on the other hand, can be expressed in terms of a different set of absolute measures, such as the number of ads per unit of time or the average ad size, as well as similar (to general advertising) relative metrics. Lastly, if present, the effect of advertising is very unlikely to be contemporaneous with sales (i.e., general advertising tends not to contain any "calls to action," hence there is no reason to believe that exposure to an ad would compel a consumer to take a reasonably immediate action) which suggests the need to lag the relationship between sales and advertising, usually by one, two or three weeks.

Keeping all of the above considerations in mind, the process of "untangling" the potential advertising impact is as follows: First, estimate a range-based un-promoted level of sales, as described above; second, compute a conservative baseline, which is an estimate of total marketing-attributable incrementality (actual sales − upper confidence limit of un-promoted baseline); third, estimate and deduct the impact of individual, non-advertising marketing activities; fourth, relate the "leftover" or residual marketing action-attributable incrementality to variability in lagged advertising intensity, such as lagged share of voice. Regarding the last step,

Week	Advertising Impact			Share of Voice: TV			Share of Voice: News		
	Positive	None	Negative						
	Residual Incrementality			Carrier A	Carrier B	Carrier C	Carrier A	Carrier B	Carrier C
1				27.1	53.6	8.8	65.7	34.3	0.0
2				25.7	56.3	9.4	61.4	38.6	0.0
3				21.4	55.7	9.0	43.0	21.9	0.0
4				17.5	54.1	9.4	18.9	61.3	0.0
5				12.5	63.6	8.5	25.3	55.2	0.0
6				11.7	63.2	10.6	7.9	66.6	0.0
7				14.5	58.3	10.2	0.0	75.8	0.0
8				14.5	50.5	12.7	0.0	56.4	15.3
9				17.1	45.6	11.0	11.8	37.8	23.6
10				23.4	47.6	8.8	31.4	43.4	20.5
11				32.0	50.4	9.1	45.5	42.5	8.4
12				35.3	43.0	14.0	26.8	31.4	30.4
13				33.9	41.2	14.3	5.8	63.0	13.3

Figure 11.10 Impact Indexing

since there is no tangible sales–advertising link, the assessment is limited to pattern comparisons—in this case, a positive relationship would be revealed by a persistent, cross-time pattern of increases in advertising being associated with appropriately lagged increases in sales.

As illustrated by the sample comparison table (see Figure 11.10 above) depicting one quarter (13 weeks) of outcomes, the comparison of residual incrementality with the variability in *Share of Voice: TV* and *Share of Voice: News* suggests no evidence of a consistent, positive impact of advertising on sales, which is taken as an indication of a lack of a persistent and measurable impact of advertising on sales.

12 Database Scoring

One of the key defining qualities of database analytics is its process orientation—the insights derived from the exploration and the analysis of historical outcomes and related data form an informational launch pad for future decisions. This takes place through a variety of means, including the delineation of the most influential drivers of buyers' behavior, identification of the most impactful—in the sense of return on marketing investment—promotional activities and the "translation" of behavioral predictions into database-resident customer/prospect selection mechanisms. The last of those mechanisms, known as "database scoring" is the focus on this chapter.

To most, the term "scoring" tends to conjure up images of assessment, appraisal, evaluation or competition, which is understandable given the many situations where what we do is "scored" or we keep track of a "score." However, within the confines of database analytics, to "score" is to apply a (statistical) model-based algorithm to individual records in a database. Hence, "database scoring" is the mechanics by means of which earlier-derived interdependencies are applied to customer or prospect (database-resident) lists to aid in future promotional efforts. More on that in the ensuing chapter.

Model Calibration

The usual goal of the database analytical process is to develop a stand-alone informational entity capable of providing ongoing decision insights. The resultant *model* is an explicit, formalized expression of relationships of interest, the intent of which is to offer decision support. Within the database analytical process described in this book, models are generally used as means of objective record (e.g., customer) categorization, which ultimately gives rise to differentiated promotional treatments and other tailored business actions. For instance, a model estimating customer-specific promotional response propensity or future spending levels can be used as the basis for differential promotional investment allocation—i.e., higher propensity and/or future spending customers would be allocated a larger share of the available spending than their lower propensity/value counterparts.

Models offer a simplified depiction of relationships of interest, typically explaining some but not all of the behavior of the systems they portray. Specifically, the highly dynamic nature of business processes and behaviors coupled with incomplete[1] data (almost always containing some degree of error) suggest that model-based explanations and predictions will always contain some degree of imprecision. For all those reasons, the objective driving the initial model development, as well as its subsequent calibrationis the maximization of the ratio of *explained-to-unexplained variability*, which is accomplished through the previously discussed identification and inclusion of all potentially explanatory data (see Chapter 8) and solid model specification (see Chapter 10).

Model Derivation vs. Model Calibration

Although the two terms—model derivation and calibration—are sometimes used interchangeably, operationally they are quite different.

Model derivation is the process of building and testing a mathematical model. Its goal is to describe and mathematically formalize all relationships—subject to data and modeling constraints—that explain the maximum amount of variability in the data. In a more practical sense, the goal of model derivation is to develop objective, rational bases for making predictions regarding the future value or the future state of a phenomenon of interest, such as brand sales, customer repurchase or promotional response propensity. The segmentation models outlined in Chapter 9 or the various predictive structures detailed in Chapter 10 are among the most commonly seen examples of models derived within the realm of database analytics.

Model calibration, on the other hand, entails adapting the earlier-derived model to more recent (time) version of (the otherwise the same, composition-wise) data. Overall, there are two types of model calibrations: model refresh and model adaptation. *Model refresh* calibrates an existing model on the most recently available data (that presumably became available since the model was built). Its goal is to preserve the model's classificatory accuracy or explanatory power by incorporating the most recent trends captured in the data. *Model adaptation*, on the other hand, entails tailoring the model's coefficients to a specific, typically somewhat more homogenous population. For instance, a model derived on a representative cross-section of brand buyers may subsequently be calibrated for specific sub-groups, such as frequent vs. occasional buyers. The goal here is to enhance the model's classificatory accuracy or explanatory power in a more narrowly defined context.

Operationally, model calibration—regardless of its purpose—does not alter the composition of the model, but merely updates the coefficients of individual predictors. In other words, model calibration retains all of the original predictors while adjusting their weights. In practice, however, it is possible for model calibration to effect the composition of the model by changing any one of the predictor weights to zero,[2] although the likelihood of that is generally quite remote.

Regardless of its type, model calibration is a short-term customization approach. Over a longer term, most models need to be *restaged*, which is another way of saying that they need to be re-derived. In general, model restaging should be considered when either of the two conditions occurs: First, when the previously unavailable data becomes available and it is believed that its inclusion would positively contribute to the quality of the model. Second, when a different functional structure of the model is being contemplated (raw input data can remain the same as the original), such as when the previously not-included interaction terms are considered.

Database Scoring

Most database analytical models are derived from a sample of all database records. Samples, rather than entire populations are used for a variety of reasons ranging from practicality and convenience (i.e., a large database may contain many millions of records, making statistical model building time- and computing-resource-intensive), to representativeness and projectability. A sample-based model derivation, however, necessitates the "exporting" of a complete model to the entire database population (from which the sample was drawn). The resultant process of applying a sample-derived model onto the entire database population of interest is called *scoring*.

In a mathematical sense, a model is an algebraic equation formally stating the relationship between the phenomenon being investigated (e.g., predicted) and its predictors, as well as between/among individual predictors. The model coefficients—or weights attributed to individual predictors—are an expression of the strength (the magnitude of the coefficient) and the direction (the sign of the coefficient) of the relationship between individual predictors and the target of the analysis. In addition, a model also encapsulates inter-predictor relationships, such as the degree of inter-correlations as well as the general manner in which the predictors are related to each other. Taken as a whole, the combination of the specific predictors and their weights is sometimes referred to as an *independent variate*, which represents the best available (given the data and method used) prediction of the phenomenon of interest. Given all that, *database scoring*, as the term is used in the context of the database-analysis-supported knowledge creation process described in this book, is the process of solving sample-derived algebraic equations for each record comprising the database population of interest.

Although we tend to think of database scoring as a relatively complex endeavor, in fact, scores can range from a simple categorization (such as one-time vs. repeat brand purchaser) that does not require the development of formal, multivariate statistical models, to complex, inference-based probability-reflecting estimates. In either case, the physical outcome of database scoring is the adding of one or more of new fields to the database.

The scoring process itself entails a couple of key considerations. The first one pertains to a model's *refresh cycle* as an indicator of the lifespan of the computed information, while the second one points to the need for—or lack thereof—the specification of any *sub-group homogenizing calibration*.

Refresh Cycle

The model's refresh cycle reflects the frequency with which the model's coefficients are updated, to take into account any new data that became available since the model was initially calibrated. There are no clearly stated, general "rules" governing the frequency with which statistical models used in business need to be updated, as the optimal frequency is a function of the data being used in the model (i.e., some data types, such as the UPC-scanner-based data accumulates on a more-or-less continuous basis, while other types, such as SEC filings accumulates on a periodic basis, e.g., quarterly or annually), the usage situation (e.g., ongoing promotional targeting or optimization vs. periodic value or risk scoring) and ultimately, the underlying methodology (e.g., a multivariate regression-analysis-based model vs. a multivariate categorization schema).

In view of the obvious complexity of the above implied 3-way refresh cycle determination (data type–usage situation–methodology), it is recommended that the database analytical models' refresh cycle determination should be instead driven by the *general product type repurchase frequency*. For frequently repurchased products, such as many of the consumer packaged goods, where subsequent repurchases are characterized by relatively low levels of involvement, a refresh cycle should allow for a sufficient number of new data points to accumulate, in order for the newly captured data to be able to "compete" with an established trend. In other words, if the current model-expressed relationships are based on the analysis of, let's say 12 months of purchase data, the refresh dataset should contain no less than 3–6 months of purchase data. Trying to refresh a model with an insufficient amount of new data may produce spurious results and lead to potentially erroneous conclusions.

In the case of infrequently purchased product categories, many of which are characterized by high involvement decision making process accompanying each purchase occasion, the refresh timing decision should be approached differently. Here, the average length of the repurchase cycle should be used as a proxy for the model refresh cycle. Hence if a particular product is purchased, on average, once every 6 months, a model should not be refreshed more frequently than twice a year.

Sub-Group Calibration

In most instances, models are developed with generalized applications in mind, such as the overall customer base value maximization. At the same time, getting the most benefit out of the resultant knowledge often demands some degree of model homogenization, such as adjusting it to a more narrowly defined goal or a sub-population.

Consider a repurchase propensity model, which estimates the probability of brand repurchase for all records (customers and/or prospects) in the database. First, a model is derived from a representative sample of the database-contained records, since the goal, quite naturally, is to identify all high repurchase propensity current buyers and (potentially) prospects. But then what if we wanted to limit our scope to only the high repurchase propensity buyers representing only certain geography, ethnicity or any other homogenizing category? On the one hand, we could simply limit our selection of the previously defined high propensity buyers and/or prospects to the sub-category (e.g., an ethnic group) of interest to us. The flaw in this approach, however, is that our categorization and selection bases do not match, which may lead to misclassification. Specifically, if we based our propensity categorization on the overall average (i.e., all ethnicities combined), but the one ethnicity that is of interest to us right now exhibits above-average purchase propensity, using the overall average-based categorization would lead to the understating of the number of high propensity customers of particular ethnicity of interest to us.

In order to avoid a potential misclassification, the overall sample-derived model should be calibrated on a more homogenous subset, reflecting the desired focus. In the above example, the model that was originally derived from the representative cross-section of all customers should be adapted to the more homogenous characteristics of the specific ethnicity of interest. Operationally, the values of the independent variate's coefficients should be re-computed on a more homogeneous sample. The resultant repurchase propensity categorization will then, in effect, be re-calibrated from an ethnically generic to an ethnically specific base.

Data Considerations

Quite frequently, building robust multivariate predictive models entails considerable data engineering. As detailed in Chapter 7, this may involve missing value imputation, various linear and nonlinear transformations, indicator creation and other steps made necessary by data deficiencies. Obviously, the data improvement steps were limited to the modeling sample only, which means that before the sample-derived model is applied to the larger database population, the same data engineering steps need to be replicated for the larger population.

It is also important to keep in mind that database scoring will likely result in less than 100% coverage—i.e., not all records contained in the focal population will be scored. Consequently, one or more of the following will likely be encountered:

- **Persistent Missing Value Problem.** Some records may have missing values on all or most of the metrics used in scoring, which will generally render them scoring-inappropriate. For instance, if the scoring equation is comprised of 7 different variables and 5, 6 or all 7 of them are missing for a particular case, it is not advisable to include that case in scoring. Of course, there are a number of different techniques that could be used to impute those missing values (see Chapter 7 for review), but regardless of which one is used the resultant value will be merely an estimate containing some degree of error. Considering that the model equation is also an estimate containing some degree of error, it is entirely possible that using error-containing value estimates as inputs into the error-containing scoring equation will yield either highly unstable or inaccurate estimates.
- **Transformation-Induced Missing Data.** One of the undesirable side-effects of certain transformations, such as those using natural logarithms, is that they may contribute to data challenges. For instance, natural logarithms are undefined for values that are smaller than 1, as well as for all negative values, which means that employing that type of transformation may contribute to missing value propagation, if the original values fall within the undefined range.[3] Although these generally fall under the situations where we have to take the "bad with the good," it is nonetheless something that should be considered ahead of time.

Coefficient Interpretation

Depending on the type of statistical technique used and the pre-modeling data preparation steps that were taken, some or all of the final model's coefficients may need to be restated prior to final deployment. For instance, if a model utilizing logistic regression required logarithmic transformations of all or some of its predictors, the so-transformed variables' coefficients will be expressed in a logarithmic form and will need to be converted with the help of anti-log transformations. Unless that step is taken, the model coefficients will not be interpretable as effect magnitudes or elasticities.

Mini-Case 12.1: Consumer Coupons and Look-Alike Modeling Scoring

Recall the case outlined in the *Behavioral Predictions* chapter: Faced with the goal of devising more effective usage of couponing as a new customer acquisition tool, a ready-to-eat (RTE) breakfast cereal brand decided to make use of the "look-alike" data analytical approach, where current customer-derived insights are used as the basis for identifying "similar looking" non-customers, who in turn are to become targets of acquisition efforts. To that end, a logistic regression model was built with the goal of yielding a mechanism for automated scoring of non-customer lists, in terms of individual-level probability of becoming high-value customers. The resultant model is summarized in Figure 12.1 (for brevity, not all statistically significant predictors are included in the illustration). The task at hand now is to convert the statistical outcomes into a predictive facility—more specifically, a computerized algorithm which can be used on recurring basis.

The first step is to create an algebraic expression that can be coded into a data storage and management application, such as SAS, SPSS, SQL or even Excel. Given that the dependent and predictor variables in logistic regression is expressed as log of the odds ratio, the formulation of the scoring model is somewhat more complex than it would be in the case of linear regression. For the model exemplified above, the development of a scoring mechanism for estimating the probability of individual non-customers becoming high-value customers entails two distinct steps: 1. computing of *raw scores* (which is formulated as log of odds ratio, or $\log(p/1-p)$), and 2. converting of raw scores into logistic *distribution-fitted probabilities*, as shown below.

Raw Score = 34.086 + Age_35–44*0.022 – Age_65–74*0.061 + LOR_2–5Yrs* 0.057 – LOR_10Yrs*0.312 – Gender_F*0.319 + Gender_M*313 – Children_ 2–3*0.273 + Lifestyle_Fitness*0.037.

The so-computed raw score represents a log of the odds ratio, which is a somewhat esoteric measure that cannot be directly interpreted as probability (odds are ratios of two frequencies, while probabilities are ratios of individual frequencies to the overall total). Hence, the raw score needs to be converted into directly interpretable probabilities, as follows:

$\text{Probability}_{HighValueCustomer}$ = Exp (Raw Score) / (1 + (Exp (Raw Score))).

Predictors	B	S.E.	Wald	df	Sig.	Exp (B)
Age_35-44	.022	.007	10.816	1	.001	1.022
Age_65-74	-.061	.017	12.979	1	.000	.941
LOR_2-5Yrs	.057	.015	14.190	1	.000	1.058
LOR_10Yrs	-.312	.046	44.912	1	.000	.732
Gender_F	-.319	.091	12.373	1	.000	.727
Gender_M	.313	.136	5.280	1	.022	1.367
Children_2-3	-.273	.047	34.386	1	.000	.761
Lifestyle_Fitness	.037	.015	5.782	1	.016	1.038
Constant	34.086	4.372	60.797	1	.000	636.000

Figure 12.1 Logistic Model

The result of the two-step scoring is a probability-expressed estimate, computed for each prospective customer independently of all other prospective customers, of becoming a high-value customer. Of course, probability is a continuum, which means that it is often difficult to draw a line between "high" and "low" probability, which is usually the case when scoring a large file of prospects (which may be comprised of millions of records). Hence, following the computing of probability scores, there is a need to pinpoint an optimal cutoff point for what can be taken as sufficiently high probability, which is best accomplished with the help of *ROC curve* (the acronym stands for "receiver operating characteristic," which has no particular meaning in marketing database analytics but merely indicates the tool's origin, which is information processing, or more specifically, signal detection theory). The idea behind the ROC-curve-based comparison is simple: To identify the optimal trade-off between magnitude of the probability score (the "sensitivity" dimension in the ROC curve graph, depicted in Figure 12.2) and the share of the total scored universe (the "specificity" dimension). Another way of looking at the ROC curve analysis is as a way of maximizing the *prospect-to-high-value customer conversion rate* by "cherry picking" a subset of prospects in such a way as to get the most conversions while using the fewest prospects. In the graph itself, the straight diagonal line represents random selection (i.e., the absence of a model)—here, selecting fewer or more prospects has a constant impact on conversion. That means that, for instance, the first 10% of randomly selected prospects would yield approximately

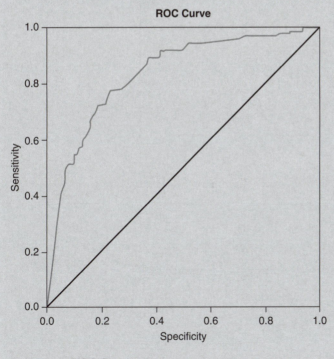

Figure 12.2 ROC Curve

the same prospect-to-high-value customer conversion rate as the second 10%, the third 10%, and so on.

On the other hand, the curve represents the benefit of using model-generated probabilities as the basis for cross-prospect differentiation: Here, selecting different probability value delimited groupings has a distinctly different impact on the overall conversion. Sorting the individually scored records in ascending likelihood-score order would result in groupings where the first 10% of prospects yielded the highest aggregate conversion rate, followed by the second 10%, then third 10%, etc. Graphically (see Figure 12.3), the greater the distance between the curve and the straight diagonal line, the greater the conversion rate associated with that particular subset of prospects. Hence, the points of maximum inflection are indicative of maximum probability value vs. % of total (prospect) universe trade-off—the dotted line in the second of the two ROC curve graphs (Figure 12.3) captures that logic. The "sensitivity" value of approximately 0.73 has a corresponding "specificity" value of approximately 0.2, which means that roughly 73% of the expected prospect-to-high-value customer conversions can be captured by focusing on only the top 20% of the model-scored prospects. In terms of improving the efficacy of the couponing-based new customer acquisition efforts, this represents a significant improvement in efficiency.

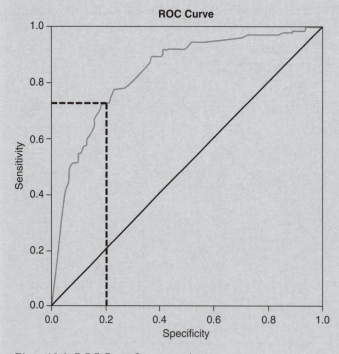

Figure 12.3 ROC Curve Interpretation

13 From Findings to Knowledge

Although the overall analytical proficiency is probably the strongest predictor of the quality of data-analysis-derived decision-guiding insights, it is the ability of the organization to "absorb" the so-created knowledge that determines the value of analytics to an organization. The most ingenious analysis, best-fitting models or most eye-opening findings will have little business value, unless they are put to a productive use. The attainment and preservation of *informational advantage*, discussed in the opening chapter, is contingent on two, equally important factors: 1. the ability to create competitively advantageous and decision-aiding knowledge, and 2. the consumption of that knowledge. The previous chapters were all focused on the former—in this chapter, we turn our attention to the latter.

The ensuing discussion addresses some of the more commonly encountered impediments to taking the full advantage of analytic findings. It is important to note that those "barriers to usage" combine obstacles that need to be overcome by the prospective users of analytic insights, such as brand managers, as well as some interpretational "hang-ups" of marketing analysts.

Knowledge Implementation

The point made repeatedly throughout this book is that database analytics is about the creation of unique, competitively advantageous knowledge. In a business sense, it means transforming raw, generic data into unique insights capable of shedding explanatory light on past outcomes and directing future courses of action. As a result, the bulk of the ideas outlined in earlier chapters was directed toward the "how-to" of effective analytics, which, as discussed in Chapter 2, makes up the lion's share of the knowledge creation process discussed in this book. However, from the business standpoint, putting the resultant knowledge to work is just as important. After all, knowing without doing is of little business value, since it is unlikely to lead to any tangible benefits.

Although not as self-evident, making use of analyses-generated insights is also quite important from the standpoint of statistical analyses, for two, distinct reasons. First and foremost, it makes possible the in-market validation of analyses-derived recommendations. For instance, the efficacy of predictive models can be calibrated by contrasting the expected outcomes (i.e., model-predicted) to actual outcomes, such as purchase rates. The second statistical-analyses-related results implementation benefit is a bit more abstract: Result implementation lays the foundation for *successively approximating* expansion of the knowledge base.

In-Market Validation

The crafting of business recommendations stemming from the analysis of data is an inferential process built on the notion of probability. Originally defined by a French mathematician, Pierre Simon Laplace, *"The probability of an event is the ratio of the number of cases favorable to it, to the number of all cases possible when nothing leads us to expect that any one of these cases should occur more than any other, which renders them, for us, equally possible."* In that sense, data-based recommendations represent the "best guess" at the appropriate, or in the case of the knowledge creation process, the most competitively advantageous course of action.

The in-market validation combines the elements of the (previously discussed—see Chapter 11) action-attributable incrementality quantification and the deployment of knowledge, which amounts to the "translating" of the often abstract relationships and coefficients into well-defined courses of action. The upcoming section offers an in-depth treatment of this topic.

Expansion of the Knowledge Base

Consider Figure 13.1, showing an outline of the now-familiar database analytical process. As depicted by the process flow, the initial roll-out of the database analytical insights-driven business actions represents a culmination of a single cycle of the knowledge creation process, which in turn kicks off the follow-up stage. In that sense, the implementation of the results of database analytics, such as the fielding of carefully constructed marketing promotions aimed at increasing the value or the productivity of the customer base, should ultimately lead to a "re-thinking" of the original analytical plan, with a resultant carry-over into data requirements setting, follow-up analyses and database re-scoring. In principle, the business knowledge creation process continues in perpetuum, to the degree to which the requisite data remains available.

In a conceptual sense, the best way of thinking about the *ongoing learning loop* characteristic of the database analytical process is in the context of the notion of *successive approximations*. The basic idea conveyed in this frequently used notion (in fields as diverse as behavioral psychology and electrical engineering) is that empirical data analyses do not instantaneously yield the best insights, but rather deliver progressively more accurate estimates, with each subsequent estimate representing an improvement over the previous one. The growing body of empirically derived and in-market-tested insights (shown as the "feedback loop" in Figure 13.1) will lead to progressively more accuracy and depth in the generated knowledge, which will ultimately evidence itself in superior decision making; i.e., sustainable competitive advantage.

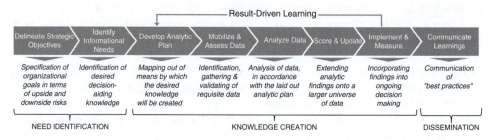

Figure 13.1 The Database Analytical Process

The cumulative learning is possible because the individual components of the broadly defined database analytical process, such as *informational needs identification*, *analytic planning* and *data mobilization* are all highly interdependent, with decisions made in antecedent stages shaping each of the successive stages. An obvious, near-term informational benefit of this "analytic coordination" is the creation of competitively advantageous data insights, rather the proliferation of generic, low-impact informational tidbits. A somewhat less obvious longer-term benefit of the analytic coordination is a gradual buildup of the organization's knowledge base, ultimately contributing to not only the sustaining but also the strengthening of the firm's competitive advantage.

No Pain—No Gain

Change is never easy. In an organizational sense, learning to "trust the numbers" represents one of the most challenging aspects of the database analytical process, largely because it requires a considerable departure from intuitive decision making, which for many business managers is the only decision mode they ever knew. The required transition can be likened to learning to fly a plane by relying on instruments, rather than visual or physiological (e.g., a feeling of descending or turning) clues and references. Because all of us grow so reliant on our own senses, we generally find it quite difficult to trust mechanical gadgets when they contradict what our own "instruments" tell us. Yet, doing just that is a critical component of safely piloting a plane. Similarly, learning to trust empirically generated insights requires a concerted effort on the part of the decision makers, but the rewards can be considerable—just ask Walmart, Capital One, Marriott, Harrah's Entertainment or any other of the analytically excellent organizations mentioned in the opening chapter.

Deployment

Putting results of empirical database analyses into action can take many different forms, ranging from product redesign to promotional mix changes and could even include expansion or divestiture decisions. In many instances, as the knowledge accumulates, the resultant decisions may take on an increasingly broad scope.

Regardless of the scope, however, results of empirical analyses usually need to be "translated" business terms and/or processes. What is important here is not just the conversion of *numerical effect estimates* into *applicable business terms*, but also the proper framing of these results in terms of (any) applicability limits. In general, no empirical results are universally and indefinitely true and applicable, which means that the deployment of these learnings needs to encompass explicit usability limits. It might sound somewhat counterintuitive, but excessive reliance on rigid, standard measures assessing the decision making worthiness of analytically derived insights should be approached carefully. In particular, the use of statistical significance tests as the basis of differentiating between important and trivial insights needs to be approached especially cautiously. Some of the reasons behind that recommendation were outlined in Chapter 8—a more explicit treatment of this topic, as it relates to the implementation of analytically generated insights is presented below.

Also important is a proper framing of numerical coefficients. Recall the two examples discussed in Chapter 11. Example 1 illustrates the often-seen tendency to report as valid statistically computed sales lift that lacks (statistical) significance. Example 2 brings to light the even more commonly observed tendency of ascribing statistical significance levels to exact (point estimates, in statistical jargon) values. Both can have a profound impact on the validity and the reliability of the resultant knowledge and both are highly dependent on the application of statistical significance tests.

Effect Quantification vs. Significance Tests' Applicability Limits

Although the proliferation of their usage might suggest a universal acceptance of statistical significance testing (SST) as an effect validation standard, that is not at all the case. In fact, it is hard to think of another statistical concept that continues to generate as much controversy among methodologists. Although widely used on the one hand, these tests' validity and credibility as an impact confirmation tool continue to be assaulted, particularly in the academic/scientific literature. Some of the most pungent points of view relating to that debate are outlined below.

To start, acknowledging the ongoing methodological debate still in need of a resolution, a sweeping review of SST applications by one researcher concludes that "*. . .researchers have inappropriately utilized statistical significance as a means for illustrating the importance of their findings and have attributed to statistical significance testing qualities it does not possess*" (Daniel, 1998, p. 23),[1] echoing an earlier conclusion that "*. . .it is more difficult to find specific arguments for significance testing than to find arguments decrying their use*" (Henkel, 1976, p. 87).[2] Alarming conclusions like these prompted the establishment of the Task Force on Statistical Inference to study the issue and make usage recommendations. The group's initial conclusion was to recommend that significance testing be abandoned as a hypothesis testing tool, which stance was later softened to instead urge caution in the tests' application and interpretation. Interestingly, even proponents of SST are careful to qualify its applicability by declaring on one hand that "there is nothing wrong with statistical tests themselves," while qualifying the tests' applicability by continuing to say that significance tests are valid "*. . . when used as guides and indicators, as opposed to a means of arriving at definitive answers*" (Huberty, 1987, p. 7).[3] Unfortunately, as detailed earlier, that somewhat fine line rarely gets clearly noticed in practical (i.e., business analyses) SST applications.

To a large degree this is due to the fact that in purely scientific research, not arriving at definite answers is a reasonable constraint, but it is not so in the context of practical business applications, such as marketing program impact measurement. The usually significant level of capital expenditures associated with large-scale promotional programs translates into heightened expectation of definite program performance answers. The inability of significance tests to support such informational needs is among the key indications of the lack of *program measurement objectives–SST applicability* fit discussed earlier in this text.

This is not to say that statistical significance testing should never be used as a business analysis tool, as there are situations where SST can deliver robust and reliable insights. I *am* suggesting, however, that it is irresponsible to "default" to it as the measurement norm without explicitly considering its merit in the context of specific business objectives, data and generalizability constraints. This can be accomplished by assessing the goodness-of-fit between measurement objectives and SST applicability limits using the evaluative dimensions listed and discussed below.

1. Sample size dependence.
2. Replicability fallacy.

3. Exact quantity fallacy.
4. Representativeness fallacy.
5. Impact fallacy.

Why these specific criteria and why are they important? The short answer is that they represent potentially the most influential misapplications of the statistical significance testing to the creation of robust and competitively advantageous business insights. Their "fallacy" stems from the degree to which each of those specific factors tends to represent a practical business analysis misapplication of a distinct theoretical notion—in other words, some of the commonly accepted practical applications are in fact in direct violation of the individual concepts' theoretical rationale. Both the validity and the reliability of the data-derived insights can be severely impacted by any of these fallacies.

The ensuing discussion is built around questions highlighting the potential pitfalls, followed by clarifying discussions and corrective recommendations. Although not always explicitly stated, individual recommendations combine the academically rooted methodological considerations with practically acquired cumulative empirical experience.

Sample Size Dependence

Question:
What will be the impact of SST sample size dependence on the validity of the findings?

Discussion:
It is apparent from SST formulations that the likelihood of detecting statistically significant differences increases as a direct function of sample size, so much so that the initially statistically insignificant *treated–control* differences can gain statistical significance with relatively modest sample-size increases. In general, keeping everything else the same and doubling the sample size will lead to more-or-less doubling of the probability of finding statistically significant results; tripling the sample size will lead to approximately tripling the probability of finding statistically significant results, etc.[4] In many instances, a sample size of several hundred records will lead to inordinately trivial differences becoming statistically significant.[5]

Promotional programs generally involve large sample sizes, as their business viability depends on scale. Not surprisingly, in the context of many typical programs even the most trivial cross-group differences will attain statistical significance casting doubt on SST's ability to differentiate between spurious and persistent effects. To counter that, it is often argued that a clear distinction be drawn between "statistical" and "practical" significance, which is almost always a highly subjective undertaking. As argued in Chapter 8, the "statistical" vs. "practical" significance split is an artifact of SST misapplication in the first place, in addition to which, the necessity of drawing such an arbitrary line of demarcation leaves one pondering the very value of significance testing as an objective benchmark.

Recommendation:
Make sure group-level sample sizes are in the range of 150–500 usable records; if any of the group-level sample sizes are in excess of 500 records, select a smaller subset of 500 or fewer records using a random, stratified or other appropriate sampling technique.

Replicability Fallacy

Question:

Should statistical significance be used to project the current program's results onto future replications of the current program?

Discussion:

In spite of misperceptions to the contrary, statistical significance testing does not support longitudinal generalizations, or result replicability. If a particular program generated statistically significant sales incrementality, it is not correct to ascribe any confidence (in a statistical sense) to the expectation of that program generating similar results when replicated in the future. SST is limited to generalizing sample-based results to the population from which the sample was drawn at a given point in time—and that's all.

For example, if we started out with a population of 2 million first-time buyers from which we selected a random sample of 200,000 to be targeted with a particular offer, we could expect to generalize any statistically significant results onto the original 2 million starting universe. We could not, however, draw any conclusions regarding future replicability of the results, which is a considerable limitation from the marketing point of view. The reason future-pointing generalizations are not plausible is due to the test statistics' cross-sectional rather than longitudinal emphasis. In other words, the t-test, χ^2 or the F-test (used to detect persistent vs. spurious differences between/among group means or proportions) utilize cross-individual and a single point-in-time information—not cross-individual and cross-time patterns. Consequently, significance testing supports sample-to-universe, but not today-to-future generalizations. This is an example of SST application and interpretation limits running counter to business users' (e.g., promotional program managers') informational needs and it is one of several reasons for why significance testing is not a universally applicable tool.

Recommendation:

Do not use statistical significance testing as the basis for making result replicability claims; use it only to generalize sample-based findings onto a larger population (from which the sample came) but without any future-pointing implications. You might have reasons to believe that similar-to-current results can be expected in the future, but SST should not be used to substantiate those claims.

Exact Quantity Fallacy

Question:

Should the results of a statistical significance test be applied to an exact quantification of the program impact (e.g., a buy rate of x%)?

Discussion:

This topic has already been covered in a sufficient level of detail earlier in this book, thus the current remarks are a summary of the previously made observations (see *Example 2: Ascribing Statistical Significance to Exact Values*, discussed in Chapter 11). As discussed there, it is common to interpret statistical significance in the context of what is technically referred to as a "point estimate," which is statistical jargon for describing an exact quantity such as an incremental buy rate of 15%. In spite of it being a relatively common practice, statistical significance cannot be ascribed to an exact value—it can only be associated with a range of values known as a *confidence interval*. This means that it is incorrect to associate confidence levels (e.g., 90%, 95% or 99%) with a specific numerical quantity, such as a sales lift of 15%, as doing so will likely produce misleading or outright inaccurate results.

Recommendation:
Do not apply statistical significance to exact impact quantifications, such as a response rate of x%; limit its application to range-based estimates.

Representativeness Fallacy

Question:
Should statistical significance be used to verify the representativeness of the program targeted sample (i.e., to attest to the degree to which the sample looks like the population from which it came)?

Discussion:
Again, despite common misperceptions to the contrary, statistical significance testing does not measure the degree to which a sample represents the population (from which it was drawn). The only way to make that determination is to develop a carefully constructed sampling plan on the front end and take appropriate sample-to-population cross-validation steps on the back end. All too often, however, there is a tendency to use the results of significance testing to validate the sample representativeness, which is erroneous. As a matter of fact, the frequently seen and somewhat counterintuitive "negative incrementality" results are indicative of some level sample-to-population incomparability, more so than they are manifestations of a promotional program depressing sales (which, frankly is hard to accept on its face value).

Recommendation:
Do not use SST as a basis for verification of the program sample's representativeness; develop a robust sampling plan as a basis for selecting program targets and follow up with a sample-to-population cross-validation.

Impact Fallacy

Question:
Should statistical significance be used as a proxy for business importance of results in question?

Discussion:
Frequently, the term "statistical" is dropped and the results are described as being "significant," rather than merely "statistically significant." Particularly in the business context, the former might be taken to mean "being of practical relevance and/or importance," which is a considerably stronger characterization than might be warranted, especially when put in the context of the previously discussed SST's

sample-size dependence. Imagine the following scenario: A large-scale (read: large sample size) marketing initiative testing an unorthodox offer generates statistically significant results, which are then presented as being "significant" with the statistical descriptor dropped to enhance user-friendliness of the results intended for a non-technical audience. The unorthodox offer is then heralded as the approach to replace current practices. . .

Let's now take a look at what information might have been skipped over: Although the response rate to the above "unorthodox" promotional initiative was low it was higher that its control group, by a small amount, but because of the larger sample size the trivial size lift was statistically significant (see *Sample Size Dependence* discussion above). In addition, there might have been profiling differences between treated and control groups, introducing another and confounding source of cross-sample variability, which is another way of saying that the observed treated vs. control difference might be, at least in part, due to the inherent differences between the two groups. Moreover, once the confidence level around the lift was calculated as required (see the *Exact Quantity Fallacy*), what appeared as a small but positive lift as a point estimate all but disappeared once expressed as a range. That coupled with the inability to make future replicability generalizations (see the *Replicability Fallacy*) showed the "unorthodox" treatment as a risky venture with still unproven promise.

Recommendation:
Do not use statistical significance as a proxy for business impact; consider an alternative approach discussed later in this chapter.

Framing of Coefficients

As mentioned earlier, there is a tendency to report as "real," sales lifts lacking statistical significance, and to ascribe statistical significance levels to exact, rather than ranges of values. Keeping in mind the potential misuses of the broadly defined statistical significance testing discussed above, even when a particular quantification (e.g., a relationship between two measures expressed as a correlation, an impact quantification expressed as dependence) lends itself to statistical significance "validation," the resultant interpretation of numerical coefficients calls for close scrutiny.

Rule #1

Numeric coefficients lacking statistical significance (i.e., those falling short of a stated threshold, such as $\alpha = 0.05$) are spurious and should not be interpreted as anything other than random noise.

Rule #2

Exact quantities (such as sales lift or bivariate correlation) should not be ascribed a level of significance. Confidence intervals (see Chapters 8 and 10 for details) should be computed for each quantity, and statistical effects should be expressed as ranges of values.

The above rationale is straightforward: In situations where statistical significance testing can be used within its applicability limits and its use is deemed beneficial, the notion needs to be interpreted correctly to ascertain valid practical interpretation of findings.

Updating

As illustrated in this book, in order to deliver the most value to an organization, database analytics should be viewed as a process, rather than a singular event. Consequently, the results it generates should be additive as singular contributions and also lead to a progressively more robust organizational knowledge base. In other words, the individual analysis-generated business insights ought to make incremental contributions to the overall organizational informational reservoir. In a more abstract sense, they could be thought of as representing successive approximations to the optimally effective business decision making model.

In contrast to most of the procedures and approaches described in the previous chapters, the task of updating the firm's knowledge base with results of successive database analytical "cycles" is somewhat softer in a procedural sense, while at the same time it is highly dependent on the type of analysis driving a particular update cycle. Overall, the importance of cycle-specific updating is a function of the expected stability of findings, with the need to update being inversely related to said stability—i.e., the more stable the results, the lower the update need.

There are four broad types of analysis (detailed in Chapters 8 through 11) that could be employed as a part of the database analytical process described in this book: Exploratory Analyses, Segmentation, Behavioral Predictions and Incrementality Measurement (see Figure 13.2.). It seems intuitively obvious that Exploratory Analyses, as described in Chapter 8, will yield the most stable results, while Incrementality Measurement, as described in Chapter 11, will be the most update-intensive, because of its "action–result" capture orientation. In general, Segmentation results will usually be updated with a relatively low frequency as well, but for a different reason. Most firms use the results of segmentation analysis as basis for crafting a part of its customer/ competitive strategy, which makes frequent segmentation updates relatively undesirable as it would translate into corresponding changes to the strategy as well as its execution, which under most circumstance would be cost-prohibitive. Thus in a practical sense, it is appropriate to conduct segmentation updates on less frequent basis.

In contrast to segmentation, behavioral predictions are more tactical in nature, which makes more frequent updates both more practically feasible and desirable. A typical application of a behavioral prediction is a customer type-based treatment differentiation. Here, a typical update is represented by a re-calibration of a predictive model (see

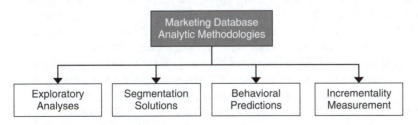

Figure 13.2 Types of Updatable Analyses

Chapter 8) used to estimate record-level response propensities. An update, again under most circumstances, would translate into some amount of re-shuffling of the customer base and a resultant re-designation of high- vs. low-value customers. In practice, the same strategy and offers could be used, but would be targeted at a different group of customers.

The last of the four general types of analyses, Incrementality Measurement, calls for the highest update frequency. In fact, each set of results should be added to the previous. However, in contrast to segmentation or behavioral predictions updates (where the focus is on refresh and replacement of old values by new ones), successive incrementality estimates are additive in nature and knowledge insights are generated from the accumulated total, rather than the most recent results.

Hence it follows that update considerations should take place in the context of the type of analyses, the type of update action required (i.e., accumulation vs. replacement) and lastly, update frequency, as summarized in Table 13.1.

Table 13.1 Update Decision Criteria

Type of Analyses	Update Action	Update Frequency
Exploratory Analyses	Adding to the "catalogue" of observed patterns and relationships. *Action: Accumulation.*	Lowest
Segmentation	Re-definition of segments and/or refresh of segment profiles. *Action: Replacement.*	Low
Behavioral Predictions	Adding new and/or refresh of existing record-level propensities. *Action: Accumulation or replacement.*	Medium
Incrementality Measurement	Adding new "action–response" results to the existing catalogue. *Action: Accumulation.*	Highest

Mini-Case 13.1: Deploying Database Marketing as a New Customer Acquisition Tool

Database marketing is a relatively recent promotional tactic leveraging stored current customer and prospect information as the basis for designing targeted, direct-to-consumer purchase-inducing programs. It is one of the most efficient and effective methods of systematically growing brand sales, as it supports result-based pairing of consumers and promotional investment. In other words, the higher expected future-value targets, representing either the current customers or prospects are allocated a larger share of the promotional investment than their lower-value counterparts, which is the essence of *look-alike* targeting (which is a tactical application of the earlier discussed look-alike modeling). Using that approach, the initial analysis of the current buyer base gives rise to the identification of high- and low-value customer segments, which in turn supports profile-based similarity matching, where consumers (i.e., potential buyers) who most closely resemble the high-value customers (i.e., current buyers) are identified and set apart from the rest.

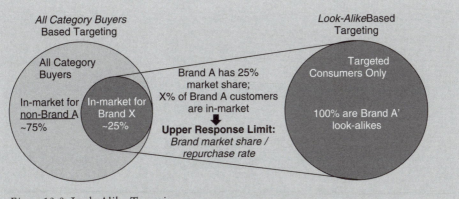

Figure 13.3 Look-Alike Targeting

Finally, the resultant promotional efforts are directed toward those high-value customer look-alikes, as illustrated in Figure 13.3.

The rationale of look-alike-based prospect selection is compelling, especially when compared to an undifferentiated approach (selecting prospects at random), which tends to be highly ineffective, especially when looked at through the prism of the cost per acquired buyer metric. The *efficacy differential* separating these two new customer acquisition approaches is well-illustrated by an automobile repurchase example, in which case, most of the "in-market" (a probabilistic estimate based on time since the last purchase, which is knowable because vehicle registration data is commercially accessible) prospective buyers are not likely to be interested in Brand X. Targeting the entire in-market universe of prospective buyers, i.e., all category prospects, would lead to a considerable dilution of promotional resources, as the more-or-less fixed amount of resources would have to be divided across a very large base. That means that the same amount of resources would be allocated to all prospects, regardless of how likely or unlikely they might be to be interested in Brand X. To make things even worse, the anticipated response rate to just about any promotional offer will also be diluted, as illustrated in Figure 13.3, as 75% of all of those who are in the market for a new car are not likely to be interested in Brand X.

Given these and other disadvantages of an undifferentiated acquisition strategy where all category buyers (e.g., all current auto owners who are deemed to be in-market) are effectively presumed to be equally good prospects, Brand X elected to make use of the look-alike-based campaign logic (graphically shown in Figure 13.4) by limiting its promotional efforts to only the "pre-qualified" prospective buyer segment, which is comprised of that subset of the total best resembling its current owners. Operationally, the said resemblance was estimated based on a comprehensive, multivariate profiling composite, which made use of all available and applicable metrics and allowed all prospects to be rank-ordered based on their individual score of *current brand buyer resemblance*, as illustrated here. The advantage of the look-alike targeting approach was twofold: First, it led to a greater concentration of promotion-based persuasion on the highest brand purchase propensity

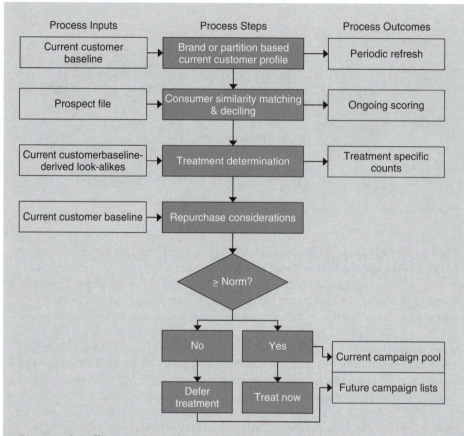

Figure 13.4 Differentiated Acquisition Logic: Getting Started

consumers, which in practice translated into more impactful (i.e., expensive) promotional materials. Second, it made possible further propensity-based treatment (i.e., offer type) and spending (i.e., offer value) differentiation. More specifically, the pre-qualified universe of prospective buyers meeting the minimum threshold of brand purchase propensity was further subdivided into high, medium and low opportunity groupings (highest, second highest and lowest, correspondingly, brand purchase propensity scores), which made possible even greater "fine-tuning" of the new customer acquisition strategy. The generalized flowchart shows the overall logic (Process Steps) as well as the requisite inputs (Process Inputs) and informational outcomes (Process Outcomes) of the overall process. It is important to note that the decision making steps depicted here describe only the "initial touch" considerations, which means the making of the initial promotional offer, based on the initially available data. Given the ongoing character of the database analytical process detailed in this book, the results of the "initial touch" shaped the design of the follow-up promotional steps. In an analytic sense, the initial look-alike-based selection strategy was extended longitudinally, which resulted in a repeatable, ongoing prospective buyer targeting process, graphically illustrated by the multi-step, extended diagram shown in Figure 13.5.

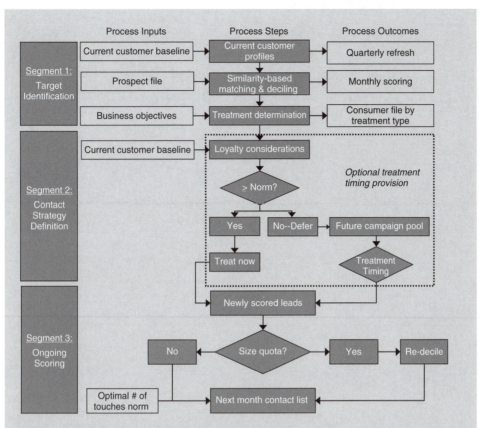

Figure 13.5 Differentiated Acquisition Logic: Ongoing

Although the logic illustrated by the extended diagram (see Figure 13.5) has the appearance of complexity, it is relatively intuitive and easy to implement. The process is comprised of three distinct segments: 1. *target identification*, built around look-alike modeling; 2. *contact strategy definition*, spelling out the specifics of the differentiated treatment investment allocation strategy; and 3. *ongoing scoring*, where the look-alike model-derived propensity scores are updated using recent behavioral patterns. Each of the segments is made up of multiple steps joined together by sequential logic; the entire process is a closed-loop system meant to repeat its steps until externally halted. The rationale embedded in this specific application (manufacturer-originated automotive marketing) can be easily generalized, which is to say it can be used to develop similar approaches in other product or service categories. The central notion of that rationale is an idea that customer retention as well as new customer acquisition efforts should be guided by the desire to align investment levels (i.e., per customer/prospect promotional spending) with anticipated benefits, which parallels the familiar return on investment considerations. In this sense, the knowledge derived from the database analytical processes described in this book can and should be used to provide empirical basis for making these decisions.

PART III

Dissemination

14 Organizational Knowledge Sharing

The final stage in a single iteration of the marketing database analytical process detailed in this book is the dissemination of database-analyses-derived insights throughout the organization. In a conceptual sense, this step can be reduced to a deceptively simple equation:

Knowledge sharing = Right insights + Right audience.

The reason it is *deceptively* simple is because what constitutes the "right" insights and audience is far from self-evident.

Another reason why getting the "right" insights to the "right" audience is not necessarily a simple task is due to the combination of multiplicity of delivery facets and the cross-user aptitude, preference and usage circumstances. Stated differently, analytic insights can be shaped into a wide range of informational inputs and individual organizational users might have distinctly different informational needs and preferences. Hence it follows that developing a sound understanding of the latter will be invaluable in the effective "packaging" of the former. An in-depth discussion of the key considerations and specific recommendations is presented next.

Analytic Insights and Decisioning

To a varying degree, organizational decision making is hierarchical, the result of which is that managers' informational needs tend to reflect their individual scopes of responsibility. At the same time, much of what comprises marketing information can be shaped into an array of otherwise considerably dissimilar presentation formats. Hence it follows that the goal of effective knowledge dissemination should be twofold: First, to identify specific "shared need" target audiences, and secondly, to design the "right" informational content and presentation for each audience type. Doing so is the necessary prerequisite for transforming competitively generic information into competitive advantage-creating knowledge.

In practice, custom fitting information to end users' needs entails determining the appropriate level of detail and the scope of coverage, and then matching the so-delimited slice of the total available information with the audience most likely to benefit from those insights. The lack of alignment between the end users' specific informational needs and the scope, coverage and the delivery format can significantly diminish the value of data-analyses-derived insights, effectively wasting organizational resources and forgoing potential opportunities hidden in the "lost in translation" insights. The most brilliant and innovative analyses won't yield much value unless they are expressly incorporated into the decision making process.

In short, the key to effective knowledge sharing is the understanding of "who needs what." Overall, those with more tactically focused, narrower responsibilities usually need more disaggregate, detailed insights, while those with broader, more strategic responsibilities will be better served by more highly "processed," or summarized and contextualized insights. A growing recognition of functional and other within-organization informational need dissimilarities is beginning to manifest itself in changing management practices and informational system developments. In terms of the former, the access to information has been gradually broadened throughout organizations—for instance, key brand and promotional performance metrics that used to be made available only to senior-most managers are now routinely communicated to a broad range of middle and even staff managers. Responding to these changes, information systems vendors, such as those offering database reporting tools, began to develop a broader range of information processing and delivery platforms. Of particular interest—and applicability—to the promotional knowledge creation process detailed in this book are *management dashboards* and *scorecards*, both of which are ideally suited to the demands of the marketing analytical reporting. Their origins and present-day functionality are outlined next.

Business Intelligence Systems

The 1990s witnessed a strong growth and a proliferation of business intelligence (BI) systems, which are computer applications purporting to help decision makers use communication technologies, data and statistical/analytical models to identify and solve problems. The origin of the first BI systems can be traced to enterprise data warehousing projects embarked on by most large organizations throughout the 1980s and 1990s (see Chapter 6 for a discussion of *data warehouses* and related data organizational structures). By far the most common reasons driving these initiatives were to bring together multiple legacy systems, and to develop user interface tools to support data analyses and reporting.

The bulk of the BI systems can be categorized as either *model-* or *data-driven*. The model-driven systems are built around data modeling capabilities, such as optimization algorithms, predictive models, decision simulations or decision trees. As such, these systems are geared toward drawing inferences and generalizing beyond the confines of the available data—in other words, they are focused on the prescriptive aspects of the analysis of data.

Unlike the model-based systems, data-driven systems are constructed around the more conceptually straightforward data mart or data warehouse-based summarizations, typically utilizing online analytical processing, or OLAP engines. These systems do not attempt to draw inferences from data, but merely try to summarize it. In other words, in contrast to the more prediction-minded model-based BI systems, the data-driven systems tend to be primarily descriptive in nature.

Regardless of the underlying data processing capabilities, BI systems ultimately produced standardized (i.e., fixed format, template-based) reports. Once structured, a standardized report template was usually reproduced on a periodic (most often weekly or monthly, but also as frequently as daily) basis, conveying snapshots of a fixed set of initially chosen operational metrics, such as sales or inventory levels, giving the organization an easy access to the key up-to-date business performance metrics. Though beneficial to some users some of the time, by-and-large, the BI systems-originated reports were nothing more than collections of ad hoc, unconnected informational tidbits incapable of discerning *cause–effect* relationships. In other words, though this basic reporting functionality yielded some insights into "what-is," it largely left the questions of "why" unanswered. Consider a period sales report capturing weekly or monthly sales and promotional expenditure levels. Though providing a convenient summary of the said metrics, such a report says nothing about sales incrementality relating the impact of promotional spending on sales. In short, it fails to answer one of the most (if not *the* most) important questions pertaining to promotional mix effectiveness.

Ongoing Evolution

The ongoing advancement of these early database reporting capabilities has been largely guided and shaped by a few key functional shortcomings. First and foremost was the previously mentioned lack of an explicit assessment of the causeneffect mechanisms, which is an impediment on the road to a direct assessment of treatment-attributable incrementality. Their second key limitation-turned-driver of progress was their focus on highly disaggregate level of analysis (i.e., focus on detailed metrics), coupled with a skew toward completeness (i.e., inclusion of all available metrics, whether related or not) over interrelatedness. In other words, rather than "telling a story," a typical database report emphasized data-dump. And third, since such reports generally offered no specific conclusions, they were not targeted at any particular type of informational need. In short, they are constructed around all that was knowable, rather than noteworthy.

The underlying reasons were a mix of business considerations and technical specifications. In terms of the former, vendors were trying to recoup their development cost as rapidly as possible, to which end mass standardization was a logical choice. However, these were not the only reasons behind the early BI database reports' generic informational structure. More specifically, a number of the vendors designed their offerings around somewhat limiting and inflexible treatment of input data matrices. In more operational terms, the reporting functionality was usually built around row (cases), but not column (metrics) summarization, which placed considerable limitations on the assessment of the underlying causal factors. In other words, a "typical" business report could not draw a clear line of differentiation between important and trivial metrics, or between persistent and spurious associations.

The good news is that the next generation of the basic BI-supported reporting, known as *dashboards* and *scorecards*, successfully tackled and surmounted the vast majority of the limitations of the original BI-supported reporting infrastructure.

To a large degree, the development as well as the ongoing evolution of dashboards and scorecards has been guided by the limitations of the BI systems they effectively replaced. More specifically, it was guided by the desire to offer a more explicit assessment of causal relationships, while also providing an expressed differentiation between persistent and spurious effects. At the same time, the target audience for these informationally richer insight delivery mechanisms has also steadily expanded beyond the initially narrowly defined set of top executives. And so while the management information systems of the 1980s and 1990s were targeted only at a handful of the senior-most decision makers, nowadays, dashboards and scorecards serve the informational needs of a wide range of organizational managers. In fact, the rapid proliferation of their use is illustrative of the true utility of decision-aiding knowledge, which is to inform and guide a wide range of tactical decisions.

Dashboards and Scorecards

The earliest precursor of what is now known as *dashboards* began to appear in the mid-1980s, and it was then known under the moniker of *executive information systems* (EIS). True to their designation (i.e., "executive"), the circulation of the EIS was typically limited to the very highest levels of organizations' management, such as CEO or Chairman of the Board. Consequently, their success was limited, in large part because their readership was so limited, but also because their data analytical foundations were still relatively immature. However, a couple of decades is quite a long time in the information field, and so a lot has changed since the early EIS days. First and foremost, the next generation of what used to be known as executive information systems are no longer targeted at just a handful of the very top managers—in fact, the qualifier "executive" is rarely used in reference to dashboards and scorecards, both of which were pushed down through the organization to provide relevant information to a particular manager, rather than just the top two or three executives. Second, the scope of both has been expanded to cover a broader cross-section of a particular decision domain, all the while being expressly focused on decision-guiding, persistent effects, while forgoing lesser important details.

Figure 14.1 depicts the relationship between basic BI reports, dashboards and scorecards, in term of their respective level of detail and the informational scope.

As shown in Figure 14.1, the evolution from basic database reporting capabilities toward the more summarization-oriented dashboards and scorecard entails a decrease in informational detail along with the associated gains in the scope of captured information. So, while basic report preparation carries with it a relatively light metric selection burden, dashboard and scorecard development places a progressively more significant metric selection burden on analysts.

Usage: Dashboards vs. Scorecards

Overall, there are a number of distinct similarities between management dashboards and scorecards, while at the same time there are clear usage and application differences. In terms of similarities, both dashboards and scorecards rely heavily on data integration and visualization, geared toward conveying critical, decision-aiding insights. At the same time, considerable differences exist between these two communication tools in terms of

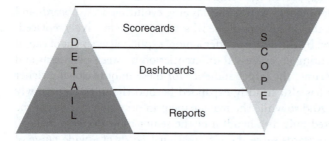

Figure 14.1 Scope vs. Detail

"how" the data is being integrated and "for what purpose." Hence, the key to developing a robust understanding of when one should be used vs. the other lies in clearly delineating their usage and application differences.

First and foremost, dashboards purport to inform their users *what* they are doing, while scorecards are geared toward telling their users *how* they are doing. In other words, dashboards communicate performance and scorecards chart progress, which ultimately means that the former are more tactically focused, while the latter are more strategic. More specifically, the difference between these two modes of information visualization is most evident in the context of their *purpose, inputs* and the *visual format.*

Purpose-wise, the overall goal of a dashboard is to display performance-related information, while the goal of a scorecard is to show progress on stated organizational objectives. It means that while the former is a performance monitoring tool, the latter can be considered a performance management instrument. In a typical promotional context, this difference parallels the distinction between campaign result tracking (dashboard) and the overall performance of the entire promotional mix (scorecard).

Input-wise, dashboards tend to be built around singular events described in terms of narrowly operationalized metrics, while scorecards tend to offer a cross-event, summary view emphasizing performance proxies often referred to as *key performance indicators* (KPIs). In promotional terms, the distinctiveness between these two types of inputs parallels the difference between the performance of a single promotional campaign and the overall impact of promotional efforts comprised of multiple campaigns. Hence, a dashboard-type mechanism is appropriate for an ongoing tracking of distinct promotional events, while a scorecard-type instrument should be considered as the means of wrapping—and summarizing—the performance of multiple promotional events. In that sense, dashboards' contents—i.e., its metrics—are usually tailored to the characteristics of a campaign and as such, will likely vary across campaigns. On the other hand, scorecards' campaign performance indicators will tend to be more "fixed," which is largely a requirement of maintaining longitudinal continuity of the progress measurement process. In general, scorecard performance indicators can be categorized as either lead or lag indicators. The former (exemplified by customer satisfaction scores or the number of planned campaigns) track factors that are expected to impact future outcomes, while the latter (exemplified by sales or profit incrementality) measure the impact of past activities.

The third of the key dashboard–scorecard points of differentiation is the use of information visualization. This is an important consideration given that roughly 70% of the sense receptors in the human body reside in our eyes, which makes us particularly adept at processing properly structured visual stimuli (hence the expression that "a picture is worth a thousand words"). On that note, though both dashboards and scorecards take advantage of visual display of information, the latter tends to make a more extensive use of it. Given that the amount of information that needs to be "packed" into a scorecard can be considerable, especially for a larger organization with a diverse and active promotional mix, "catching the eye" of the reader can be a critical step in successfully disseminating analytical insights. As pointed out earlier, impactful information visualization is particularly important for the more summary-oriented scorecards.

Choosing Between Dashboards and Scorecards

In the information sense, scorecards can be considered to be a subset of dashboards. Consider the following process depiction:

Figure 14.2 The Complete Marketing Database Analytics Process

The promotion analytics process detailed in this book is anchored in the delineation of strategic objectives of the organization, in terms of its point of departure, and in the development of a cumulative reservoir of competitively advantageous knowledge communicated via a dashboard, which demarks the marketing database analytic process' logical point of arrival. Of course, as discussed earlier, this is an iterative process and hence what is shown in Figure 14.2 is just a point-in-time snapshot. Each iteration will produce a set of findings, which will be built around treatment-attributable action incrementality (see Chapter 11 for the discussion of incrementality measurement). The resultant knowledge will then be disseminated throughout the organization with the help of an appropriately designed scorecard. In essence, the results of a singular promotional campaign will be captured and communicated here.

Complementing the scorecard-based single campaign reporting will be the cross-sectional (i.e., across campaigns taking place around the same time) and longitudinal (i.e., successive campaigns) accumulation of results, leveraging business dashboards. The key to a successful campaign scorecarding and cumulative dashboarding lies in a close synchronization of the two communication templates in terms of the composite metrics and reporting dimensions standardization.

First and foremost, it is not required that the analytics-supported scorecards and dashboards be limited to only a common set of metrics—it is, however, important that both contain a common core of metrics. Considering that as mentioned earlier, in practice, insights communicated via a scorecard can be considered to be a subset of what might be included in a dashboard, a scorecard should contain all metrics comprising a dashboard, but not necessarily the other way around. In other words, scorecards will tend to contain more campaign-specific details than dashboards, which is useful from the standpoint of understanding the uniqueness of individual events, while maintaining the necessary cross-campaign comparability.

To structure an effective reporting template, the following core business impact considerations need to be addressed:

- Type of campaign/program.
- Net effect: Treatment-attributable incrementality assessment.
- Contributing factors: Other business outcomes.
- Reporting periodicity.

Type of Campaign

Consider the discussion of the purchase funnel discussed earlier. Depending on their characteristics and the stated purpose, promotional campaigns may offer more or less direct means of assessing their treatment-attributable incrementality, but it is generally feasible to put in place an objective assessment schema to enable cross-campaign comparisons. However, the type of measurement as well as the resultant precision will clearly vary as a function of the type of program and its stated promotional goals. For instance, a general advertising campaign aimed at increasing the brand's awareness will yield different, and less precise, impact assessment options than a direct mail program targeted at stimulating near-term sales. It follows that the dashboard and scorecard design process should start with an explicit categorization of the program/campaign type, in the context of the purchase funnel. The recommended simple categorization schema is presented in Figure 14.3.

In effect, all promotional programs can be grouped into two non-overlapping categories: 1. those targeted at building awareness, and 2. those geared toward incenting near-term purchases. Although as suggested by the notion of the purchase funnel, all promotional efforts are ultimately driven by the desire to grow sales, individual promotional activities—i.e., single promotional campaigns and/or programs—are usually targeted at a specific part of the funnel (see Chapter 10 for a full discussion). Consequently, a stand-alone promotional campaign will rarely attempt to both create the awareness of a brand/product and stimulate near-term purchase, for a variety of reasons, most notably, because of the nature of promotional media employed. For instance, awareness building is typically pursued through general advertising which does not offer an easy way of distributing *message-attributable* purchase incentives. The reason for that is certainly not that a TV commercial cannot announce to the TV-watching world a, let's say, 20% discount on all purchases of Brand X for the next 30 days—it is rather that there is no way of differentiating between purchasers who saw the commercial and acted on it and those who either did not see the said commercial or would have purchased the brand regardless. And conversely, direct promotional media, such as direct mail, could certainly be used as means of creating brand awareness, but considering that, on average, its cost ranges from a low of $1 per piece (for a letter-type piece) to more than $10/piece (for the so-called "dimensional" piece, which is a box-type mailing), it would make for a very expensive proposition in the market of 100+ million households. . .

Given the rationale presented above, promotional activities can be categorized—for the purpose of developing knowledge disseminating scorecards and dashboards—into either of the two mutually exclusive categories shown in Figure 14.3, as the first step in the process of developing insight reporting templates.

Figure 14.3 Purchase-Funnel-Based Categorization

Net Effect

Let us re-visit the purchase funnel-framed impact evaluation logic first presented in Chapter 10, shown in Figure 14.4.

As detailed earlier, the individual components of the promotional mix, such as general advertising, direct mail or personal selling (shown as Impacting Medium in Figure 14.4) are most productive when aligned with specific components of the purchase funnel. Furthermore, given the inherent differences among promotional media, the choice of impact-assessing metrics (Evaluative Metrics) and the overall approach to impact quantification (Evaluative Logic) will be dictated by the specifics of a particular promotional campaign/program being evaluated.

In other words, the task of designing robust scorecards and dashboards entails a careful consideration of the specifics of impact quantification: What type of promotional media does a given campaign/program fall under? Which stage of the purchase funnel is it intended to influence? What are the key characteristics of the broadly defined evaluative logic, and what type of evaluative metrics are being employed?

A scorecard, which is primarily focused on communicating event-specific outcomes, such as response or purchase rates associated with a particular promotion should be more tailored to the specifics of the said event. On the other hand, a dashboard purporting to provide a cross-event summary will need to emphasize outcome commonalities shared by the individual events which it will encompass. In other words, dashboard metrics should be thought of as representing a "common denominator" of individual scorecards.

Furthermore, in the instances when the goal of a dashboard is to communicate the impact of marketing events stretching across multiple stages of the purchase funnel depicted above, its design will need to include the additional component of the cumulative impact of each of the successive events. Consider a direct mail campaign comprising several individual mailings, or "touches." In principle, the goal of each individual mailing is the same, which means that from the evaluative standpoint it is important to quantify the share of the total outcome that can be attributed to each mailing. In a conceptual sense, this parallels the notion of partial R^2 used in regression models outlined in Chapter 10, which captures the contribution made by each variable to the model's overall explanatory power. In both instances, objective, standard (i.e., scale-neutral) metrics allows an analyst to properly evaluate each successive event and/or entity in the context of the cost–benefit evaluative framework.

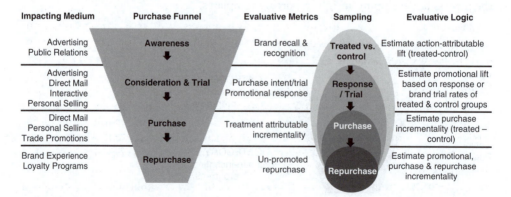

Figure 14.4 General Evaluative Logic of Promotional Campaigns

Associative Factors

The primary objective of both dashboards and scorecards is to address causal impacts of promotional stimuli on business outcomes, or factors that directly contribute to the observable outcomes. However, it may also be instructive to incorporate an assessment of corollary, or associative measures, which are metrics relating to the outcome of interest in a non-causal manner. In the language of empirical analyses, associative factors are correlated with outcomes of interest, but are not presumed to have a causal effect on the said outcomes.

Given the indirect nature of their relationship with outcome metrics, the assessment of the impact of associative factors should highlight their proxy value. In other words, the presence of these factors should be an indication of outcomes of interest, but in and of themselves, associative factors are not the drivers of observed outcomes. Measurement- and metric-wise, there are significant differences between causal and associative factors. In terms of the measurement approach, the impact of causal factors is assessed through action-attributable incrementality, which captures the amount of increase (i.e., lift) in the outcome of interest that is due to specific causal factors. On the other hand, associative factors have no impact, in the measurement sense, but instead they offer correlative evidence of changes in the observed outcomes, which is the proxy function mentioned earlier. This suggests that associative factors are somewhat more appropriate for scorecards than for dashboards.

In a broader promotional sense, associative factors can play an important role in what has come to be known as the "360° view of the customer," which is the ability to integrate into a single informational reservoir the multiple—and often quite diverse— aspects of a single customer's behavior. The 360° customer view necessitates the broadening of the analytical scope to consider not only the most direct, but also a broader range of corollary factors, thus incorporating associative factors alongside causal factors will offer the benefit of not only broadening the analytical scope, but also of expressly differentiating direct drivers of key outcomes from effect indicators.

Reporting Periodicity

Perhaps the most practical consideration involved in scorecard and dashboard design is that of reporting periods. Unlike the systemic issues discussed earlier, periodicity is strictly a practical decision reflecting the firm's promotional strategy. There are two key issues governing that decision: the length of a single time interval and the frequency of reports.

As a general rule, the length of a single reporting time interval should encompass the duration of promotions being evaluated, assuming those promotions have stated effective dates (in general, many near-term sale-incentivizing promotions, such as coupons or temporary price reductions have stated "start" and "end" dates, while typical awareness-building campaigns, such as general advertising might only have implied "start" and "end" dates, which in case of advertising would correspond to the length of purchased media time). This suggests some key differences in the scorecard and dashboard design. Scorecards should combine (somewhat) concurrent promotional campaigns/events with approximately similar durations, while dashboards should amalgamate findings from individual scorecards, which means across time, as illustrated in Figure 14.5.

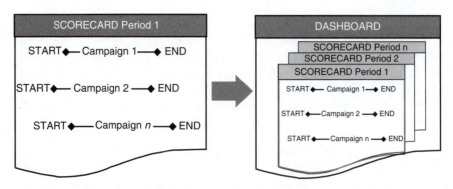

Figure 14.5 Scorecard vs. Dashboard Periodicity

Effective Presentation

To be effective as a communication mechanism, both dashboards and scorecards need to exhibit several distinct characteristics. Overall, these characteristics can be grouped into *visual design* and *content design* considerations.

Visual Design Considerations

Most notably, their design needs to be intuitive and personalizable; their construction guided by a combination of informational parsimony and visual simplicity. Furthermore, they need to make an appropriate use of visual cues, such as color and universally understood symbols, and, whenever possible, combine singular informational elements into patterned displays.

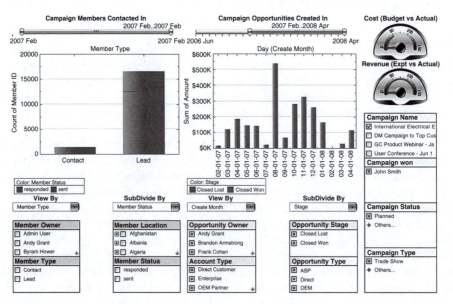

Figure 14.6 Sample Dashboard

The dashboard example (shown in Figure 14.6) communicates the overall summary of the combined impact of all direct mail campaign executed during the course of a year. Although there are many plausibly useful dashboard designs, a "typical" marketing scorecard should be built around the following dimensions:

1. **Aggregate Scores.** Commonly shown as the familiar-looking automotive gauges, this aspect of the report is intended to convey the combined performance of all campaigns (executed in the course of the year) on the three key performance dimensions: *response rates*, *repurchase rates* and *lift*. Typically, the results have been deciled to enable implicit longitudinal comparisons—in other words, to express performance in relative terms (i.e., in relation to past performance).
2. **Drivers of Response and Repurchase.** Often leveraging another commonly used data visualization tool—a bar chart—the goal of this component is intended to highlight *causal factors* demonstrating the most pronounced impact on promotional response as well as the subsequent repurchase. To avoid excessive visual clutter, each of the graphical elements "hides" descriptive details that can be activated (in an electronic version, of course) by clicking or positioning a cursor appropriately.
3. **Treatment-Attributable Incrementality.** The intent of this section is to offer a summary view of (appropriately estimated) impact of the individual promotions. The emphasis here is not so much on absolute outcomes (e.g., 2.1% lift neither universally good or bad), but rather on relative contrasts, where different promotional programs are compared in terms of their ultimate impact.
4. **Highlights.** This is a bit of a "catch-all" category, which can be used to communicate learning that can be most helpful in planning and/or executing future promotions. Associative factors described earlier fall into this category.

The recommended general outline discussed above is one of the many potential dashboard designs. Its goal is to illustrate the key dashboard and scorecard design considerations mentioned earlier, most notably informational parsimony, visual simplicity and intuitive design. In general, the actual scorecard and dashboard template should be tailored not just to individual organizations, but to the informational needs of specific audiences within an organization. Thus the same fundamental information might be circulated throughout the organization in several different formats, all with the goal of increasing its utilization. At the same time, reporting templates should exhibit a fair amount of cross-time stability to aid in longitudinal comparisons, thus enabling more accurate longer-term performance trending.

Report Deployment: A Normative Framework

As much as an eye-catching and easy to "see" design is critical to capturing the intended stakeholders' attention, powerful informational content is a necessary prerequisite to assuring the desired impact. The following framework offers a universally applicable structured set of considerations that can be used to guide the development process.

The Normative Report Design Framework presented here is built around the three key dimensions of *function*, *what to report* and *how to report*, as depicted in Figure 14.7.

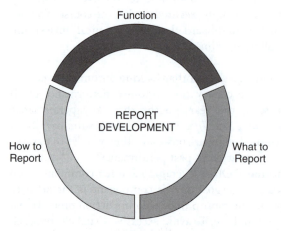

Figure 14.7 Report Development Considerations

Function

In the context of the promotion analytical process outlined in this book, a report can serve one of two key functions:

1. Assess and communicate performance.
2. Compile an aggregate overview.

Assess and Communicate Performance

The essence of product or service promotion is the execution of multiple initiatives, such as direct marketing programs or general advertising campaigns, geared toward influencing buyers' or prospective buyers' decisions. As discussed in earlier chapters, this entails different degrees of use of organizational resources, which in turn necessitates the estimation of each initiative's incremental contribution to the overall revenue stream. In terms of reporting, the broadly defined scorecard template is the most appropriate information communication tool.

The promotional scorecard (the *promotional* qualifier is used to differentiate it from other types of reporting mechanisms) leverages the general scorecard template outlined earlier, which emphasizes longitudinal (i.e., cross-time) and cross-sectional (i.e., across individual initiatives) measuring and reporting consistency. It emphasizes initiative-specific impact assessment centering on action-attributable incrementality for the direct assessment of the net effect, i.e., cause–effect relationships, of factors of interest, while also conveying the corollary impact of associative factors. Overall, the promotional scorecard summarizes and communicates the impact of clearly defined factors within a clearly defined timeframe.

Aggregate Overview

Taking a broader view of promotional efforts necessitates the development of a complementary—to the earlier discussed promotional scorecard—reporting template. To the degree to which, on period-by-period basis, marketing can be viewed as a sum of the initiatives that were executed during a particular time interval, the aggregate impact of promotional initiatives can be assessed with the help of a promotional dashboard. However, to be effective, a promotional dashboard requires more upfront developmental effort—in particular, it requires the operationalization of the evaluative logic summarized in Figure 14.4.

As discussed earlier, a dashboard can be viewed as a summarization of multiple scorecards (see Figure 14.5), which in itself may lead to an (incorrect) belief that the dashboard construction amounts to nothing more than simply summarizing the specific scorecards falling within the desired focus (time and promotion type-wise). Unfortunately, there is a bit more involved here, specifically, the purchase-funnel-related considerations. Consider the differences between the upper and lower parts of the funnel (Figure 14.3) in the context of the evaluative logic depicted in Figure 14.4. The direct impact measurement of promotional activities designed with the upper funnel in mind—i.e., awareness and consideration—tends to be far more elusive than is the assessment of promotional activities geared toward the lower funnel, such as purchase or repurchase. Hence, the impact of the former is measured in terms of its effect on the latter, which is to say that the performance of the upper funnel promotions is expressed in terms of their persuasive impact of "converting" awareness and consideration (upper funnel) into purchases (lower funnel). At the same time, the impact of the lower funnel promotions is measured in terms of purchase incrementality. Consequently, combining individual scorecards will often mean amalgamating the somewhat different types of outcomes into a singular reporting schema.

Another, though not as critical a challenge pertains to potentially different mixes of causal vs. associative factors that may be associated with individual scorecards. In fact, that too has the potential of showing a pattern of significant differences between upper and lower funnel promotions, as the more "tangible outcome"-related lower funnel promotions are less dependent on the proxy qualities of associative factors.

In view of these and other potential challenges associated with the development of robust promotional scorecards, it is imperative to consider the functional qualities of report design in the context of the remaining two dimensions of the normative report design framework outlined here. The impact of "what to report" and "how to report" dimensions on the report design is discussed next.

What to Report

Once chosen, a promotional scorecard or a promotional dashboard template needs to be populated with the "right" information. More specifically, as captured in the knowledge creation process detailed in earlier chapters, tailoring the generic information to the specifics of the *user–decision* conjoint (i.e., who is the user of information and what are the specifics of the decision that is being made) is the necessary requirement to creating decision-guiding, competitively advantageous knowledge. In short, clear decisions regarding what is to be the content of those report are extremely important. In a normative sense, both the scorecard and the dashboard that are to be built for a clearly defined audience within the organization need to be shaped in accordance with the following set of considerations:

* User group's needs.
* Materiality of content.
* Completeness of conclusions.

User Group's Needs

It is intuitively obvious that user groups within an organization are going to differ—quite considerably, at times—in terms of their informational needs. The needs of senior executives are rarely the same as those of line managers, both in the sense of scope as well as detail, just as the informational needs of database analysts will usually differ from those of brand managers in terms of the type of information. At the same time, all of those stakeholders have a vested interest in the performance of marketing promotions, though they all may contribute quite differently to their success. Yet all too often, they all have to drink from fundamentally the same spring of insights.

As suggested earlier, to become competitively advantageous knowledge, promotional information needs to be molded to the specific informational needs of its users. As expected, it starts with the delineation of the key user groups, followed by the demarking each of the group's information-type-specific needs, both in terms of content as well as the format. In fact, the content dimension should already be available, if the analysis used to generate the about-to-be disseminated findings were conducted in accordance with the Marketing Database Analytical Process, first outlined in Chapter 2 and recalled in Figure 14.8.

In practice, one of the more effective approaches is to prepare a sample dashboard and a scorecard, hold a brainstorming session with each group to adapt these templates to their needs. The final version of the templates should be approved by each group prior to the first "live" report being issued.

Materiality of Content

The informational content of a dashboard or a scorecard needs to demonstrate an appreciable impact on the decision making process of each user group. In other words, the content of a report has to be material, which is defined here as the degree to which any analysis-derived insights enhance the uniqueness and/or the depth of the stakeholders' knowledge.

The materiality of content should be determined in the context of the two types of influences outlined earlier: the causal and associative factors. Oftentimes, the causal factors that are deemed material to the decision making process are relatively self-evident when evaluating the impact of promotions. Depending on the specifics of the campaign, it could be treatment-attributable sales incrementality, repurchase rate or an increase in unaided recall or recognition, to name a few of the more common ones. On the other hand, the choice of the most appropriate associative factors tends to be quite a bit more fuzzy for two reasons: One, there are simply a lot more correlative than causal factors to choose from, and two, the distinction between "important" and "trivial" can be somewhat arbitrary.[1]

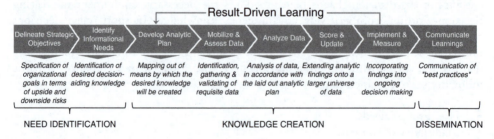

Figure 14.8 Marketing Database Analytical Process

Completeness of Conclusions

To paint an informationally complete picture, the report's coverage of its insights and any definitions of their interpretational boundary should be sufficient to make a positive contribution to the quality of its users' decisions. More specifically, the report's completeness is a function of its scope, boundary and the time interval covered.

The scope of a promotional scorecard should almost always be narrower than the scope of a promotional dashboard. In general, it is advantageous to limit the scope of the former to either a single promotion or a relatively homogenous type of promotions. The scope of a promotional dashboard will necessarily be broader to accommodate cross-promotional comparisons, but it too should be limited to somewhat similar types of promotions. Mixing and matching fundamentally dissimilar promotional types, such as general advertising and direct-to-consumer couponing will erect barriers to meaningful promotional comparisons by diminishing the number of viable causal and associative factors.

How to Report

As it is often the case, how information is packaged has a significant bearing on its end user utility. Of particular interest are the following dimensions:

- Accuracy
- Reliability
- Clarity
- Cross-sectional and longitudinal comparability.

Accuracy

Without the doubt, accuracy is the single most important aspect of promotional reporting. Inaccurate conclusions can lead to a wide range of undesirable consequences, from missed opportunities to misallocation of considerable organizational resources.

To be deemed accurate, dashboard- or scorecard-reported insights have to stem from correct interpretations of unbiased analyses of robust data. In a more operational sense, correctness of conclusions means that: the underlying data has been evaluated in terms of its credibility, representativeness and size; any statistical-method-related assumptions (such as those relating to distributional properties of data) have been validated and met; the margin of error of findings is not wide enough to potentially influence conclusions (for instance, the confidence interval for treatment attributable incrementality does not include "0" in its range); and the shown conclusions are valid interpretations of the data and can be replicated, if needed. The basic premise and the goal of the promotion analytical process depicted above in Figure 14.8 is to lay the procedural and methodological groundwork to ensure the accuracy of data analytical findings.

Reliability

Closely related to the notion of accuracy, reliability also ranks prominently among the report-defining dimensions outlined here. Technically, it is defined as the underlying facts and analytical processes that form the basis for findings and conclusions contained in a report being compiled, analyzed and disclosed in a way that could withstand quality review.

In the context of sample-based business analyses, the notion of reliability takes on particular significance. In view of basic economics, under most circumstances organizations have a relatively limited interest in sample-only findings, instead focusing on the degree to which these findings are true of a larger universe. For instance, it is encouraging that a sample of 1,000 trial buyers showed a 12% promotion-attributable purchase incrementality, though what is critically important is whether or not a full-scale rollout of that promotion will lead to a comparable sales gains. In that sense, the reliability of findings can often mean the generalizability of sample-based results, which in contrast to the earlier discussed accuracy of findings (which are binary in nature—i.e., are or are not true) should be projected on a *low–high* continuum.

Let's consider the aforementioned sample of 1,000 trial buyers. If the confidence interval-expressed promotion-attributable sales incrementality (see Chapter 11 for an in-depth discussion of treatment-attributable incrementality) includes "0" in its range, e.g., −0.3% to 3.9%, the reliability, or generalizability of such findings should be called into question. In other words, the range of the estimated impact suggests the possibility of no lift at all (since "0", or no lift falls within the estimated range), which translates into *low* reliability findings. In the way of contrast, if the said range was, let's say 1.3% to 3.9%, the findings should be considered more highly reliable.

Clarity

A lesson that many analysts find hard to remember is that oftentimes it is not just *what* the results are, but *how* we communicate them. Any scorecard- or dashboard-reported insight should be informationally unambiguous and interpretationally understandable to its stakeholders. Although as argued earlier, information should be tailored to the user type-specific needs (in order to become competitively advantageous knowledge), in principle, any user group tailored report should be understandable to any other user group. There is a vast difference between the usability and the understandability of results—just because a particular is not directly of interest to a particular audience does not mean that it should not be understandable to that audience.

Cross-Sectional and Longitudinal Comparability

For most organizations, promotional scorecard and promotional dashboard preparation is an ongoing process, where each set of reports captures a snapshot of promotional activities. It follows that it is important for an individual scorecard to be comparable with other scorecards, as well as an individual dashboard to be comparable with other dashboard. To ensure the ongoing comparability of each of these two types of reports demands cross-sectional and longitudinal standardization.

Longitudinal standardization is the invariance of the key report elements with regard to the passage of time—in other words, a dashboard or a scorecard report prepared today should be built around the same key elements as the same type of report prepared in the past. Cross-sectional standardization demands that reports encapsulating different promotion types could be compared in terms of their key outcomes. This means that, for instance, upper-funnel promotion-focused reports should be comparable, in terms of their key impact metrics, with lower-funnel promotion-focused reports. It is by no means an easy task in and of itself, but the earlier drawn line of demarcation separating causal and associative factors is further compounding the level of difficulty.

Longitudinal standardization requires solid planning and executional discipline to identify—and to stick with—a set of key evaluative causal factors, such as promotion-attributable sales and/or revenue incrementality measures. However, a different set of principles should be applied when considering associative factors. Here, cross-time change should be the focal point. In other words, as time passes and innumerable influences continue to shape competitive landscape and consumer preferences, the importance of different associative factors is expected to change, and it is those "changing promotional circumstances" that are of interest. The rationale behind this conclusion is relatively simple: The broadly defined role of marketing promotions does not materially change over time, which means that its assessment, in terms of specific metrics, should also remain relatively unchanged. It is hard to imagine circumstances under which promotion-attributable incrementality would not be the best way of assessing the business value of marketing promotions. At the same time, the circumstances surrounding successive promotions can likely change over time, which means that so should the metrics capturing those effects. Consequently, the cross-time measurement of associative factors should account for changing patterns in the importance of those metrics.

Mini-Case 14.1: Communicating with Non-Technical Audiences

The vacation ownership concept, commonly known as "timeshare," originated in the 1960s and has since grown to become one of the most popular leisure travel options. The popularity of timeshares has multiple roots, but perhaps the most salient selling point is the idea of home-away-from-home comfort and convenience, relative to traditional hospitality accommodations. A typical modern timeshare features spacious, home-like floor plans and amenities, including fully equipped kitchens (inclusive of washer and dryer) with dining area, offered in a resort setting with swimming pools, tennis courts, spas and other amenities. Product-wise, there are two broadly defined sets of offerings: 1. the traditional *interval week*, where a consumer purchases the use of a particular unit for one or multiple weeks during the year; and 2. a *point-based system*, where a consumer purchases a pool of points which can be redeemed in a wide array of ways. The latter of the two options has gained popularity in recent years because if offers far greater time (of year), location and accommodation flexibility. In total, there are nearly 2,000 timeshare resorts in the U.S., spread over 47 states—the quintessential vacation spot, Florida, is home to about 23% of that total, followed by South Carolina and California, each with roughly 8% share. Household penetration-wise, little over 4% (or about four million) of U.S. households own a timeshare, which translates into roughly 96 million of potential prospects. . .

Clearly, the "true" universe of potential buyers is considerably smaller, as the level of affluence and vacation accommodation preferences vary widely across households, all of which is well-known to a leading developer of timeshare properties (a large hospitality company). What was somewhat less known were the specific owner vs. non-owner differences, which precipitated a comprehensive descriptive study focused on the delineation of a set of attributes that could be used to construct a prototypical profile of an "ideal" prospective owner. An important consideration in the ensuing analysis was the usability of findings, as the majority of the study's constituents were not comfortable interpreting technically involved outcomes of statistical analysis. Hence the results of the analysis, a limited extract of which is shown here, were presented in a maximally non-numeric fashion, all the while communicating the numeric conclusions. In the example shown in Figure 14.9, the star-highlighted metrics (Age > 50, Income > $85k, Homeowner and College Grad) are all attributes that are characteristic of owners, who as a group, have a significantly higher (i.e., above the mean level) proportion of individuals exhibiting those traits.

The second part of the analysis was focused on gaining insights into the effectiveness of new customer acquisition efforts, starting with a comparative assessment of several recent mail campaigns (see Figure 14.10). Each campaign was described in terms of the same set of three metrics, including *lift* (campaign-attributable net increase in purchase rate), *statistical significance level (Sig. level)* and

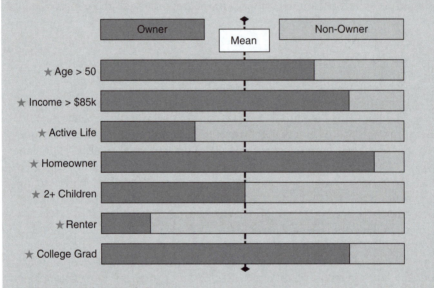

Figure 14.9 Index-Based Contrasts

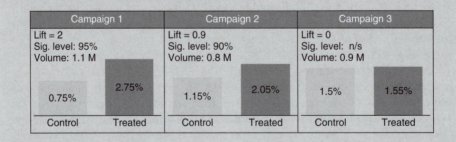

Figure 14.10 Cross-Campaign Comparisons

volume. The side-by-side comparison revealed that Campaign 1 clearly outperformed the other two campaigns, which posed an obvious question: What factors made Campaign 1 more successful?

An In-Market Performance assessment (see Figure 14.11) exemplified a side-by-side comparison of the three campaigns, in terms of several key Evaluative Metrics, including *open rate* (% of the total offer recipients who open the mailing), *action taken* (% of total offer recipients who took the desired action, such as making a tour reservation), *offer redemption* (% of total offer recipients who redeemed the offer for a free or discounted resort stay) and *purchase rate* (% of total offer recipients who became owners). Evaluation-wise, the more fully filled (½ vs. ¼) the individual performance icon, the better the particular campaign's performance on that attribute (as shown in the In-Market Performance graphic, Campaign 1 excelled at compelling recipients to open the mailing and ultimately making a purchase).

Taking the explanatory inquiry a step further, to be complete, the explanation demands linking the "who" with the "what" of the winning campaign, to bring about a deeper understanding of the mechanics of the persuasion process. *Purchase funnel* is a widely used explanatory approach designed to elicit relevant insights that can further an understanding of the unique combination of respondent and campaign attributes that resulted in a comparatively well-performing campaign (see Figure 14.12). In principle, purchase funnel parallels the four-step persuasion process of awareness, consideration, trial and purchase, but this general framework is usually adapted to the specifics of a particular project—here, the focus of the analysis was on linking consideration (as operationalized by recipients openning the offer letters), offer redemption (as measured by recipients' taking the promoted action), and purchase. As used in the context of this study, the purchase-funnel-based analysis aimed to delineate the specific campaign attributes that exhibited a measurable impact on increasing the offer's appeal, as well as the attributes of respondents that could be linked to systematic gains in successive campain

In-Market Performance			
Evaluative Metric	**Campaign 1**	**Campaign 2**	**Campaign 3**
Open rate	●	◕	●
Action taken	◔	◔	◐
Offer redemption	◔	●	◐
Purchase rate	●	◑	◔

Figure 14.11 In-Market Performance

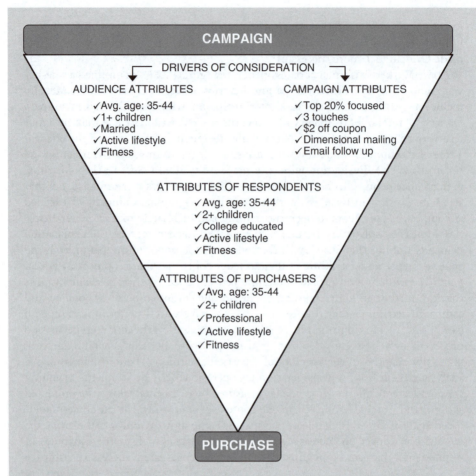

Figure 14.12 Promotional Funnel

thresholds of (offer) consideration, action and purchase. Hence, Drivers of Consideration are broken down into audience and campaign attributes, where in each case, the most salient (i.e., statistically significant) attributes were singled out. In a similar vein, Attributes of Respondents and Attributes of Purchasers represent those traits that systematically increased reponse and purchase rates, respectively. The inverted triangle is meant to symbolize the nested logic of the underlying analytical processes, where purchaser attributes are framed within a broader set of respondent attributes, which in turn are contained in a broader context of consideration attributes.

15 In Closing

In aggregate, business organizations spend billions of dollars annually to store and maintain the ever-expending volumes of data, driven by the belief that data is an organizational asset. However, many data-rich companies put more into data, in terms of ongoing expenditures, than they get out of it, in terms of decision-aiding knowledge. In that sense, what is believed to be an asset can in fact be a drag on organizational earnings. . . Does it sound extreme? Well, data does not appreciate (in fact, as it ages it tends to lose relevance) or pay dividends—which means that data can only be considered an asset to the degree to which it yields decision-aiding insights.

Yet, as exemplified by a cross-section of companies mentioned in the introductory chapters, when intelligently mined and used, data can be a source of a considerable competitive advantage. But mining the organization's own data is not the only way of gaining an informational edge—the world's greatest repository of information, the Internet, also can and should be leveraged to deepen the knowledge derived from in-house data.

Sputnik and Internet

In 1958, a year after the Soviet Union successfully launched the first satellite, Sputnik I, President Dwight Eisenhower issued an executive order to create a new federal agency, called Advanced Research Projects Agency (ARPA).[1] Tasked with pursuit of break-through technologies, ARPA's long-term mission was to spearhead efforts to regain the technological lead in the arms race; in the near-term, the agency was charged with helping to protect the U.S. against a space-based nuclear attack. Among the new agency's early conclusions was the belief that a part of the solution should be the development of a country-wide communications network, which subsequently became one of its first major projects. Leveraging the new techno-idea of *packet switching* and a special computer called Interface Message Processor, ARPA built a working prototype, or a nucleus of such a network—the ARPANET—which went live in October of 1969. And so, the world's first network of connecting remote computers was born. The first ever (remote) computer-to-computer message exchange took place between two research labs, one at the University of California at Los Angeles and the other one at the Stanford Research Institute; soon after, multiple other sites went "on line." The seed of the Internet was sown.

In 1990, the original ARPANET was officially retired and its communication load transferred to the NSFNET (National Science Foundation Net). The NSFNET was soon connected to the CSNET, which linked universities around North America, and then to the EUnet, which connected research facilities in Europe. But at that point, the Internet was still largely a "special purpose vehicle," used mostly by scientists wishing to disseminate and exchange information in a rapid fashion. It was not until a complementary technology was introduced that the Internet's popularity truly exploded on a global scale. That complementary technology was the World Wide Web and its impact was so profound that it ultimately led the U.S. Government to transfer the management of the Internet to independent organizations in 1995. Today, the Internet and the Web are as essential to business as spreadsheets or calculators.

All of its many benefits notwithstanding, the Web has some distinct shortcomings. First and foremost, the volume of "stuff" that is "out there" is truly overwhelming, as illustrated by the fact that a search for a popular topic will usually result in millions of matches. Even seemingly narrowly defined searches can return prohibitively large number of pages—typically well beyond what most of us are willing to tread through. Furthermore, given the advent of search engine marketing, which includes methods such as search engine optimization, paid placement, contextual advertising and paid inclusion, the content that appears at the top of the list is not necessarily the most pertinent. In a sense, the explosive growth of the Web created a dilemma that is similar to the one posed by large databases, namely, the volume of the available information can be an impediment to finding something that is of value. However, that may change soon.

The Semantic Web

The Web continues to evolve toward becoming an "intelligent agent." As envisioned by the World Wide Web Consortium, the evolutionary extension of the World Wide Web will be the Semantic Web, in which the *semantics*[2] of information is defined, making it possible for the Web to "understand" the requests of both people and machines and provide the exactly relevant content. Not only is the Semantic Web going to greatly reduce the earlier discussed problem of too much irrelevant content being delivered to search engines, but it will also lead to greater automation of the Web-enabled knowledge creation.

It goes without saying that it is an enormous undertaking. In its current state, the World Wide Web is an interconnected network of applications, such as individual databases, documents, websites, etc. Each of these applications contains varying amounts of data, but what is networked is not the data contained in each application, but the applications hosting the data, which is the primary reason for the relative inaccuracy of the current search engines. In contrast to the current World Wide Web, the Semantic Web is intended to be an interconnected network of data, rather than applications. According to the World Wide Web Consortium, ". . .*The vision of the Semantic Web is to extend principles of the Web from documents to data. Data should be accessed using the general Web architecture using, e.g., URI-s; data should be related to one another just as documents (or portions of documents) are already. This also means creation of a common framework that allows data to be shared and reused across application, enterprise, and community boundaries, to be processed automatically by tools as well as manually, including revealing possible new relationships among pieces of data.*"

The emerging Semantic Web technologies will be used in a wide range of applications and areas, such as *data integration*, where data in dispersed locations and dissimilar formats can be integrated into a single, seamless application; *resource discovery and classification* to provide better, domain-specific search engine capabilities; *cataloging* of the content and content relationships available at a particular Web site, page, or digital library. Furthermore, the intelligent Web software technologies will be leveraged by "smart" software agents to facilitate knowledge sharing and exchange, as well as content rating, and to describe collections of pages that represent a single logical "document." Imagine the possibilities that this extent of informational enablement creates for marketing management and planning: Virtually "on the fly," we will be able to compile multiple sources of consumer information, product and/or service preferences and ratings and purchase patterns, to name just a few. And so while the emergence of the Internet made it possible to physically connect informational domains across the globe, and the World Wide Web contributed to enriching the quality of content, the Semantic Web will distill the often overwhelming volume of raw data into contextualized insights.

Marketing Management and the Semantic Web

The emerging, breakthrough technology will create new and exciting marketing planning and process improvement opportunities. At least initially, it will be likely seized by a small handful of progressive organizations, the "early adopters," for whom the Semantic Web-sourced informational advantage will create a noticeable *performance gap*, which will eventually force the majority of their competitors to follow. The small, nimble organizations are likely to be the early adopters of the Semantic Web technology precisely because they are nimble (i.e., can adapt more easily) and also because, in general, they have less invested in legacy processes and systems, which is to say, they have less to lose and more to gain. In more general terms, the expected adoption of the emerging Semantic Web technologies will likely parallel the process described by the *diffusion of innovation* process, which is a broad theory characterizing the spread of new ideas and products through a social system.[3]

It is important to keep in mind that it is not the Semantic Web as such that will give rise to competitive advantage—it is the combined effect of effective "in-house" analytics *and* the "external" insights that will be made available by the "intelligent" Web. Individually, the marketing database analytical process discussed in this book and the emerging intelligent technologies of the Semantic Web will have a profound impact on the efficacy of marketing decisions—however, the synergies that will result from thoughtfully amalgamating the two sources of decision-aiding knowledge are a potential game-changer for organizations.

Notes

1 The Informational Advantage

1 Perhaps the most familiar example of transactional data to most of us is the *point-of-sale*, or POS, transaction recording taking place in a retail setting. A customer paying for his/her purchases creates multiple transactional records, with each item comprising the shopping basket creating a separate electronic record.

2 The 12-fold threshold was reached using a very long stretch of thin paper, resembling toilet paper, using what is known as "single direction folding." A number of people, however, questioned the validity of this mark, believing that a "proper" folding approach entailed folding a sheet in half, turning it 90° and then folding it again. Using the "proper" folding method, it has been shown that a single sheet of thin paper can be folded 11 times, with the first 8 folds accomplished manually and the remaining 3 with the help of mechanical equipment (a steam roller and a fork lift).

3 see Bruce Rosenblum and Fred Kuttner, *Quantum Enigma, Physics Encounters Consciousness* (New York: Oxford University Press, 2008).

4 Quinn, J. B., P. Anderson, and S. Finkelstein (1996), "*Managing Professional Intellect: Making the Most of the Best*", Harvard Business Review, 74, no.2 [March-April], (1996): 71–83.

5 Born around 428 BC, Plato was a Classical Greek philosopher and mathematician, as well as a founder of the Academy in Athens, the first institution of higher learning in the Western world. Along with his mentor, Socrates, and his student, Aristotle, Plato helped to lay the foundations of Western philosophy. As a student of Socrates, Plato was as much influenced by his thinking as by what he saw as his teacher's unjust death.

6 The processes governing making the said choices are the subject of an interdisciplinary field known as "decision theory," which is concerned primarily with goal-directed behavior in the presence of options, under the assumption of non-random selection. In a very broad sense, decision theories fall under two general umbrellas: normative and descriptive. A *normative decision theory* is a theory about how decisions should be made, and a *descriptive theory* is a theory about how decisions are actually made. Obviously, the availability of decision-guiding knowledge is essential to each of the two sets of theories.

7 Microwaves are very short wavelength/frequency electromagnetic waves, much smaller than those used in radio broadcasting.

8 Purposeful; derived from the Greek word *telos*, meaning *end* or *purpose*.

9 The trial and the resultant abjuration of Galileo before the Holy Congregation of the Catholic Church at the convent of Minerva on June 22, 1633.

10 See Patricia S. Churchland and Terrence J. Sejnowski, *The Computational Brain*, (Cambridge, MA: MIT Press, 1992)

11 In the database jargon, the key properties of a database transaction are referred to as *atomicity, consistency, isolation* and *durability*, or ACID.

12 In the jargon of statistical analysis, the impact of individual factors looked at in isolation (from other variables) is often referred to as a *main effect*, whereas the joint impact of several factors is referred to as an *interaction effect*.

13 In principle, the term "algorithm" is sufficiently broad to include virtually all statistical techniques. However, as used here, *statistical techniques* refer to general problem solving

methods readily available to anyone, while *computational algorithms* denote custom-built computational methods. For example, cluster analysis is a statistical technique widely used for grouping customers into segments; it is typically included in many of the popular statistical analysis software packages (e.g., SAS or SPSS) and as such readily available for anyone to use. A proprietary approach to customer value quantification, developed "in-house" and not readily available to others is an example of a computational algorithm.

14 Most notably, the difficulty of integrating these typically special-application-oriented systems with the growing number of other applications.

15 In fact, a typical report layout is somewhat reminiscent of a car dashboard (hence the name), given the heavy reliance on dials and gauges as means of communicating the information. See the *Organizational Knowledge Sharing* chapter for an example of a management dashboard report.

16 *Pluralitas non est ponenda sine necessitate*, Latin for "entities should not be multiplied unnecessarily."

17 These include standard POS (point-of-sale) transaction recording systems or third-party data vendors such as AC Nielsen (consumer packaged goods) or RL Polk (automotive), or Standard & Poor's Compustat (quarterly, annual and ad hoc SEC filings submitted by all publicly-traded firms).

18 This is particularly the case with transactional data, where the *recency* of behavioral outcomes is one of the key factors in deriving robust explanatory/predictive insights. It is a manifestation of the intuitively obvious notion that behaviors are most influenced by factors and events closest to them in time.

19 see Thomas H. Davenport, "Competing on Analytics," *Harvard Business Review* 84, no.1 (2006):98–107.

20 First reaching the milestone in 2005, subsequently passed by ExxonMobil in 2006 (largely because of a sharp, near-term rise in the cost of crude oil), but shortly thereafter regaining the #1 spot.

21 As detailed in the subsequent chapters, a "typical" transactional database can contain hundreds of individual metrics and millions of rows of data, which represents an exponential increase from the size of datasets that were used as a backdrop to deriving various data analysis processes and approaches.

22 For instance, the so-called *scanner* data captured as a result of electronic scanner-equipped retail outlets (which nowadays can be found in virtually all mid-size and larger retail stores) exhibits vastly different properties from consumer surveys, geodemographics or promotional response history. The key differences are detailed in the *Data Basics* chapter.

2 The Marketing Database Analytics Process

1 *Epistemology* is the study of nature of knowledge and processes that create it.

2 *Measurement theory* is a branch of applied mathematics, often used in data analysis. Its basic premise is that measurements (defined as a process of assigning numbers or other symbols to entities in such a way that relationships of those numbers or symbols reflect relationships of the attributes of entities being measured) are not the same as attributes being measured, thus in order to draw conclusions about attributes one must take into account the nature of the correspondence between attributes and their measurements.

3 Organizational Objectives and Informational Needs

1 In his best-known work, *The Republic*, Plato describes his vision of an ideal city-state, Kallipolis, and argues that in order for his idealized vision to come true, "*philosophers {must} become kings. . .or those now called kings {must}. . .genuinely and adequately philosophize.*"

2 This is certainly not a complete listing of the potential sales growth tactics, but merely a sample illustration

3 As detailed later in this book, data append match rates can range from a high of about 80% or so to a low of about 2%, depending on the type of data.

4 Skills and Tools

1 Third-party data appends are usually added into the in-house data through household name and address matching, which almost never is 100% accurate due to households moving and random data errors. In addition, many of the household-level metrics are not available for all households. As a result, a key evaluative metric used in assessing the efficacy of the third-party data appends is the "match rate," which is the proportion of in-house household-level records that were successfully appended with a particular measure. In some instances, the match rate can be prohibitively low, bringing into question the analytic reliability of the low match rate metrics (more on that in the next chapter).

2 The terms "test" and "experiment" are used here interchangeably, as in the context of marketing analytics their meaning is synonymous as both refer to setting up specific contrasts and capturing the resultant data.

3 Fully discussed in the *Analytic File Creation* chapter, the *effective* sample size is the notion used in reference to the most narrowly defined, i.e., the most disaggregate sub-sample contained within the overall sample. For instance, the overall consumer sample can usually be broken down into multiple sub-samples based on anything from purchase history or propensities, demographics, geography, etc.

4 Since *statistical modeling* is a subset of *statistical analysis*, these two terms can be used synonymously in the context of analyst skill sets. A distinction will be drawn between the two as a part of the discussion of targeting and behavioral analyses considerations presented in the *Behavioral Predictions* chapter.

5 Some scores might have natural bounds, such as standardized propensity scores expressed as probabilities which can only range from 0 to 1 (or 0% to 100%), while others, such as lifetime value scores can have more qualitatively-bounded ranges requiring judgment-based evaluations.

6 Data Basics

1 Charles Babcock, "Data, Data Everywhere," *Information Week*, January 9, 2006.

2 As envisioned by the World Wide Web Consortium, an international community devoted to the development of Web standards, the Web continues to evolve toward becoming an "intelligent agent," where semantics (the meaning of information) is defined, making it possible for the Web to "understand" both people and machines and thus provide the exactly relevant content.

3 Explicitly numeric data are coded as digits; implicitly numeric data are coded as alphanumeric (a combination of digits and letters) characters that are convertible into digital format. For instance, Gender is often coded as "F" for females and "M" for males, which can be easily converted into a numeric format, such as "1" and "2," respectively.

4 Although in principle the initial hypotheses could be based on the analyst's current level of understanding of the issues at hand, using exploratory, qualitative data infuses a higher level of objectivity into the knowledge-building process.

5 Some statistical software vendors, such as SPSS, offer text mining modules as add-ons to their statistical analysis solutions. However, their functionality is limited to semantics exploration, rather than performing matrix type operations required of most statistical techniques.

6 As discussed later, other data attributes, namely its scaling properties will determine the applicability of different types of statistical techniques that could be used.

7 The bulk of those requirements are aimed at protecting consumer privacy; for instance, businesses are prohibited from disclosing individually identifiable financial data, which can be circumvented by creating segment-level summaries.

8 A UPC (Uniform Product Code) barcode is usually made up of 10 digits, where the first five digits identify a manufacturer while the remaining five denote the specific physical product (not just a brand). For example, a single UPC code would identify a 2-liter bottle of caffeine-free diet Coke manufactured by Coca-Cola, while a different UPC code would identify a 2-liter bottle of diet Coke.

9 A "transaction" here is defined as recording (i.e., scanning) of a single UPC, not the entire consumer purchase. Thus a shopping trip is made up of as many individual transactions as

there were individual UPCs scanned. Outside of the bar-coded product sales, a transaction is often defined as a single consumer purchase, which might be comprised of several items. For instance, a single consumer purchasing several movie tickets will usually count as a single transaction.

10 In fact, the "over" and "under" estimate cancelling phenomenon required squaring of the error terms to enable desired data analysis.

11 One terabyte is equal to one trillion individual characters (i.e., digits or letters or combination of both).

12 In a practical sense, it simply amounts to reducing the amount of information in the data.

13 More specifically, categorical variables cannot be designated as dependent or target variables in certain type of multivariate statistical models.

14 Shelby D. Hunt, *Modern Marketing Theory: Critical Issues in the Philosophy of Marketing Science* (Cincinnati, OH: South-Western Publishing, 1991), 86–89.

15 Of course, organizations can and do offer products and services to governmental and non-profit sectors as well, but the focus of this text is on describing the knowledge creation processes used in support of for-profit, non-governmental sectors.

16 It should be pointed out that, according to the most recent U.S. Census estimates, only about 42% of all households fall under the "traditional family" classification, which is the household type that is most likely to engage in the group decision making. The remaining 58% is split more or less equally between "non-traditional families" (married couples without children, single parents with children and unmarried couples) and "non-family households," i.e., roommates or people living alone. The last category—those living alone—accounts for nearly a quarter of all U.S. households.

17 According to one vendor of database appliances, Netezza, its Netezza Performance Server delivers 10–50 times the performance (measured in processing speed) of traditional data warehouse systems as offered by Oracle, IBM or Teradata. The performance gains are generally attributed to multiple, micro data processing units replacing a single, central CPU-based batch processing. It should be pointed out, however, that the greatly increased processing efficiency can make certain other operations, such as selecting of a representative database sample, somewhat more cumbersome.

18 www.worldwidewebsize.com.

19 One terabyte = one trillion (1012) bytes and one petabyte = one quadrillion (1015) bytes.

20 Qualitative research methods are focused on developing an in-depth understanding of phenomena of interest by using subjective methods, such as a researcher's interpretation of the meaning of stated opinions and perceptions, implied or explicit symbolism, etc.; focus groups are perhaps the best known application of qualitative research in business. In the vast majority of cases, conclusions of qualitative research are non-generalizable, which is to say that the sample-derived findings and conclusions cannot be taken as being representative of a larger population, primarily because qualitative research emphasizes depth (of insight) over representativeness (of conclusions).

21 Although popularized by the recent emergence of social communication platforms such as Facebook or Tweeter, social networking is a general idea of grouping of individual, either by means of self-selection or "naturally delimiting" context such as universities, communities, professional organizations, etc., which as such has been a subject of sociological inquiry for the past several decades.

22 Discussed in more detail later, *syntax* refers to the arrangement of words in sentences which, together with the meaning of the individual words, gives sentences their meaning.

23 Consider the earlier-mentioned examples of the largest repositories of textual data—Facebook's social networking, Google's search or the Library of Congress databases—the overwhelming majority of the individual files comprising those gargantuan databases is made up of free-flowing text lacking discernible structure.

24 As is well-known, the primary advantage of machine processing is speed, not creativity. The vast majority of computer processing algorithms are designed to apply the same processing logic to all cases (rows of data)—when that is not the case, i.e., when input files do not follow a pre-determined and recurring structure, the otherwise highly efficient algorithms' performance degrades rapidly.

25 The "mining" label is meant to connote the exploratory focus; in general, data mining is focused on search for patterns and/or relationships in typically very large databases, such as

UPC-scanner-originated purchase databases amassed by retailers. With that in mind, text mining can be viewed as a subset of data mining, as it focuses on search for patterns and/or relationships in text data.

26 SPSS is now a subsidiary of IBM.

27 Ethnographic research is a group of qualitative research techniques utilizing researcher's immersion in subjects' way of living (e.g., culture), with the goal of developing an understanding of subjects' experience from their point of view.

28 Data about data; the term (metadata) is quite broad as it is used in a wide array of contexts. Within the confines of executive risk-related text mining, its meaning is synonymous with "meta content."

29 The so-called "360° view of customers," "customer focused" or "customer centric" approaches to customer relationship management, or CRM, rest upon organizations' ability to compile a singular data analytical infrastructure, where different aspects of customer knowledge are all "tied together." The ultimate goal of multi-source analytics is to yield a complete (or as complete as possible, given all available data) understanding of consumer behavior, which means the linking of consumers' opinions/attitudes (the bulk of which are text coded), demographics as well as other salient motivational factors with product and service purchases (which tend to be numerically coded) and other marketplace behaviors.

30 Consider, for instance, a term such as "price discount"—in a broader context, it could be used to communicate that a price discount had no impact on purchase intent or the opposite. Obviously, the ultimate informational value of the "price discount" term is highly dependent on the context in which the term was used.

31 *Semantics* is the study of meaning, focused on establishing the relationship between words, expression or symbols and what they stand for; *linguistic semantics* is the study of language-based communication.

32 In a broader sense, text can be transformed into a wide variety of other media, such as pictures, video, etc. In fact, in educational research, "text transformation" is used in the context of enhancing printed text to aid in students' efforts to comprehend the meaning of text.

33 Many database applications make heavy use of libraries of terms that are used to describe a particular condition, state or an outcome. In effect, the structured textual data represents selections made from a predefined listing of applicable terms.

34 A key simplicity-related consideration is reflected in the notion of "overfitting," which is a condition where the algorithm is too tailored to the specifics of the training data and does not generalize well to new data.

35 Knowledge-based classification systems are usually built around phrasal pre-processing and pattern matching that is guided by tailored (to a specific subject area) classification rules; given that, expert-imbued knowledge provides the basis for probability-expressed matching.

36 Perhaps the best way to think about this scenario is to consider it in the context of regression analysis, where the a priori identified outcomes are operationalized as *dependent* variables (or quantities, the variability in which we seek to explain), while the a priori identified stimuli are operationalized as *independent* or *predictor* variables, the variability of which is viewed as causing the variability in the dependent variables.

37 Transaction-recording data, such as those sourced from barcode scanners, capture data at the most disaggregate level—i.e., at the level of an individual item, rather than (the more aggregate) brand level—hence the number of individual variables can be quite large, as for instance, retail outlets tend to carry thousands or even tens of thousands of individual items. Furthermore, transactional data is multiplicative in nature—each individual selling item, such as 48 oz. box of Honey Nut Cheerios, is usually ascribed with several sales-related attributes, such as price, discount (if any), time of sale, place of sale, etc.

38 Conceptually, the notion of "marketing ecosystem," as used in this text, is distinct from a broader concept of "business ecosystem." As discussed by James F. Moore in his 1996 book, *The Death of Competition: Leadership & Strategy in the Age of Business Ecosystems* (New York: Harper Business), the latter can be thought of as ". . .an economic community supported by a foundation of interacting organizations and individuals—the organisms of the business world." Examples of business ecosystems abound in manufacturing (e.g., supplier networks in the automotive or aerospace industries), information technology (e.g., networks of developers for computer operating systems, such as iOS, Android or Windows), service (e.g., underwriters, consultants, brokers and analysts working together within risk management)

and virtually all other industries. In contrast to the cross-organization-focused business ecosystems, marketing ecosystems are primarily intra-company focused.

39 This definition borrows from the work of Peter Drucker, as encapsulated by his famous quote: "The purpose of business is to create and keep a customer"—Peter Drucker, *The Essential Drucker: The Best of Sixty Years of Peter Drucker's Essential Writings on Management* (New York: HarperCollins, 2001).

40 A cross-industry study by a consulting firm of Booz & Company in partnership with the Association of National Advertisers, the Interactive Advertising Bureau and the American Association of Advertising Agencies.

41 The terms "marketing mix" dates back to 1948 (N. Borden's article "The Concept of Marketing Mix"), while the *four Ps* classification was first proposed by E. J. McCarthy in 1960. The familiar four Ps classification has been subsequently expanded to *seven Ps* by adding the notions of physical evidence, people and process, though the seven Ps classification is rarely used in business.

42 To be truly interactive, media such as television have to either allow the user to alter the viewing experience (e.g., choose a perspective from which a viewer is watching a sporting event) or offer a "return path," or means of returning information to the broadcaster. As it relates to marketing, it is the latter of the two—the return path—that is changing the previously one-way (i.e., advertisers *talking at* consumer) promotional channels into two-way interactions (i.e., advertisers *conversing with* consumers).

43 Literally, "dark and light"; a popularized Eastern philosophical concept capturing how seemingly contrary forces can be both interconnected and interdependent).

44 According to the Booz & Company's "Marketing & Media Ecosystem 2010" study, 88% of marketers are planning to increase their spending on digital (online) media and 52% are planning to increase their spending on mobile media, while nearly 50% of marketers are planning on reducing their print spending, with another 40%+ planning to cut back on their TV advertising expenditures.

45 When two or more files are merged, missing values will be generated for some of the variables in non-overlapping cases. As discussed in the upcoming chapters, most statistical analysis do not permit missing values, which means that either the cases containing missing values have to be eliminated or missing values have to be imputed, both of which can have potentially adverse consequences (discussed in more detail in the next chapter).

7 Analytic File Creation

1 Oftentimes such data is referred to as "secondary" in recognition of the fact that its capture is a by-product of other functions. Though technically correct, the term "secondary" also tends to perpetuate misperceptions about the value of the data (i.e., not as good as could be; not as useful as could be, etc.) which is unfortunate as well as unfounded, since the secondary data tends to be among the most accurate and valuable of all data assets. For that reason, this text will use the term "incidental" instead.

2 It is also referred to as "primary" data, in recognition of the fact that it is collected for a very specific purpose. Again, the everyday connotation associated with the term "primary" may be potentially misleading as it may be taken to attribute the qualities to these data, such as a higher level of importance, that are unwarranted or even untrue.

3 For example, the outside vendor-sourced geodemographic variables have an average "hit rate" of anywhere from about 5% for certain special interest metrics, such as magazine subscription propensity, to about 50% for general purpose metrics, such age, house ownership, etc. The coverage will be far lower for direct-capture survey information, mostly due to high costs, which can run in excess of $10 per completed survey.

4 An in-depth discussion of the applicability of statistical significance testing to marketing is offered in the *Beware of Significance Tests!* section.

5 In a nutshell, it means that small changes in the initial conditions can have disproportionately large impact on the system—i.e., a butterfly flapping its wings can set off a chain of events that can ultimately cause a hurricane.

6 It should be noted that the stratified sampling scheme also relies on random selection, but in pre-specified proportions. In contrast to purely random selection, stratified sampling breaks

the entire database down into distinct segments (such as customer type groupings) called strata, following which, a representative, random sample is selected from each strata.

7 For the purposes of the data it makes available to the public, the U.S. Census Bureau uses an 8-tier hierarchical system: *nation*, naturally the most aggregate level, is broken down into *regions*, which are then divided into *divisions*, which in turn are divided into *states*, which are broken into *counties*, then *census tracts*, *block groups* and finally, *blocks*.

8 The evolving legislative landscape continues to shape and redefine the organizations' access to consumer data, largely in response to mounting privacy considerations. For example, the recently enacted Shelby Act severely restricts the access of companies to consumer auto registration data compiled by R.L. Polk and Company from state automotive registries.

9 Physical-distance-based outlier identification typically utilizes the so-called Mahalanobis distance, which relates the arithmetic mean of the data and the sample covariance matrix as basis for identifying outlying data points. On the other hand, an approach based on a difference of magnitudes quantifies the discrepancy between the sample-wide average and a record-specific actual value which is then evaluated in the context of the allowable upper and lower intervals.

10 A continuous variable is one for which, within the limits of its ranges, any value is possible. Common database analytical metrics of sales and age are both examples of continuous variables. Likert-type survey items (measuring the degrees of agreement/disagreement with specific statements) are also often assumed to be continuous, even though the scale itself is comprised of a finite number of discrete categories. In general, of the four types of measurement scales—nominal, ordinal, interval and ratio—the latter two are typically categorized as continuous, while the first two are characterized as discrete.

11 K. V. Mardia, "Measures of Multivariate Skewness and Kurtosis with Applications." *Biometrika* 57, no.3 (1970):519–530.

12 In a perfectly symmetrical, non-skewed distribution, the mean, median and mode are equal.

13 See Andrew D. Banasiewicz, "Marketing Pitfalls of Statistical Significance Testing." *Marketing Intelligence and Planning Journal* 23, no.5 (2005):515–528.

14 Based on Tabachnick, B. G and L. S. Fidell, *Using Multivariate Statistics*, 3rd ed., (New York: Harper Collins, 1996).

15 See note 14 above.

16 These analyses used regression-based missing value imputation processes to fill in randomly created missing values (i.e., the values were deleted for the purpose of the experiment), the results of which were then validated via ascribed-to-actual comparisons.

17 For example, F. S. Switzer, III, P. L. Roth, and D. M. Switzer, "Systematic Data Loss in HRM Settings: A Monte Carlo Analysis." *Journal of Management* 24, no.6 (1998):763–779; and D. B. Rubin, *Multiple Imputations for Nonresponse in Surveys* (New York, John Wiley, 1987).

18 This particular limitation would be circumvented if the variables of interest, i.e., the X and Y metrics being correlated, had no relationship (operationally, 0 correlation) with other variables. Although theoretically possible, that is extremely rare in practice.

19 D. B. Rubin, *Multiple Imputations for Nonresponse in Surveys* (New York, John Wiley, 1987).

20 A linear combination of predictor, or independent variables, such as the combined set of the right hand-side metrics in a regression model.

21 In multivariate statistical analysis, behaviors are usually used as dependent variables, i.e., variables being explained, while causes usually play the role of independent variables, i.e., the drivers of the observed behaviors.

22 Since the information-richer quantitatively coded variables can always be re-coded into qualitative ones, quantitatively coded variables do not face such limitations. However, since the process of quantitative-to-qualitative re-coding results in permanent informational reduction as the information richer quantitative variable is reduced into the information-poorer qualitative one, the quantitative-to-qualitative re-coding is non-reversible. It goes without saying that qualitatively coded variables cannot be re-coded into quantitatively coded ones.

8 Exploratory Data Analyses

1 Technically, the *null* hypothesis is the "default" belief stating that there are no differences, dependence or other relationships; in other words, it postulates that two or more variables are

not related. If true, it is interpreted that nothing other than chance is operating to produce an effect seen in a particular dataset.

2 Statistical significance tests are in principle a "pass–fail" mechanism, which means there is no implicit "degree" of significance that might be attributed to individual relationships, in spite of the evident numeric differences across individual tests (i.e., significant at .01 vs. .001). As a result, once a given relationship is deemed to be statistically significant, its level of a significance test-imputed importance is the same as that of all other (statistically significant) relationships.

3 Among the most commonly used data mining techniques are fuzzy query and analysis, case-based reasoning, neural networks and data visualization. Fuzzy, in contrast to crisp, query and analysis tries to extract the intent from a relatively vague semantics of a database query (e.g., finding "good" customers vs. identifying all customers whose spending is greater than a specified threshold); case-based reasoning allows analysts to identify records that are similar to specified targets; neural networks attempt to emulate human brain's learning processes to extract insights out of raw data; data visualization offers graphical interpretation of complex relationships in multidimensional data.

4 John Tukey, *Exploratory Data Analysis* (Reading, MA: Addison-Wesley, 1977).

5 *Collinearity is an excessively high correlation between predictor variables in multiple linear regression.* This concept will be discussed more fully in Chapter 10.

6 The Delphi Method is a structured process for collecting and distilling knowledge from a group of experts, hence it is also sometimes referred to as the "jury of executive opinion." The basic idea behind this particular method is that in areas where the development and/or validation of objective scientific laws is not possible, human judgment can be considered a legitimate and useful decision making input. The term "Delphi" refers to the hallowed site of the most revered oracle in ancient Greece (which in the opinion of some, is an unfortunate choice of a label).

7 Since histograms show categories of data, continuously measured variables typically need to be grouped into categories to allow the frequency of data values to be tabulated. Not doing so will distort the appearance of the graph making it unreadable due to a very large number of distinct values appearing with very low frequency. There are no set ways of grouping continuous variables, as the best method is in part a function of the type of data. For instance, purchase data (e.g., captured by UPC-code readers or other POS systems), could be divided into a number of equally sized categories by subdividing the range of values into the chosen number of categories. On the other hand, survey-captured data, such as consumer preferences or attitudes could be easily categorized by summing scale responses (e.g., although the commonly used Likert scale is assumed to be continuous, responders select specific categorical responses on the *agree–disagree* continuum).

8 *General Linear Model*, discussed in more detail in the *Behavioral Predictions* chapter.

9 It may seem somewhat counterintuitive that a range defined by stated end-points would have an infinite number of values but the basic idea here is that any interval bounded by extremes can still be divided into ever-smaller subsets.

10 Technically, it is also important to distinguish between a sample and a population mean. Sample mean is the actual computed value based on the data contained in a particular dataset or a database. The population mean, on the other hand, is a more abstractly defined expected value of a random variable. In database analytics the term mean is synonymous with sample mean.

11 Assumes it is computed in a sample (as opposed to the population).

12 Sample standard deviation; it can also be expressed as a square root of variance.

13 SAS and SPSS do not have a limit on the number of categories, thus it is possible to end up with very large matrices.

14 A cell is a unique conjoint, or a combination, of a variable and a level. For instance, a 2×2 test would be comprised of 4 individual cells, as there are 2 variables each with two levels.

15 Some of that rationale is evident in what is known as *partial correlation*, which is (still) a bivariate relationship, but one that is computed net of the effects of one or more of the potentially confounding variables. In that sense, partial correlation should be treated as a special case of the general bivariate correlation.

16 Examples include such well-known, yet elusive concepts as intelligence, expertise or satisfaction, all of which are typically measured with multiple-indicator survey studies

(largely because it is believed that no single item is a perfectly reliable measure of those constructs). Thus when multiple items are all intended to measure the same underlying concept, ascertaining the relationships between those items is obviously of informational value to researchers. However, more methodologically robust approaches, such as the confirmatory factor analysis are now the preferred method of studying those relationships.

17 Standardization involves subtracting means from the original values and dividing the residual by the standard deviation.

18 There are a few notable exceptions to that rule in the context of structural equations modeling (SEM) techniques, but these techniques fall outside of the scope of this book.

19 Kendall's tau is also an appropriate choice and will typically yield practically the same results (both Kendall's and Spearman's correlations carry out the same computation, just by somewhat different means). In the past, Spearman's coefficient tended to be preferred to Kendall's because it is computationally less taxing, though that is obviously a moot point currently. That said, Spearman's has more recognition, thus it is preferred.

20 *Type II* error entails incorrectly accepting a false null hypothesis. The previously discussed prohibitively small sample size is among the more common causes of the Type II error.

21 In contrast to the earlier-detailed three-prong shortcomings of tests of statistical significance associated with exploratory data analyses, applying SST tests to causal analyses discussed here generally raises concerns only in terms of the effective sample size and the resultant potential of deeming as significant relationships whose significance is inflated in the sample size used in the analysis.

22 Specifically, it is one of the fundamental building blocks of the maximum likelihood based structural equation modeling, which is a method of simultaneously estimating multiple relationships.

23 see the *principle of parsimony*.

24 For an in-depth discussion of misapplications of statistical significance tests see Andrew D. Banasiewicz, "Marketing Pitfalls of Statistical Significance Testing." *Marketing Intelligence and Planning Journal* 23, no.5 (2005):515–528.

25 Some sources tend to use factor analysis and principle component analysis interchangeably, even though the term principal component technically refers to factor (i.e., a variable grouping) extraction technique, giving the latter more specific meaning. In this book, the more general name of *factor analysis* will be used.

26 For an excellent, easy-to-follow discussion of this technique see J. E. Hair, R. E. Anderson, R. L. Tatham, and B. Black, *Multivariate Data Analysis*, 5th ed. (Upper Saddle River, NJ: Prentice Hall, 1998).

27 This should be intuitively obvious, since successive factors can only be based on the residual variance, left after the extraction of preceding factors.

28 Also known as the *latent root*, the eigenvalue (a German-sourced term which when translated means "own value") represents the sum of squared factor loading, shown on the diagonal of the factor loading matrix, which is a measure of the amount of variance explained by a factor.

29 This exemplifies simple *correspondence analysis* (CA), limited to only two metrics at a time. *Multiple correspondence analysis* is a multivariate extension of the simple CA methodology to allow three or more variables to be considered concurrently.

30 It is commonly held that that Pearson's correlation does not assume normality, at least so long as the underlying distributions have finite variances and covariances, which is to say that the statistic can be taken as a consistent estimator under relatively general conditions. However, a comprehensive examination carried out by Kowalski [Charles J. Kowalski, "On the Effects of Non-Normality on the Distribution of the Sample Product-Moment Correlation Coefficient." *Journal of the Royal Statistical Society* 21, no.1 (1972):1–12.] presents convincing and comprehensive evidence suggesting that Pearson's r correlation is not robust to departures from normality.

9 Segmentation

1 The term *decision tree* has a relatively broad usage, going far beyond the descriptive classification outlined here. Of those, the most closely related are *regression trees*, exemplified by Multivariate Adaptive Regression Splines (MARS) which is a more methodologically

advanced predictive extension of the basic classificatory methodology developed in the 1990s. In machine learning, a decision tree is a commonly used name for a predictive model which maps observations about an item to conclusions about the item's target value. Lastly, the broad field of *decision theory* also uses decision trees, particularly in the area of risk management, to map out possible decisions and their likely consequences.

2 Usually called geodemographics, in reference to the fact that they represent geography-level demographic generalizations.

3 In contrast to objectively determined behaviors, attitudes are far more difficult to accurately measure simply because of the lack of observable, objective and universally applicable manifestations.

4 In most instances, a cluster-analysis-based solution will either need to be re-computed to take into account newly added records (which in turn may lead to a reshuffling of the initial solution) or it will simply be treated as a "snapshot" picture of the structure of the customer base.

5 Readers interested in the usage-focused review of some of the key multivariate statistical techniques might want to consider J. E. Hair, R. E. Anderson, R. L. Tatham, and B. Black, *Multivariate Data Analysis*, 5th ed. (Upper Saddle River, NJ: Prentice Hall, 1998). Those wishing to reference a more in-depth review of a wide-range of multivariate statistical concepts are encouraged to consider Trevor J. Hastie, Robert J. Tibshirani, Jerome Friedman, *The Elements of Statistical Learning: Data Mining, Inference and Prediction* (New York: Springer, 2001).

6 The concept of statistical significance cannot be applied to point estimates as doing so would suggest an absence of random error in the data analysis, which is virtually impossible in sample-based inferential statistical analysis. Statistical significance can only be applied to confidence intervals, as in sample-based analyses the true (meaning, exact) values of coefficient cannot be known with certainty and can only be estimated as being contained somewhere within a range of values bounded by upper and lower confidence intervals, which are computed by factoring the random error (a standard measure of sampling imprecision) into coefficients' point estimates. That said, as detailed in Chapter 8, the concept of statistical significance should be approached with caution under any circumstances.

7 Continuously measured = ratio or intervally scaled metrics.

8 Discretely measured = nominal or ordinal scales.

9 (mean − actual)^2; the squaring is necessary to prevent the cancelling of positive (actual > mean) and negative (actual < mean) deviations.

10 It is often helpful to use the standard z-scores (mean = 0 and standard deviation = 1) in place of raw values to remove scale differences and allow for easier cross-metric comparisons.

11 Or metric-aggregates; for instance, several disaggregate metrics could be grouped together into a higher-order factor (typically, either based on previous knowledge or as a result of data reduction analysis, such as the principal component analysis), which would subsequently be treated as a single entity.

12 In a multi-way split classification tree, each variable can assume a different number of categories, thus a two-way split can be followed by a three-way split, which can be followed yet a different category or the same number of categories. One of the disadvantages of this approach is that it exhibits a heightened likelihood of creating spurious categories, which can lead to interpretational difficulties.

13 In general, the definition of linear effects models is far broader, encompassing such commonly used methods as linear regression and others, but here it is limited to only include the methodologies that are appropriate to database segmentation related analyses.

14 The emphasis here is on *automatic* estimation, since in principle the linear effects models, such as logistic regression or multinomial logit can certainly encompass an estimation of non-linear effects.

15 One *terabyte* equals to approximately one trillion of individual characters, where a character could be a single digit, such as '1.' The prefix 'tera' has a Greek origin, meaning "monster."

16 A *treatment* is defined as any loyalty program-originated communication, offer or incentive intended to stimulate purchase.

17 For more details see Andrew D. Banasiewicz, "Acquiring High Value, Retainable Customers." *Journal of Database Marketing* 12, no.1 (2004):21–31.

18 For example, barcoded transactional data tends to be organized around the product-store-time continuum; consumer surveys are organized around individual responders and marketing program responses are event-based.

19 Specifically, it requires a customer-level quantification of transactional profitability and repurchase propensity to identify high value buyers.

20 Product category is comprised of all brands offering functionally substitutable products; for instance, all ready-to-eat breakfast cereal brands comprise the ready-to-eat breakfast cereal product category.

21 Henry Assael, *Consumer Behavior and Marketing Action* (Cincinnati, OH: South-Western Publishing, 1995), 558–559.

22 Although at least some of the transactional information is collected at the individual consumer level, the database de-duplicating (redundant record cleansing) and aggregating (rolling up of individual transactions to total value) processes effectively transform individual- into household-level information. In addition, third-party overlay data (e.g., geodemographics, lifestyle, etc.) is usually only available at a household or even a more aggregate level.

10 Behavioral Predictions

1 More specifically, the bulk of the business data is captured through automated transaction recording systems, such as point-of-sale UPC scanners or Web activity-tracking technologies.

2 In practice, interaction terms are often limited to bivariate (two-variable) terms as higher-order interactions and become quite cumbersome to interpret. Also, pragmatically speaking, the higher the number of variables linked together to form an interaction term, the lower the likelihood that such multi-way interactions will turn out to be statistically significant.

3 There is an ongoing controversy among methodologist regarding the trade-off between adhering to the assumption of predictor independence at the cost of poorer model fit vs. effectively violating that assumption (by means of introducing interaction effects of variables that are already in the model as stand-alone predictors) but at the same time enhancing the model's goodness-of-fit. In applied business analyses the latter choice is preferred.

4 This name reflects that, mathematically, interactions represent a *product* of *n* stand-alone metrics; i.e., a two-way interaction is a product of variable 1 _ variable 2.

5 Probably the best-known (among non-economists) economic principle, which suggests that each additional unit of input (holding everything else to be unchanged) will produce less and less additional output.

6 These are typically investor-filed civil lawsuits, predominantly in federal courts, asserting fraudulent behavior on the part of officers and directors of publicly traded companies, which then led to investor loss (a "class" represents a group of investors banding together for the purpose of jointly pursuing retribution). The much-publicized Enron, WorldCom and Tyco scandals represent examples of large securities class actions.

7 Applied business analyses at times make use of lower levels of significance, such 80%, which most of the time is in response to the desire to show as "significant" a compelling explanatory factor, which falls short of one of the traditionally used significance thresholds. This is a potentially dangerous practice, particularly when coupled with a large sample size. Given that the probability of finding statistically significant relationships increases as a function of sample size (see Chapter 5 for detailed discussion), also lowering the probability of interpreting as significant otherwise spurious associations will greatly increase the likelihood of coming to an unsupported (by the data) or outright erroneous conclusion.

8 First presented in the 1943 paper "A Theory of Human Motivation," it contends that all human needs can be grouped, hierarchically, into *basic* and *higher* needs. Often graphically expressed as a pyramid, the theory places the physiological needs (basic sustenance, sleep, sex) at the bottom, followed by safety (security of body and/or employment), belongingness/love (friendship, family), esteem (confidence, achievement) and self-actualization (morality, problem solving). The reaching of each successive stage is predicated upon a satisfactory completion of the precedent stage(s).

9 In marketing lingo, a *defector* (also referred to as an *attritor,* a marketing personification of the term *attrition,* used to describe customer loss) is a former customer who has since switched to a competing brand. The aggregate rate at which customer defection takes place is often referred to as the *attrition rate.*

10 Of course, this assumes that a particular product/service has a functionally substitutable alternative offered by another supplier. And indeed, the vast majority of consumer and industrial products do indeed have one or more competitors, although there are instances of at least temporary monopolies in highly specialized industries, such as biotechnology.

11 In fact, in order to calibrate a statistical model capable of robustly differentiating between the two customer types, the two samples should exhibit a fair amount of invariance across multiple characteristics.

12 This is particularly common in retail, i.e., scanner data analysis. In most instances, a transaction can only be attributed to a specific customer or a household if it is associated with some personally identifying device, such as a loyalty reward card, otherwise a transaction will only be defined by the *time–place–product* conjoint (the so-called "reverse append" process, where a purchase paid for with a bank credit card could be linked to a specific customer or a household, is no longer allowed).

13 Frederick F. Reichheld, *The Loyalty Effect: The Hidden Force Behind Growth, Profits, and Lasting Value* (Cambridge, MA: Harvard Business School Press, 1996).

14 George E. Belch, and Michael A. Belch (2004), *Advertising and Promotion: An Integrated Marketing Communications Perspective*, 6th Edition, (New York: McGraw-Hill/Irvin, 2004).

15 Microsoft, *Groundbreaking MSN-Sponsored Study Proves Online Ads Boost Branding and Offline Sales* (Redmond, WA: Microsoft, 2004), available from http://www.microsoft.com/presspass/press/2004/mar04/03–25AdsBoostBrandingPR.asp.

16 Direct, "Online Product Research Drove Offline Spending." *Direct Magazine,* 2004, available from http://directmag.com/news/Online-Product/index.html, as of October 13, 2004.

17 Philip Kotler, and Gary Armstrong, *Principles of Marketing*, 7th ed. (Englewood Cliffs, NJ: Prentice Hall, 1996).

18 Leon G. Shiffman, and Leslie Kanuk, *Consumer Behavior,* 8th ed. (Englewood Cliffs, NJ: Prentice Hall, 2003).

19 Michael R. Solomon, *Consumer Behavior: Buying, Having and Being,* 6th ed. (Englewood Cliffs, NJ: Prentice Hall, 2003).

20 Jupiter Research, *Automotive Purchase Funnel: Integrate Data Sources to Improve the Consumer Research Experience* [online report]. (Darien, CT: Jupiter Research, 2003).

21 Russell, J. Thomas, Glenn Verrill and W. Ronal Lane, *Kleppner's Advertising Procedure,* 10th ed. (Englewood Cliffs, NJ: Prentice Hall, 1988).

22 Most notably, this includes non-attributable magazine, newspaper or billboard communications, which are ones not containing promotionally coded coupons or promotion-specific call-in phone numbers.

23 David Sheppard Associates, *The New Direct Marketing: How to Implement a Profit-Driven Database Marketing Strategy*, 3rd ed. (New York: McGraw-Hill, 1999).

24 *eMarketer*, "Media Spending Outlook 2003: A Review of the Latest Projections, Surveys, Data and Trends in the Online and Offline Media Landscape." *eMarketer* (2002). http://www.emarketer.com.

25 Philip Kotler, *Marketing Management: Analysis, Planning, Implementation and Control*, 9th ed. (Englewood Cliffs, NJ: Prentice Hall, 1997).

26 Public Relations Society of America official Web site, www.prsa.org, as of October 6, 2004.

27 Based on a compilation of industry sources including Cannondale Associates, eMarketer and Advertising Age; excludes personal selling and public relations.

28 Based on averaging of multiple analysts' estimates, including J. P Morgan, McCann, Myers Group, Jupiter, Veronis and Direct Marketing Association (direct marketing only)

29 Oxbridge Communications, *National Directory of Magazines* [a proprietary industry report] (New York: Oxbridge Communications, 2003).

30 Cannondale Associates, *Annual Trade Promotion Study*, a private research source. (Wilton, CT: Cannondale Associates, 2003).

31 Advertising Research Foundation Webcast, October 26, 2004, available from www.arfsite.org/conferences/webcasts.html

32 See Daniel O'Keefe, *Persuasion: Theory and Research*, 2nd ed. (Beverly Hills, CA: Sage, 2002); Michael E. Roloff, and Gerard R. Miller, eds., *Persuasion: New Directions in Theory and Research* (Beverly Hills, CA: Sage, 1980); Kenneth E. Andersen, *Persuasion: Theory and Practice* (Boston, MA: Allyn and Bacon, 1978).

33 Samuelson, Paul A. and William D. Nordhaus, *Economics*, 17th ed. (New York: McGraw-Hill, 2001).

34 See e.g., George E. Belch, and Michael A. Belch, *Advertising and Promotion: An Integrated Marketing Communications Perspective*, 6th ed. (New York: McGraw-Hill/Irvin, 2004).

35 See Andrew D. Banasiewicz, "Acquiring High Value, Retainable Customers." *Journal of Database Marketing* 12, no.1 (2004):21–31.

36 Captures the impact of media mix elements on individual channels reflecting the differing roles some marketing media play across purchase funnel stages (e.g., advertising's impact on *awareness* vs. *consideration*, or direct mail's impact on *consideration* vs. *purchase* stages)

37 See Andrew D. Banasiewicz, "Marketing Pitfalls of Statistical Significance Testing." *Marketing Intelligence and Planning Journal* 23, no.5 (2005):515–528.

11 Action-Attributable Incrementality

1 In contrast to that, profit contribution determination can be quite a bit more involved in the context of impact measurement as it entails the apportionment of the share of the overall promotional expenditures of the action of interest (e.g., a promotion), over and above the non-marketing fixed and variable production and delivery costs.

2 The two terms, incrementality and lift, are used interchangeably as both describe an increase in the outcome of interest—such as sales—measured as a deviation from a pre-established base.

3 A non-directional hypothesis test involves determining if a phenomenon of interest has any impact, positive or negative, on the focal outcome.

4 For example, the current regulations require that all prospects whose credit was queried need to be made a credit offer as a result, which precludes setting aside a random control group.

5 Analytically-distinct segments are sub-groups that are expected (based on past analyses or theoretical considerations) to exhibit somewhat unique behavioral or attitudinal patterns. What comprises an analytically distinct segment can vary across situations or the type of investigation.

6 Negative incrementality, although conceptually possible is practically not tenable, because it suggests that a particular business action depressed the outcome of interest, such as sales. Under most circumstances that would be a relatively far-fetched conclusion, given that most so-measured business actions are promotions offering some positive value (e.g., price reduction coupons, etc.) to prospective redeemers/buyers. In the vast majority of cases I am familiar with, negative incrementality (lift < 0) is an indication of either the presence of an unaccounted for moderating factor or treated–control sampling frame incommensurability.

7 Although the "no difference" null hypothesis, where treated buy rate = control buy rate, is probably most common as it requires no specific a priori knowledge, the test–control relationship can also be expressed directionally, e.g., "treated buy rate > control buy rate" or "treated – control buy rate x%"—although it is rarely done so for reasons of operational efficiency or lack of sufficient a priori knowledge.

8 This is more globally referred to as *falsificationism,* according to which knowledge claims cannot be definitively proven as being true (since it would take an infinite number of tests), thus the best we can do is to fail to reject the claim(hypothesis) in question, leading to its tentative acceptance, at least until contrary evidence is presented.

9 These are arbitrary numbers used only to illustrate the concept; confidence interval can be easily calculated with formulas available in most basic statistics textbooks.

10 Defined here as consumers who, on average, contribute the least to the brand's profitability while at the same time exhibit the strongest propensity to switch brands, generally in response to competitive promotions. These consumers are often referred to as *switchers*.

11 In practice, the very term "new buyer" or "new customer" can be quite misleading as it claims something that rarely, if ever, has truly been validated. In fact, in most situations it is only known that the particular purchaser—i.e., the new customer—is not among the buyers contained within the analytical dataset, which is limited both in terms of completeness as well as its timeframe.

12 Database Scoring

1 Not all potential influencers of observed behaviors or outcomes are quantifiable, which means that the vast majority of database modeling endeavors will yield a somewhat incomplete explanation.
2 Naturally, all predictors in the originally derived model have non-zero coefficients as otherwise they would not make it into the model.
3 The most commonly used remedy is to add a constant, such as '1.'

13 From Findings to Knowledge

1 L. G. Daniel, "Statistical Significance Testing: A Historical Overview of Misuse and Misinterpretation with Implications for Editorial Policies of Educational Journals." *Research in the Schools* 5, no.2 (1998):23–32.
2 C. G. Henkel, *Tests of Significance* (Newbury Park, CA: Sage, 1976).
3 C. J. Huberty, "On Statistical Testing." *Educational Researcher* 16, no.8 (1987):4–9.
4 This is due to an increase in a number of error degrees of freedom which is a direct function of sample size.
5 The basic logic of significance testing involves comparing actual (such as the observed difference between treated and control buy rates) to expected (statistically derived) values based upon which a test statistic (such as *t-test*) is computed along with its respective probability (i.e., the *p* value). Expected values are arrived at by means of dividing the total amount of variability by sample size, which means that the larger the sample size the smaller the expected value. It can be easily shown that as the sample size increases, the magnitude of the expected value will continue to diminish. Naturally then, as a given observed value (e.g., buy rate differential) is compared to an ever smaller expected value, the likelihood of the former being deemed "statistically significant" will continue to increase.

14 Organizational Knowledge Sharing

1 Recall the discussion of the limitations of significance testing presented in Chapter 8 (*Beware of Significance Tests!*) and the basic characteristics of tests of association discussed earlier. The size of the analytical universe used in many, if not most practical business applications will tend to be relatively large, which in turn will result in relatively small, magnitude-wise, associations being deemed statistically significant, the net effect of which will be a potentially large pool of associative factors characterized by large differences in the magnitude of effects. In short, an analyst will need to decide, more or less arbitrarily, which of the multiple statistically significant associative factors warrant inclusion in a dashboard or a scorecard.

15 In Closing

1 Established in 1958 as ARPA, the Agency's name has subsequently been changed to the Defense Advanced Research Projects Agency (DARPA) in 1972, then back to ARPA in 1993 and back again to DARPA in 1996. There is no indication that another round of name flip-flapping is imminent. . .
2 The meaning of information; *semantics* is a formal area of the study of linguistics.
3 It was first introduced in 1962 by Everett Rogers in his book, *Diffusion of Innovations*. He theorized that the spread of new ideas (products, technologies, services, etc.) through society followed the so-called S-curve, where the small group of early adopters embraced the new idea first, followed by early majority, late majority and laggards, until the idea became common. Rogers' theory proved to be quite predictive in a variety of situations, so much so that many organizations now invest quite a bit of effort into identifying and persuading those most likely to be the early adopters, in hopes of speeding up the adoption process of their technologies, products or services.

Bibliography

Andersen, K. E., *Persuasion: Theory and Practice*. Boston, MA: Allyn and Bacon, 1978.

Assael, H., *Consumer Behavior and Marketing Action*. Cincinnati, OH: South-Western, 1995.

Ayres, I., *Super Crunchers: Why Thinking-by-Numbers Is the New Way to Be Smart*. New York: Bantam Books, 2007.

Babcock, C., "Data, Data Everywhere." *Information Week*, January 9, 2006.

Banasiewicz, A. D., "Acquiring High Value, Retainable Customers." *Journal of Database Marketing* 12, no.1 (2004):21–31.

Banasiewicz, A. D., "Marketing Pitfalls of Statistical Significance Testing." *Marketing Intelligence and Planning Journal* 23, no.5 (2005):515–528.

Belch, G. E., and Belch, M. A., *Advertising and Promotion: An Integrated Marketing Communications Perspective* (6th ed.). New York: McGraw-Hill/Irvin, 2004.

Cannondale Associates, *Annual Trade Promotion Study*. Wilton, CT: Cannondale Associates, 2003.

Churchland, P. S. and Sejnowski, T. J., *The Computational Brain*. Cambridge, MA: MIT Press, 1992.

Daniel, L. G. "Statistical significance testing: A historical overview of misuse and misinterpretation with implications for editorial policies of educational journals." *Research in the Schools* 5, no.2 (1998):23–32.

Davenport, T. H., "Competing on Analytics." *Harvard Business Review* 84, no.1 (2006):98–107.

David Sheppard Associates, *The New Direct Marketing: How to Implement a Profit-Driven Database Marketing Strategy* (3rd ed.). New York: McGraw-Hill, 1999.

Direct, "Online Products Research Drove Offline Spending." *Direct Magazine* (2004) , available from http://directmag.com/news/Online-Product/index.html, as of October 13, 2004.

Drucker, P., *The Essential Drucker: The Best of Sixty Years of Peter Drucker's Essential Writings on Management*. New York: HarperCollins, 2001.

eMarketer, "Media Spending Outlook 2003: A Review of the Latest Projections, Surveys, Data and Trends in the Online and Offline Media Landscape." *eMarketer* (2002). http://www.emarketer.com.

Hair, J. E., Anderson, R. E., Tatham, R. L., & Black, B., *Multivariate Data Analysis*. Upper Saddle River, NJ: Prentice Hall, 1998.

Hastie, T. J., Tibshirani, R. J., and Friedman, J., *The Elements of Statistical Learning: Data Mining, Inference and Prediction*. New York: Springer, 2001.

Henkel, C. G., *Tests of significance*. Newbury Park, CA: Sage, 1976.

Huberty, C. J., "On Statistical Testing." *Educational Researcher* 16, no.8 (1987):4–9.

Hunt, S. D., *Modern Marketing Theory: Critical Issues in the Philosophy of Marketing Science*. Cincinnati, OH: South-Western, 1991.

Jupiter Research, *Automotive Purchase Funnel: Integrate Data Sources to Improve the Consumer Research* [online report]. Darien, CT: Jupiter Research, 2003.

Kotler, P., *Marketing Management: Analysis, Planning, Implementation and Control* (9th ed.). Englewood Cliffs, NJ: Prentice Hall, 1997.

Kotler, P., and Armstrong, G. *Principles of Marketing* (7th ed.). Englewood Cliffs, NJ: Prentice Hall, 1996.

Kowalski, C. J., "On the Effects of Non-Normality on the Distribution of the Sample Product-Moment Correlation Coefficient." *Journal of the Royal Statistical Society* 21, no.1 (1972):1–12.

Levitt, S. D., and Dubner, S. J., *Freakonomics: A Rogue Economist Explores the Hidden Side of Everything*. New York: William Morrow, 2005.

Mardia, K. V., "Measures of Multivariate Skewness and Kurtosis with Applications." *Biometrika* 57, no.3 (1970):519–530.

Microsoft, *Groundbreaking MSN-Sponsored Study Proves Online Ads Boost Branding and Offline Sales*. Redmond, WA: Microsoft, 2004. http://www.microsoft.com/presspass/ press/2004/mar04/ 03–25AdsBoostBrandingPR.asp.

Moore, J. F., *The Death of Competition: Leadership & Strategy in the Age of Business Ecosystems*. New York: Harper Business, 1996.

O'Keefe, D., *Persuasion: Theory and Research* (2nd ed.). Beverly Hills, CA: Sage, 2002.

Oxbridge Communications, *National Directory of Magazines* [a proprietary industry report]. New York: Oxbridge Communications, 2003.

Plato, *The Republic*.

Quinn, J. P., P. Anderson, and S. Finkelstein, "Managing Professional Intellect: Making the Most of the Best." *Harvard Business Review* 74, no.2 [March-April], (1996): 71–83.

Reichheld, F. F., *The Loyalty Effect: The Hidden Force Behind Growth, Profits and Lasting Value*. Cambridge, MA: Harvard Business School Press, 1996.

Roloff, M. E., and Miller, G. R., eds., *Persuasion: New Directions in Theory and Research*. Beverly Hills, CA: Sage, 1980.

Rosenblum, B., and F. Kuttner, *Quantum Enigma: Physics Encounters Consciousness*. New York: Oxford University Press, 2008.

Rubin, D. B., *Multiple Imputations for Nonresponse in Surveys*. New York: Wiley, 1987.

Russell, T. J., *Kleppner's Advertising Procedure*. Englewood Cliffs, NJ: Prentice Hall, 1988.

Samuelson, P. A., and Nordhaus, W. D., *Economics* (17th ed.). New York: McGraw-Hill, 2001.

Shiffman, L. G., and Kanuk, L., *Consumer Behavior* (8th ed.). Englewood Cliffs, NJ: Prentice Hall, 2003.

Solomon, M. R., *Consumer Behavior: Buying, Having and Being* (6th ed.). Englewood Cliffs, NJ: Prentice Hall, 2003.

Switzer, F. S. III, P. L. Roth, and D. M. Switzer, "Systematic Data Loss in HRM Settings: A Monte Carlo Analysis." *Journal of Management* 24, no.6 (1998):763–779.

Tabachnick, B. A. and L. S. Fidell, *Using Multivariate Statistics* (3rd ed.). New York: Harper Collins, 1996.

Thomas, R. J., Verrill, G., and Lane, W. R., *Kleppner's Advertising Procedure* (10th ed.). Englewood Cliffs, NJ: Prentice Hall, 1988.

Tukey, J., *Exploratory Data Analysis*. Reading, MA: Addison-Wesley, 1977.

Index